Winner of the Jules F. Landry Award for 1984

When the War Was Over

When the War Was Over

*The Failure of Self-Reconstruction
in the South, 1865–1867*

Dan T. Carter

Louisiana State University Press

Baton Rouge and London

Typeface: Linotron Monticello
Typesetter: G & S Typesetters Inc.
Printer and binder: Edwards Brothers, Inc.
Publication of this book has been assisted by a grant from the Andrew W. Mellon Foundation.

Library of Congress Cataloging in Publication Data

Carter, Dan T.
  When the war was over.

  Includes index.
  1. Reconstruction. 2. Southern States—History—1865–1877. I. Title.
E668.C28 1985   975'.041   84-21315
ISBN 0-8071-1192-9
ISBN 0-8071-1204-6 (pbk)

Portions of Chapter VI appeared previously, in slightly different form, in an article, "The Anatomy of Fear: The Christmas Day Insurrection Scare of 1865," published in the August 1976 issue of the *Journal of Southern History* (XLII, pp. 345–64). The author is grateful to the Managing Editor for permission to reprint this material.

To my Mother and Father

Contents

Acknowledgments

Identifying all those who helped me in the research and writing of this book is rather like drawing up an invitation list to a southern wedding. Either I must include almost everyone from the eleven Confederate States (plus the District of Columbia and Maryland) or limit the proceedings to close friends and immediate family. I gracelessly opt for the latter.

George Callcott remains my friend even though he initially encouraged me to write a book on this subject. Summer research grants from the National Endowment for the Humanities and the University of Maryland Research Committee made it possible for me to complete the initial research. Jocelyn Shaw typed the first version of the manuscript before I decided to abandon this project. Beverly Jarrett persuaded me to take it up once again and a sabbatical from Emory University allowed me to do additional research and to rewrite the manuscript. Patsy Stockbridge heroically typed the final version so that my friend and colleague James L. Roark could read the manuscript and pencil sarcastic comments next to some of my more outlandish conclusions and observations. And Judith Bailey was the editor every author hopes to find.

I will not acknowledge in detail the many debts I owe my wife, Jane, and my children, Alicia and David, lest I become hopelessly maudlin. They performed many loving and supporting acts, the greatest of which was to refrain from asking me when I would finish the book.

Abbreviations

AA	Alabama State Department of Archives and History
AH	*Agricultural History*
AHQ	*Alabama History Quarterly*
AHR	*American Historical Review*
AMA	American Missionary Association Archives, Armistad Research Center, Dillard University
ASR	*American Sociological Review*
BRFAL	Selected Series of Records, issued by the Commissioner of the Bureau of Refugees, Freedmen and Abandoned Lands, 1865–1872, in Record Group 105, National Archives
CS	*Caribbean Studies*
CWH	*Civil War History*
DR	*De Bow's Review*
DUL	William R. Perkins Library, Duke University
ETHSP	*East Tennessee Historical Society Publications*
EU	Emory University Library, Special Collections
Fa	*Farmer*
FCHQ	*Filson Club Historical Quarterly*
FF	*Field and Fireside*
FHQ	*Florida Historical Quarterly*
GA	Georgia State Department of Archives and History
GHQ	*Georgia Historical Quarterly*
HW	*Harper's Weekly*
JAH	*Journal of American History*
JEH	*Journal of Economic History*
JMH	*Journal of Mississippi History*
JNH	*Journal of Negro History*
JSH	*Journal of Southern History*

LC   Library of Congress
LH   *Lincoln Herald*
LL   *Land We Love*
LSU   Department of Archives and Manuscripts, Louisiana State University
MLJ   *Mississippi Law Journal*
MM   *Merchant's Magazine and Commercial Review*
MQ   *Mississippi Quarterly*
MSA   Mississippi State Department of Archives and History
NA   National Archives
NAR   *North American Review*
NCA   North Carolina Department of Archives and History
NCHR   *North Carolina Historical Review*
NEM   *New England Magazine*
NOC   *New Orleans Chronicle of Medical Education*
OR   *The War of the Rebellion: A Compilation of the Official Records of the Union and Confederate Armies* (130 vols.; Washington, D.C., 1880–1901). Unless otherwise noted, all citations are to Series 1.
PMHS   *Publications of the Mississippi Historical Society*
PSHA   *Proceedings of the Southern Historical Association*
RG   Record Group
SCL   South Caroliniana Library, University of South Carolina
SCA   South Carolina State Department of Archives and History
SCB   *Sanitary Commission Bulletin*
SCHM   *South Carolina Historical Magazine*
SCu   *Southern Cultivator*
SHC   Southern Historical Collection, University of North Carolina at Chapel Hill
SP   *Southern Planter*
SPR   *Southern Presbyterian Review*
SUS   *Susquehanna University Studies*
SUL   Syracuse University Library
SwHQ   *Southwestern Historical Quarterly*
TC   *Technology and Culture*
THQ   *Tennessee Historical Quarterly*
THR   *Textile History Review*
TrCHP   *Trinity College Historical Society Papers*
UGL   University of Georgia Library
UTA   University of Texas Archives
UVa   Alderman Library, University of Virginia
VMHB   *Virginia Magazine of History and Biography*
WMQ   *William and Mary Quarterly*
WTHSP   *West Tennessee Historical Society Papers*
WTHY   *West Texas Historical Yearbook*

When the War Was Over

Introduction

I N T H E months after Appomattox, white southerners confronted hundreds of unsettling questions about their future. This book is the story
of those white southerners and how they responded to a world turned
upside down. It is about race. It is about economics. Above all, it is
about politics and political leadership. The conclusions of this study will
probably offend a number of my colleagues; I am offended by some of the
implications one can draw from my conclusions.

Perhaps my uneasiness can best be illustrated by recounting the story of
Henry Garrett, a Natchez planter's son who left the University of Mississippi in 1861 to enroll in the University Grays. His earliest entries ended
on the June date of his enlistment with an emotional promise to "seek a
glorious death" in defense of his new country. When Garrett resumed writing in his diary in August of 1865, however, it was clear that four years of
war under Jeb Stuart had shown him enough heroism to last a lifetime. In
time he would reminisce of the glories of the Lost Cause, but his initial
recollection of the war was a listing of the names of his friends who were
scattered in graves across three southern states. His account of his return to
his home was a spare catalogue of chaos and devastation, complete with the
proverbial chimneys "standing like blackened sentinels" over the ashes of
Mount Ida, his childhood home.

For the next four years Garrett drifted aimlessly, failing first as a planter,
then as a schoolteacher, and finally as a lawyer. And as he slipped down the
scale of respectability and into poverty he bitterly chronicled the rise of

those less principled and "honorable," but far more adept in the survival skills of a precarious postwar world.[1]

Even when we make allowances for self-pity and melodramatic posturing, the story of Henry Garrett and thousands of other fellow Confederates is affecting. It became a staple of melodrama and literature as well as professional historical writing between 1900 and 1940. Not surprisingly in this century of war it is a story with enormous appeal around the world. *Gone with the Wind*, after all, is as popular in Japan as it is in the United States.

And yet I, like most contemporary historians, find it difficult to develop great empathy for a generation of white southerners who went off to war to destroy the Union and guarantee the future of human slavery. Even worse, they came home defeated but unrepentant. Humility was seldom a virtue of white southerners.

Even during those years when most white Americans sympathized with the defeated white South, the political leadership of the brief era of "Presidential Reconstruction" did not fare well at the hands of professional historians. Early twentieth-century writers might treat them as victims of "radical" excesses, but all but the most prosouthern apologists found it difficult to wax enthusiastic about a leadership whose policies seemed to have played directly into the hands of the Republican opponents of a courageous Andrew Johnson. If none were willing to echo the 1865 complaint of one of Johnson's cabinet members ("The entire South seems to be stupid and vindictive"), most would certainly have accepted the gentle reprimand of James W. Garner, a Mississippi historian. Their policies were "folly," said Garner, and their political obstinacy gave Republican radicals a "pretext to subvert the partially reconstructed state governments and return the South to despotic rule."[2]

Historians of the past thirty years, while hardly sympathetic to Garner's political outlook, have often agreed. As historians living through the "second reconstruction" of the post–World War II era have rehabilitated the reputations of those Republicans who fought for equal rights, the reputation of these southern post–Civil War leaders has sunk even lower. They were blind to the consequences of the war, concluded John Hope Franklin, "pursuing most of their prewar policies as though there had never been a war." These "planter politicians" discredited Johnson's entire program by their "irresponsible behavior," agreed Kenneth M. Stampp, "reducing the Johnson plan of reconstruction to a shambles." Most recently, Michael Perman has recognized the moderate character of the region's postwar

1. Henry Garrett Diary, Claiborne Manuscripts, LC, March 25–June 5, August 18, 1865, January 3–February 11, 1866, September 3–19, 1870.
2. James Wilford Garner, *Reconstruction in Mississippi* (New York, 1901), 116–17.

leadership, but he has argued that their very moderation was an obstacle to solving the political crisis of the war and the Reconstruction era. Only their removal from power could have brought about "harmony between the sections."[3]

Many of these criticisms are well taken. The men who sought to bring the South back into the Union in 1865 and 1866 were racists, oblivious (for the most part) to the human aspirations of black southerners. They were certainly fanatically opposed to the notion of black political participation and willing to do almost anything to thwart federal involvement in what they, in their more tactful moments, described as the "domestic affairs" of the southern states. They were certainly politically insensitive. Like Mark Anthony I do not come to praise these men.

On the other hand, I do believe that in our desire to illuminate the bitter persecution of black Americans during these years and throughout our history we run the risk of accepting uncritically the partisan judgments and assertions of their enemies.

At the risk of making a reading of the book unnecessary, let me summarize some of the points I have tried to make. First, I argue that there emerged in the fall of 1865 a southern postwar leadership which, though quite diverse, shared a number of characteristics. A surprising minority had either been neutral during the war or had overtly opposed the Confederacy. But the majority had been reluctant secessionists who had initially opposed secession and then, when it was an accomplished fact, supported the new nation.

They are best remembered from their policies on race; specifically for their enactment of the infamous black codes of 1865. As a result, historians have generally dismissed them as blindly reactionary on all issues of race. I would argue that, at least within the context of white southern thought, they promoted distinctly conservative policies. Their notions about the future of the freed men and women in their midst were an amalgam of despair, frustration, and hatred. But these emotions were often leavened by a dash of antebellum paternalism and a realistic awareness that the nation would never accept a return to those antebellum legal codes that had placed free blacks a half step away from slavery.

Finally, I would contend that, in our understandable focus upon the racial dimensions of postwar politics, we have ignored the extent to which this postwar leadership turned grudgingly but surely from a slave to a free

3. John Hope Franklin, *Reconstruction: After the Civil War* (Chicago, 1961), 53; Kenneth M. Stampp, *The Era of Reconstruction, 1865–1877* (New York, 1965), 72–73; Michael Perman, *Reunion Without Compromise: The South and Reconstruction, 1865–1868* (Cambridge, 1973), 346–47.

society. This is only the beginning of the story of postwar adjustment and reconstruction. Nevertheless, I believe that a careful examination of these critical months after Appomattox raises questions about recent historians' assumptions that postwar elites formed an ideologically cohesive planter class, adamantly intent on resisting any change in their society. Collectively, the men who led the region in the aftermath of the war were cautious and conservative by temperament. And they often responded to emancipation with the same stubborn resistance that marked other nineteenth-century landed classes that were faced with the loss of control over their labor. There are important insights to be gained from viewing emancipation in a broad comparative framework, but only if we remember that these southern masters without slaves were not Brazilian "seignors" or German "Junkers" or counterparts of British planters. They were Americans, even though they sometimes denied it. And in the absence of slavery, they lacked the cohesive ideology and self-identity that characterized nineteenth-century rural landed elites in other societies.[4]

Although they were hardly united on all issues, a surprising number were veterans of the old Whig party. And, whether ex-Whig or not, they often shared a whiggish sympathy for state-sponsored economic development. In practical terms, this sometimes meant nothing more than the use of the power of the state government to stabilize the plantation economy by controlling the freed population, restoring the region's commercial infrastructure, and promoting the development of railroad transportation to improve access to staple-crop markets.

I have concluded, however, that we have ignored the significant role of a substantial number of postwar southerners (including many planters) who endorsed tax and credit policies that would promote industrial as well as agricultural development. Even more surprisingly, they appeared ready to accept the destruction of the South's plantation economy and its replacement by an agricultural society dominated by more efficient small-scale farmers.

Of course most white southerners tenaciously clung to the past, and even the vision of these self-reconstructionists was deeply flawed. The decade of the 1880s revealed the shallowness of their "New South" ideas as well as the enormous difficulties in carrying them through in the face of traditional economic interests, poverty, and inertia. But it will not do to dismiss the southern leaders of Presidential Reconstruction as racists and

4. For a recent study that emphasizes some of the important similarities between these landed classes, see Eric Foner's collection of published lectures, *Nothing But Freedom: Emancipation and Its Legacy* (Baton Rouge, 1983).

incompetents. In important ways, they represented the most constructive and creative response white southerners were able to make to their defeat and to the revolution of emancipation. That may be the most depressing observation we can make in viewing the history of the postwar South.

I / Social Disorder and Violence in the Land of the Vanquished

O N M ARCH 2, 1865, Confederate officers mustered the eleven hundred men of the Galveston, Texas, garrison on an open field near
the main barracks. Shortly after 2 P.M., a private in Dege's Artillery Battery, flanked by the post commander and an army chap-
lain, marched to the center of the field. At the sight of the mule-drawn
wagon with its open coffin, the young soldier began weeping, then recovered his composure and stood at attention as an officer read the findings
of the court martial. "You have been found guilty of willful desertion from
the Army of the Confederate States of America," he concluded, "and it is
the judgement of this court that you be executed without delay as a just
punishment for your crime and a fitting example for your comrades." With
the sharp rattle of a rifle volley, Antone Ricker, age seventeen, was dead.[1]
Two weeks later as Nathan Bedford Forrest maneuvered his troops west of
Columbus, Mississippi, to avoid encirclement by Union troops, three of his
soldiers defiantly called him out from his breakfast at a Mississippi farm-
house where he had set up temporary headquarters. They "told him dey
wasn't going to fight no more," Henry Gibbs recalled nearly seventy years
later. Forrest "served de law on em," remembered the former slave, who
had brought the general his breakfast that morning. "Dem three men stood
in a row," said Gibbs, and at the roll of a drum, a firing squad aimed, "dey
fired and de three men was no more."[2]

1. *Flake's Bulletin* (Galveston, Tex.), March 3, 1865; Houston *Tri-Weekly Telegraph*,
March 6, 1865.
2. *OR*, Vol. II, Pt. 2, pp. 1124–25; George G. Rawick (ed.), *The American Slave: A*

Such executions were designed to stem the spreading wave of desertions in the Confederate army, but they succeeded only in advertising its disintegration. The Confederacy was dying and neither draconian measures nor patriotic exhortations could stem the spreading defeatism of soldiers and civilians alike. As late as December of 1864, a South Carolina planter had commented that most of his friends were like ostriches, plunging their heads into the sand. Even those who suspected the worst were "reticent, not daring to speak what they think."[3] The continuing list of Confederate defeats in January and February finally flushed peace advocates into the open. Although their criticism was often expressed in cautious and veiled language, it reflected the widespread loss of confidence in the future of the Confederacy. By March, a peace movement of sorts existed in every southern state and rumors of "special conventions" were rife throughout the region.

Such defeatism enraged those Confederate patriots who demanded last-ditch resistance. Capitulation was "unthinkable," argued the Richmond *Whig*, for any settlement short of independence would leave the "cultivated and refined ladies" of the South "subject to their own slaves, overawed by negroes in Yankee uniforms . . . and forced . . . to the embrace of brutal Yankee husbands." Other opponents of surrender railed against "traitorous croakers and submissionists" and outlined nightmarish scenarios of slave insurrections, Negro supremacy, property confiscation, and the inevitable "savage cruelty" that would be inflicted by the "fiendish Yankees." The Confederacy, said one southerner, represented all that remained between anarchy and "constitutional law and conservatism" in America.[4]

Those who found it hardest to face the prospect of defeat during the fading weeks of the Confederacy coupled each confirmed disaster with the hope of some miraculous reprieve. The outlook was bleak, a Georgia soldier admitted after he learned of the fall of Fort Fisher on January 15. But he eagerly endorsed the suggestion of the Richmond *Enquirer* that the

---

Composite Autobiography, Supplementary Ser. 1 (12 vols.; Westport, Conn., 1977), VIII, 824–25.

3. James Hemphill to Robert Hemphill, December 30, 1864, in Hemphill Collection, DUL. Southerners' private diaries and correspondence as a rule reflected a gloomy pessimism at odds with their public statements. For example, see George Anderson Mercer Diary, SHC, January 15, 1864; David Schenck Diary, SHC, February 19, 1864; A. R. Rowzie to Thomas Ruffin, March 4, 1865, in Thomas Ruffin Papers, SHC.

4. Richmond *Whig*, February 11, 1865; Houston *Tri-Weekly Telegraph*, April 24, 1865; Columbia *Carolinian*, n.d., quoted in Yorkville (S.C.) *Enquirer*, February 1, April 26, 1865; Columbia (S.C.) *Phoenix*, April 22, 1865; Selma *Daily Messenger*, March 30, 1865; Mobile *Daily Advertiser and Register*, January 24, February 8, 1865; Richmond *Daily Dispatch*, January 20, 1865; Lucy Walton Diary, DUL, April 14, 1865.

South agree to gradual emancipation in return for a treaty of recognition by the major European powers. "An Alliance with France or England would certainly secure our recognition and independence," he said wistfully. Even as Lee fell back from Petersburg, the southern press reported that daily casualties from Grant's army had reached the thousands, with resistance to the war growing throughout the North. By the time such accounts reached the hinterlands of the South they had become even more exaggerated. "Lee has joined Johnson and torn Sherman all to pieces; Sherman's loss is 60,000 men," reported a Mississippi planter on April 13, four days after the surrender of the Army of Northern Virginia. A Virginia schoolgirl, depressed at the steady advance of Sherman's army, found encouragement in a dispatch from Confederate army chaplains reporting a "decided increase in religious interest" throughout the Army of Northern Virginia. God might yet rouse himself from his unexplained torpor and send the Yankees pell-mell back across the borders of the Confederacy.[5]

"It is wonderful the multitude of lies which are circulated to disapate [sic] depression," observed the Reverend Samuel Agnew. "Bitter pills are considerably improved by sweetening." But no amount of manufactured news could conceal the reality of defeat. "The people, soldiers and citizens are whipped." A Georgia soldier on leave from his company in mid-April was jolted from the solace of his neighbor's predictions of victory when a local black newspaper vendor demanded ten cents in coin or ten dollars in Confederate currency for a copy of the Augusta *Daily Constitutionalist.*[6]

Even with the surrender of the armies of Lee and Johnson in mid-April the dream of continued resistance remained alive. "The End is Not in Sight," claimed the *Constitutionalist* on April 18 as it argued that the independence of the South could still be won by the Trans-Mississippi Army of Kirby Smith. As Jefferson Davis fled westward from Richmond, a handful of diehards sounded the call for further resistance. "Our cause is not dead," insisted Brigadier General Thomas Munford in a special order to his troops. "We have sworn a thousand times by our eternal wrongs, by our sacred God-given rights . . . that we would be free. . . . Can we kneel down by the graves of our dead, kneel in the very blood from sons yet fresh and kiss the rod which smote them down? Never! Never!" Let those who were that last "organized part of the army of Northern Virginia" strike the

5. James Appleton Blackshear Diary, EU, January 26, 1865; Richmond *Daily Enquirer,* December 29, 1864; Columbia *Carolinian,* n.d., quoted in Augusta *Daily Constitutionalist,* April 16, 1865; Samuel Agnew Diary, SHC, March 12, April 13, 1865; Lucy Walton Diary, March 12, 1865.

6. Samuel Agnew Diary, April 16, 17, 22, 1865; James Appleton Blackshear Diary, April 18, 1865.

first blow, which, "by the blessings of our gracious God, will yet come to redeem her hallowed soil." Twelve hundred miles away, Kirby Smith, the commander of that army of the west, insisted that his forces would secure "the final success of our cause."[7]

Those who were able to look realistically at the condition of the armies of the Confederacy had no such illusions. On May 3 at a conference at his headquarters in southwest Alabama, the same Nathan Bedford Forrest who had executed deserters six weeks earlier listened incredulously while Mississippi governor Charles Clark and former Tennessee governor Isham Harris outlined plans for retreating across the swollen Mississippi to link forces with Smith's army. Forrest abruptly stood and interrupted the two. "Men, you may all do as you damn please," he said, "but I'm a-going home." When Harris insisted that Forrest take the field to repel the advancing Union forces, Forrest reminded him that his detachment would soon be outnumbered ten to one. "To make men fight under such circumstances would be nothing but murder," he argued. Looking Harris in the eye, he concluded, "Any man who is in favor of a further prosecution of this war is a fit subject for a lunatic asylum."[8]

Forty miles from where General Joseph E. Johnston would surrender the last significant body of Confederate forces east of the Mississippi, William Horn Battle had been shocked to hear his son advocate continued resistance at any price. Battle, near the end of a long career as lawyer, legislator, judge of the North Carolina Superior and Supreme Courts, and professor of law at the University of North Carolina, scornfully dismissed such "nonsense." What was meant by the plea that southerners should "rouse themselves?" he asked his son, Kemp. Had they not already been roused? "Were they not intoxicated by political nonsense before 1861 & stimulated to volunteer in running amok with Christendom upon the subject of slavery?" And when that "fever" wore off, "were they not spurred on . . . by all means of force & fraud?" It was absurd, the senior Battle concluded, to suppose that entreaties, addresses, and proclamations could restore the vital energies of the Confederacy. "I really feel like swearing when I hear such foul bluster ventilated in my presence. It is the language of officials—of exempts—of old men who have made investments—of speculators—of ladies—it is a parrot cry—there is no sense—no apprehension of mercy— no appreciation of the past, no consideration of the future about it—and I

7. OR, Vol. XLVI, Pt. 3, p. 1395; Robert L. Kerby, *Kirby Smith's Confederacy: The Trans-Mississippi South, 1863–1865* (New York, 1972), 412. As Smith's biographer notes, the soldiers' response to his bombastic oration was to desert by the hundreds.

8. Jason Niles Diary, SHC, May 6, 1865.

can relieve myself only by swearing when I hear it. Do not ever mention it again—as you love me; for I fear I should be tempted into profanity."[9]

"I do not pretend to disguise how hard, oppressive [and] cruel this all may be," agreed Judge William Pitt Ballinger of Texas. "But if, as an inexorable fate it cannot be averted, then it is best to submit to it, and not inflame it with bitter passions." It was advice that even the most partisan newspaper advocates of the Confederacy would echo in their editorials by mid-May. Resistance, John Dumble of the Macon *Daily Telegraph* told his readers, would lead only to disaster. "Our own purpose for ourselves, and our advice to others, is to acquiesce with what cheerfulness we may in the decrees of fate and the dispensations of Providence."[10]

It was a "strange and uncertain time," a Florida physician said of those days before military occupation began. Union policy had been amply reported in the southern press, but such precedents as existed were clouded by the assassination of Lincoln and the elevation of a vengeful Andrew Johnson to the presidency. A few southerners, terrified by wartime propaganda of Yankee atrocities, steeled themselves for the arrival of their conquerors. "I wish that they were here now," a North Carolina woman confided to her fiancé. "I can endure anything better than the suspense." Men of property and outspoken supporters of the Confederacy were free to reflect upon the punishments that might be administered to them as defeated revolutionaries: confiscation, political disfranchisement, even imprisonment. And among almost all white southerners, there was uneasiness over the future of the three and a half million black people whose bondage had been at the heart of the four years of struggle.[11]

If the widespread wartime propaganda of Yankee atrocities unnerved white southerners, most quickly learned that this was the least of their troubles. The South in the late spring and early summer of 1865 was a land without law. "We have no currency, no law, save the primitive code that might makes right," a frightened Georgia woman wrote in her diary. With everything in a state of disorganization, "the props that hold society are broken." When the editor of the nearby Macon *Telegraph and Confederate*

9. William Horn Battle to Kemp Battle, April 10, 1865, in Battle Family Papers, SHC.
10. William Pitt Ballinger Diary, UTA, May 13, 1865; Macon *Daily Telegraph*, May 11, 1865. Dumble had been the refugee editor of the Memphis *Daily Appeal* during much of the war and had counseled resistance until the end. See T. H. Baker, "Refugee Newspaper: The Memphis *Daily Appeal*, 1862–1865," *JSH*, XXIX (1963), 333–35.
11. Ethelred Philips to James J. Philips, April 22, 1865, in James John Philips Papers, SHC; Addie Worth to William H. Bagley, March 24, May 4, 1865, in Bagley Family Papers, SHC; Emma Mordecai to George W. Mordecai, April 21, 1865, in George W. Mordecai Papers, SHC; George W. Munford to Mrs. E. T. Munford, April 21, 1865, in Munford-Ellis Family Papers, DUL; Bessie Cain Diary, April 16, 1865, William Newton Mercer Diary, April 10, 1865, both in LSU; William Pitt Ballinger Diary, May 13, 1865.

abandoned his presses in late April, 1865, two printers who remained behind managed to publish an abbreviated edition on May 4. Although the syntax and grammar of this one-page broadside fell short of the usual standards of the old *Telegraph*, the printers were able to communicate their near hysteria. The people of Georgia and of the South "face a prospect of anarchy and barbarien warfare," warned the two men. Without the existence of "wholesome restraints" society was threatened with reversion to a state in which "every man is forced back onto his own resources, without the protecting arm of the law." And in a vague but unmistakable reference to emancipation, they reminded their readers of the blood bath that had followed the "revolutionery upheavels in the Caribbean."[12]

There was to be no repetition of the tragic events that marked Haitian emancipation and independence, however. When violence occurred, it was more likely to result in the death of blacks than of whites. But violence there was, and it affected every aspect of the lives and thinking of southerners—rich or poor, black and white. Under the best of circumstances it would have taken weeks to reestablish some form of organized government in the South, but these were hardly the best of times. Like most Union leaders, Secretary of War Edwin Stanton did not want to grant even a shadow of legality to the collapsing Confederate government, and he had emphasized to Union officers that all police power in the South had reverted to the United States Army. Individuals who held local civil positions should "report themselves to the military authorities . . . to wait the action of the General Government," he declared in late April and early May. Southern officeholders who violated these instructions were liable to trial before a military tribunal.[13]

However advisable these orders were from a political and military point of view, it was to be some time before military garrisons could be established throughout the Deep South. In a few areas where unionists were particularly strong or where army officers were willing to exercise judgment, judges, sheriffs, commissioners, and justices of the peace had been allowed to perform their duties under the antebellum laws of the state (excepting, of course, those laws dealing with slavery). General George H. Thomas, who directed operations in Tennessee and in parts of northern Georgia, Alabama, and Mississippi, adopted such a policy in early 1865, and the practice was fairly common in parts of North Carolina. But though these contraventions of Stanton's instructions were never explicitly repudiated by the War Department, they reflected exceptional circumstances. In

12. Eliza Andrews, *The Wartime Journal of a Georgia Girl, 1864–1865*, ed. Spencer Bidwell King (Atlanta, 1976), 198; Macon *Daily Telegraph*, May 4, 1865.
13. *OR*, Vol. XLIX, Pt. 2, pp. 646–47, 810.

the interregnum between the end of the war and the creation of provisional governments by Andrew Johnson, the army was law. Yet despite the best efforts of the War Department, it was to be weeks before garrisons could be stationed throughout the South. And their effectiveness would always be limited by the size of the region and the relatively limited numbers of mobile cavalry troops that could be deployed for police purposes.[14]

The collapse of the Confederate armies alone guaranteed an upsurge of crime as hungry veterans set out on the long march back to their homes. There was something "painful and pathetic," noted one South Carolinian, in seeing these once proud men scrambling for handouts and reduced to petty thievery as they straggled southward. A chagrined Joseph E. Johnston could do nothing as Lee's veterans wandered aimlessly through the lines of his still-intact army in late April, stealing mules and horses as they went and filching clothes hung out to dry.[15]

For the most part, soldiers seemed to concentrate upon the "impressment" (as they called it) of Confederate and state stores. "I lived four years on goobers, parched corn and rotten meat," one former soldier defiantly told a newspaper editor, "and I saw nothing wrong with taking blankets & such from the commissary as they would have been confiscated anyhow by the Yankees when they arrived." What often began as acts of organized groups, however, degenerated into something approaching anarchy. When homeward-bound soldiers rifled Confederate stores in Augusta, Georgia, in mid-May, they were soon joined by a mob of wagon-driving thieves who shattered store windows and seized private as well as public property while town officials stood by helplessly.[16]

A week earlier, Thomasville, Georgia, had been the scene of three days of disorder as disbanding soldiers passed through the town on their way west. On the night of May 6 more than fifty armed men stole eighty-nine mules and seven horses from the loosely guarded Confederate depot. Two nights later, on May 8, four hundred former soldiers attacked the Confederate storehouses under the guard of a handful of Confederate officers who remained at their posts. At the issuing commissary and the railroad commissary, they broke into two warehouses and "carried away from 75,000 to 125,000 pounds of corn." After rifling these goods, they "demolished all books, papers and office furniture they could find . . . [and] then declared

---

14. *Ibid.*, Vol. XLVII, Pt. 3, pp. 14, 460–61, 502–44; James E. Sefton, *The United States Army and Reconstruction, 1865–1877* (Baton Rouge, 1967), 11–12.

15. McCarter Journal, LC, 92–93; Joseph E. Johnston to Zebulon Vance, April 24, 1865, in Zebulon Vance Papers, NCA.

16. *OR*, Vol. XLVII, Pt. 3, pp. 595–96; Augusta *Chronicle and Sentinel*, n.d., quoted in Houston *Tri-Weekly Telegraph*, June 15, 1865.

their intentions to burn the town." Fortunately, they did not carry out their threat, but they did break into private stores and the end result was destitution and fear in the community.[17]

Such riots occurred in several small communities in the Deep South, becoming particularly widespread in Texas in May and June when the belated surrender of Kirby Smith's army and the absence of Union troops created a military and political vacuum. The practice of "liberating" Confederate storehouses had already become so common that Confederate governor Pendleton Murrah had issued a proclamation in mid-May ordering county sheriffs to collect and preserve all government property for "equitable distribution." But irregular committees—in most cases undisciplined mobs—ignored Murrah's order, broke into storehouses, and scattered materials in the streets. At La Grange and San Antonio, crowds plundered and looted food, clothing, firearms, and most ominously, whiskey and "spirits of all kinds." When a group of paroled soldiers arrived in Houston to find that the Confederate storehouse had already been looted and its contents distributed, they threatened to burn the Texas town. Frightened citizens hastily returned a portion of the materials to the soldiers who were fed and offered accommodations by an intimidated mayor and city council. A correspondent for the New Orleans *Times* reported that "ex-confederate soldiers have fought four years without pay, and now they propose to pay themselves."[18]

In that process of self-payment, the soldiers preferred to steal from the defunct Confederate government, observed one South Carolinian, but when public property was no longer available, they "preyed on the horses & mules of citizens who they chose to think had more than their fair share." Eliza Andrews, a young Georgia woman, watched a filthy and bedraggled veteran walk up to her neighbor in broad daylight and calmly commandeer the old man's only draft animal, ignoring his pathetic pleas that it would result in the starvation of his family. As the soldier rode past Miss Andrews, he said with a grin, "A man that's going to Texas must have a mule to ride, don't you think so lady?"[19]

The sanctity of private property had already been severely undermined by wartime foraging practices and the tendency of Union and Confederate forces to regard the belongings of civilians as legitimate prizes of war. By 1865 Union soldiers in general and William Tecumseh Sherman's troops in

17. *OR*, Vol. XLIX, Pt. 2, pp. 7683–85; Macon *Daily Telegraph*, May 16, 1865.
18. *OR*, Vol XLVII, Pt. 3, pp. 595–96; Houston *Tri-Weekly Telegraph*, May 24, 31, June 6, 9, 16, 1865; *Flake's Bulletin*, June 28, 1865; New York *Herald*, May 20, 21, 1865; New Orleans *Times*, n.d., quoted in New York *Times*, June 18, 1865.
19. Eliza Andrews, *Wartime Journal*, 199; McCarter Journal, 93–94.

particular had earned themselves a place in history for the thoroughness with which they emptied the larders, personal strongboxes, and table silver from southern plantations and households. But they were scarcely inferior to their gray-coated opponents who thundered down upon plantations and swept away livestock, meat, grain, and forage, often commandeering the very wagons on which to carry the goods and leaving behind only scrawled and worthless receipts. Half of Georgia's northern counties had been turned into a wasteland by outlaw bands of soldiers and deserters, as well as Union and Confederate forces, concluded one Georgia newspaper in January of 1865. Riding together in small bands, they roamed from "house to house, from county to county plundering the scanty stores of the distressed and impoverished people."[20]

One South Carolina slave in the path of Sherman's troops recalled repeated Yankee raids in the last year of the war, raids that put everyone, black and white, on short rations. But Isaac Walker found little distinction between the blue-coated soldiers and the Confederates. The latter, he recalled, were "just about as hard and wolfish as de' Yankees." On one occasion they had unceremoniously rounded up several cows and much of the plantation's grain. "They say de Yankees was close behind them," recalled Walker, "and they just as well take things as to leave all for de' Yankees. Spect dat was true for de Yankees come next day and took de rest of de hog meat, flour and cows."[21] In such a setting, the distinction between legal and extralegal acts was well eroded by the end of the war.

In the short run these bands of "jayhawkers" posed the greatest threat to social order. Some of these groups had operated during the war with nominal allegiance to either the Confederacy or the Union, but they seldom answered to a precise chain of command. In Florida, William W. Strickland of Taylor County deserted in mid-1863 and formed a band of fifty raiders who operated under the romantic title of the Royal Rangers. For nearly two years, Strickland's company plundered plantations along the Gulf Coast, supplying Union blockaders with food and military intelligence. It is highly doubtful, however, if Strickland considered himself answerable to any authority beyond his own whims. Once, when the Royal Rangers easily eluded a Confederate attempt to corner them, Strickland sent his enraged pursuers a cheeky note offering to raise stock for the Confederate army if he and his men received an exemption from all military service. He had tried the Union side, he told Confederate Colonel Henry Capers, "but I find it is like the Confederate—more wind than work." When the war

20. Milledgeville (Ga.) *Confederate Union*, January 3, 1865.
21. Rawick (ed.), *The American Slave*, Ser. 1, Vol. III, p. 173.

ended, Strickland returned to his home, but many of his men moved up the coast and joined other former guerrillas to terrorize portions of northwest Florida and southern Alabama.[22]

Typically, these outlaw bands were composed of conscripts and deserters from the Confederate army who had begun their thievery as a means of survival and then, in the words of a Mississippi planter and minister, "continued practices countenanced by the customs of war." They existed in every part of the South, but they were most widespread in Texas, in the mountainous regions of North Carolina, Georgia, and Alabama, and throughout central and northern Mississippi. Conditions had deteriorated so sharply in Mississippi by the spring of 1865 that Confederate and Union army units tacitly cooperated in suppressing these irregular outlaw bands.[23]

With the war ended, Union army officers were able to turn their full attention to the eradication of these outlaws. General Thomas, commander of the Division of Tennessee (including Kentucky, Tennessee, Georgia, and Alabama), gave his subordinates latitude to use any measures necessary to end these depredations. In turn, Brigadier General H. M. Judah made these policies more explicit in instructions to his men. "Hunt down all guerillas and lawless depredators upon private property." When dealing with one particularly stubborn band of thieves, he was even more ruthless. "Take no prisoners," he instructed a cavalry officer, and there is ample evidence that his direction was followed to the letter. When one detachment of federal cavalrymen cornered thirteen alleged thieves near Charlotte, North Carolina, in late May, they gave the men no chance to surrender. "The guerillas were desperate characters," reported Captain Robert O'Shea with some pride, and "not one of their number escaped the penalty of their crimes." He was confident, he reported, that the "salutary results will prove a warning to others."[24]

By October of 1865, military officials, while acknowledging the continued existence of outlaw bands in northern Mississippi, northern Ala-

22. *OR*, Vol. LIII, Pt. 1, pp. 316–20; Walter L. Fleming, *The Civil War and Reconstruction in Alabama* (New York, 1905), 122–23; J. T. Sprague to Gen. O. O. Howard, December 31, 1866, (copy), in BRFAL, Microcopy 742, Roll 3, frame 168.

23. *OR*, Vol. XLVIII, Pt. 1, pp. 238–64, 431–33, 1073; Samuel Agnew Diary, May 1, 1865; Nimrod Porter Diary, SHC, February 2, 1865; T. Conn Bryan, *Confederate Georgia* (Athens, 1953), 137–55; Bessie Martin, *Desertion of Alabama Troops from the Confederate Army: A Study in Sectionalism* (New York, 1932), 24–26; Fleming, *Civil War and Reconstruction in Alabama*, 108–30; James W. Silver (ed.), "The Breakdown in Morale in Central Mississippi in 1864: Letters of Judge Robert S. Hudson," *JMH*, XVI (1954), 99–120; New Orleans *Picayune*, March 29, 1865. See also the extensive correspondence in 1864 and early 1865 on this subject in Mississippi Governors' Papers, MSA.

24. *OR*, Vol. XLIX, Pt. 2, pp. 465, 805, 855, Vol. XLVIII, Pt. 3, p. 545, Vol. XLVII, Pt. 3, pp. 64, 396, 460–61, 502–87.

bama, and Texas, insisted that most groups had been dispersed. "Every-thing in this country shows a state of pacification," one army officer wrote from western Virginia. "The worst band of guerillas . . . have all been killed or surrendered." One western North Carolina Confederate had filled his wartime diary with angry denunciations of the "Yankee nation and all its minions." By June he was enthusiastically praising the security brought by the once-hated bluecoats. "Before their arrival we were threatened by armed mobs of Confederate soldiers, deserters, & c., but the Yankees put them down where they were."[25]

It was one thing to destroy semimilitary outlaw bands, however, and quite another to reverse the forces set in motion by four years of civil war. Union soldiers had often become inured to violence in four years of war, but northern travelers—particularly more genteel New England journalists—were horrified at the level of violence they encountered while traveling through the postwar South. A shaken Whitelaw Reid, touring the region as a reporter for the Cincinnati *Gazette*, told his readers that it was difficult to brush against a white southerner "without being bruised by his con-cealed revolver." In a twenty-four-hour visit to Albany, Georgia, in Novem-ber, 1865, a Boston *Advertiser* correspondent claimed to have witnessed half a dozen fistfights, shootings, knifings, and drunken brawls. And when Sidney Andrews made the mistake of trying to break up a knife fight be-tween a black man and a white on the town's main street, he nearly touched off a lynching in which he was to be the guest of honor. With the assistance of a sympathetic hotel owner, he fled from a drunken mob one step ahead of "knives, pistols and horsewhips." Little wonder that the Boston journalist assured his northern readers that it was impossible to describe such "filthy poverty, such foul ignorance, such idiotic imbecility, such bestial instincts, such groveling desires" as characterized a substantial portion of the popula-tion of the South.[26]

It is not surprising that northern journalists, army officers, government officials, and politicians—influenced by a generation of abolitionist propa-ganda—sometimes saw the turmoil and social conflict of the postwar South

25. *Ibid.*, Vol. XLVI, Pt. 3, pp. 868, 921, 1079; Schenck Diary, May 31, 1865; McCarter Journal, 92; John Hammond Moore (ed.), *The Juhl Letters to the Charleston "Courier"* (Athens, 1974), 41.
26. Sidney Andrews, *The South Since the War As Shown by Fourteen Weeks of Travel and Observation in Georgia and the Carolinas* (Boston, 1866), 288–300, 336; Whitelaw Reid, *After the War: A Southern Tour* (Cincinnati, 1866), 422; John Richard Dennett, *The South As It Is*, ed. Henry M. Christman (New York, 1965), 266–67. For a particularly vivid account of law-lessness and violence encountered by another northern traveler, see the testimony of Mordecai Mobley, a U.S. land agent, before the Joint Committee on Reconstruction. *House Reports*, 39th Cong., 1st Sess., No. 30, Pt. 1, p. 1921.

in a historical perspective. In the somewhat melodramatic words of one Ohio abolitionist, it was the "inevitable fruit of a decadent people, nurtured by the poisonous milk of slavery and filled with the arrogant bluster of lords of the manor who know no restraints on their savage appetites." A Virginian born and reared in New Jersey was slightly more restrained, but he found the same basic flaws in the "Southern character." If white southerners had a grudge against a man, black or white, "they will plan all manner of schemes to gratify their grudge," said Jonathan Roberts of Falls Church, Virginia. "Law they do not respect for its moral obligations"; only brute force could keep them from exercising their violent passions against all who challenged them. Twenty-five years before the war, a New England writer had sardonically described those "Southern gentlemen" who spent their time "chewing tobacco, drinking mint juleps in the morning and toddy at noon, horse-racing, fisticuffing and other like genteel accomplishments." Given the antebellum assumptions that shaped the attitudes of many northern travelers, they expressed little surprise that white southerners were so violent since they had done nothing before the war but, in the words of one Union soldier, "walloped niggers, fawned on the ladies and fought duels."[27]

If northern journalists were conscious of the historical roots of southern violence, they were nevertheless inclined to interpret lawlessness as a campaign of terror against unionists and helpless freedmen. Novelist John William De Forest, an agent for the Freedmen's Bureau in up-country South Carolina, disagreed. He recognized the racism underlying physical assaults by whites against blacks, and he occasionally saw political motivations in the attacks of whites against whites. He was much more inclined, however, to interpret these conflicts as part of a deep-rooted cultural pattern that had been reinforced by the upheavals of war and postwar Reconstruction. As a veteran army officer, De Forest seldom reacted with the naïveté of a Sidney Andrews or a Whitelaw Reid, but even De Forest was astonished at the level of mayhem in his district. The numerous affairs in "which the low-down whites butcher each other seldom receive much notice from the Southern papers," he observed. Whenever such an affair was

27. Cleveland *Leader*, September 18, 1865; *House Reports*, 39th Cong., 1st Sess., No. 30, Pt. 2, pp. 34–35; Russell H. Conwell, *Magnolia Journey: A Union Veteran Revisits the Former Confederate States*, ed. Joseph C. Carter (University, Ala., 1974), 133; Conwell, "The Southern Gentleman," *NEM*, VII (1834), 78. From somewhat different perspectives, George Tindall and C. Vann Woodward have explored the myths and images that have characterized the northern view of the South. Tindall, *The Ethnic Southerners* (Baton Rouge, 1976), 22–58; Woodward, *America Counterpoint: Slavery and Racism in the North-South Dialogue* (Boston, 1971). Howard R. Floan describes the literary origins of these images in *The South in Northern Eyes, 1831 to 1861* (Austin, 1958).

over, "the respectable portion of the community, if it is interested at all, thanks God and takes courage." Although much of this violence was directed by whites against blacks, De Forest concluded that these incidents were not simply a manifestation of racism. Poor whites "simply kill them in the exercise of their ordinary pugnacity." Before the war, such a murder would have ignited the anger of a prominent slaveowner. "Now, the negro is no better than they [the poor whites] are, and they pay him the compliment of fighting him as an equal."[28]

Nor was such behavior limited to the poor. "Self-respect, as the Southerners understand it," said De Forest, "has always demanded much fighting." As bureau officer for the Greenville District, he gradually became familiar with the histories of many prominent families. "I declare positive that I was amazed at the number of persons who bore marks of frays and the number of houses which had been rendered memorable by scenes of blood." After describing the violent histories of half a dozen well-to-do upcountry planters, he nevertheless concluded that the Greenville area was a "nest of turtledoves" and a "haven of Quakers compared with Abbeville, Newberry and half a dozen other districts." Southerners might point to the rampant crime of northern cities, but De Forest denied that the two could be compared. "Our tragedies are crimes . . . ; their tragedies are gentilities which the public voice does not condemn and for which the law rarely exacts a penalty."[29]

However much white southerners might deny the "exaggerated and unwarranted calumnies" of northern observers, their own correspondence reflected an all too easy acceptance of violence as a legitimate means of resolving disagreements. Francis Warrington Dawson, the Englishman who served on the staff of the Richmond *Examiner* during the war and eventually became editor of the Charleston *Daily Courier*, described with the enthusiasm of a recent convert his daily confrontations with opponents through the end of the war and the beginning of the postwar years. And his activities were only a pale reflection of his fellow "gentlemen" on the staff of the Richmond *Examiner*. Early in 1866 the editor of the rival *Enquirer*, Nathaniel Tyler, implied that Dawson's editor, H. R. Pollard, had defrauded the state through inflated printing costs. Pollard promptly sought out Tyler and found him in the lobby of the Virginia Statehouse. After a brief exchange of gunfire ("Nobody was hurt except George Washington's statue which had the top of its cane shot off"), the sergeant at arms managed to end the brief affray and both sides withdrew with their honor

28. John William De Forest, *A Union Officer in the Reconstruction*, ed. James H. Croushore and David M. Potter (New Haven, 1948), 153–54.
29. *Ibid.*, 181–82.

intact. But the issue had scarcely been settled before the irrepressible Pollard set out to punish E. P. Brooks, the New York *Times* Richmond correspondent. Brooks had published an "insulting letter," reported Dawson, and when Pollard found him in the lobby of a Richmond hotel, the editor of the *Examiner* "cow-hided him heartily." Friends of the northern journalist threatened retribution, and "we armed ourselves with revolvers, went down and lounged about, but could see nothing of the cowardly rascals." Concluded Dawson: It was a "characteristic episode in Southern life and meets with the hearty approval of the community." Had he survived, Dawson would presumably have been less enthusiastic about the unchivalric response of Dr. Thomas B. McDow, who refused to accept a caning at Dawson's hands in 1889. The doctor, a "foreigner" and presumably unfamiliar with the etiquette of such matters, pulled out a revolver and killed Dawson.[30]

In some respects, therefore, the violence that characterized southern society in the wake of Appomattox was simply a continuation of traditional patterns, however exacerbated by the turmoil of civil war, emancipation, and postwar racial adjustment. But there were critical differences in the perceptions of most white southerners. Those bloody personal encounters, or "affairs of honor," that so horrified northern visitors were not reflections of illegality as much as extralegality. The rural nature of the South, the plantation system of slavery, and the existence of a strong unwritten code of behavior acted in concert to restrict the power of "ordinary law" and to enlarge the areas of life governed by informal social restraints. Andrew Jackson's mother had summarized a major part of this unwritten code among whites when she told her son: "Never tell a lie, nor take what is not your own, nor sue anybody for slander or assault and battery. *Always settle them cases yourself.*" Despite the lack of visible manifestations of the law, there was in reality a complex body of customs—an unwritten code of folkways—that governed the nature and limits of such conflict. Whether acted out with the punctilious regard for the code duello or the uninhibited enthusiasm of an eye-gouging, nose-biting backwoods brawl, it was usually violence within socially defined limits.[31]

Frederick Law Olmsted, that veteran observer of the antebellum South,

30. Francis Warrington Dawson to Mother, June 7, 1866, in Francis Warrington Dawson Papers, DUL; *Virginia House Journal*, 1865–1866, pp. 212–15; Charleston *News and Courier*, March 13, 14, June 30, 1889; E. Culpepper Clark, *Francis Warrington Dawson and the Politics of Restoration: South Carolina, 1874–1889* (University, Ala., 1980), 215–18.

31. Charles S. Sydnor, "The Southerner and the Laws," *JSH*, VI (1940), 12; Dickson Bruce, Jr., *Violence and Culture in the Antebellum South* (Austin, 1979); Bertram Wyatt-Brown, *Southern Honor: A Study in Ethics and Behavior in the Antebellum South* (New York, 1982).

understood that these customs, although lacking the apparatus of government enforcement, were ultimately based upon the ease with which "vigilance" committees could be mobilized to express community will. Nevertheless, he was still surprised by the peculiar strength of southern folkways as opposed to institutional "stateways." In backcountry communities where "law and government is almost unknown," where many of the people were poor and illiterate and "accustomed to the use of the most certain deadly weapon," he found it remarkable that "law has so much power and its deliberate movements and provisions for justice to the accused parties are so much respected."[32] It was the collapse of these folkways that so unnerved white southerners in the months after Appomattox.

In northeastern Mississippi, a Presbyterian minister laconically noted in his diary a bloodcurdling litany of assaults, murders, and thefts in his once peaceful neighborhood. In one entry, he described the fate of an elderly neighbor who was dragged from his home by five former soldiers and hanged from a tree until he finally revealed the location of a concealed strongbox where he had hidden his meager savings. What was more ominous, marauding bands, which had begun their practices out of desperation, had begun to appreciate the opportunities afforded by a society in which there were no sheriffs, no laws, and no courts. "Lawlessness seems to be the order of the day," he concluded on May 12. It was the identical phrase used by a fellow southerner three hundred miles away—on the same day. And in the state of Texas, the editor of the Houston *Telegraph* admitted that "lawlessness and absolute robbery" pervaded much of the state between Houston and the Rio Grande.[33]

Even in a state like South Carolina, relatively untouched by the war until 1865, arriving Union military forces found "widespread outlawery" throughout the state. Six months after the war had ended, the public roads of large sections of the two Carolinas were still unsafe to travel. In Edgefield, South Carolina, the local military commander concluded with disgust that the "concentrated meanness of the state had evidently been put in the Edgefield District." Ten months after a garrison was stationed in that western South Carolina community, Brevet Lieutenant Colonel John Devereux admitted to his superior officer that he was unable to control two bands of outlaws who operated with impunity. The final insult had come when he was stopped in broad daylight, near Augusta, Georgia, wearing his uniform as a United States officer. The highwaymen stole his pocketbook,

32. New York *Daily News*, July 8, 1853; Frederick Law Olmsted, *A Journey in the Backcountry* (New York, 1860), 44.

33. Samuel Agnew Diary, May 8, 12, 1865; James Appleton Blackshear Diary, May 12, 1865; Houston *Tri-Weekly Telegraph*, June 15, 1865.

pocketwatch, and horse, and as a final indignity, they forced him to hand over his boots, leaving Devereux to walk back to Augusta in his stocking feet. Although Devereux might think he had been assigned to the worst post in the state, newspaper accounts, complaints to the governor, and directives of the military authorities made clear the extent to which robbery and violence had become a way of life for many South Carolinians.[34]

Moreover, there is some evidence that the actual level of crime may have been consciously underreported. When North Carolina's first elected postwar governor, Jonathan Worth, continued to read reports in the state's newspapers of robberies and murders, he wrote to editors of friendly journals warning that continued accounts of these depredations would jeopardize the South's chances for reentering the Union. At least one, W. J. Yates of the Charlotte *Democrat*, assured the governor that he would carefully screen all such reports and refrain from publishing all but the most notorious incidents in order to "maintain the good name and character of the state."[35]

A less discreet New Bern, North Carolina, newspaper editor filled his columns with descriptions (some of them clearly fanciful) of widespread assaults and robberies. More than a year after the end of the war, he observed to his readers that it was impossible for southerners to pick up a local newspaper without being "horror-stricken with the details of some terrible atrocity, highway robbery or daring murder." Before the war these were unusual occurrences worth noting, he said, "but lately they have become of such frequent occurrence that a traveller by private conveyance or the dweller in remote areas holds his life by a frail tenure." If something was not done, "it will be as unsafe to travel our public roads as in poor Mexico."[36]

Observers sometimes differed as to which area of the South was most unsettled and crime-ridden. Benjamin G. Truman, traveling through the South on behalf of President Johnson in the fall of 1865, insisted that "Mississippians have been shooting and cutting each other all over the state to a greater extent than in all the other states of the Union put together." General William E. Strong, on the other hand, while aware of the mark set by Mississippians, insisted that Texas richly deserved this dubious honor. And at various times other travelers nominated Georgia, South Carolina, Tennessee, North Carolina, and Alabama. One former Union soldier from Cin-

34. Bvt. Lt. Col. Devereux to Maj. H. W. Smith, February 28, 1866, in BRFAL, South Carolina, Box 23.
35. W. J. Yates to Gov. Jonathan Worth, January 24, 1866, in Jonathan Worth Papers, NCA.
36. New Bern (N.C.) *Journal of Commerce*, October 20, 1866.

cinnati, visiting in Florida, was convinced that this state was the most lawless he had seen in all his travels in the South. Fortunately, he said, the
"outlaws and bushwhackers have no-one on which to inflict their sundry
cruelties except alligators, snakes, swamp rats and fellow outlaws (since
that is all that seems to live in this miserable place)."[37]

White southerners of influence and position might regret—even de-
plore—the mistreatment of former slaves, but they were quick to insist that
the greater threat was posed by the "insolence" and "insubordination" of
the millions of blacks in their midst. And however much it might horrify
the more refined sensibilities of New England newspapermen, the continued tendency of white southerners to resort to pistol, bowie knife, or
gutta percha cane to settle their personal disputes aroused little alarm. If
the victor was a southern gentleman and the victim an impudent northern
newspaperman, such incidents might even seem pleasantly exciting. When
Francis Warrington Dawson described H. R. Pollard's thrashing of New
York *Times* correspondent E. P. Brooks to a drawing room filled with
southern ladies, they "clapped their hands with joy" at his account of how a
"miserable Yankee had been so well thrashed by a Southern gentleman."
As Dawson quickly perceived, such incidents added a welcome dash of excitement to an otherwise drab and depressing postwar existence.[38]

What frightened white southerners was the growth of a different kind of
violence: crimes against property and crimes against individuals that took
place outside the framework of traditional community mores. It was regrettable but understandable if one gentleman killed another over a real or
imagined personal insult. It was not even regrettable if a white southerner
was forced to take violent action to remind black southerners of their
proper place. It was terrifying, on the other hand, if a man was dragged
from his home by unknown assailants, and his property was destroyed or
stolen. And the traditional means of restoring order—harsh punishment by

37. New York *Times*, February 4, 1866; New York *Herald*, January 21, 1866; Devereux to
Smith, February 28, 1866, in BRFAL, South Carolina, Box 23; Macon *Gazette*, August 16,
1865; Savannah *Daily Republican*, September 1, 1865; Robert Johns to Andrew Johnson,
May 31, 1865, in Andrew Johnson Papers, LC. Measuring the level of crime is notoriously
difficult. Often perceptions of lawlessness bear little relationship to the actual level of lawbreak-
ing. Nevertheless, the level of petty thievery and crimes of violence undoubtedly increased dramatically during and after the war. One historian who has examined this issue in one state concluded that estimates of violence and social disorder have been far too low. Jesse Parker Bogue,
"Violence and Oppression in North Carolina During Reconstruction, 1865–1873" (Ph.D. dissertation, University of Maryland, 1973), 2–3. And in a recent article surveying postwar
homicide rates in more than twenty countries, Dana Archer and Rosemary Gartner have concluded that criminality has sharply increased following large-scale wars. "Violent Acts and
Violent Times: A Comparative Approach to Post-war Homicide Rates," *ASR*, XLI (1976),
973–83.
38. Dawson to Mother, June 11, 1866, in Dawson Papers.

a community court or the even swifter punishment of a vigilance committee—were barred by the presence of the Union army and the demoralization of the white majority.[39]

Parts of the South remained relatively calm and untroubled in the months after Appomattox; at no time was the region threatened with complete anarchy. But the prevalence of crime and social disorder created a pervasive sense of fear and uncertainty, a state of mind reflected in the jeremiads of many white southerners. Like all Americans, "we have been boastful on account of our material means . . . wealth and physical powers," observed the Louisiana historian Charles Étienne Gayarré as the war drew to its end. "We now see how we have destroyed it with our own hands." He cited and agreed with the prediction of British historian Thomas B. Macaulay that there would ultimately be "more horror perpetrated, more blood shed and more barbarism exhibited [in America] than had ever been seen in Europe, even in the days of Attilla." The war, he warned his old friend J. D. B. De Bow, was only a foretaste of the future.[40]

Such apprehension was not without its beneficial side effects. The fear of anarchy had been a major factor in leading most southern military and civilian leaders to ignore Jefferson Davis' last call for a campaign of guerrilla warfare.[41] At the same time it created a willingness on the part of white southerners in the short run to accept almost any form of government that would restore order to a disordered land. In contrast to these limited benefits, the fear of social anarchy, when joined to the mental dislocation wrought by emancipation, economic chaos, and political uncertainty, reinforced the repressive legacies of slavery and created a setting in which violence and repression could flourish. As a young German-speaking Texas Confederate watched his frantic commanding officer station cannon on the streets of Houston in an attempt to intimidate rampaging former Confederate troops, he had been filled with apprehension. "I do not know if peace will put an end to all of this for us," he wrote his father, "or whether it won't be as when a predatory animal is shot: the last convulsions are the most dangerous."[42]

39. There were exceptions to the military's refusal to tolerate such committees, as when a frustrated cavalry officer stationed in Camden, Arkansas, unable to track down a band of guerrillas, urged local citizens to form a "public safety" committee and give a "long rope and a short shrift" to "jayhawkers, murders and robbers." *OR*, Vol. XLVIII, Pt. 1, pp. 847–48.

40. Charles Étienne Arthur Gayarré to J. D. B. De Bow, April 20, 1865, in J. D. B. De Bow Papers, DUL.

41. See especially the final letters of advice written by members of Jefferson Davis' cabinet in mid-April of 1865. *OR*, Vol. XLVIII, Pt. 3, pp. 813–34.

42. Minetta Altgelt Goyne (ed.), *Lone Star and Double Eagle: Civil War Letters of a German-Texas Family* (Lubbock, Tex., 1982), 172–73.

II / Self-Reconstruction Begins: The Failure of Strait-Sect Unionism

IN THE weeks after Abraham Lincoln's assassination, white southerners waited for Andrew Johnson's first substantive policy announce-
ments with understandable uncertainty and uneasiness. To hear Vice-
President Johnson speak on the subject of secession, Carl Schurz later
recalled, "one would have thought that if this man ever came into power,
the face of the country would soon bristle with gibbets and foreign lands
swarm with fugitives from the avenging sword of the Republic." Southerners of more modest means could take heart from the fact that he had directed his darkest threats against the "great planters" who had lorded it
over their poor neighbors and sneered at Negro equality even though
"mulatto children" surrounded their homes, "the product of concubinage,
compared to which, polygamy is a virtue." An old Tennessee rival claimed
that no emotion—fear, love, disgust, or jealousy—matched the hatred
Johnson had felt for the southern "aristocrat." If "Johnson were a snake,"
concluded Isham Harris, "he would lie in the grass to bite the heels of rich
men's children." Throughout his long political career, he had hated gentlemen by instinct. As he said on April 3, he would be lenient with the poor
and with honestly deluded southern soldiers, but as for the rich and influential secessionists, he declared, "I would arrest them—I would try them—
I would convict them and I would hang them." However consoling this
class bias might be for the common southerners, it was hardly reassuring to
men of property.[1]

1. Frank Moore (ed.), *Speeches of Andrew Johnson, President of the United States. With a Biographical Introduction* (Boston, 1865), xxxv; Clifton Hall, *Andrew Johnson, Military Gover-nor of Tennessee* (Princeton, 1916), 22, 174, 221; John M. Palmer, *Personal Recollections of*

The president's May 29 Proclamation of Amnesty and Pardon—his first major statement on postwar policy—appeared to be a chilling reflection of his mistrust of wealthy southerners. Although the majority of southerners who supported the Confederacy were to receive a pardon as soon as they had taken the oath of allegiance to the United States and promised to obey the Emancipation Proclamation, there were fourteen categories of exceptions. The largest excluded those former rebels with twenty thousand dollars' worth of property from the generous provisions of Johnson's amnesty policy, barred them from public life, and threw them into a legal limbo in which they remained subject to all the penalties of treason. While northern Republicans tended to focus upon the effect of these exemptions upon the suffrage, unpardoned southerners were initially far more concerned about their property holdings. Altogether fifteen thousand southerners filed pardon applications, more than half of them threatened by the "twenty thousand dollars" clause. Even if one took the optimistic position that the president would avoid extensive treason trials, excepted southerners were barred from any licensed profession such as the law and their property remained subject to confiscation.[2]

Even as he threatened with one clause, however, the president offered clemency with another. Pardons would be "liberally extended" on an individual basis, he declared, "consistent with the facts of the case and with the peace and dignity of the United States." And to make his point even clearer, he met with delegations of apprehensive southerners during the months of June and July to assure them that, his wartime threats notwithstanding, his postwar policy included neither gibbets nor banishment.[3]

The president's conservative approach to Reconstruction was further reflected in the character and political outlook of the seven men he selected during June and early July as provisional governors for the two Carolinas, Georgia, Florida, Alabama, Mississippi, and Texas. Although the significance of these appointments was unclear in the summer of 1865 they were to prove critical in establishing the limits of Andrew Johnson's plans to "reconstruct" the South. The president would intervene in southern politics on several occasions in 1865 and 1866, but he always preferred that white southerners initiate policies within the guidelines he had outlined.

John M. Palmer: The Story of an Earnest Life (Cincinnati, 1901), 127; Carl Schurz, The Reminiscences of Carl Schurz (3 vols.; Garden City, N.Y., 1913), III, 95; Life, Speeches, and Services of Andrew Johnson, Seventeenth President of the United States (Philadelphia, 1865), 118–20.

2. James D. Richardson (comp.), A Compilation of the Messages and Papers of the Presidents, 1789–1897 (11 vols.; Washington, D.C., 1896–99), VI, 213–18; Jonathan T. Dorris, "Pardon Seekers and Brokers: A Sequel to Appomattox," JSH, I (1935), 291.

3. In fact, Johnson had foreshadowed his policy on May 8 when he recognized the tenuous Pierpont regime in Virginia without preconditions. New York Times, May 9, 1865.

Given that latitude and the fact that all legitimate political power seemed to flow from the president through the provisional governors in the initial stages of Reconstruction, it was only mild hyperbole for North Carolina's David Swain to claim that W. W. Holden (and, by implication, other provisional governors) exercised authority "not merely greater than known to his predecessors, but greater than ever were claimed for an English monarch since 1688."[4]

What was soon apparent, however, was the widely disparate backgrounds and outlooks the seven men brought to their postwar appointments. W. W. Holden of North Carolina, James Johnson of Georgia, Benjamin F. Perry of South Carolina, and Andrew Jackson Hamilton of Texas came from the same yeoman, small-farmer constituency that had sustained the president throughout his career. But William Marvin of Florida was far more at home with business friends and colleagues from his native New York than with the piney-woods farmers of Florida. Although Lewis Parsons made his home in the up-country of Alabama, his closest ties were to the emerging merchant-business-railroad class of his state, a political and economic orientation suggested by his lifelong allegiance to the old Whig party. And William Sharkey of Mississippi was almost a caricature of the class that had earned Johnson's hatred. Sharkey had been a well-to-do slaveowner and prominent southern Whig before the war, and his early years in the hills of eastern Tennessee had seemed to reinforce rather than modify his commitment to political elitism, a commitment reflected in his outspoken advocacy of a property ownership requirement for all voters.[5]

If there was a common characteristic that cut across these differences, it was the fact that the seven were all at least minimally acceptable to the majority of the white citizens of their respective states. James Johnson of Georgia, Lewis Parsons of Alabama, and William Sharkey of Mississippi had remained at their homes during most of the war, maintaining a discreet silence on political issues. William Marvin of Florida was technically a consistent unionist since he had spent much of the war behind federal lines as a United States district judge, but his conservative wartime and postwar statements made him acceptable to all except the most unreconciled Florida rebels. Although North Carolina's W. W. Holden had led his state's peace

4. David L. Swain to William Alexander Graham, July 4, 1865, in William Alexander Graham Papers, NCA. Reconstruction was already underway in Virginia, Arkansas, Tennessee, and Louisiana, although the future of the wartime unionist governments was still uncertain in the summer of 1865.

5. For the best description of the selection process that Johnson followed, see Michael Perman's "Southern Politics and American Reunion, 1865–1868" (Ph.D. dissertation, University of Chicago, 1968), 125–60. Sources on the background of Johnson's appointees may be found in the footnotes that follow.

movement in 1863 and 1864, he had earlier endorsed secession, and he maintained close relations with some of the state's most prominent Confederate officials throughout the war. And Benjamin Perry of South Carolina had actively supported the Confederacy once secession was an accomplished fact, serving in important civil and military positions. Only Andrew Jackson Hamilton of Texas had been an outspoken and uncompromising unionist throughout the war, and his appointment may have stemmed from Lincoln's stated wish that Hamilton be named provisional governor for Texas.[6] Collectively, therefore, the seven men represented that substantial body of southerners who had opposed secession until late 1860 but had then either gone with their state or avoided public condemnation of the new Confederate government. They did not represent the handful of consistently loyal white southerners who had captured the admiration and imagination of a patriotic North.

The frantic efforts of various southern factions to disown their role in secession and appropriate the title of unionist reminded a former Alabama governor of the ludicrous consequences of an antebellum deer hunt. These deer drives were what the lawyers called an *in solido* business, said Andrew Moore—what one man killed all shared. In this particular hunt two acquaintances had set themselves up in adjacent deer blinds and waited for the frightened animals to pass. At the sound of a gunshot and an animal crashing to the ground, one of the hunters rushed to the scene to claim his share. Instead, he found that his crestfallen companion had "dropped by a splendid shot . . . a fine and most valuable horse." "My God," said the chagrined marksman, "*we* have killed a horse." "The devil," replied his previously greedy friend, "*you* killed the horse. I had nothing to do with it."[7]

From the outset, most Republicans were totally unimpressed with the efforts of reluctant secessionists to appropriate the title of unionist. As one Ohio newspaper editor angrily responded, a definition that included men simply because they were reluctant members of the "original band of thieves" who had attacked the Republic in 1860 would "dishonor the thousands of *true unionists* who sleep the endless sleep in martyr's graves." Nevertheless, Johnson's appointees always saw themselves as victims of the passions aroused by their rabble-rousing antebellum opponents, the secessionists. It was those secessionists who had unnecessarily plunged the South into a needless and disastrous war. And it was the secessionists who had thus abrogated their right to play an important role in the politics of the postwar South. If these reluctant secessionists or unionists, as they now

6. New York *Times*, June 9, 1865.
7. Montgomery *Advertiser*, September 28, 1865; Cleveland *Leader*, October 7, 1865.

conveniently described themselves, blamed their old political enemies for the calamities of the region, however, they also emphasized forgiveness and reconciliation, not punishment and proscription. Like the president who had appointed them, they envisioned neither gibbet nor banishment for their fellow southerners.

The president's generous amnesty policies and the moderate background of his gubernatorial appointees complemented the limited political demands he outlined for southern restoration into the Union. The nature and extent of these preconditions for southern reentry shifted slightly under changing conditions through the fall of 1865. When some North Carolina unionists complained, for example, of plans to postpone repudiation of state war debts, Johnson made repudiation a precondition for readmission into the Union. And growing northern concern over restrictive legislation directed against the freedmen led the president to insist that basic civil rights, short of suffrage, be granted to the emancipated slave. Basically, however, white southerners had only to renounce the pernicious doctrine of secession, accept emancipation, repudiate their war debts, and swear an oath of loyalty to the government they had foolishly abandoned.[8]

Johnson's conciliatory actions, as opposed to his angry threats, should have been a clear indication by midsummer that he had no ambitious plan to reshape postwar southern politics and postwar southern society. A handful of radical Republicans, sensitized by four years of sparring with the cautious Lincoln quickly recognized the conservative implications of the president's policies, but they remained powerless for the time being. Moderate Republicans, lulled by the president's tough talk and his conciliatory conversations with Republican party leaders, had no desire to challenge the new head of their party. As veterans of the long tug-of-war between Lincoln and the conflicting elements of their fractious party, they assumed that Johnson could always modify the direction of his policy if the results proved unsatisfactory.[9] They were wrong.

It was not that the president opposed all change within the South. Like

8. Eric McKitrick's superb study *Andrew Johnson and Reconstruction* (Chicago, 1960) remains the best account of Johnson's approach to the reconstruction process although it should be supplemented by LaWanda Cox and John Cox, *Politics, Principle, and Prejudice, 1865–1866: Dilemma of Reconstruction America* (Glencoe, Ill., 1963).

9. Johnson consciously or unconsciously encouraged the self-deception of Republican moderates by implying that his program was conditional rather than final. See for example George S. Boutwell's *Reminiscences of Sixty Years in Public Affairs* (2 vols.; New York, 1902), I, 103–104. For a detailed discussion of the relationship between Johnson and the Republican party during the critical summer of 1865, see Michael Les Benedict's *A Compromise of Principle: Congressional Republicans and Reconstruction, 1863–1869* (New York, 1974), 100–16; Andrew Johnson, *Speech of Governor Andrew Johnson on the Restoration of State Government* [pamphlet] (Nashville, 1864), 6.

any surviving antebellum southern politician, Andrew Johnson had made his peace with slavery, but he was then and he remained during and after the war an enemy of the class structure that had developed as a by-product of the peculiar institution. In a bitter antebellum debate with South Carolina's James Hammond, for example, Johnson had indirectly attacked many of the assumptions underlying the proslavery argument. It made no sense, he had declared on the eve of the war, for men to justify slavery on the grounds that slaves performed "menial tasks." For this assumed that "every man who does not own slaves, but has to live by his own labor, is a slave." When the war began and Johnson chose the Union over the Confederacy he was able to speak even more frankly, without concern for the political delicacies of the slavery issue. And he argued that slavery had always been an "iniquitous system," not so much because of the damage it had done to the slaves, but because it allowed a handful of wealthy individuals "by means of forced and unpaid labor" to monopolize the lands and wealth of the South. ("Damn the negroes," exploded Johnson when he first learned of the Emancipation Proclamation. "I am fighting these traitorous aristocrats, their masters!") Slavery had been the linchpin of that system, believed Johnson, and with it gone, the natural laws of political economy operating in a democratic society would lead to a social and economic revolution. "If you cut up these large cotton farms into small-sized farms," argued Johnson, the end result would be an agricultural renaissance in the South. And beyond the farm population, it would "give more good citizens to the commonwealth, increase the wages of our mechanics, enrich the markets of our city, enliven all the arteries of trade, improve society and conduce to the greatness and glory of the state."[10]

Johnson's views on race did change during the war. As military governor of Tennessee in 1863, he endorsed a postemancipation black code that would have thrown the freed slaves of Tennessee directly under the control of their former owners. By the time of his election as vice-president, he had endorsed, in vague terms, "personal liberty, education, compensation for labor, and [unrestricted] choice of economic pursuit." Even as he left for Washington in the winter of 1864–1865, however, he was convinced some form of special legislation for the freedmen was essential, and this assumption shaped Johnson's postwar policies and pushed him toward a lenient treatment of the South's traditional leadership. As Great Britain's minister to the United States reported to his government, the president had not simply rejected a significant political role for the freedmen, he was con-

10. Leroy P. Graf and Ralph W. Haskins (eds.), *The Papers of Andrew Johnson, 1858–1860* (10 vols. to date; Knoxville, 1972), III, 158–60; G. W. Bacon, *Life and Speeches of President Andrew Johnson* (London, 1866), 68–69.

vinced that the very survival of the South's black population and the region's economy was jeopardized by the suddenness of the emancipation process. Released to their own devices, the former slaves would become "idle, thievish and dissipated." Their only hope was to remain under the tutelage and control of the South's large landowners—their former masters. In Johnson's view (claimed Sir Frederick Bruce) the freedmen's well-being would be far better protected by relying upon the "interests" of southern planters than on "ignorant Northern sentimentalists" and the "Radical majority in Congress," who hoped to use the freed population as a "means to prolong their tenure of power."[11]

Johnson's racism and his vague beliefs in the efficacy of "natural laws" were matched by his insensitivity to the growing national concern over the civil and political rights of the emancipated slaves. As the wartime military governor of Tennessee and as Lincoln's vice-president, Johnson was familiar with the history of the wartime debate over Reconstruction policy, but he seemed unaware of the complex process by which Lincoln had compromised his differences with that portion of the Republican party most concerned with the rights of the freedmen and most suspicious of the trustworthiness of defeated white southerners.[12] For Andrew Johnson, the great challenge to the indissoluble Union had ended in April and May of 1865, and the way was open for a rapid national reunification and the restoration of state and local governments. The army and the Freedmen's Bureau might assist in maintaining order and easing the transition from war to peace and from a slave economy to a free one, but the obligations of the federal government did not extend beyond these limited duties and the re-creation of loyal state governments.

One measure of Johnson's reluctance to intervene in the affairs of the provisional governments may be gauged from a conversation he held with Benjamin Perry following the South Carolina unionist's appointment. As the two men walked to the door at the end of the interview, Perry recalled, Johnson asked "that I write him occasionally and let him know how I was getting on in reconstructing the state." To Perry, the implication was pleas-

11. Sir Frederick Bruce to Earl of Clarendon, February 9, May 6, 1866, in Eric Foner (ed.), "Notes and Documents, Andrew Johnson and Reconstruction: A British View," *JSH*, XLI (1975), 368–69; John Y. Simon and Felix James (eds.), "Andrew Johnson and the Freedmen," *LH*, LXXIX (1977), 74–75; John Cimprich, "Military Governor Johnson and Tennessee Blacks, 1862–1865," *THQ*, XXXIX (1980), 459–70; Hans Trefousse, *Impeachment of a President: Andrew Johnson, the Blacks, and Reconstruction* (Knoxville, 1975), 43.

12. For a summary of the importance of these wartime reconstruction efforts, see Herman Belz, *Reconstructing the Union: Theory and Policy During the Civil War* (Ithaca, 1969). Peyton McCrary, *Abraham Lincoln and Reconstruction: The Louisiana Experiment* (Princeton, 1978), shows how moderate and radical Republicans were particularly affected by events in that Delta state.

antly clear: such reports were a matter of courtesy, but he was not account-able to the president on most matters. Unlike Perry, who was anxious to have a free hand, Virginia's Governor Francis Pierpont complained that he was repeatedly forced to make critical decisions with "no instruction or ad-vice of any kind from the President." A revolution had occurred in the American political system between 1860 and 1865, but Andrew Johnson's lifelong commitment to a federal compact with a central government of lim-ited powers remained unshaken.[13]

Whatever the motivation underlying Johnson's unwillingness to adopt a coercive policy toward the South, his decisions inevitably made white southerners less concerned over the necessity of pacifying uneasy north-erners. They should have been more aware of the limits of the president's authority in outlining conditions for readmission into the Union, but it is hardly surprising that they were not. Quite apart from an understandable tendency to accept the most painless prescription for reunion, white south-erners knew that the president had widespread support among north-erners—Democrats as well as Republicans. It was this consciousness of the president's general political popularity that made them insensitive to the subtle limitations of northern political support. In time they would receive a painful lesson in the realities of national postwar politics, but for the time being they were free to undertake their experiment in self-reconstruction.

Initially white southerners were most preoccupied with bringing order to chaos. Throughout the summer of 1865 frightened planters and busi-nessmen, office-hungry petitioners, confused and uncertain army officials, and even more confused interim state officials crowded the stiflingly hot streets of Raleigh, Columbia, Milledgeville, Tallahassee, Montgomery, and Jackson. Faced with their constant harassment, at least one provisional gov-ernor resumed his celebrated antebellum drinking patterns and another suffered a temporary collapse from overwork.[14] The short-run need to re-store some semblance of state and local government consumed most of the working time of Johnson's appointees, and few had time to thoughtfully outline the political philosophy that shaped their postwar policy. But their decisions, however haphazard they appeared at times, formed the frame-work for the kind of postwar society they envisioned. And the first and

13. Benjamin Perry, *Reminiscences of Public Men, with Speeches and Addresses* (Greenville, S.C., 1889), 248–49. See also William H. Seward to Benjamin Perry, September 6, 1865, in Benjamin Perry Manuscripts (Microfilm, 2 reels, SHC, 1967); Richard Lowe, "Republicans, Rebellion, and Reconstruction: The Republican Party in Virginia, 1856–1870" (Ph.D. disser-tation, University of Virginia, 1968), 192.
14. John L. Waller, *Colossal Hamilton of Texas: A Biography of Andrew Jackson Hamilton, Militant Unionist and Reconstruction Governor* (El Paso, Tex., 1968), 97–98; Raleigh *Progress*, August 23, 1865.

most critical decision was made at the outset. With the exceptions of North Carolina's W. W. Holden and Texas' Andrew Jackson Hamilton, Johnson's appointees refused to rely upon the hard core of southern unionists who had remained loyal to the federal government throughout the war.

This implicit rejection of the so-called strait-sect unionists was one of the first of a long list of actions that would alienate a suspicious northern public and gradually erode the popularity of the president's plan to reconstruct the South. Throughout the war, noted Whitelaw Reid, northerners had believed in the existence of a "strong Union Party in the South." And this belief had grown stronger as southern antiwar sentiment increased in 1863 and 1864. Nor was the notion of widespread dissidence simply a creation of the hesitant peace movements of 1863 and 1864. Throughout the 1850s and well into the war, many northerners were unwilling to acknowledge the broad support for the secession movement. John Cairnes, though an Englishman, captured this cast of mind in 1863 when he argued that the rebellion had been the handiwork of a "controlled despotism" wielded by a "compact oligarchy, supported by their four million slaves and dominating the white majority." The rebellion was "merely a shell [and we] have but to crack it to find it hollow," insisted one abolitionist in 1864. If given the chance, he concluded, "nine-tenths of the rank and file of the rebel army would gladly lay down their arms and go peacefully back to their homes today." Even President Johnson, as military governor of Tennessee, argued that the small farmers and yeomanry of the South had been "decoyed" and "driven into the rebellion."[15] Most numerous in the border South, these national loyalists supposedly existed in great numbers throughout the South, particularly among the ranks of the small farmers living outside the rich lands of the black belt and relatively untainted by the enervating blight of slavery.

There were such southern unionists, and they generally expected to

15. Whitelaw Reid, *After the War: A Southern Tour* (Cincinnati, 1866), 298; John E. Cairnes, *The Slave Power: Its Character, Career, and Probable Designs; Being an Attempt to Explain the Real Issues Involved in the American Contest* (London, 1863), 103; Edmund Kirke, *Down in Tennessee and Back by Way of Richmond* (London, 1864), 124; Cleveland *Leader*, May 18, 1865. For accounts of the wartime peace movements, see Walter L. Fleming, "The Peace Movement in Alabama During the Civil War," *SAQ*, II (1903), 114–24, 246–60; Ted R. Worley, "The Arkansas Peace Society of 1861: A Study in Mountain Unionism," *JSH*, XXIV (1958), 445–56; Henry T. Shanks, "Disloyalty to the Confederacy in Southwestern Virginia, 1861–1865," *NCHR*, XXI (1944), 118–35; William T. Auman and David R. Scarboro, "The Heroes of America in Civil War North Carolina," *NCHR*, LVIII (1981), 327–63; Marc W. Kruman, "Dissent in the Confederacy: The North Carolina Experience," *CWH*, XXVII (1981), 293–313; Roberta F. Cason, "The Loyal League in Georgia," *GHQ*, XX (1936), 125–53.

dominate the politics of the postwar South. For them, the late spring and early summer of 1865 was a time of celebration. That "damned old Confederacy has finally gone up the shoot," proclaimed a jubilant Thomas DuVal of Texas. And with the collapse of that treasonable conspiracy, patriotic unionists would lead the way through the "wilderness of reconstruction." In Louisiana, one of the first states to begin the process of restoration, unionists who had fled behind U.S. Army lines returned to their homes filled with optimism. Union men and "Union men *only*" would be in power, one wartime refugee insisted. The secessionists had had their day; now that the Union cause was triumphant, "let us have ours."[16]

To many consistent unionists the collapse of the Confederacy was an opportunity for long-delayed satisfaction at the expense of their political opponents. "It is astonishing & at the same time amusing to see how meek & mild all those violent fellows now are," observed one north Mississippi unionist with mock surprise. During the last dark days of the war, his Confederate neighbors had assured him they would leave the country if the North won. "I have been trying to keep them to their words, but they don't want to recollect." A. W. Joyce of Stokes County, North Carolina, traveled into nearby Salem on Independence Day, 1865, to hear a round of fiery speeches attacking the "infamous wretches" who had led his state into the war. The diehard Confederates sat quietly for the most part, he said, wearing "long faces like hired mourners at a burying," though there was an "occasional groan like a horse with cholic [*sic*]" when speakers described a suitable hanging for Jeff Davis.[17]

Mixed with this good-natured sense of vindication was a generous dose of vindictiveness, which, as in the case of Andrew Johnson, gave the illusion of southern radicalism. Throughout the war, Ethelred Philips of Marianna, Florida, filled his correspondence with denunciations of the "damned secesh" who had destroyed his beloved Union. Of these rebels he hated none so much as John Milton, the fire-eating Confederate governor of Florida. When Philips learned that Milton had taken his life in April of 1865 the Marianna physician was beside himself with joy. The "damned scoundrel," reported a gleeful Philips, had "put the muzzle of his gun to his

16. Thomas DuVal Diary, UTA, April 10, May 10, 1865; Mrs. Maj. Barlow to James Govan Taliaferro, July 25, 1867, in Taliaferro Family Papers, LSU; Jeremiah Clemens to Andrew Johnson, April 21, 1865, Huntsville [Ala.] Citizens to Andrew Johnson, June 6, 1865, Sampson County [N.C.] Union League to Andrew Johnson, June 22, 1865, all in Andrew Johnson Papers, LC.

17. Thomas Surget to Stephen Duncan, June 12, 14, 1865, in Stephen Duncan Papers, LSU; A. W. Joyce to W. W. Holden, July 5, 1865, in Governor William Woods Holden Papers, NCA.

eyes, pulled the trigger with his toe & sprinkled his brains over the ceiling of his room—by far the best act of his bastardly life."[18]

Other southern unionists shared Philips' bloodthirsty desire for revenge—none more than William G. "Parson" Brownlow of Tennessee, who transformed vengeance into a state religion and exemplified the bitterness of those antisecessionists who had been persecuted during the war. In the summer of 1865 when a group of former Confederates in East Tennessee pleaded for protection from the reprisals of revenge-seeking unionists, Brownlow responded by insisting that "every field of carnage, every rebel prison, every Union man's grave unite with a violated law and demand the penalty, and if the courts do not administer it, an outraged people will." The persecutors of union men had "forefeited all right to protection and life," continued Governor Brownlow. "I am not among those who would restrain their vengeance against their oppressors, so long," he hastened to add, as their revenge was kept within "reasonable bounds." As one delegate to the Tennessee constitutional convention of 1865 succinctly put the matter, "The only right they [the rebels] have is to be hung." John Carper's enthusiasm for public hangings was shared by other unionists. "I am opposed to pardoning any of them," insisted North Carolina's Warren Powell. "I had rather hang every one."[19]

Such bitter political animosity grew directly out of the wartime conflict in Tennessee, the most divided of southern states. Through the introduction of martial law in 1862, Confederate forces had maintained a semblance of authority, but by mid-1863 eastern Tennessee and much of the rest of the state was a battleground for nonuniformed gunmen quite apart from the armies of the North and South. James Welch Patton exaggerated only slightly when he described a "reign of terror" throughout 1864 and 1865 during which Confederate vigilantes rode through the countryside, armed to the teeth, arresting men on suspicion of hostility to the new government and shooting others down. At the same time, the unionists, in retaliation, formed secret "bushwhacking" societies, shot Confederates from ambush and destroyed their property. One Tennessean who lived through the years remembered them vividly nearly a half century later. "It was the reign of terror—war at every man's door, neighbor against neighbor," recalled David Sullins. "Neither property nor life was safe by day or night."[20]

18. Ethelred Philips to J. C. Philips, October 24, 1865, in James John Philips Papers, SHC.
19. Knoxville *Whig*, June 7, 1865; Nashville *Dispatch*, January 12, 1865. Warren Powell to Holden, October 23, 1865, in Holden Papers.
20. James Welch Patton, *Unionism and Reconstruction in Tennessee, 1860–1869* (Chapel Hill, 1934), 63; David Sullins, *Recollections of an Old Man: Seventy Years in Dixie* (Bristol,

These experiences in Tennessee were repeated on a smaller scale in other southern states. Texas, like Tennessee, had been bitterly divided at the outset of the war with unionist sentiment particularly strong in North Texas and in the German communities of San Antonio, Seguin, and New Braunfels.[21] Throughout 1862, the violence of the intrastate civil strife increased as disgruntled unionists resisted Confederate authority while patriotic secessionists attempted to crush any opposition to the war. State officials repeatedly placed sections of the state under martial law. In the late summer of 1862, a group of sixty-three German-born Texans left for Mexico rather than agree to serve in the hated Confederate army. Less than a day's march from the Rio Grande, however, a detachment of Texas soldiers surprised the German-Texans as they rested on the banks of the Nueces River. About a dozen escaped, thirty were killed, and another twenty were wounded in the brief battle between the poorly armed unionists and the Confederate force. When the battle was over, the Texas group assembled the wounded Germans in a copse near the Nueces River and executed them to the last man.[22]

Four months later, secessionists in North Texas learned of a "plot" of unionists to resist the Confederacy. Vigilantes rounded up more than 150 alleged conspirators, lynched 25 without benefit of hearing, and sent another 55 to their death with the dubious imprimatur of a "citizens court" that briefly heard evidence before dropping each man off the end of a wagon with one end of a rope tied around his neck and the other end to a high tree limb. Before the hysteria had subsided, nearly a hundred Texans were hanged, thirty-two from the same tree at Gainesville, Texas. The draconian measures of these vigilantes and state authorities succeeded in ending any overt resistance by Texas unionists, but hardly inspired enthusiastic unanimity within the state. In the wake of the "Slaughter of the Nueces" and the "Great Hanging at Gainesville," several thousand Texans

---

Tenn., 1910), 262. For an overview of the turmoil in Tennessee and its effects on postwar politics, see Charles F. Bryan, "The Civil War in Tennessee: A Social, Political, and Economic Study" (Ph.D. dissertation, University of Tennessee, 1978); Thomas Alexander, "Neither Peace nor War: Conditions in Tennessee in 1865," *ETHSP*, XXI (1949), 33–51.

21. See Rudolph L. Biesele, *The History of the German Settlements in Texas* (Austin, 1930), and Walter L. Buenger, "Secession and the Texas German Community: Editor Lindheime vs. Editor Flake," *SwHQ*, LXXXII (1979), 379–402.

22. Robert W. Shook, "The Battle of the Nueces, August 10, 1862," *SwHQ*, LXVI (1962), 31–42; Robert Hamilton Williams, *With the Border Ruffians: Memories of the Far West, 1852–1868* (New York, 1907), 232–59. After the war, German-Texans were an important element in the Republican party, but their unionism seems to have been stronger than their Republicanism. See Chap. 1 of James Alex Baggett's "The Rise and Fall of the Texas Radicals, 1867–1883" (Ph.D. dissertation, North Texas State University, 1972); Carl H. Moneyhon, *Republicanism in Reconstruction Texas* (Austin, 1980), 10, 122–24, 171, 178–82.

fled the state and more than two thousand served in the Union army.[23] Until the end of the war, Confederate vigilantes continued the policy of persecution against suspected unionists. As late as April of 1865, a mob, with the connivance of local officers, hanged ten German prisoners who were accused of disloyalty.[24]

Gilbert Kingsbury of Brownsville, Texas, had consistently opposed secession throughout the 1850s. The somewhat eccentric rancher and self-proclaimed expert on all matters relating to "agriculture, commerce, education and politics" engaged in no overt acts against the new government when it was created, but he found it impossible to contain his contempt for the "political buffoons" who headed the Confederacy. In March of 1863, a neighbor and friend warned him in time to make his escape before the arrival of a vigilance committee created to stamp out disloyal sentiments in the Lone Star State. Although Kingsbury later insisted that he had engaged in no overt acts of resistance against the Confederate government, each day in exile he expected to hear it proclaimed that he had "strangled a score of infants, robbed an army of blind beggers, instigated the John Brown raid & led the incendiaries and carried the torch and poison into the towns of northern Texas." His disposition was not improved by the fact that the mob, frustrated by his successful escape, had sacked the Kingsbury family home, burned his eleven-hundred-volume library (the largest in South Texas), and carried off the marble monuments from the nearby family burial plot to use as stepping stones. Understandably, Kingsbury had something less than fraternal compassion for his defeated fellow Texans when he returned to his home in mid-1865.[25]

North Carolina lacked some of the frontier crudeness of Texas but not the violence. Even in that settled seaboard state bloody wartime conflict between unionists and secessionists spilled over into the postwar era. On the day after Lee surrendered at Appomattox, two patriotic Confederate

23. Robert L. Kerby, *Kirby Smith's Confederacy: The Trans-Mississippi South, 1863–1865* (New York, 1972), 93–95; Sam Acheson and Julie Ann Hudson O'Connell (eds.), "George Washington Diamond's Account of the Great Hanging at Gainesville, 1862," *SwHQ*, LXVI (1963), 331–414; James Smallwood, "Disaffection in Confederate Texas: The Great Hanging at Gainesville," *CWH*, XXII (1976), 349–60; Frank Herbert Smyrle, "Unionism, Abolitionism, Vigilanteism," (M.A. thesis, University of Texas, 1961); Smyrle, "Texans in the Union Army, 1861–65," *SwHQ*, LXV (1961), 235; Claude Elliott, "Union Sentiment in Texas, 1861–1865," *SwHQ*, L (1947), 455.

24. Ella Lonn, *Foreigners in the Confederacy* (Chapel Hill, 1940), 437.

25. Gilbert Kingsbury to Milton K. Kingsbury, May 30, 1862, Gilbert Kingsbury, Speech, June [?], 1867, both in Kingsbury Family Papers, UTA. Kingsbury's references to the "torch and poison" in North Texas refers to a slave insurrection panic in 1860 in which secessionists accused unionists of poisoning the state's water wells, burning its towns, and planning a campaign of rape and pillage by the state's slaves. See William M. White, "The Texas Slave Insurrection of 1860," *SwHQ*, LII (1949), 261–85.

citizens had taken a unionist suspected of cooperating with federal troops, tied him to a tree, and beat him to death with chains. The year before, twenty-two North Carolinians had been executed for disloyalty to the Confederacy. These men had originally enlisted in a home-guard defense battalion, but when they were pressed into general service in the Confederate army, these lukewarm Confederates deserted and joined the Second North Carolina Loyal Volunteers serving under the flag of the United States. After twenty-two of the men were captured in an engagement near New Bern, North Carolina, Confederate General George S. Pickett of Gettysburg fame ordered the men tried with unseemly haste before a Confederate court martial at Kingston, North Carolina. After perfunctory proceedings, all were hanged from a single gallows.

At least they had received a trial of sorts. In January of 1863, in a raid on the remote Appalachian valley of Shelton Laurel, frustrated Confederate troops tortured women, children, and old people into revealing the hiding places of fifteen local men suspected of disloyalty to the Confederacy. The following day, troops of the Sixty-fourth North Carolina Regiment marched thirteen men to the banks of a local creek (two had escaped during the night), executed them, and left their bodies in a shallow grave. One of the "men" was thirteen years old. The bitter memory of the Shelton Laurel massacre, the mass Kingston execution, and hundreds of other lesser incidents remained with North Carolina unionists in the west long after Appomattox. To Confederates these men were deserters or guerrillas; to hardcore unionists, however, they were martyrs of Confederate persecution and the top of an iceberg of continued conflict, particularly in western North Carolina.[26]

It was not surprising that the passions aroused by such no-holds-barred conflict spilled over into the postwar era. The Republican leadership in Congress was particularly receptive to reports of the persecution suffered by southern unionists. At times, the hearings before the Joint Committee

26. Jesse Parker Bogue, "Violence and Oppression in North Carolina During Reconstruction, 1865–1873" (Ph.D. dissertation, University of Maryland, 1973), 188–207; *House Executive Documents*, 39th Cong., 1st Sess., No. 98, pp. 324–25. The civilian leadership in North Carolina drew a sharp distinction between the Shelton Laurel and Kingston episodes. In the former case, Augustus S. Merrimon, a good friend of Confederate governor Zebulon Vance, exposed the massacre and tried for two years (with Vance's support) to bring the guilty officers to justice. A. S. Merrimon to Zebulon Vance, February 16, 1863, *OR*, Ser. 1, Vol. XVIII, p. 867. For a superbly evocative study of the Shelton Laurel massacre, see Phillip Shaw Paludan's *Victims: A True Story of the Civil War* (Knoxville, 1981). Some historians have linked the growing antiwar sentiment in North Carolina from 1861 to 1865 to the state's high desertion rate, but Richard Reid has denied any such connection. See his "A Test Case of the 'Crying Evil': Desertion Among North Carolina Troops During the Civil War," *NCHR*, LVIII (1981), 253.

on Reconstruction in 1866 would become little more than a sounding board for complaints of persecution suffered by white unionists in the post-war South. There was certainly discrimination against unionists; the difficulty always lay in separating fact from exaggeration. A year after the war had ended, forty Camden, North Carolina, men complained to President Johnson and to congressional Republicans that they were being persecuted for their service as Union soldiers. According to their petition, they had been arraigned on such trumped-up charges as selling without a business license, "moral turpitude and adultery," and assault and battery. When federal judge G. W. Brooks examined Camden County court records, however, he discovered that only two of the forty had been indicted and only one had been convicted. He was fined twenty-five dollars for selling whiskey without a license.[27]

Understandably, that same Republican leadership was less concerned when unionists had managed to gain the upper hand and used their position to exact revenge for wartime grievances. Something of the flavor of bitter reprisals could be gathered from the report of a company of Missouri volunteers who were detailed to Howard and Boone counties in Missouri toward the end of the war to locate and destroy the "notorious guerilla leader Jim Jackson and his nefarious band." Under the command of "Captain" James D. Meredith, the twenty-man cavalry unit never found Jackson, but their account of the casual way in which they devastated the countryside was a chilling reflection of the hatreds engendered by years of civil conflict. On the basis of the vaguest rumors and hearsay, Meredith and his men calmly put the torch to the homes of citizens on the grounds that they had harbored "bushwhackers." On one occasion, they burned the home of a widow who had allegedly sheltered the sister of a Missouri rebel. Toward the end of his raid, while passing through a small community, they stopped at the home of a woman whose son was reported to be part of Jackson's group. ("I have forgotten the name," reported Meredith.) When she "expressed herself in the most disloyal manner," the commander wrote, "I burned the house." While technically under the authority of the federal

27. See, for example, the lengthy list of citations in the committee's report under the heading: "Union Men, Northern and Southern, Manifestations of Hostilities to—" *House Reports*, 39th Cong., 1st Sess., No. 30, Pt. 4, pp. 180–81. See also Raleigh *Daily Sentinel*, June 1, 4, 1866; Jonathan Worth to Nereus Mendenhall, September 10, 1866, in James Gregoire de Roulhac Hamilton (ed.), *The Correspondence of Jonathan Worth* (2 vols.; Raleigh, 1909), II, 773; Worth to Benjamin Hedrick, September 18, 1866, in Benjamin Hedrick Papers, DUL. Edward Hobson McGee gives a particularly thoughtful review of this issue in his "North Carolina Conservatives and Reconstruction" (Ph.D. dissertation, University of North Carolina, 1972), 159–63.

government, such volunteer forces spent most of their time exacting vengeance for past wrongs.[28]

Shortly after the war, North Carolina's provisional governor Holden was particularly embarrassed by the documented cases in which unionists, resentful over wartime harassment and persecution, used their new position to jail their old enemies on flagrantly trumped-up charges. During the same period, vengeful unionists in Choctaw County, Mississippi, formed a Loyal League, ostensibly to "suppress crime, keep down rebellion and keep order and discipline among the negro population." In fact, members of the league acted primarily to intimidate political opponents and local Mississippians who had been loyal to the Confederacy.[29]

The question of unionist persecution was further complicated by the tendency of United States officers—and Republican congressmen—to see postwar violence and disorder purely in the context of politics or racism. Saint Clair County, Alabama, was torn by bloodshed and violence for more than a year after the war had ended. As late as July of 1866, one bitter "unionist" complained that a band of former rebels had "set the civil law at defiance" and embarked on a campaign of persecution against those who "reverenced the grand old flag and dared to set their faces against the contemptable [sic] rebels who are counselling disunion once more." Complaints became so serious from local army officials that Governor Robert Patton ordered an investigation by Marcus Cruikshank of Talladega, Lewis Parsons' old law partner. Cruikshank found ample evidence of lawlessness, with dozens of instances of burned homes and gin houses, a dozen whippings, and at least three unsolved killings. At one point, state judge W. B. Wood had abruptly terminated a grand jury investigation and fled to the safety of a neighboring county.[30]

28. *OR*, Vol. XLVIII, Pt. 1, pp. 1332–34. Union officers became so concerned over such incidents that they considered disbanding these unionist militia units, but the absence of alternative police forces during the immediate aftermath of the war and the political repercussions that would have come from disbanding them made this inexpedient. *Ibid.*, pp. 197–98, 431–33, 458–59, 476–79, 501–502.

29. Holden to Yadkin County Justices of the Peace, September 13, 1865, Holden to Randolph County Sheriff, September 16, 1865, Holden to Randolph County Justices of the Peace, September 16, 1865 (copies), all in Governor W. W. Holden's Letterbooks, NCA; William C. Harris, *Presidential Reconstruction in Mississippi* (Baton Rouge, 1967), 36; William T. Blain, "'Banner' Unionism in Mississippi: Choctaw County, 1861–1869," *MQ*, XXIX (1976), 207–20.

30. Ross Phillips to Patton, July 21, 1866, J. N. Settles to Maj. George E. Brewer, September 24, 1866, Judge W. B. Wood to Patton, November 3, 1866, J. J. Giers to Patton, July 31, 1866, A. M. Gibson and J. W. Moore to Patton, August 16, 1866, B. T. Pope to Gov. Robert M. Patton, September 3, 1866, William C. Hunter, Gen. S. Davis, and B. S. Smoote

And as army officers had complained, there were political overtones to the conflict. In his reports to the governor, Cruikshank described two competing irregular bands, each numbering from fifty to a hundred men. One group, the "Tories," had been unionists during the war. The other consisted of loyalists who had faithfully supported the Confederacy. But even though the violence and occasional gunfights were couched in political terms, Cruikshank soon discovered that the murders and whippings went back to before the Civil War, even before the secession crisis. These disturbances were rooted in "long time feuds" involving "bad blood" between families and community factions. When they erupted, usually after a clash between a "few reckless—and generally whiskey drinking—young men," it would have taken the wisdom of Solomon, argued Cruikshank, to untangle the web of contributing factors. Certainly, it was absurd to see them as political clashes between unionist and secessionist factions.[31]

Taken as a whole, southern unionists engaged in relatively few acts of repression against their Confederate enemies and inflicted even fewer casualties, but this was due less to their principle of abstention from violence than to their weak numerical position.

And it was their decided minority status in most southern states, rather than their ethical position on the morality of retribution, that threatened these consistent defenders of the Union in their efforts to shape postwar developments in the South. In Georgia, a sizable number of individuals were embittered over the devastation caused by the war and resentful of the Empire State's traditional antebellum leadership which they blamed for maneuvering Georgia into rebellion. But they sharply divided between a group of southern Georgia urban unionists centered in Savannah and the small-farmer element of North Georgia. President Johnson's choice as provisional governor, James G. Johnson, had the potential for unifying these disparate groups. A Whig unionist during the 1850s, he refrained from open opposition to the Confederacy, but he had never given his support to the secessionist movement and his views on most subjects were vague enough to have left him with a free hand to act without embarrassment. Although he condemned the political leaders who had dominated the state for the previous twenty years, Johnson seems to have been politically paralyzed by an extremely limited conception of the powers he had been granted as provisional governor. For a time, he expressed doubt that he had any power to alter existing appointments to civil positions. Even when he

---

to Gov. Lewis E. Parsons, July 24, 1865, A. W. Dillard to Col. J. J. Seibels, July 31, 1865, Jasper Ridge to Parsons, October 10, 1865, all in Alabama Governors' Papers, AA.

31. Marcus H. Cruikshank to Patton, July 29, August 3, 1866, *ibid.*

began to fill vacant offices under explicit authorization from the president, he acted timidly, without political decisiveness of any kind.[32]

Benjamin Perry of South Carolina was not so timid in his views of the powers he had been granted as provisional governor. The bluff-talking Greenville legislator and former newspaper editor had distinguished himself in the unionist cause through nearly thirty years of consistent opposition to the nullification and secessionist doctrines of his fellow South Carolinians. Neither his dedication to the Union nor his personal courage had been challenged after 1832 when he had shot and killed a rival newspaper editor in a duel that stemmed from his antinullification editorials. As Perry later remarked, that duel had ended all "secret slanders" by the nullifiers and in this way it produced a "greater courtesy in society and a higher refinement." In 1860, in the face of bitter criticism from fellow South Carolinians, he opposed disunion even when it was apparent that Lincoln would be elected. Almost alone among South Carolinians, he drew a careful distinction between Republicans and abolitionists, and he argued that Lincoln's election would change little. The interests of the South would remain protected by the guaranties of the Constitution.[33]

Only when it was apparent that the overwhelming majority of his fellow South Carolinians were committed to secession did he reluctantly accept disunion as an "inevitability." By the spring of 1861 he had transferred his allegiance to the new Confederacy, urging his fellow unionists to join the army and supporting the selling of state and Confederate war bonds. He never wavered in his support of the new government until it ceased to exist in April of 1865. Despite Perry's wartime service to the Confederacy, Johnson believed that the South Carolina editor's antebellum record of consistent unionism and the respect he had retained within the state made him the logical choice as South Carolina's provisional governor.

Moreover, Perry had led much the same small-farmer constituency that had supported the president in Tennessee. Throughout his political career he opposed the planter wing of the South Carolina Democratic party, denouncing the political domination that the low country had maintained through the antiquated and malapportioned parish system. It might be

32. Olive Hall Shadgett, "James Johnson, Provisional Governor of Georgia," *GHQ*, XXXVI (1952), 2–9; Joseph Parks, *Joseph E. Brown of Georgia* (Baton Rouge, 1977), 336–37; Wesley Floyd Busbee, Jr., "Presidential Reconstruction in Georgia, 1865–1867" (Ph.D. dissertation, University of Alabama, 1972), 85–92.

33. Benjamin Perry Journal, Perry Manuscripts, August 23, 1832; Lillian A. Kibler, *Benjamin F. Perry, South Carolina Unionist* (Durham, N.C., 1946), 135; Charleston *Courier*, August 13, 20, 1860; Benjamin Perry, Speech before Anderson, S.C., rally (Unidentified newspaper clipping, October 10, 1860, in Benjamin Perry Scrapbook, Perry Manuscripts).

most accurate to say that Perry represented the small-farmer constituency of the up-country, but he himself often claimed to speak for the masses, as opposed to the tight-knit aristocracy that dominated the state's politics. When a young Charleston aristocrat condemned public education in 1853 because "it can only make laborers idle and vicious," Perry's angry response was representative of his lifelong views. William R. Taber and his supporters were men who stood "not only against human liberty," charged an angry Perry, but in "opposition to Republicanism, to civilization and the spirit of the age."[34]

And even though he remained within the planter-dominated Democratic party of the state, he often spoke positively of selected aspects of Henry Clay's American system, particularly those "democratic and industrial reforms" that would benefit the nonslaveholders. During the 1850s in florid Fourth of July orations he spoke for industrial development (particularly textile manufacturing) in Piedmont South Carolina. In the legislature he advocated state support for railroad construction and increased expenditures for the totally inadequate "free school" system within the state. He clearly saw himself arrayed on the side of "human liberty . . . , republicanism . . . , progress . . . , civilization and the spirit of the age."[35]

As provisional governor, Perry allowed himself the satisfaction of scolding the secessionists for their "madness and folly" in bringing on a disastrous civil war, but in one of his first official acts, he confirmed in their offices all of the civil officers of the state, and he took a similarly conciliatory attitude to the question of amnesty. "I determined to refuse no application for pardon," he later recalled, "where the applicant took the oath of allegiance and expressed himself loyal to the United States." When President Johnson hestitantly questioned this policy, Perry argued that it was impossible to discriminate against those who had supported secession since only a handful of South Carolinians had opposed the "revolution."[36]

Perry lacked the driving ambition of his North Carolina counterpart, W. W. Holden. He had spent a lifetime representing an up-country minority, and he saw little chance that this minority could be transformed into a stable political majority in the factionalized but essentially conservative po-

34. William A. Schaper, *Sectionalism and Representation in South Carolina*, ed. E. M. Lander, Jr. (New York, 1968), 433.
35. Kibler, *Benjamin Perry*, 302–12; Daniel Hollis, *University of South Carolina* (2 vols.; Columbia, S.C., 1952–56), I, 348–49.
36. Perry, *Reminiscences*, 229–41, 264. The best analysis of Perry's political strategy may be found in John L. Bell, Jr., "Andrew Johnson, National Politics, and Presidential Reconstruction in South Carolina," *SCHM*, LXXXII (1981), 354–66. For Perry's proclamation of July 20, 1865, outlining his policies, see the Winnsboro (S.C.) *Tri-Weekly News*, July 29, 1865.

litical climate of South Carolina. Instead he was content with achieving a goal that had eluded up-country South Carolinians for more than half a century: reform of the state's archaic political structure and practices. The property-holding requirements for state legislators, the practice of secret voting in the legislature, the restriction to the legislature of the power to elect both the governor and the presidential electors, and above all else, the old parish system under which the low-country planters had been disproportionately represented in the upper house—all were part of the system that had "made South Carolina the leader in the Rebellion" and had kept political power in the "conservative hands of the low country" rather than the "progressive hands of the up country."[37] Perry's agenda for change was a logical outgrowth of his political career, but it did little to resolve the issues raised by the war and the Reconstruction.

If Perry, like W. W. Holden and James Johnson, spoke for the up-country unionists of the South, Mississippi's provisional governor William L. Sharkey represented a different constituency and a different approach to the reconstruction of his state's politics and society. Like most of his fellow provisional governors, the former chief justice of the Mississippi Supreme Court had opposed disunion throughout the 1850s. Even after John Brown's raid at Harpers Ferry and Lincoln's election led most white Mississippians to conclude that their future security could best be guaranteed by secession, Sharkey preferred the unpleasant prospect of a Republican president to the potential anarchy of a revolutionary movement, however committed to maintaining the status quo. When the war began, Sharkey retired to his Hinds County home and devoted his time to a desultory law practice and the management of his small plantation. A prominent Whig before the war, he avoided political statements of any kind and publicly maintained a position of passive acceptance toward the new government.[38]

From the outset of his self-imposed political silence, patriotic Confederates suspected Sharkey's loyalty. Officials of the new government went so far as to arrest him for refusing to sell needed agricultural goods to Confederate army officers, although formal charges were never filed. Two years later, however, the neutrality ended when Sharkey swore an oath of allegiance to the United States government in the wake of Grant's successful

37. Schaper, *Sectionalism and Representation, passim*; Charleston *Daily Courier*, September 29, 1865; Perry, *Reminiscences*, 276–77.
38. Sharkey outlined his reasons for opposing secession in William L. Sharkey to Henry Dickinson, September 3, 1859, in McGavock Family Papers, SHC. For his position through the period up to secession, see Percy Lee Rainwater, *Mississippi, Storm Center of Secession, 1856–1861* (Baton Rouge, 1938), 69–70, 103–104, 149–50, 175–76.

campaign against Vicksburg. As he told a correspondent for the New York *Times*, Jefferson Davis had warned early in the war that the fall of Vicksburg and Port Hudson would mean the destruction of the Confederacy. "Now," said Sharkey, "I take him at his word." Under the circumstances, a healthy dose of pragmatism seems to have been as important in Sharkey's thinking as his commitment to the Union. If his unionism was not as impeccable as that of Andrew Jackson Hamilton of Texas or William Marvin of Florida, it still compared favorably with the Confederate service of Perry and the inconsistent record of W. W. Holden.[39]

Sharkey's conservatism had led him to balk at secession, and that same conservatism shaped his postwar policy in Mississippi. Superficially it represented the most clear-cut postwar example of a resurgent southern "whiggery." In Mississippi as in North Carolina, antebellum Whigs had generally balked at disunion; Mississippi's Democrats led the fight for secession. With those Democrats discredited by defeat, old-line Whigs saw their opportunity to humiliate and destroy their antebellum adversaries and to rebuild a postwar Whig party composed of the "only true union element in this state." And in the weeks after his appointment, Sharkey received letters from his old Whig friends urging him to expel every Democrat from office and to appoint only Whigs in their place. "I have not forgotten the struggles we have had with a rule or ruin Democracy," argued William M. Pollan of Copiah County, Mississippi. With a national bank, an expanding program of internal improvements, and a protective tariff, the way seemed clear for an affiliation with the conservative elements of the Republican party. Though few shared Pollan's enthusiasm for affiliation with northern Republicans, other antebellum Whigs insisted that there was still an opportunity to revive the moribund Whig party, perhaps under the title of the Conservative party.[40]

Sharkey's background as a staunch Whig (albeit one with a southern accent) and his identification with Mississippi's commercial and planter elements made him amenable to state and federally supported programs of agricultural, commercial—even industrial—development. He was particularly sensitive to the problems of the Delta planters who faced a precarious future because of the wartime collapse of the state's levee system. But

39. *Dictionary of American Biography*, IX, 21–22; Frank W. Klingberg, *The Southern Claims Commission* (Berkeley, 1955), 110–11; New York *Times*, September 26, 1863. Relatively wealthy, Sharkey was not a particularly large slaveholder. According to the census of 1860, he had only eighteen slaves, and he prudently refrained from making additional purchases once the war had begun.

40. In his excellent study of Mississippi during Presidential Reconstruction, William Harris describes the role some Whigs expected to play in postwar politics. Harris, *Presidential Reconstruction in Mississippi*, 44–51.

Sharkey was nearly seventy, an aging veteran of an earlier political era, and he seemed at times to be most concerned about recouping his own wartime economic losses. At the same time, his close involvement with a group of Tennessee Democrats in a scheme to secure a refund of the controversial federal tax on raw cotton seems to have softened his lifelong hostility to Democrats.[41]

For the short run, he concentrated on the restoration of minimal state services and the adoption of legislation that would define the "obligations and rights" of the state's newly freed black population. The latter was, as Sharkey observed, a "particularly delicate task" since it was essential that northern voters be satisfied of white southerners' good intentions toward their former slaves. Only through the passage of "wise and judicious legislation" could the "negro garrisons and other evidences of military rule . . . be removed from the state." He had no illusions that he could enact an ambitious program of self-development or that he could resuscitate a moribund Whig party, and he lacked the political ambition that would have been required for a reshuffling of Mississippi politics.[42]

Provisional governor Lewis Parsons of Alabama sprang from the same antebellum whiggish background, but he was willing to take greater political risks than Sharkey. Both Parsons and his close friend and elected successor Robert Patton had linked their antebellum careers with two of Alabama's most powerful businessmen, Daniel Pratt and J. W. Sloss. Veterans of the Whig party, Parsons and Patton combined support for Henry Clay's American system with the grievances of their fellow North Alabamians. Both men (particularly Patton) had been involved in a series of ambitious antebellum schemes for railroad construction and industrial development. The war disrupted these ambitious goals, but neither Parsons nor Patton abandoned their policies. Ever sensitive to the uncertainties of wartime politics, Patton raised money for the Confederacy while he maintained discreet contacts with General Ulysses Grant through his unionist brother-in-law, J. J. Giers. By the end of the war, both Parsons and Patton had made invaluable contacts with conservative northern Republicans while retaining the respect of their fellow Alabamians.[43]

The policies of the two men made their priorities clear. First, the federal

41. L. Marshall Hall, "William L. Sharkey and Reconstruction, 1866–1873," *JMH*, XXVII (1965), 13–17.

42. J. S. McNeily, "From Organization to Overthrow of Mississippi's Provisional Government, 1865–1868," *PMHS*, I (1916), 14–55; Harris, *Presidential Reconstruction in Mississippi*, 45; Sharkey to William A. Graham, August 9, 1866, in Graham Papers.

43. Horace Mann Bond, *Negro Education in Alabama: A Study in Cotton and Steel* (Washington, D.C., 1939), 39–50.

authorities—whoever they might be—had to be pacified and conciliated. As the ever-practical Giers cautioned Patton at one point during the growing conflict between Johnson and the Congress, no matter what the provocation, it was his duty to act cautiously and discreetly so as to retain "sufficient influence with the members of the dominant party to obtain favorable terms on matters of vital importance to our State; such as the postponement of the Direct Tax, Extension of Railroad Loan Grants, & c."[44]

Secondly, Parsons and Patton moved quickly in the months after the war to build a political base that would sustain their ambitious program. Although they never explicitly defined their political strategy, their policies reflected a desire to move beyond the limited base of North Alabama unionists (who made up less than 15 percent of the state's white population) toward a broader coalition of wartime unionists, emerging industrial interests, and the "conservative" as opposed to fire-eating planter elements of South Alabama. To the up-country farmers, both Patton and Parsons offered unionist rhetoric and support for postwar legislative representation based upon white population alone. This was combined with an ambitious plan of direct aid to destitute whites in the up-country (blacks were considered the responsibility of the Freedmen's Bureau) and promises of state-supported railroad construction to end the economic isolation of the state's northern counties. To the black belt planters who had succumbed to the enticement of the secessionist movement, Parsons and Patton expressed a willingness to forgive their indiscretions. And both men promised to use their influence in Washington to lobby against the 2.5¢-per-pound punitive tax placed on southern cotton growers. This was no symbolic issue. Between 1865 and 1868, Alabama cotton producers paid $10.4 million to the federal government, a figure four times the total revenues collected by the provisional government.[45]

To the emerging industrial entrepreneurs and railroad promoters to whom they were most closely tied, Parsons and Patton promised legislative support for favorable incorporation and tax legislation and generous railroad subsidies. And at a time when the bestowal of federal land grants could mean the difference between success and failure for ambitious railroad promoters, the two men committed themselves to vigorous lobbying

44. J. J. Giers to Patton, November 16, 1866, in Alabama Governors' Papers.
45. The estimate of unionist strength was made by William H. Smith, the North Alabama lawyer-farmer who served as the state's first postwar Republican governor. *Report of the Joint Committee on Reconstruction*, III, 11; Marjorie Howell Cook, "Restoration and Innovation: Alabamians Adjust to Defeat, 1865–1867" (Ph.D. dissertation, University of Alabama, 1968); James L. Watkins, *King Cotton: A Historical and Statistical Review, 1790 to 1908* (New York, 1908), 151. Patrick J. Hearden, *Independence and Empire: The New South's Cotton Mill Campaign, 1865–1901* (De Kalb, Ill., 1982), 34.

in Washington on these matters. In supporting the "state's" interest in these concerns, particularly railroad land grants, issues took on a rather concrete significance for both Parsons and Patton since both were so deeply immersed in the formation of new and combined railroad and business corporations. Even at a time when Americans took a generous approach to questions of conflict of interest, Parsons and Patton's financial and political interrelationships skirted the bounds of propriety. Patton, for example, simultaneously filled the offices of governor of the state and president of the Central Mining Company. At the same time much of his energy as chief executive seems to have been devoted to the interests of the Mills Valley Railroad, lobbying for land grants in Washington and soliciting special tax legislation from the state legislators. Union General Wager Swayne was at least half right when he described Patton as an "economical old merchant who . . . would neither deceive nor be deceived."[46]

Only in North Carolina was there a convergence of circumstances that offered opportunities for a significant postwar role by the state's consistent unionists. And there the key individual was William Woods Holden, twice-rejected candidate for governor, a man whose ambitions were matched only by his political ingenuity. Holden had been selected by Johnson for obvious reasons. Both had championed the yeoman, nonslaveholding classes of the South. They shared a common social outlook. And even though Holden had initially supported the Confederacy, his peace agitation after 1863 and the harassment he suffered made him, in Johnson's eyes, a logical choice for leading the reconstruction of North Carolina politics.[47]

46. Patton was one of the principle stockholders in the Mills Valley Railroad and became president of the company immediately after leaving office. Horace Mann Bond attempted to untangle Patton's complicated political and economic connections in "Social and Economic Forces in Alabama Reconstruction," *JNH*, XXII (1938), 290–348, but there are a number of significant errors in Bond's account. A brief but accurate description of the way in which the railroad issue cut across Presidential Reconstruction into the era of "Radical" Reconstruction in Alabama may be found in Sarah Woolfolk Wiggins, *The Scalawag in Alabama Politics, 1865–1881* (University, Ala., 1977), 42–45. The "Railroad File" and "Industry File" in Robert M. Patton Papers, Alabama Governors' Papers, contain unusually candid letters between Patton and a number of lobbyists, promoters and businessmen. One thing is certain, neither Parsons nor Patton regarded their activities as improper. For the antebellum period, see J. Mills Thornton III, *Politics and Power in a Slave Society: Alabama, 1800–1860* (Baton Rouge, 1978), 267–342.

47. The most satisfactory biography of Holden is Horace W. Raper's "William Woods Holden and the Peace Movement in North Carolina," *NCHR*, XXXI (1954), 493–516, but Raper's conclusions should be supplemented by the more critical perspective of Richard Yates in his "Governor Vance and the Peace Movement," *NCHR*, XVII (1940), 1–25, 89–113. Most recently William C. Harris has made a defense of the integrity and ability of Holden in his article, "William Woods Holden: In Search of Vindication," *NCHR*, LIX (1982), 354–72. Equally useful is the surprisingly candid correspondence in Holden's Letterbooks, *NCA*. The public explanations for his shifts in policy may be found in his newspaper, the Raleigh *Standard*. His autobiography, published in 1911, is far less useful.

At the outset of his administration, Holden insisted to the people of North Carolina that the South would never be readmitted into the Union until the "straitest sect" of unionists were in control of the state and the "secessionists," "destructives," and "factionalists" were excluded from power. Such a policy required some political prestidigitation since a rigid definition of the term *strait sect* would exclude Holden and many of his closest allies. For example, Thomas Settle of Rockingham, the man who would be Holden's legislative floor leader, had enlisted in the Confederate army in the flush of patriotic enthusiasm that swept North Carolina in 1861. Even worse, Settle had then become a state solicitor who vigorously prosecuted unionists and "slackers." The dilemma was solved by an elastic definition of strait-sect unionism. All those who had tacitly abandoned the Confederacy as of 1864, when Holden publicly launched his peace campaign, were acceptable unionists. Those who supported the Lost Cause until the end— whatever their antebellum antecedents—were certifiably secessionist. Although such a tortured definition only further convinced conservatives of Holden's untrustworthy and Machiavellian motivation, it considerably broadened his potential power base by neatly encompassing his closest supporters.[48]

To some extent, Holden's postwar political strategy was patterned after that of Tennessee's Parson Brownlow. With the solid support of East Tennessee unionists, Brown had won election in March of 1865 and consolidated his political strength by disfranchising potential opponents as they returned from service in the Confederacy. But Brownlow had a much larger reservoir of unconditional unionist strength than Holden. Tennessee had furnished more than thirty thousand white soldiers for the Union army, and the eastern part of the state was overwhelmingly opposed to the Confederacy by 1863. But the months between Brownlow's inauguration and the beginning of Holden's provisional governorship was a brief but critical time of transition. By the late summer of 1865 disfranchisement no longer seemed a feasible policy. Instead Holden would have to use more traditional means of political survival.[49]

48. (Raleigh) *North Carolina Daily Standard*, October 13, 23, 1865. As Otto Olsen has observed, such a definition inevitably strained the political relationships between Holden and more consistent northern unionists who arrived in 1865 and 1866. At the same time, those true strait-sect North Carolina unionists were also uneasy at the prospect of a coalition with the Holdenites. Olsen, *Carpetbaggers Crusade: The Life of Albion Winegar Tourgée* (Baltimore, 1965), 38–48; D. W. C. Johnson to Holden, June 25, 1865, James R. Ellis to Holden, June 25, 30, 1865, Thomas B. Long to Holden, June 29, 1865, Warren Powell to Holden, June 28, 1865, all in Holden Papers.

49. Klingberg, *Southern Claims Commission*, 43. For information on the Brownlow administration, see E. Merton Coulter, *William G. Brownlow, Fighting Parson of the Southern Highlands* (Chapel Hill, 1937); Thomas B. Alexander, *Political Reconstruction in Tennessee*

These traditional levers of political power were not inconsiderable. The president assured Holden that he would have the authority to approve or reject pardons for all North Carolinians and Holden believed that his authority to block presidential pardons was critical. Many of the "oligarchs" were still unsubdued and unrepentant, he had concluded, and though he expressed no enthusiasm over a confiscation policy, "I think it is a good plan to hold their pardons in suspense."[50]

Holden was determined to use patronage to liberally reward his supporters and proscribe his enemies. In keeping with this policy, he had scarcely taken office in early June before he announced plans to review the "character and loyalty" of every public official in North Carolina. Like many southern states, North Carolina had invested heavily in antebellum railroad construction and the state held a substantial interest in six lines—the Atlantic, the North Carolina, the Wilmington and Weldon, the Central North Carolina, the Raleigh and Gaston, and the Western North Carolina railroads. In mid-July, Holden named his supporters to head the six lines. Later that same month, he reshuffled the board of directors of the Bank of North Carolina.[51]

Even more important in Holden's reorganization was his review of the appointments of the justices of the peace in the state's eighty-five counties. These men were not only authorized to try minor civil and criminal cases but also had the power to organize the county courts. And these courts, apart from their judicial role, appointed sheriffs, constables, county clerks of court, trustees, wardens of the poor, overseers of the roads, and tax assessors. Altogether this amounted to more than three thousand direct and indirect appointments.

Holden undertook the patronage review with a systematic zeal that reflected favorably on his basic administrative skills and his ingenuity. With the mail system inoperative and the traditional methods of communication seriously impeded by the war, he sent his secretary to Raleigh's hotels and boardinghouses for a list of travelers from across the state who could be cajoled into serving as unpaid messengers for the governor. Still, it was a massive undertaking. Even though Holden had been active in North Carolina politics since the 1840s, he was unfamiliar with the hundreds of individuals who remained uncertain in their minor positions, and he knew only a small minority of the thousands who sought appointment. Faced with the

---

(Nashville, 1950), 79–97; James B. Campbell, "East Tennessee During the Radical Regime, 1865–1869," *ETHSP*, XX (1948), 84–102; E. G. Feistman, "Radical Disfranchisement and the Restoration of Tennessee," *THQ*, XII (1953), 135–51.

50. Holden to Andrew Johnson, July 26, 1865, in Andrew Johnson Papers.

51. Raper, "William Woods Holden," 509–10.

pressing task of filling these vacancies, Holden experimented with a number of ways of evaluating applicants and current officeholders. For a time he used the old subscription list of his newspaper, the *Standard*, on the somewhat dubious assumption that his readers were the most likely "loyal" North Carolinians. But his followers soon warned him that this was an unreliable measure of loyalty. "There are some men in this county that take the Standard and they are your enemies," claimed one of Holden's western supporters. In fact, he argued, many of the most devoted unionists were either illiterate or too poor to subscribe to any newspaper.[52]

On at least one occasion, Holden used the investigative powers of the Union army to evaluate existing officeholders in two North Carolina counties. Colonel Elliott Wright, using a half dozen informers whose names had been suggested by Holden, compiled dossiers on the 113 men serving as justices of the peace in Sampson and Duplin counties. Wright's agents concluded that seventeen of the men were clearly unfit for office, having either been fire-eating advocates of secession in 1861 or given to "expressions of disloyalty" in the weeks after the collapse of the Confederacy.[53]

For the most part, however, Holden relied upon the network of friends and supporters he had established during his twenty years in state politics. He wrote to each, asking for the names of potential magistrates who were "known for their devotion to conservatism and the union" and would contribute to "good feeling" in politics. (This latter phrase seems to have been a euphemism for Holden supporters since the governor complained of North Carolinians who contributed to "bad feelings" by opposing his policies.) From the responses he received, Holden had his secretary collate the lists in an attempt to arrive at a slate of acceptable officeholders.[54]

Equally critical to Holden's ambitious postwar plans was his use of the pardoning power. Nothing was so chilling to a wealthy North Carolinian as the news that his invaluable pardon had been "delayed" (never denied in Holden's terminology). It was public knowledge that Andrew Johnson had agreed to allow his provisional governors the power to recommend or to thwart presidential pardons, but time after time Holden went through the charade of assuring frightened constituents that he wanted to help but was unable to assist because of the political implications of their case, even as

52. R. G. D. Pickler to Holden, June 17, 1865, in Holden Papers.
53. Col. Elliott Wright to Holden, June 13, 1865, *ibid.*
54. See especially Holden's notation on the letter of M. A. Newton to Holden, June 20, 1865, *ibid.* For a revealing insight into Holden's systematic use of patronage, see Holden to R. Dunn, July 14, 1865 (copy), D. W. C. Johnson to Holden, June 25, 1865, J. C. Monk to Holden, June 20, 1865, Newton to Holden, June 20, 1865, John J. Myrick to Holden, June 27, 1865, Ellis to Holden, June 30, 1865, Long to Holden, June 29, 1865, Warren Powell to Holden, June 28, 1865, all *ibid.*

he instructed his secretary to refrain from forwarding their pardons to Washington.

Holden's not so subtle use of the pardoning power could be seen in the case of Paul Cameron of Hillsboro, one of North Carolina's wealthiest antebellum slaveowners. By the summer of 1865, the soft-spoken Cameron was reconciled to the loss of the nine hundred slaves with which his family had farmed their antebellum plantations. He was obsessed, however, with the conviction that his large landholdings might be confiscated. He had never held political office, devoting his time and energies to managing the family's far-flung agricultural holdings. His most prominent public position had been his nonpolitical role as president of the North Carolina Railroad during the war. Nevertheless, he had been an advocate of secession as early as 1859, and he had supported the Confederacy vigorously throughout the war, condemning the peace movement led by Holden.[55]

Less than two weeks after Holden's appointment, Cameron met with the provisional governor and sought his support for a presidential pardon. While he appeared unwilling to commit himself, Holden was polite, even cordial, and he urged Cameron to submit an application for pardon through the governor's office. When six weeks had passed and Cameron still had heard nothing, he became more concerned. His suspicions were increased when Holden declined to meet with him on grounds of "pressing state business." After a further request for some definite information on the status of his pardon, Holden's secretary, Tod R. Caldwell, wrote the apprehensive Cameron to offer a few "helpful suggestions." Already, he observed, there was a hue and cry that Holden was being too lenient in endorsing the pardon of known secessionists. If he should pardon the richest disunionist in the state, the governor might "lose the confidence of the President." Holden was willing to assist Cameron, but he needed "cooperation." The secretary continued: "I had a long conversation with the Governor today about your case. He intimated that you held your destiny in your own hands. . . . Your position might be helped by your making a public speech in your county among your own friends and constituents, counselling submission to and cooperation with the federal and state authorities." Orange County citizens were holding a meeting in the county courthouse in late August, noted Caldwell, "and it would be well for you to have the substance of your speech published in the Hillsboro Recorder." Of course, Caldwell hastily added, this letter was written "on my own responsibility entirely, and it is not intended by any means to commit the governor," who

---

55. Samuel Ashe, *A Biographical History of North Carolina from Carolina Times to the Present* (7 vols.; Greensboro, 1907–11), III, 48–56.

would certainly not "assume the right to dictate terms." Nevertheless, with suitable "cooperation," he concluded, "you can quiet your fears about the confiscation of your property."[56]

If there were any doubts about what was expected of him, they were removed a week later when George W. Mordecai wrote Cameron of conversations with the governor's assistant. His pardon had been held hostage by Holden, concluded Mordecai, Cameron's close friend and president of the Bank of North Carolina. "Unless you get up a public meeting in Orange [County] for the purpose of endorsing & approving the Governor's course . . . [and] make a speech at the meeting . . . , the Governor will not recommend a pardon."[57]

When Holden's successor, Jonathan Worth, took office later that year, he found a file cabinet containing more than three hundred pardon requests that Holden had refused to forward to Johnson—among them was Cameron's. Although some of the three hundred had been prominent secessionists, Holden had refused to recommend pardons for some of the state's most distinguished unionists, including a number of individuals who had continued to oppose secession even as Holden signed the ordinance that separated North Carolina from the Union. The one thing the three hundred had in common was their refusal to publicly endorse Holden.

But the wily Holden was soon undercut by Andrew Johnson. George Mordecai, like other North Carolina conservatives, knew the falsity of the provisional governor's claims that he had to be cautious in endorsing pardons. Although Johnson had expressed some uneasiness over "Northern impressions" that too many unrepentant rebels were being recommended for pardons, he had generally supported the policy of appointees who endorsed almost any applicant who would pledge future support to the Constitution. The solution, therefore, was to bypass Holden completely and send a pardon request directly to the president through an intermediary of prominence and unquestioned stature. Mordecai recommended David L. Swain, former governor of North Carolina (1833–1836) and president of the University of North Carolina. On September 27, Swain managed to wade his way through an array of pardon seekers for a brief meeting with the president, presenting petitions on behalf of himself, Cameron, and the distinguished North Carolina jurist Thomas Ruffin. The harassed Johnson did not even read the papers before scribbling a note to his attorney general ordering that the pardons be prepared for his signature.[58]

56. Tod R. Caldwell to Paul C. Cameron, August 17, 1865, in Paul Cameron Papers, SHC.
57. George W. Mordecai to Cameron, August 26, 1865, *ibid.*
58. Andrew Johnson to Holden, August 22, 27, 1865, Holden to Andrew Johnson, Au-

Even before Swain's successful direct intervention with the president, Holden's plans for controlling the pardon weapon had been shaken by the president's haphazard endorsement of individual petitions. "We are losing from the fact that pardons are granted on personal application," complained Holden to his representative in Washington. At the same time, "the cases of special friends for whom appeals are made are not finally acted on."[59]

As the results from his use of the pardoning power became increasingly counterproductive, Holden's attempts to restructure the state's politics through patronage also faltered. In part, the problem was simply mechanical. Holden's primitive bureaucracy, which consisted of a full-time secretary, was woefully inadequate to the task of evaluating and replacing thousands of minor officials. Five months after the war had ended, Holden was still receiving plaintive letters from justices of the peace inquiring about the validity of their wartime commissions. As his harassed secretary acknowledged, entire counties had been overlooked in the chaos of political reorganization.[60]

Nor were Holden's chances for political success enhanced by the growing public distrust of his integrity and motivation—suspicions skillfully exploited by his conservative opponents. Even in a tumultuous political era when political principles shifted erratically, Holden's ideological gymnastics led more than one North Carolinian to agree with the question put to Andrew Johnson. "What confidence can we put in a man who is first a 'Methodist'—then an 'Episcopalian'—one year a Democrat, next a Whig—then a 'know nothing'—a ranting secessionist, then a Unionist?" Still others were willing to endorse the cruder theory of the Raleigh *Sentinel*'s Octavius: "If the powers that be announce this afternoon that Jackasses shall

gust 26, 1865 (copy), all in Holden Papers; Samuel F. Phillips to Kemp Battle, September 16, 1865, in Battle Family Papers, SHC; John Berry to Graham, October 12, 1865, Swain to Graham, October 14, 1865, both in Graham Papers; Worth to Hedrick, January 18, 1866, in Hedrick Papers; Thomas Wagstaff, "Andrew Johnson and the National Union Movement, 1865–1866" (Ph.D. dissertation, University of Wisconsin, 1967), 130–31. For a more sympathetic analysis of Holden's pardoning policy, see McGee, "North Carolina Conservatives and Reconstruction," 106–12.

59. Holden to Dr. R. J. Powell, September 13, 1865 (copy), in Holden Papers. Benjamin Perry endorsed every application that crossed his desk, and only once did Johnson fail to comply with his request. See Perry, *Reminiscences*, 276–77. Horace Raper pinpointed the inherent weakness of Holden's policy. Once he supported pardon for his potential opponents, the "fear of punishment and the confiscation of property was gone; thus Holden's opponents were free to act and bring discredit upon his administration" and, it might be added, to act with even greater anger and vindictiveness. Raper, "William Woods Holden," 116.

60. See especially Holden's correspondence for September and October when he became increasingly preoccupied with the task of political campaigning. There are strong parallels between Holden's strategy and tactics and those of fellow unionist Andrew Jackson Hamilton of Texas. And there are similar parallels in the factors that led to their downfall. See Moneyhon, *Republicanism in Reconstruction Texas*, 21–53.

be kings, a certain 'Honorable' Governor will be braying through the streets before sundown."[61]

By the fall of 1865 widespread and vocal opposition to Holden existed throughout the state, and one of his own appointees, State Treasurer Jonathan Worth, had begun plans to challenge the provisional governor. Holden's plan to reshape North Carolina's politics had failed.

It was a failure composed of many elements. For a brief period after Appomattox, dazed and panic-stricken southerners had been willing to defer without question to the president and his appointees. As they recovered their political self-confidence and began to understand the president's commitment to independent postwar state government, they no longer felt it necessary to defer to a provisional governor whose reputation for the ideological quick-change was to be equaled only by Joseph Brown of Georgia. This shift in public mood in North Carolina and throughout the South led a number of contemporary observers to conclude that Johnson destroyed any chance to change the configuration of southern politics in 1865 when he failed to capitalize upon white southerners' initial mood of pliancy—a conclusion historians of the last generation have often echoed.[62] The argument is an appealing one, but it should be remembered that there is little evidence of any national consensus in 1865 on the kinds of changes that should have been made in southern society. Moreover, it seems unlikely that the stunned acquiescence of white southerners would have been a suitable foundation on which to build far-reaching changes in southern politics. In part, southern resistance increased as whites seized upon Johnson's moderate plan of reconstruction; in part, their growing recalcitrance was an inevitable consequence of the passage of time and their awareness of Republican intentions.

Holden's inability to gain the support of a majority of white North Carolina voters reflected his own political liabilities as well as the inherent weakness of relying upon hard-core unionists—however broadly defined. Holden's popularity with the voters of North Carolina had never matched his ambitions. He had been unable to gain the Democratic nomination in 1858 in his first race for the governorship. In Holden's one statewide race in 1864, his opponent Zebulon Vance trounced him by a more than four-to-one margin.[63] Stretching his definition of strait-sect unionism to include

61. Jennie Brin to Andrew Johnson, December 1, 1865, in Elizabeth Gregory McPherson (ed.), "Letters from North Carolina to Andrew Johnson," *NCHR*, XXVIII (1951), 71–72; Raleigh *Sentinel*, October 23, 1865.

62. See, for example, Whitelaw Reid's oft-quoted comments, *After the War*, 296–97.

63. Clarence Clifford Norton, *The Democratic Party in Antebellum North Carolina, 1835–1861* (Chapel Hill, 1930), 230–32; Glenn Tucker, *Zeb Vance: Champion of Personal Freedom* (Indianapolis, 1965), 366.

all North Carolinians who had wearied of the war by 1864 still left him far short of a majority of voters. And no manipulation of the patronage and pardoning powers could overcome this elementary fact of electoral arithmetic.

Still, no matter how small their numbers, these most consistent unionists had expected to play a critical role in the creation of a new political order. And they were unimpressed with the argument that they were too few to accomplish this end. As one North Alabama loyalist argued, "If there are only a half a dozen true men in the county, they should be appointed to office in preference to the secessionists." The desperate poverty of most southerners after the war made once haughty and independent men plead desperately for even the most minor appointments. Under these circumstances, the reluctance of most provisional governors to replace local magistrates and court officials profoundly disillusioned the strait-sect unionists for practical as well as ideological reasons.[64]

Faced with the inescapable and politically unpalatable fact that hardcore unionists were a minority, politically ambitious southerners nevertheless realized the necessity of pacifying a suspicious North only gradually becoming aware of the limitations of southern unionism. Most of Johnson's appointees (and most of the political candidates of 1865 and 1866) attempted to redefine unionism and return it to an antebellum context. Even southerners who had accepted the principle and right of secession but had cautioned delay (the cooperationists as opposed to the "immediatists") considered themselves unionists. As Alexander Stephens, former vice-president of the Confederacy, explained in a lengthy application for pardon, he had opposed the secessionists at every turn. "No living man . . . exerted his powers to a greater extent . . . to prevent these troubles and the late deplorable war than I did," he argued. Like most southerners, however, he accepted the "Crawford, Troup and Jefferson State Rights School of Politics," and when Georgia seceded, he had no alternative but to follow his state even though the war was "inaugurated against my judgement" and "conducted on our side against my judgement."[65] Between the strait-sect loyalists and the reluctant (but active) secessionists were a whole range of unionists who so defined themselves because their advocacy of a peaceful settlement preceded the final collapse of the Confederacy.

64. Wiggins, *Scalawag in Alabama Politics*, 9.
65. Myrta Lockett Avery (ed.), *The Recollections of Alexander H. Stephens; His Diary, Kept When a Prisoner at Fort Warren, Boston Harbour, 1865, Giving Incidents and Reflections of His Prison Life and Some Letters and Reminiscences* (New York, 1910), 187–204. Stephens' pardon petition, like others submitted by southerners in 1865 and 1866, was not always faithful to the precise facts of his political career. Applicants for pardon had an understandable tendency to

Like most northerners, frustrated veterans of half a decade of "rebel persecution" saw no justice in such a definition. These "quondum [*sic*] rebels & would be union men . . . are something like the N.Y. Democracy," warned Jacob Hawkins of Louisiana. "They dress like union men, look like union men, talk like union men and have ears like union men but they don't smell much like union men."[66]

Even more depressing was the retention of out-and-out secessionists in political offices. Thomas Wilson, a Clarke County, Alabama, farmer, walked the three miles to the Gainestown courthouse in early August, 1865, to take the oath of allegiance. There he discovered Lorenzo James, one of South Alabama's most vocal secessionists, pompously administering the oath of allegiance to the government of the United States. In 1862 James had led a vigilance committee that smashed into Wilson's home, dragged him and his eighty-year-old father out of the house, administered twenty lashes and then sent them to a dank Mobile jail for two weeks until the two men publicly repented of their "sinful, unionist ways." And this, said an angry Wilson, was the material from which Alabama would be restored.[67]

By the end of 1865, the disillusionment was complete for radical southern unionists. If the men who had vilified and denounced the government and waged war upon it for four years were to be "pardoned, enfranchised and qualified to hold the offices upon terms of equality with the loyal men of the state, then the triumph of the Union over the late rebellion will have been in vain," concluded one Virginia loyalist. Ethelred Philips, the Florida celebrant of Governor John Milton's gory suicide, pronounced his malediction upon the "wretched" provisional state government and the federal government that sustained it. He had no love for those who called the United States "their" government, he told his brother, and "no interest in their fate." "I . . . never intend to read another page of their history. In making no discrimination between us and the vile secesh, the real authors of our ruin, they have succeeded . . . in utterly extinguishing all attachment to the Union."[68] The disappointment was perhaps greatest in Alabama, where strait-sect unionists had initially thought Parsons would back them exclu-

emphasize their devotion to the Union. But these records are invaluable in outlining their definitions of *unionism, loyalty* and *secessionism*.

66. Jacob Hawkins to Taliaferro, September 22, 1865, in Taliaferro Family Papers.
67. Thomas Wilson to Parsons, August 9, 1865, in Alabama Governors' Papers. After receiving several complaints from Clarke County unionists, Provisional Governor Parsons removed James from office. Citizens delegation to Parsons, September 5, 1865, *ibid*.
68. Lowe, "Republicans, Rebellion, and Reconstruction," 201; Ethelred Philips to James J. Philips, January 21, 1866, in Philips Papers. Because of his bitter racism, Philips had no sympathy for those unionists who were willing to move into the Republican party.

sively, but from every southern state came complaints that opponents of the Confederacy had been denied the legitimate fruits of victory.[69] The contempt expressed for them by the patriotic former Confederates was understandable. The editor of the Nashville *Banner* had described the loyalists of the South as the "merest trash that could be collected in a civilized community," while the Richmond *Times* was even more scathing. It would be absurd, said the *Times*, to ask southerners to place their government in the hands of a handful of men who were "beneath the contempt of the lowest camp followers . . . of the Federal Army." Opposition came, however, from unexpected sources. Whitelaw Reid, the *Nation*'s correspondent in the South, had begun his postwar travels prepared to sympathetically support the southern unionists, but he was soon uneasy at the prospect of their political control of the South. Such men were filled with dreams of revenge and plans to disfranchise and exclude most white men within their states in order to maintain political power. This was necessary, noted Reid, because they were, by their own acknowledgment, a "very small minority and it remains to be seen how long a minority, however loyal, can govern in a Republican country."[70] Even Henry Winter Davis, coauthor of the Wade-Davis bill, insisted that wartime policies had to be adjusted in the postwar South. To rely only upon those who had consis-

69. It would be impossible to cite all the primary sources that reflect the anger and disappointment of strait-sect unionists in the postwar South. The governors' papers of almost every southern state for the summer of 1865 contain dozens—in the case of Alabama, hundreds—of unionists' complaints. For some of the more useful secondary sources see Sarah Woolfolk Wiggins, "Unionist Efforts to Control Alabama Reconstruction, 1865–1867," *AHQ*, XXX (1968), 61–64; Floyd Ewing, "Origins of Unionist Sentiment on the West Texas Frontier," *WTHY*, XXXII (1956), 21–24; Elliott, "Union Sentiment in Texas," 450–68; James Alex Baggett, "Birth of the Texas Republican Party," *SwHQ*, LXXVIII (1974), 1–20; Baggett, "Rise and Fall of the Texas Radicals," 1–71; Moneyhon, *Republicanism in Reconstruction Texas*, 21–52; Harris, *Presidential Reconstruction in Mississippi*, 13, 16, 33–36, 40–41; Lowe, "Republicans, Rebellion, and Reconstruction," 200–203; John Allen Meador, "Florida Political Parties, 1865–1877" (Ph.D. dissertation, University of Florida, 1964), 30–36; Elizabeth Studley Nathans, *Losing the Peace: Georgia Republicans and Reconstruction, 1865–1871* (Baton Rouge, 1969), 2–15; James Douglas Smith, "Virginia During Reconstruction, 1865–1870: A Political, Economic, and Social Study" (Ph.D. dissertation, University of Virginia, 1960), 1–33. Although the complaints of postwar unionists are couched in the wartime vocabulary of *unionist* and *rebel*, much of the hostility is rooted in antebellum political divisions and in family and local political feuds that defy easy generalization.

70. Nashville *Banner*, n.d., quoted in Knoxville *Whig*, March 21, 1866; Richmond *Times*, January 6, 1866; Whitelaw Reid, *After the War*, 20. Reid's scepticism concerning the reliability and trustworthiness of southern Unionists was shared by the majority of northern correspondents traveling in the South (though part of their hostility was rooted in a kind of social snobbery as well as in their political calculations.) See also John Richard Dennett, *The South As It Is*, ed. Henry M. Christman (New York, 1965), 119; Sidney Andrews, *The South Since the War as Shown by Fourteen Weeks of Travel and Observation in Georgia and the Carolinas* (Boston, 1866).

tently opposed the Confederacy would be a political impracticality. It would place the governments of the southern states in the hands of a tiny minority, a "mere handful of the population . . . , wholly incompetent to form or maintain a state government."[71]

By the early fall of 1865, radical southern unionists had only two alternatives. One was to oppose the whole notion of reestablishing state governments in the South. The overwhelming portion of the white southern "body politic" had been "nursed on slavery and . . . looked to secession as its foster mother," argued Gilbert D. Kingsbury of Brownsville, Texas. Civilization did not "march to the beat of a drum," and its conquests were not completed by "repeals and enactments nor by rigging a platform at a party caucus." The South was in the midst of a great revolution. "We are not dusting a sideboard with a feather, but turning up the earth from its substratum." Revolutions took time to nurture and support. Under such conditions, "loyal" southerners should wait.[72]

But there were compelling reasons why such a strategy was undesirable. Not only were the great majority of southerners convinced that economic recovery could only come with the establishment of stable state governments, most unionists were convinced that time was *not* on their side. As northern support dwindled, it would be the secessionists who would profit. And in fact, it was the most bitter opponents of any form of reconstruction who supported the strategy first suggested by A. P. Aldrich of South Carolina, who urged fellow southerners to wait passively until the "radical" Republicans had overreached themselves and triggered a reaction among northern conservatives that would lead to the return of constitutional government.[73]

There was another alternative, one to which the dynamics of postwar politics seemed to point: the enfranchisement of the freedmen. Parson Brownlow of Tennessee, for example, had been a bitter antebellum and wartime racist. And quite apart from his own feelings on the subject, he was conscious of the antiblack sentiments of his East Tennessee constituency. (If the federal troops are removed, said a Knoxville unionist, "the buzzards can't eat up the niggers as fast as we'll kill them.") As late as April of 1865 he supported the colonization of blacks outside the state and he repeatedly complained of black depredations and "insolence." As he saw his political strength falter, however, he moved expediently during the summer of 1865 toward a reluctant acceptance of black suffrage. A small number of

71. Henry Winter Davis to Edward McPherson, May 27, 1865, in Edward McPherson Papers, LC.
72. Gilbert D. Kingsbury, Speech, June [?], 1867, in Kingsbury Papers.
73. A. P. Aldrich, quoted in Sidney Andrews, *The South Since the War*, 43.

outmaneuvered Louisiana and Virginia unionists made a similar about-face in 1865.[74] But this was hardly the response of most southern unionists, whatever their background. Throughout the summer and fall of 1865, for example, unhappy unionists from across the South wrote northern Republicans to plead for their help in blocking the take-over of the Johnson governments by "unregenerate rebels." When they mentioned the issue of race, they sometimes compared blacks favorably to their hated political opponents. More commonly, they railed against the notion that blacks should be given the suffrage. John Robinson, a Goldsboro, North Carolina, unionist, insisted that he meant no harm to the freedmen, but he did not believe they were a suitable raw material for reconstructing North Carolina. "I believe I am sufficiently conversant with the habits of both races to know that they cannot live together in harmony," Robinson wrote to Thaddeus Stevens.[75]

The racial attitudes of southern unionists were probably better and certainly no worse than those of their political opponents, but this racial fear and hatred from the outset undermined any basis for a genuine political coalition. Even as he pressed for an end to the war in the winter of 1865, William Woods Holden railed against the prospect of emancipation. It would result in "negro and white equality, in amalgamation and in the horrors of a St. Domingo's Insurrection." Although he abandoned his defense of slavery in the aftermath of the war and, as provisional governor, insisted that he knew "neither black nor white" in the performance of his duties, he showed little solicitude for the problems of the freedmen. In November of 1865 after a military court imposed a twelve-month jail sentence on a white North Carolinian for shooting a black alleged horse thief, Holden was beside himself with rage. Such a "harsh and unreasonable punishment as that imposed upon Mr. [J. P.] Marcus is calculated to set the whites against the whole negro race," Holden complained, and it would only increase the "numerous instances of outrages committed by freedmen upon the whites." At

74. John V. Cimprich has described the shifting attitudes of Tennessee politicians toward slavery in "Slavery Amidst the Civil War in Tennessee: The Death of an Institution" (Ph.D. dissertation, Ohio State University, 1977). See also Brownlow's fervent defense of slavery as the "natural condition of negroes" in William G. Brownlow and Abram Pryne, *Ought Slavery to Be Perpetuated: A Debate Held at Philadelphia, September, 1858* (Philadelphia, 1858), 101–103; Joseph E. Walker, "The Negro in Tennessee During the Reconstruction Period" (M.A. thesis, University of Tennessee, 1933), 16; Patton, *Unionism and Reconstruction*, 124–25; Lowe, "Republicans, Rebellion, and Reconstruction," 202; Joe Gray Taylor, *Louisiana Reconstructed, 1863–1877* (Baton Rouge, 1974), 70–79.

75. John Robinson to Thaddeus Stevens, February 22, 1866, in Thaddeus Stevens Papers, LC; Benjamin Higgins to John Sherman, October 25, 1865, in John Sherman Papers, LC. Both Sherman and Stevens received numerous letters from southern unionists. With a few noteworthy exceptions, they made no attempt to conceal their hostility toward the freedmen.

the same time, the least mention of black suffrage angered the North Carolina unionist. Black suffrage, no matter how limited in scope, he argued in March of 1866, would result in a "government of darkness and failure." The "despicable argument" that freedmen should be included in the political body of the state not only "ignores hundreds of thousands of white Unionists in the South, but it puts the freedmen above them." It was, Holden insisted, a "libel upon the union men of the South."[76]

Most white southern unionists shared Holden's outlook. Ultimately their ambitions and their hatred for their traditional political enemies would lead them to accept black suffrage but there is little evidence of willingness to do this in their postwar public statements or their private correspondence. If they had been predisposed to support a coalition with the South's newly emancipated freedmen, however, the radical unionists would have destroyed any chance of broadening their political base within the white community. They were trapped in a political cul-de-sac. Holden's inability to develop postwar policies that would allay the fears and suspicions of a victorious North *and* gain the support of his fellow North Carolinians was a sobering dress rehearsal for all those southerners who sought to govern the region in the aftermath of the war.

On the other hand, the ineffectual role of the southern strait-sect unionists in the shaping of postwar society did not mean that nothing had changed, for war, defeat, and emancipation had set in motion an unpredictable chain of upheavals. "Everywhere foolish men plead for a return to the union as it was," observed a Georgetown, South Carolina, planter. Joshua had made the "sun stand sill in Gibeon and the Moon at Ajalon [*sic*]," but Benjamin Wilson reminded his fellow southerners of the biblical footnote: there had been "no day like it before or since." The sun would not stand still in 1865, and neither the Union nor the South would remain as it was before the war.[77]

76. Raleigh *Standard*, February 3, 1865, March 22, 1866; Holden to A. Jackson, November 2, 1865, in Provisional Governor's Record Book, 1865, North Carolina Governors' Papers, NCA. One would be hard pressed to find antiblack statements by other provisional governors that matched Holden's. See his interview in the London *Times*, November 30, 1865, and his correspondence for the last six months of 1865, particularly his letter to Gen. Thomas H. Ruger, September 23, 1865, and to Gen. O. O. Howard, September 26, 1865, both in Holden Letterbooks.

77. Benjamin Wilson to James L. Orr, June 7, 1866, in South Carolina Governors' Papers, SCA. Wilson's reference here is to Joshua 10: 12 – 14.

III / Southern Realism and Southern Honor: The Limits of Self-Reconstruction

I T W A S a subdued group of Mississippians who gathered in Jackson in mid-August of 1865 as delegates to their state's postwar constitutional convention. Four and a half years earlier, members of the secession convention had met in the same building, amid a carnival atmosphere of marching bands, torchlight parades, and nightly serenades, to dissolve the bonds between Mississippi and the United States of America. Even before that earlier convention had signed the proclamation of January 15, 1861, the jubilant population had begun a week-long celebration. "Bring out the cannon," one editor had written enthusiastically, "and let it roar out its loud reverberating approbation." With the exception of a handful of dispirited cooperationists, most delegates had seemed disturbed only by the tardiness that had made the Mississippi ordinance second to that of South Carolina.[1]

In 1865 there were no bands and parades, no "fair hands and lovely forms" to applaud the creation of a new Mississippi, and most Mississippians had heard enough cannon fire to last a lifetime. What fools they had been, one Confederate veteran and delegate recalled as the convention opened. The secessionists had expected a "holiday march," but when they found instead gunpowder and lead, with death everywhere, the "sport was lost." "I am sick of war," declared William Martin of Natchez, "tired of

---

1. Percy Lee Rainwater, *Mississippi, Storm Center of Secession, 1856–1861* (Baton Rouge, 1938), 215; Robert W. DuBay, *John Jones Pettus, Mississippi Fire-Eater: His Life and Times, 1813–1867* (Jackson, Miss., 1975), 84; Thomas H. Woods, "A Sketch of the Mississippi Secession Convention of 1861—Its Membership and Work," *PMHS*, VI (1902), 91–104.

fighting the battles of those who enticed me and others with speeches and when the day of our calamity came, deserted us to our fate."[2]

Few moments more aptly captured this combination of common sense and frank acceptance of southern defeat than the emotional speech of former Confederate general Samuel McGowan on the second day of the South Carolina constitutional convention. During the morning session, delegate A. P. Aldrich, leader of a handful of irreconcilable opponents of any concessions to the North, offered a resolution to recess the convention without taking any action, on the grounds that it was better to "endure patiently the evils which we cannot avert or correct and to await calmly the time and opportunity to affect our delivery from unconstitutional rule." Aldrich had not taken his seat before McGowan was on his feet in rebuttal. The Abbeville planter, wounded at Cold Harbor and Second Manassas, had returned to the war as a brigade commander in 1863. At Chancellorsville he was wounded for a third time. Despite his injuries, he had rejoined his regiment and was at Appomattox when Lee surrendered. McGowan would have no part of Aldrich's resolution, he told his fellow delegates, for it implied duplicity on the part of the South. "It is not true that South Carolina carries a dagger underneath her vestments; not true that she stands with obedient words on her lips and disloyal spirit in her heart," he declared. The state had been the first to secede, and its citizens had waged war with all their energies and material resources. But "whatever may have been charged against her, no one has ever dared charge her with double dealing." The state was now so poor that it was "no figure of speech to say she has lost everything but honor." To pass Aldrich's resolution, McGowan declared, would "bow in the dust the head of every one of her true sons." Thumping his desk for emphasis, the general angrily concluded: "She has seen enough of war; in God's name I demand that she shall not be made to appear as if she still coveted fire and sword." A roar of applause from the gallery seconded McGowan's impassioned plea, and the Aldrich resolution was tabled by an overwhelming majority.[3]

The task seemed clear-cut as the constitutional gatherings convened in

2. Cincinnati *Commercial*, September 13, 1865.
3. Sidney Andrews, *The South Since the War as Shown by Fourteen Weeks of Travel and Observation in Georgia and the Carolinas* (Boston, 1866), 43–44; Ulysses Robert Brooks, *South Carolina Bench and Bar, 1846–1947* (Columbia, S.C., 1908), 121; Jon L. Wakelyn (ed.), *Biographical Dictionary of the Confederacy* (Westport, Conn., 1977), 297–98. The Aldrich-McGowan exchange is also compelling evidence that, just as southerners misunderstood and misrepresented northern public opinion, northerners were likely to do the same with southern attitudes. The New York *Tribune* and the Cleveland *Leader*, for example, described the Aldrich resolution, implying that his action had the support of the majority of delegates, and then failed to note the overwhelming vote against it.

August and September. The South had staked everything—including slavery—on the right to secede and to form a new Confederacy. A somber James L. Orr told the South Carolina convention, "We first failed at the ballot-box, and now we have failed on the battle field." The conqueror, said the longtime state political leader, had made the terms of settlement: "abolish slavery by our own enactment, declare that it shall never be reestablished, treat our freedmen well, popularize our constitution." On the whole, said Orr, these terms were remarkably liberal. "Might we not have fared much worse?" Instead of persistently and stubbornly resisting, "let us be wise men by graceful and ready acquiescence in the results of the war."[4]

Orr's forthright statement of the requirements of the hour was repeated across the South. As one Mississippi delegate, a once-wealthy slaveowner, concluded, the South had fought to preserve slavery and to maintain the "right" of secession. "Having assisted at the interment of slavery," he told his fellow delegates, "I am anxious to assist at the funeral of his twin brother secession."[5]

But it was not so simple. In the constitutional conventions of 1865, the first postwar test of the political acumen of white southerners, delegates were quickly embroiled in petty and rancorous debates over the precise terms of that "interment" of slavery and secession. The general impression conveyed to a watching nation was hardly the "graceful acquiescence" that James Orr had prescribed. Not surprisingly, the Republican party's radical minority attacked the new postwar regimes from the outset, but they were soon joined by moderate Republicans made uneasy by the statements and actions of the Johnson governments. Even Wade Hampton mocked his state's 1865 constitutional convention and its "bastard offspring," the legislature of 1865–1866, a "political 'Nullius filius' somewhat after the order of Melchesidec, without father, without mother, without descent—fit successor of a most unhonored predecessor."[6]

Southerners were not insensitive to their precarious position in 1865. In their private correspondence they repeatedly reflected an acute awareness that their words and actions were daily scrutinized by their victors. Southern newspapers were filled with warnings to be "sober and circumspect," and few convention debates began without an admonition from a delegate that they be sensitive to the suspicions of northern public opinion. Nevertheless, the great majority of white southerners seemed unable to grasp the

4. Charleston *Daily Courier*, September 20, 1865.
5. Montgomery *Advertiser*, September 13, 1865.
6. Wade Hampton III to Andrew Johnson, August 25, 1866, in Charles Edward Cauthen (ed.), *Family Letters of the Three Wade Hamptons, 1782–1901* (Columbia, S.C., 1953), 133.

breadth of the division between North and South. Like William Martin of Natchez, they were sick of war and ready to acknowledge the supremacy of the Union, but they were unwilling to condemn the political beliefs that they had maintained through the 1850s. They were reconciled to emancipation, but they would not rejoice in the death of slavery. Even as men of property recognized that the death of the Confederacy meant the destruction of $700 million in Confederate notes, bonds, and securities, they tenaciously fought to salvage a portion of the much smaller debts of the individual southern states. They simply seemed unable to grasp the fact that to most Americans outside the South secession and slavery were moral issues not subject to debate, just as the financial obligations of the southern states were "immoral" debts, "irrevocably tainted with the odor of rebellion."[7]

In the crazy quilt of these postwar politics, one can find on every hand the "stupidity" and "monumental folly" that Mississippi's lieutenant governor J. H. Jones remembered almost half a century later.[8] There is evidence as well to document the conspiratorial rhetoric of radical Republicans who saw bad faith and continued rebelliousness on every hand. But the tangled events of 1865 and 1866 offer more than a lesson in blundering and duplicity.

White southerners did not fail because they turned to the "demogogues and old fogies" (in Benjamin Truman's words) who had brought on the war itself. The notion that southerners gave power to their former secessionist leaders was first raised by the strait-sect unionists at the time of the 1865 elections and repeated faithfully by suspicious Republicans. Rejected unionists were quick to insist that their political failure in the elections for convention delegates proved that the secessionists dominated the postwar political process. According to one Alabama unionist, the "old secesh element living around the courthouses" had managed to register and vote, but the "genuine unionists—those who were originally opposed to secession—living in the distant areas" were never administered the oath and therefore could not take part in the elections. This refrain was repeated across the South by rejected unionists, who cited the low turnout of voters as evidence that the great majority of loyal southerners had been intimidated and prevented from casting their votes.[9]

7. New York *Tribune*, November 27, 1865.
8. J. H. Jones, "Reconstruction in Wilkinson County," *PMHS*, VIII (1904), 156.
9. Citizens delegation to Gov. Lewis E. Parsons, September 5, 1865, James R. James to Parsons, September 2, 1865, L. F. Hubard to Parsons, September 2, 1865, all in Alabama Governors' Papers, AA; C. R. Bishop to J. R. Kilby, September 3, 1865, in J. R. Kilby Papers, DUL; Leesburg (Va.) *Mirror*, October 5, 8, 19, 1865. See also Charlotte *Daily Times*, December 13, 1865; Fayetteville (N.C.) *News*, September 22, 1865. Benjamin C. Truman, a journalist and supporter of President Johnson who traveled through the region in 1865, submitted a

But the vote in the summer of 1865 was remarkably open and free from coercion. The low turnout was due in part to apathy, in part to the chaotic state of postwar communications in the South. Certainly there was almost no intimidation, and if—as historians would later conclude—white southerners acted with one eye nervously turned toward their northern occupiers, such prudence does not necessarily indicate duplicity or insincerity. Overwhelmingly, southern voters chose cautious and conservative postwar leaders who had opposed secession until the movement for southern independence was an accomplished fact. The clearest evidence of this predilection for antebellum southern unionists can be seen in the background of those 1865 convention delegates who had also served in their state's secession conventions. In North Carolina, of the eleven delegates who had been in Raleigh in 1861, nine had opposed separation until Lincoln's call-up of federal troops. Six of the seven Mississippi delegates who attended both conventions had voted against secession. Of the twenty-two 1865 convention delegates who had served in Georgia's secession convention, fourteen had won election by flatly opposing secession while another six had cautioned against precipitous action. Another fourteen 1865 delegates had been defeated when they ran for the secession convention as unionist candidates. Even in South Carolina, where secession had been the overwhelming choice of the people, fifteen of the twenty postwar delegates who had served in the 1860 secession convention had opposed their state's separation from the Union until after Lincoln's election. By South Carolina standards, this was unionism.[10]

Antebellum secessionists were present in every postwar convention, but they were clearly in the minority. According to one survey of the delegates in the Deep South states of Georgia, Alabama, South Carolina, and Mississippi, more than 70 percent had been unionists in 1860, while the remainder were about equally divided between cooperationists and secessionists. Presumably the proportion of unionists would have been even higher in the states of Texas and North Carolina.[11] By the fall of the year,

generally optimistic report to the president but was also critical of some of the postwar southern leaders. See "Report of Benjamin C. Truman," *Senate Executive Documents*, 39th Cong., 1st Sess., No. 43, Serial No. 1237, pp. 1–14.

10. James Gilchrist McCormick, *Personnel of the [North Carolina] Convention of 1861*, James Sprunt Historical Monographs, I (Chapel Hill, 1900), 19, 22, 29–34, 47, 51, 60–61, 76–80, 87; Wesley Floyd Busbee, Jr., "Presidential Reconstruction in Georgia, 1865–1867" (Ph.D. dissertation, University of Alabama, 1972), 94–96; Milledgeville (Ga.) *Federal Union*, April 30, 1861; Montgomery *Advertiser*, October 1, 1861; Charleston *Daily Courier*, June 16, 1865; Winbourne M. Drake, "The Mississippi Reconstruction Convention of 1865," *JMH*, XXI (1959), 223; John Porter Hollis, *The Early Period of Reconstruction in South Carolina*, Johns Hopkins University Studies, XXIII (Baltimore, 1905), 33–36.

11. See Donald H. Breese, "Politics in the Lower South During Presidential Reconstruc-

critics of the Johnson governments would complain that the great majority of the delegates were unable to sign the "ironclad" test oath, an oath affirming that they had never supported the Confederacy. But the issue was seldom raised in the summer of 1865 except by southern constitutionalists who filled the pages of the region's press with long-winded expositions of the unconstitutionality of the ironclad oath.[12]

Southern voters also tended to choose veterans of the defunct Whig party, thereby continuing a wartime trend in which voters had increasingly rejected southern Democrats and had instead elected individuals associated with the old Whig party or the short-lived Constitutional Union party of 1860 (although the John Bell movement was not simply a continuation of whiggery). South Carolina had had no Whig party worthy of the name in the 1850s. There, the men who emerged as leaders of the 1865 convention were conservatives similar in background and ideology to the antebellum Whigs whom voters favored in every other southern state. This choice was most apparent in Virginia where ninety-six of the ninety-seven members of the 1865 House of Delegates had at one time or another belonged to the Whig party. The situation was the same in the Virginia Senate. In Georgia more than 80 percent of the delegates to the convention had been members of the antebellum Whig party, though some had adopted the label "conservative" in the late 1850s. Mississippi voters preferred Whigs by almost the same majority. Of the ninety-nine delegates in 1865, seventy-one described themselves as Whigs, another eight were Democrats, and the remaining ten used a variety of labels to identify their political affiliation. In North Carolina, where the peculiar position of William W. Holden clouded the issue of party identification, Whigs nevertheless made up a clear majority.

---

tion, April to November, 1865" (Ph.D. dissertation, University of California, 1963), 158. My own findings roughly correspond with Breese's, though results can easily be manipulated because of the elusive nature of the terms *unionist* and *secessionist*. Quite apart from the cooperationists, many southerners who acknowledged the right of secession in 1859–60 were opposed to exercising the right and were quick to describe themselves as unionists after the war.

12. New York *Times*, n.d., quoted in Richmond *Whig*, October 10, 1865; Cleveland *Leader*, November 10, 1865; Raleigh *Sentinel*, October 16, 1865; James Gregoire de Roulhac Hamilton and Max R. Williams (eds.), *The Papers of William Alexander Graham* (6 vols. to date; Raleigh, 1957–), VI, 427–38. As Herman Belz noted in his study of reconstruction during the Civil War, the ironclad oath was essentially a wartime requirement to guarantee the loyalty of those reorganized governments in Louisiana and Arkansas that rested on narrow popular bases. Application of such a rigid oath was impractical in postwar circumstances, and it was the unpalatable prospect of seeing former rebels regain power that led many Republicans to move toward black suffrage rather than the use of the test oaths. Belz, *Reconstructing the Union: Theory and Policy During the Civil War* (Ithaca, 1969), 299–300. One striking aspect of the test oath question is its relative absence from public discussion throughout 1865. It is possible that northerners did not raise the issue because they assumed that southerners would have the good sense to choose leaders who met this high standard of loyalty, but the almost complete absence of any discussion of this issue by northern newspapers or their correspondents in 1865 is surprising.

Only in Alabama were the delegates divided almost evenly between Whigs and Democrats. Even in that state, the majority of these Democrats had voted for the nationalist Democrat Stephen Douglas in 1860; less than 25 percent had supported the Deep South candidate, John C. Breckinridge.[13]

The factors that led white southerners to turn to the antebellum Whigs in 1865 were a complex blend of instinct, ideology, and caution. Although a number of candidates alluded to their past party membership, in no state except Mississippi was party affiliation a critical issue. Zebulon Vance, antebellum North Carolina Whig and post-Reconstruction governor of the state, recognized this situation in 1865 when he fondly recalled the old party but insisted, "The party is dead and buried and the tombstone placed over it and I don't care to spend the balance of my days mourning at its grave." In a speech to his fellow North Carolinians he recounted a typically racist joke about the black boy who caught a huge catfish, staked him to the bank, and fished farther up the river. In his absence, another young fisherman adroitly swapped his smaller catfish and stole away. When the first fisherman returned, he pulled up his fish and declared: "Great Lord, is dis my cat? Here's where I stuck him, but *ain't he shrunk*." That was the condition of the old Whig party, said Vance, "shrunk."[14]

The most decisive factor that led southern voters to choose former Whigs was probably the general impression that these men had been reluctant secessionists and were, under the circumstances, more likely to be acceptable to northern public opinion. Colonel Elliott Wright, attached to the North Carolina district army command, investigated 113 local officeholders in the area of Sampson and Duplin counties in early June of 1865. In this heavily Democratic area, only 34 were Whigs. But of this number, 33 had opposed secession until 1861. In contrast, 16 of the 79 Democrats had been extreme secessionists, while most of the rest had been cooperationists. As a rule, he concluded ("not, however, without exceptions"), those whose "political antecedents before the war had been Whig were originally anti-secessionist and supported the war less heartily and are more unconditional in their union sentiments than those whose antecedents were Democratic."[15] It was this factor that inflated the strength of southern

13. Breese, "Politics in the Lower South," 158–62; Busbee, "Presidential Reconstruction in Georgia," 94–96; Montgomery *Advertiser*, October 1, 1865; Thomas B. Alexander and Richard E. Beringer, *Anatomy of the Confederate Congress* (Nashville, 1972), 337–48; Washington, D.C., *National Intelligencer*, December 4, 1865.

14. David Lowry Swain to Zebulon Vance, August 11, November 1, 20, 1865, all in Zebulon Vance Papers, NCA; Vance quoted in Glenn Tucker, *Zeb Vance: Champion of Personal Freedom* (Indianapolis, 1965), 450–51.

15. Col. Elliott Wright to Gov. William Woods Holden, June 13, 1865, in Governor William Woods Holden Papers, NCA.

former Whigs in 1865. Collectively, these former Whigs had been luke-warm in their support of secession (with, as Wright noted, some excep-tions). Collectively they had benefited from the South's growing war-weariness as southerners turned to the men who had cautioned against pre-cipitous action in the late 1850s.

There was also an impression, seldom stated explicitly but present throughout much of the South, that these sober, conservative men offered a promising approach to the problems of the postwar South. Their ideologi-cal grab bag of whiggish notions for economic development and postwar recovery held at least the pale prospect of action at a time of political and economic paralysis.[16] Thomas Pearsall, the Alabama business promoter who had reluctantly accepted secession in 1861, was ready to revive his ambitious antebellum plans in 1865. The southern up-country was blessed with an ideal soil, a temperate climate, and laboring men "anxious to work," he told his good friend Lewis Parsons. With the intelligent guidance of sympathetic state and federal governments, the South would ultimately become the manufacturing center of the nation and—in the process— "vastly increase the agricultural wealth of the region." But nothing could be accomplished, concluded Pearsall, until the South was restored into the Union once more and constitutional, stable government reestablished. Only the steadying leadership of southern conservatives ("men who had abandoned the union with sad reluctance") could remove the dangerous obstacles of northern hostility and southern "intemperance."[17]

The Mississippi convention, first to meet, had been in session less than a week before it was apparent how difficult it would be to remove these obstacles. The first issue that Mississippians, and later other southerners, faced was a basic one: Should the conventions repeal the secession ordi-nances of 1860 and 1861 or should they declare them null and void *ab initio*? The difference between these two phrases was initially dismissed by one northern journalist as a "distinction betwixt tweedledee and tweedle-dum." But the delegates soon grasped the difference, and ultimately, so did northern Republicans. To repeal the secession ordinances would be to im-ply their legitimacy at the time of enactment; to strike them from the stat-

16. Thomas Alexander's attempts to show the continuity of Whig leadership between the antebellum and postwar South are generally convincing, but I agree with John Mering that Whig party affiliation—after 1865—was only "one of many determinants of later political deci-sions." See Alexander, "Whiggery and Reconstruction in Tennessee," *JSH*, XVI (1950), 291–304; Alexander, "Persistent Whiggery in the Confederate South, 1860–1877," *JSH*, XXVII (1961), 305–29. Mering's response is in "Persistent Whiggery in the Confederate South: A Reconsideration," *SAQ*, LXIX (1970), 124–43. See also Richard E. Beringer, "The Unconscious 'Spirit of Party' in the Confederate Congress," *CWH*, XVIII (1972), 312–28.

17. Thomas Pearsall to Parsons, August 16, September 14, 1865, both in Alabama Governors' Papers.

ute books as null and void from the start was to assert that secession had always been an illegal act.[18]

A few southerners were willing to acknowledge just that. Secession had been a rebellion that failed, one Mississippi former Whig insisted, and he wanted it understood once and for all that it was a revolutionary act. "Peaceable secession!" he scornfully told his fellow delegates. "It meant the risking of all we had or valued." While he was sure that such a rebellion would never come again, "in God's name . . . let [the South] not go out as the fox stealthily and slyly" under the delusion that separation from the national government was a peaceful and constitutional measure.[19]

For other delegates such a position amounted to an act of constitutional self-incrimination. Any resolution nullifying the secession ordinance *ab initio* would "impute the charge of treason upon every person who obeyed the state's 1860 secession ordinance," insisted James Trotter of Panola County, Mississippi. And the language soon took on a more emotional rhetoric. Nullification *ab initio* required that the convention delegates "brand as traitors their fathers, brothers and sons who had died in battle," mourned one Texas observer. North Carolina's O. H. Ferrebee acknowledged that the war had settled once and for all in practical terms that the right of secession did not exist. But to insist that it had had no legal or constitutional basis in 1860 and 1861 was to "cast a stigma upon the 30,000 North Carolina soldiers who sleep in graves across the South." Given the choice between stigmatizing the memory of the southern war dead and satisfying the instructions of President Johnson, it is hardly surprising that the antisecession resolutions became the subject of prolonged and occasionally bitter wrangling. Ultimately the North Carolina convention (by a wide margin) and the Florida and Mississippi conventions (by narrower votes) swallowed their distasteful medicine and declared their secession ordinances null and void *ab initio*. But the South Carolina and Georgia delegates simply repealed their secession ordinances. Georgia's provisional governor James Johnson (an uncompromising opponent of the right of secession) initially failed to grasp the significance of the issue in his message to the Georgia delegates and called upon them to "cancel" the secession ordinance. Unionist Joshua Hill planned to amend the legislation to make it more explicit, but fearful of rhetorical fireworks that would arouse northern suspicions, he did nothing. The Alabama and, later, the Texas delegates compromised by declaring that the 1861 secession ordinances were null and void—as of 1865.[20]

18. Cincinnati *Commercial*, September 8, 1865.
19. Cincinnati *Commercial*, September 9, 1865.
20. Marjorie Howell Cook, "Restoration and Innovation: Alabamians Adjust to Defeat,

The debate over the dead issue of secession revealed the postwar southern leadership at its most inept: prideful, arrogant, and blinded by the constitutional dogmatism of the past. And here, as on so many issues, northern condemnation increased as southerners debated the issue. Thus, at the time South Carolina and Georgia repealed (rather than nullified) their secession ordinances, even the most radical Republican newspapers failed to raise objections.

The controversy over the repudiation of state debts reflected a far more complex blend of crosscurrents, which posed particular problems for most of Johnson's provisional governors and for the conservative leadership that emerged in the constitutional conventions. They faced compromising their deepest ideological convictions in order to satisfy a nation that first ignored the question and then, as in most postwar controversies, came to view the issue as a touchstone of loyalty.

Both the Confederate government and the member states of the Confederacy had financed the war less through taxation than through massive borrowing. The practice of concurrently printing greater and greater quantities of paper currency, coupled with the growing weakness of the Confederacy, inevitably debased the real value of the loans, but the total was still staggering by nineteenth-century standards. When the Confederate government collapsed in the spring of 1865, its financial obligations amounted to more than $700 million. Even when this figure was corrected to account for the depreciation of the currency, it totalled more than $300 million. Although some Confederate bondholders continued to dream of redeeming their worthless promissory notes, the majority of southerners seemed reconciled to the fact that the failure of the rebellion inevitably meant their Confederate bonds were worthless. As one large bondholder observed philosophically, "Every Southerner knew that we staked all on our struggle for

---

1865–1867" (Ph.D. dissertation, University of Alabama, 1968), 18; Jerrell H. Shofner, *Nor Is It Over Yet: Florida in the Era of Reconstruction, 1863–1877* (Gainesville, 1974), 41; Busbee, "Presidential Reconstruction in Georgia," 103–104; William C. Harris, *Presidential Reconstruction in Mississippi* (Baton Rouge, 1967), 55; *Journal of the Convention of the People of South Carolina, Held in Columbia, S.C., September, 1865*, 174–76; Horace W. Raper, "William Woods Holden and the Peace Movement in North Carolina," *NCHR*, XXXI (1954), 145–46; Carl H. Moneyhon, *Republicanism in Reconstruction Texas* (Austin, 1980), 37–39; *Journal of the Proceedings and Delegates in the Constitutional Convention of the State of Mississippi, August, 1865*, 220; Sidney Andrews, *The South Since the War*, 244–46. White southerners' penchant for legalistic hairsplitting and their continuing insistence upon "states' rights" are well documented. James Trotter, elected a Mississippi circuit court judge in November, 1865, ruled in several cases, notwithstanding the emancipation proclamation and the federal government's de facto liberation, that Mississippi's slaves remained "legally chattel" until the action of the postwar constitutional convention in August. John W. Kyle, "Reconstruction in Panola County," *PMHS*, XIII (1913), 68.

independence; that if we lost, we would lose our property [slaves]. We can hardly complain now about the investments we made in the entirprise [*sic*]."[21]

If the Confederacy no longer existed, however, individual state governments did continue, after a fashion, and there was a widespread assumption that some portion of the $54 million debt that individual states had incurred between 1860 and 1865 would be recognized. Few suggested that the states' wartime bonds be repaid at par. In the summer and fall of 1865, newspapers throughout the region outlined proposals for repayment on a scale based upon the bonds' actual value in gold at the time of sale. In Georgia, which had incurred one of the largest war debts, this would have meant a reduction from $17,167,776 to $6,573,917, according to the state's comptroller general. Other supporters of the wartime obligations, conscious of objections that the debt had been incurred in order to destroy the Union, suggested that the states further reduce the amount owed by removing all military expenditures from the total.[22]

During the war, Republicans had repeatedly emphasized the sanctity of the federal debt, and most party leaders were either convinced or professed to be convinced that a resurrection of the antebellum Democratic alliance between North and South would lead to a repudiation of the national debt. It is less clear that Republicans took seriously their political rhetoric that the Democrats—once returned to power—would assume the Confederate debt. Whatever their views, Republicans as well as union Democrats seldom drew a distinction between the wartime obligations incurred by the Confederacy and those that the state governments had added to their pre-existing debt obligations. On the other hand, northerners who held antebellum bonds were understandably anxious that a clear distinction be made between the "immoral" war debts (which few of them held) and the "moral" antebellum debts. Their uneasiness on these points was strengthened by memories of 1861, when the new Confederate state governments had nullified the legal obligation of Confederates to repay northern debts.[23]

21. Henry W. Ravenel Journal, SCL, May 22, 1865; Andrew McDowell to Rev. M. H. Lance, August 26, 1865, in Read-Lance Family Papers, SCL; Alvan F. Sanborn (ed.), *Reminiscences of Richard Lathers* (New York, 1907), 245.

22. For various plans for a modified repayment of the war debt, see Macon *Daily Telegraph*, October 29, 1865; Edward Conigland to Thomas Ruffin, December 4, 1865, in Thomas Ruffin Papers, SHC; Montgomery *Advertiser*, September 13, 1865; Charleston *Daily Courier*, October 12, 1865. Brief summaries of the wartime debts incurred are in John E. Johns, *Florida During the Civil War* (Gainesville, 1963), 107–11; Raleigh *Standard*, January 22, 1866; *American Annual Cyclopedia and Register of the Important Events of the Year 1865* (New York, 1870), 17–18; New York *Times*, September 29, 1865; James H. Bass, "Civil War Finance in Georgia," *GHQ*, XXVI (1942), 213–24.

23. New York *Times*, September 29, 1865; "Will the Old State Debts of the South Be

Only once did the issue surface in the early stages of Johnsonian Reconstruction. When Andrew Johnson met with South Carolina's provisional governor Benjamin Perry (and a dozen other unofficial delegates from the state), he laid down a list of requirements for the state's return to the Union. The newly organized constitutional convention, Johnson told the attentive group, had to abolish slavery by state law, ratify the proposed Thirteenth Amendment, and renounce the doctrine of secession. These were described by Johnson as "indispensable." At the same time, he told Perry, it was important that South Carolinians abandon the "aristocratical" system under which low-country planters dominated the state government, and the people were barred even from selecting presidential electors and their state's chief executive.

At the conclusion of the interview, Johnson did raise the issue of the state's war debt but in a curiously equivocal manner. Repudiation of that debt was not described as an indispensable requirement, but any state that retained the debt should not expect to meet a "favorable reception" by either his administration or the Congress, Johnson told the group. As one of the participants, John Bacon, concluded in his report of the meeting, however, in the absence of a clear and explicit command from the president any proposal for repudiation would be "warmly contested."[24]

In point of fact, repudiation was never to be discussed by the South Carolina convention because Perry—who abhorred repudiation almost as much as black suffrage—used Johnson's lack of explicit instructions on this point as his pretext to ignore the issue. He failed to mention it in his speech to the convention or later in his memoirs, even though he implied that Johnson's other recommendations for the democratization of South Carolina politics (which Perry favored) were essential if the state was to be accepted into the Union. William Sharkey of Mississippi followed the same course in that state. Thus, although both states would later be excoriated for failing to meet one of the president's "requirements" for readmission, it would be more accurate to say that Perry and Sharkey used the ambiguity and hesitancy of the president to strengthen their political and ideological opposition to repudiation. By the time Secretary of State William H. Seward made repudiation of the debt an absolute requirement for readmis-

---

Paid?" *MM*, LIII (1865), 409–12; Kenneth Stampp, *And the War Came: The North and the Secession Crisis, 1860–1861* (Baton Rouge, 1950), 29.

24. Perry gives a general description of his meetings with the president in his memoirs, but it is far less specific (and accurate) than the report John F. Bacon made to the people of South Carolina. It was published in the Edgefield (S.C.) *Advertiser*, August 16, 1865. The editors of the Charleston *Daily Courier* and the Columbia *Phoenix*—both of whom abhorred repudiation —did not publish Bacon's account.

sion, a self-satisfied Perry (who dismissed the state's war debt as "inconse-quential") was able to reply that the convention had already adjourned.[25]

In Alabama, however, strait-sect unionists in the northern portion of the state had made the repudiation of the state debt one of the litmus tests for loyalty in 1865. Most of the state's $3.8 million wartime debt was held by South Alabama bondholders, and North Alabamians seized the oppor-tunity to strike at their traditional enemies. Still sensitive to antebellum charges of "financial immorality," they were now able to make these de-mands for repudiation one of the moral issues of war. The "bloated bond-holders sat on their verandahs safe from conscription, investing their dollars rather than their sons in this vile war," said one bitter North Alabamian in the summer of 1865. Now these "speculators and Shylocks" wished to "resurrect" their bloodstained investments. "We do not have the luxury of resurrecting our sons who were forced to fight and die!" Not one penny should be paid, he insisted, "*Not one penny!*"[26]

During the early stages of the session, defenders of the state's debt de-feated a hastily drafted repudiation ordinance by urging members of the legislature to wait for the recommendations of the appropriate committee. Even at this stage, however, representatives from the mountain counties of North Alabama pressed for action.[27] The clamor for repudiation created particular problems for Provisional Governor Lewis Parsons. Ideologically, Parsons, like his successor Robert M. Patton, was steeped in a whiggish tradition in which repudiation was an anathema. At the same time, Parsons' lukewarm support for the war had given him considerable support from the North Alabama Democrats who had little use for banks or bonds, particularly those held by South Alabamians. Torn between his ideological commitment to sound financial principles and a constituency hostile to such attitudes, Parsons remained neutral. He made no mention of the war

25. Winbourne Drake, "Constitutional Development in Mississippi, 1817–1865" (Ph.D. dissertation, University of North Carolina, 1954), 314–16; William H. Seward to Benjamin Perry, November 10, 24, 1865, Perry to Seward, November 26, 1865 (copy), all in Benjamin Perry Manuscripts (Microfilm, 2 reels, SHC, 1967).

26. Huntsville (Ala.) *Advocate*, July 23, 1865; W. L. Cunningham to Parsons, November 29, 1865, in Alabama Governors' Papers. According to Walter L. Fleming, most of the debt was held in Mobile. Though he cites no evidence, his conclusion is consistent with past bond-holding practices. See William H. Brantley, *Banking in Alabama, 1816–1860* (2 vols.; Bir-mingham, 1967), II, 330–40.

27. The ordinance failed fifty-nine to thirty-four, with solid support coming only from the area north of present-day Birmingham. Typically suspicious, the New York *Tribune* (Sep-tember 22) attributed this vote to continuing "disloyalty" and "opposition to the union." In fact, there was little doubt that Alabama would abandon its war debt; the original resolution of repudiation was improperly drawn. Montgomery *Advertiser*, September 29, 1865; New York *Times*, October 10, 1865; *Journal of the Proceedings of the Convention of the State of Alabama Held in Montgomery Beginning September 12, 1865*, p. 1861.

debt in his opening message to the convention, and he declined to make a statement on the subject during the deliberations that followed. On September 28, with only desultory debate, the convention voted sixty to nineteen to abandon its war debt. Seventeen of the nineteen opponents came from the city of Mobile and nine black-belt counties.[28] Thus, southern unionists rather than the president or northern Republicans had first raised the issue of the state's war debts. And not for the first time, they had couched their grievances in the comfortable language of loyalty and disloyalty.

Even after the Alabama vote in late September, Andrew Johnson remained silent on the question. In North Carolina, W. W. Holden's newspaper, the *Standard*, had endorsed repudiation of the state's war debt in late August but made few comments about the issue during the following two months. Holden's representative in Washington interviewed the president's cabinet members in early October. With the exception of Secretary of War Edwin Stanton, they advised Holden to postpone debate on the state's war debt until more pressing controversies had been resolved. A number of delegates read R. J. Powell's letter to Holden, and this probably strengthened their reluctance to take up the issue. When a western delegate to the convention introduced a proposal in early October to repudiate the state's war debt, the convention, with Holden's tacit support, tabled the resolution by a three-to-one majority. Only a handful of delegates from the Piedmont and those from the westernmost counties supported the repudiation resolution. Without the catalyst of angry debate, the convention vote passed unnoticed in the northern press.[29]

By mid-October the "moral" issues remained unchanged, but the political circumstances in North Carolina had suddenly shifted. Jonathan Worth, the state's postwar treasurer under Holden, had decided to campaign for the governorship in the fall elections. Although Worth had loyally supported the Confederacy, his long-term allegiance to whig-unionism in the 1850s and his courageous defense of Holden against a pro-Confederate mob in 1864 had made him Holden's first choice for his postwar cabinet. Too late, Holden realized that his attempt at conciliating his old Whig opponent had jeopardized his own campaign for election in the fall. By forcing Worth and his followers to defend the revolutionary debt, Holden could discredit them and tie himself to what he believed was Johnson's critical

28. For a sensitive description of the ideological background from which Parsons emerged, see J. Mills Thornton III, *Politics and Power in a Slave Society: Alabama, 1800–1860* (Baton Rouge, 1978), esp. Chap. 5. *Journal of the Alabama Convention*, 294; Montgomery *Advertiser*, September 29, 1865.

29. *Journal of the North Carolina Constitutional Convention, 1865*, 334–35; *North Carolina Daily Standard*, October 19, 1865; Raleigh *Sentinel*, October 19, 30, 1865.

political future. All through the summer and into the fall, Worth had counseled postponement of the debt question because he realized that his strongest supporters were sharply divided on the issue. A handful of his friends wanted debt repayment on a scaled basis. Holden, however, recognized that the Alabama convention had tainted the state's war debts with the odor of rebellion.[30]

On October 17, Holden secretly telegraphed the president that the North Carolina convention had "involved itself in a bitter discussion of the State debt made in the rebellion." (In fact, there had been no debate at any time, and the subject had not even been mentioned on the convention floor after the original repudiation proposal had been tabled.) Was it not advisable, Johnson's appointee asked, "that our convention, like that of Alabama, should positively ignore this debt now and forever?" At this point, for the first time, Johnson openly committed himself to repudiation as an unconditional requirement for the readmission of the southern states, and he did so in lofty moral tones. "Every dollar of the debt created to aid the rebellion against the United States should be repudiated finally and forever," he told North Carolina's governor Holden. By this act, the people of North Carolina would "wash their hands of everything that partakes in the slightest degree of the rebellion."[31]

Reluctantly, the convention bowed to the president's directive. Two days after the exchange between Holden and Johnson, the delegates enacted an ordinance of repudiation by a vote of eighty-seven to twenty-four. To the end, a handful of delegates from constituencies across the state held out against what they argued was a "flagrant interference" in the internal affairs of North Carolina. But Worth and his supporters refused to take the bait. Despite his own strong opposition to repudiation, Worth had concluded in late August that the president would probably demand that the state abandon the debts incurred between 1861 and 1865. Worth took the

30. Worth's decision to run was made in the late summer, but he concealed his plans as long as possible. Jonathan Worth to J. C. Jason, August 12, 1865, Worth to W. B. Stipes, August 21, 1865, Worth to E. G. Reade, August 22, 1865, all in Letterpress Book, 1865–1866, Jonathan Worth Papers, NCA; Raleigh *Standard*, October 10, 13, 23, 1865. Describing motivations can be difficult. Michael Perman, for example, argues that it was Worth who precipitated the debt controversy by his plans to run for the governorship in the fall on a platform opposing repudiation. Perman, *Reunion Without Compromise: The South and Reconstruction, 1865–1868* (Cambridge, 1973), 76. There is ample evidence that Worth opposed repudiation, but I found none that he planned to make this the centerpiece of his fall campaign. Moreover, in a telegram to President Johnson on October 20, 1865, Holden frankly acknowledged that he had raised the issue in order to draw a distinction between himself and the emerging "Worth faction." Holden to Andrew Johnson, October 20, 1865, in Andrew Johnson Papers, LC. Clearly both sides were maneuvering for political advantage.

31. Holden to Johnson, October 17, 1865, in Andrew Johnson Papers; Johnson to Holden, October 18, 1865, in Holden Papers.

outcome of the dispute philosophically and discouraged all attempts by his friends to revive the question. Having acquiesced in the "confiscation" of hundreds of millions of dollars in slave property, he saw little reason to challenge Johnson over a few million dollars in state debts. Thus, the primary consequence of the North Carolina repudiation fight was to fix the issue as a test of southern loyalty—and to confirm many North Carolinians in their distrust of Holden.[32]

Repudiation may have become a moral issue for the editors of the Cleveland *Leader* and the Chicago *Tribune*, but its consequences were far more concrete to a postwar southern leadership seeking to avoid further financial losses. Moreover, in several southern states, common-school endowments had been invested in state securities. (The North Carolina and Texas funds had been more than $2 million in 1860.) Private educational institutions had also invested in state and Confederate bonds. Due West College in upstate South Carolina had a sizable endowment by antebellum southern standards. Pressured by patriotic alumnae and the state government, trustees for the little Presbyterian college had invested every penny in state securities. Repudiation destroyed the endowment.[33]

It had even broader repercussions in its effects upon a collapsing southern banking system. The threat to state bonds drove more than one postwar banker, already reeling under the financial effects of emancipation and the loss of Confederate securities, to conclude that there was little hope for survival. Throughout the summer of 1865, William A. Wright, president of the Wilmington, North Carolina, Bank of Cape Fear, resorted to every

32. Worth to W. B. Stephens, August 21, 1865, Worth to Jesse Walker, September 14, 1865, Worth to S. Whitaker, September 15, 1865, all in Letterpress Book, 1865–1866, Worth Papers; Worth to R. S. French, August 18, 1865, in James Gregoire de Roulhac Hamilton (ed.), *The Correspondence of Jonathan Worth* (2 vols.; Raleigh, 1909), 393–94. The issue had already begun to attract some scattered interest on the part of northerners, but the president's message to Holden made it a major question for the first time. As late as October, one northern newspaper editor concluded that the president's message to Holden "foreshadowed" a policy whereby repudiation of the state war debts would be made a condition of readmission to the Union. Cleveland *Leader*, October 23, 1865. And it was mid-November before Johnson eventually got around to communicating this condition to the South Carolina and Florida conventions. Seward to Perry, November 10, 1865, in Perry Manuscripts; *Journal of the Constitutional Convention of 1865 at Tallahassee, Florida*, 103–109. See also Worth to Dr. W. P. Pugh, October 28, 1865, in Hamilton (ed.), *Correspondence of Worth*, I, 445–56; *Journal of the North Carolina Convention*, 492; John Richard Dennett, *The South As It Is*, ed. Henry M. Christman (New York, 1965), 80–81.

33. William Hood to Rev. W. R. Hemphill, July 24, 1865, in Hemphill Collection, DUL; Oliver C. Bentley to Parsons, September 23, 1865, in Alabama Governors' Papers; Johns, *Florida During the Civil War*, 179; Worth to Rev. N. H. D. Wilson, September 7, 1865, in Hamilton (ed.), *Correspondence of Worth*, I, 411; John Townsend Trowbridge, *The South: A Tour of Its Battle-fields and Ruined Cities* (Hartford, 1866), 579–80; Moneyhon, *Republicanism in Reconstruction Texas*, 93.

conceivable strategem—some beyond the hazy border of legality—to avoid bankruptcy. Foreign assets and securities were converted to gold to prevent seizure by creditors, and such money, along with negotiable securities, was placed in the hands of trusted third parties beyond the reach of bank creditors. At the same time, the bank refused to pay depositors on the grounds of "temporary" nonliquidity. The threat of "villianous [sic] repudiation" was the last straw, concluded a discouraged Wright, a delegate at the 1865 North Carolina constitutional convention. It would work the "inevitable ruin of the Bank." Other bankers were equally convinced that this last jolt to their fragile banking structure would lead to bankruptcy.[34]

The stakes seemed higher because the debate over repudiation took place in the context of a broader conflict between debtor-creditor elements in southern society, a conflict that reached beyond the relatively insignificant matter of the state's war debt. A series of vexing financial complications compounded the overwhelming condition of poverty. Were mortgages and liens given for the purchase of slaves still valid? If the banks succeeded in obtaining legislative relief from payment to their creditors, did this relieve their debtors as well? Would individuals be forced to repay in gold or greenbacks debts that had been contracted in nearly worthless Confederate currency? These and dozens of other unsolved questions were laid against a setting of overwhelming destitution in which the great majority of indebted southerners were simply unable to meet their obligations. Little wonder that one Mississippi planter would suggest that southerners simply "wipe out all debts"—public and private—and "start fresh."[35]

And parlor orators revived a well-oiled rhetoric to argue that the impoverished people of the South were threatened with economic ruin at the hands of the "merchant, the banker, the speculator, the shylock" who had "purchased mortgages, liens and state bonds at ten or fifteen cents on the

34. Sanborn (ed.), *Reminiscences of Lathers*, 245. See correspondence of Wright to his head cashier, James Green Burr, June–November, 1865, (esp. October, 1865) in John MacRae Papers, SHC. Sanborn (ed.), *Reminiscences of Lathers*, 245; H. A. Schroeder to Gov. Robert Patton, July 23, 1865, January 1, 1866, both in Bryan Family Papers, DUL; G. A. Kimberly to James L. Orr, November 23, 1866, in James L. Orr Papers, SCA; A. A. Gilbert to Thomas Boone Fraser, September 19, 1866, in Thomas Boone Fraser Papers, SCL; Worth to Holden, June 16, 1865, in Holden Papers; "Some Few Considerations Touching 'the Georgia War Debt,'" [1865?], De Renne Collection, UGL; Savannah *National Republican*, October 31, 1865; Atlanta *Daily Intelligencer*, February 11, 1866; Macon *Daily Telegraph*, February 16, 1866.

35. C. B. Kerville to J. D. B. De Bow, October 12, 1866, in J. D. B. De Bow Papers, DUL. It was a view shared by a large number of southerners, claimed Trowbridge in *The South*, 488. For discussion of some of the purely "mechanical" problems involved in adjusting prewar debts, see T. P. Devereux to George W. Mordecai, June 1, 1865, in George W. Mordecai Papers, SHC. Robert T. Hubard to Willie J. Eppes, September 1, 1865, in Hubard Family Papers, SHC; *Fa*, I (1866), 169–70, 197–99.

dollar" and were now demanding that these debts be repaid in specie. Occasionally, an added note of sectionalism was introduced by arguing that many of these "rich extortioners and speculators" were Yankees who had purchased southern property and bonds and were now prepared to add economic ruin to military destruction. The banks themselves were "swindling shops" and "leeches," which had fastened themselves upon the people of the South in order "to make slaves of you!" argued a Rock Hill farmer to his fellow South Carolinians. The time had come to strike back at this "combined force of capital" too powerful for any one person to compete with in the same community. Unless repudiation was adopted, agreed a fellow up-country farmer, "enforced payments will have concentrated wealth" in the hands of "aristocrats, autocrats, and nabobs and insolent commandeers of the 'public good!'" Throughout 1865 and 1866, while the larger newspapers of the region deprecated such "irresponsible agitation," up-country newspapers such as the Huntsville, Alabama, *Advocate* and the Yorkville, South Carolina, *Enquirer* continued to condemn their states' banking interests.[36]

Not surprisingly, conservative elements in southern society—including many of the individuals most active in the Johnson postwar governments—were horrified by such rhetoric. As a rally of "concerned citizens" in Campbellton, Georgia, concluded, the death of the Confederacy made the $700 million debt of that defunct government "legally" invalid. But any attempt to abandon all of the $54 million wartime debts of the states was a "palpable violation of the Constitution." Moreover, it was "unjust and inexpedient; dangerous to personal rights, calculated to destroy confidence between man and man; paralyzing the energies of the people and opening the way to all kinds of radicalism, insecurity and mob law."[37]

Northern public opinion had conveniently compartmentalized the issues of repudiating state debts and interfering with private debts. Thus the New York *Times* would eventually scold southern constitutional conventions and legislatures both for hesitating over repudiating the state's war debts *and* for considering "stay laws," which would have delayed repayment of private debts. Southern conservatives agreed with Jonathan Worth that tampering with the state's legitimate debt incurred between 1861 and 1865 was like a cancer that would inexorably spread. Once this was nullified, there would be a "disposition to repudiate all the antebellum debt."

36. Yorkville (S.C.) *Enquirer*, August 6, 1866; (Jacksonville) *Florida Union*, October 21, 1865; Cunningham to Parsons, November 29, 1865, in Alabama Governors' Papers; Charleston *Daily Courier*, January 3, 1866.

37. Yorkville (S.C.) *Enquirer*, August 6, October 1, 25, 1866; Atlanta *Daily Intelligencer*, February 11, October 6, 1866; Montgomery *Advertiser*, October 28, 1866.

After that there would inevitably be actions taken to abridge the terms of personal contracts and debts. When Henry Ravenel of South Carolina first learned that repudiation of the state's war debt might be a condition for reentering the Union, he was deeply depressed. Repudiation was a "dangerous subject for legislators to meddle with," warned the South Carolina planter.[38]

For those anxious to rebuild the South economically, any proposal that meddled with the state's "sacred obligations" would sentence the people of the South to economic backwardness and decay. Few wealthy southerners expressed more explicitly the chain of "agrarian horrors" that might ensue than S. S. Jackson, a well-to-do North Carolina Quaker planter. Repudiation of the state debt, he warned, was but the "entering wedge to the repudiation of all private debts—and the latter to the division of the lands & mules, stock &, &, &." Though it might seem impractical in the short run, if the radicals ever succeeded in forcing Negro suffrage, the "negro vote combined with the refuse white vote would affect it." Jackson, like many timid southern conservatives, exaggerated the danger that repudiation would become contagious, but there were chilling examples to strengthen their fears. When one Georgia legislator demanded repudiation of all debts and a "fresh start," he defended the morality of his position by pointing to the repudiation of the state's war debt. Two North Carolina legislators used the same rationale.[39]

Georgia was a case study of the interaction between southerners' concern for northern sensibilities and their own ideological and political differences. As the convention opened in late October, public sentiment seemed overwhelmingly to favor a scaled-down repayment of the war debt, and newspaper reporters found only a handful of delegates in favor of outright repudiation. Positions were unchanged by Provisional Governor James Johnson's plea that the debt be nullified as one of the inevitable results of the "failure of the rebellion." Even when Governor Johnson followed Holden's lead and elicited a telegram from the president demanding that the debt be repudiated, the convention delegates angrily resisted.

In Georgia, as in North Carolina and Alabama, stances on the issue reflected sectional and class divisions within the state. The minority who favored repudiation railed against the speculators, "fat and sleak [*sic*]," who

38. Worth to J. L. Bason, August 12, 1865, in Letterpress Book, 1865–1866, Worth Papers; South Carolina Committee on Immigration, *South Carolina House of Representatives Special Committee on European Immigration, Report on the Subject of Encouraging European Immigration* (Charleston, 1866), 19; Ravenel Journal, September 11, 1865.

39. S. S. Jackson to Worth, May 10, 1866, in Worth Papers; Milledgeville (Ga.) *Southern Recorder*, February 6, 1866; Raleigh *Tri-Weekly Standard*, March 24, 1866.

"never saw the forefront of battle, who knew no loss" but were "anxious to have their pockets filled with taxes, wrung from an impoverished people." One delegate from the North Georgia mountains noted that the convention had, "without a word of debate or the twitching of a nerve," endorsed the emancipation of every slave in Georgia, ensuring the confiscation of hundreds of millions of dollars in property, though it "ruins the very fabric of society among us." Now, the same convention balked at the prospect of nullifying a few million dollars in state bonds. "We have swallowed the camel," concluded a Columbus delegate, "is it seemly or consistent for us now to strain at the gnat?"[40]

Defenders were ready to confront analogy with hyperbole. "I will not vote for the state of Georgia and this convention to cover ourselves with the slime, filth and foul odor of 'repudiation,'" declared one delegate. The state's comptroller general, Peterson Thweatt, was a bit more restrained, but even he supplemented the standard descriptions of the dire effects of repudiation on ruined widows and orphans by insisting that failure to pay at least a portion of the state's war debt would "sully the state's reputation for integrity" and "damn public and private credit beyond recognition." Thweatt's impassioned defense of the state's integrity in turn brought forth the accusation that the comptroller general was primarily concerned over the state's war debt because he had "invested in it himself." The only variation in the Georgia debates was the persistent use of the phrase "Shylock's pound of flesh," a not-so-veiled reference to Savannah's Solomon Cohen, who led the fight to repay the war debt.[41]

But Cohen was simply the floor representative for the ever resourceful Joseph E. Brown, Georgia's antebellum secession leader and war governor. With the political aptitude and flexibility that marked his long career, Brown had skillfully extricated himself from his embarrassing support of the Confederacy. Five months after his incarceration in Washington's Carroll Prison, he was the most important figure in the 1865 constitutional convention. (He would later exhibit the same adroitness by shifting to the Republican party in 1867 and back to the Democrats in 1872.) Although Brown was not a representative at the convention, reporters noted that he was on the floor every day, buttonholing friendly delegates and hourly conferring with Solomon Cohen, his close friend and longtime political ally.[42]

Two days after the president demanded nullification of the state war

40. Macon *Daily Telegraph*, November 1, 1865.
41. *Ibid.*, November 1, October 27, 1865; Savannah *National Republican*, October 31, November 5, 1865.
42. Macon *Daily Telegraph*, November 2, 1865; Savannah *National Republican*, November 7, 1865; Sidney Andrews, *The South Since the War*, 242–43.

debt, Solomon Cohen introduced a measure to sell the state-owned Western and Atlantic Railroad in shares of a hundred dollars each. The value of the railroad was put at $10.2 million. Ostensibly, the move was unrelated to the debt question (Cohen insisted he simply wanted to rescue the state from "financial embarrassment"), but one clause of the Cohen measure permitted purchase of the shares with Georgia bonds that had been issued during the war. Two days later, an up-country delegate studying the measure saw the loophole in the Western and Atlantic bill and took the floor to denounce this "cunningly devised scheme," which simultaneously assumed the war debt and robbed the state of a property worth "twice the amount offered." He minced no words in pointing to the originator of the proposal, Joseph Brown. The exposure of this transparent maneuver, as much as the intervention of the president, forced the convention into a nullification of the state's war debt on November 7 by a vote of 137–117.[43] The vote, though much closer in Georgia than in the other states, reflected similar internal divisions. Delegates from Savannah and the coastal counties voted solidly against repudiation, as did most (though not all) of the black-belt representatives. The northern tier of mountain counties from Dade and Chattooga eastward to Rabun and Habersham almost unanimously endorsed repudiation. By a narrow margin, delegates from the upper Piedmont supported payment of the state debt.[44] The mountain counties were most alienated from the state's conservative leadership. On an ideologically related issue—a relief bill for the state's banks that would absolve officers and stockholders from personal liability for their institutions' financial obligations—delegates from most of the state overwhelmingly approved the measure on the grounds that these men should not be forced into personal bankruptcy because of events over which they had no control. But representatives from the northern tier of Georgia counties unanimously opposed any form of relief for bankers.[45]

"This is bitter medicine," one Georgia delegate confided to a newspaper correspondent, "but it is not the first draught we have had to take

43. Sidney Andrews, *The South Since the War*, 242–43. According to Joseph Brown's recent biographer the war-governor owned no state bonds, having wisely (if not altogether patriotically) invested all his savings in wartime land purchases. This fact notwithstanding, there is considerable evidence that, if not Brown, certainly his friends planned to use the war bonds to take over the Western and Atlantic. Cincinnati *Commercial*, n.d., quoted in Chicago *Tribune*, November 14, 1865. For Brown it was only a plan deferred. Five years later, he skillfully coordinated an incongruous coalition of northern investors, "carpetbaggers," "scalawags," and the former vice-president of the Confederacy to lease the lucrative railroad. Joseph Parks, *Joseph E. Brown of Georgia* (Baton Rouge, 1977), 342–43, 449–66.
44. Allen Daniel Candler (ed.), *The Confederate Records of the State of Georgia* (4 vols.; Atlanta, 1909–11), IV, 335–89.
45. Macon *Daily Telegraph*, November 9, 1865.

this year." When faced with the alternative of jeopardizing their ties with President Johnson by maintaining the shredded illusion of "financial integrity," Georgia conservatives, like those throughout the South, bowed—albeit not always gracefully—to expediency. One North Carolina conservative found consolation in the fact that the federal government had forced the southern conventions to consent to this "disgraceful act of public banditry." He concluded that Johnson's mandate saved North Carolina from the stigma of voluntarily abandoning all the state's wartime obligations. Impoverished voters, he surmised, would probably have turned upon the sound-money men in the first postwar elections for the legislature.[46]

If the repudiation controversy exposed the potential political weakness of the southern conservatives who dominated the Johnson governments, it also reflected the peculiar volatility and instability of postwar politics. The conflict between repudiationists and antirepudiationists was a venerable one, reflecting long-standing class and ideological lines in the nineteenth-century South. The issue had been particularly lively in Mississippi in the early 1840s, for example. Many of the South Carolina conservatives who defended their state's war debt in 1865 would swallow their prejudices in 1877 and support the obligations incurred by radical Republicans during the Reconstruction era. When southern opponents of repudiation were able to transform this question into a test of loyalty, they strengthened the spirit of cynicism that would come to dominate postwar southern politics. The vague and imprecise requirements of Andrew Johnson's program of reconstruction always encouraged southern conservatives to manipulate appearances rather than to accept some of the more unpleasant changes required by their defeat. The political sleight of hand of the repudiationists gave conservatives a sobering demonstration that they were not the only group in postwar southern society capable of employing the threat of federal intervention to promote their own policies.

But the debates over emancipation revealed differences between North and South to be more than the product of political maneuvering. The question of slavery should have evoked little controversy. If the war had settled anything, argued the Montgomery *Advertiser*, it was that "the destruction of slavery is complete." The editor of the Macon *Daily Telegraph* told his readers in the newspaper's first postwar issue, "Hug no delusive phantom to your soul that . . . [emancipation] was simply a war measure." The "negroes are free, free forever." More than one former slaveowner shared the dream of a Confederate soldier who predicted that southern whites

46. *Ibid.*, November 11, 1865; David L. Swain to William A. Graham, December 4, 1865, in William Alexander Graham Papers, NCA.

would substitute "a system of serfdom" for slavery by "killing the mean negroes and rewarding the good," but there is almost no evidence that whites seriously expected a return to *de jure* slavery despite the accusations of northern Republicans.[47]

Yet the conventions were soon filled with persistent wrangling over the precise wording of constitutional emancipation clauses—the distinction of tweedledee and tweedledum derided by Sidney Andrews. Specifically, the convention members argued whether the states should take responsibility for abolition or should simply acknowledge the action of the federal government in ending slavery. Only in North Carolina, where the Holden faction was clearly in command, was the matter accomplished expeditiously by a simple emancipation clause. Even in North Carolina, one eastern delegate proposed that there be at least an indirect reference—"Slavery having been destroyed in North Carolina"—to the "historical fact" that the federal government had instigated emancipation. When a delegate from western North Carolina gleefully amended the sentence by adding the phrase "by the secessionists," the proposal of John Odom was lost in a round of laughter and a simple declaration of emancipation passed unanimously.[48]

In the other constitutional conventions, opposition to a forthright endorsement of emancipation sprang form two sources. First, there was the lingering hope that some form of compensation might eventually be voted by Congress. The Georgia convention inserted a clause declaring that their ordinance forever prohibiting slavery was not a "forfeiture of claims" for the loss of slave property. The first postwar Virginia legislature had earlier provided a mechanism for certifying the value of slave losses for an undefined but obvious purpose. Even so shrewd a political figure as James L. Orr of South Carolina expressed the forlorn hope that partial compensation might be extended to the South. As late as October, 1865, a delegation of New Orleans Democrats announced plans to petition Congress for compensation, and congressional candidate John Pratt of Opelousas that same month promised voters that he would vote for a program whereby former slaveowners would be paid for their "property." Such illusions may have been based upon the long association of some Louisiana planters with U.S. Army forces during the war and the fact that Lincoln initially exempted eleven

47. James Appleton Blackshear Diary, *EU*, January 26, 1865; Montgomery *Advertiser*, July 29, 1865; Macon *Daily Telegraph*, May 28, 1865. Of course, such public statements were often tailored for the impression they would create outside the South. In examining the diaries and correspondence of more than four hundred former slaveowners, however, I found few who seriously suggested that slavery might be restored.

48. Sidney Andrews, *The South Since the War*, 154–55; *Journal of the North Carolina Convention*, 28.

Union-controlled parishes from the original effects of the Emancipation Proclamation. But even this evidence of a serious belief in compensated emancipation can be exaggerated. Although the cost of filing affidavits of slave property loss in Virginia was minimal, only a handful of slaveowners petitioned. (They were former unionists.) And John Pratt ultimately withdrew from his congressional race in Louisiana for lack of support.[49]

Postwar political leaders hesitated at offering endorsement of emancipation to establish the record for ultimate historical vindication. A sizable minority of white southerners were ready to argue in 1865 that emancipation was a positive good, that it would ultimately liberate the South from the stifling economic and social effects of the peculiar institution. But a clear majority still agreed with Muscogee, Georgia, delegate John Chappell, that emancipation "renders our lands comparatively valueless, subverts our whole system of labor, [and] ruins the very fabric of society." T. N. Dawkins of Union County, South Carolina, who had opposed secession with the same vigor as Chappell had in Georgia, insisted that it was essential to note in the constitution that "immediate emancipation, with all its travail for both races, has come to us against our will and better judgment." He hoped, indeed he daily offered his prayers, that "all our fears and misgivings be proved groundless." If, however, the passage of time should prove this cataclysmic experiment a disaster—as there was every indication it would—then, said Dawkins, "posterity should at least know that we did not voluntarily set out on the road to perdition." Alexander White of Alabama made much the same argument at his state's convention. "Hereafter, when the accumulated evils which this measure will bring shall press our people to the earth, we shall have the consolation of not having been in any way accessorial to it."[50]

Northern observers present at the convention were disturbed that these southern states seemed only "grudgingly" to have taken up the "banner of liberty." On this point some delegates were sensitive to northern expectations, but the overwhelming sense of the conventions was to refuse responsibility for the death of an institution central to their society. An outspoken minority of Mississippi delegates originally proposed a resolution that censured the federal government for freeing without compensation the slaves

49. Candler (ed.), *Confederate Records*, IV, 43–44, 171; Charleston *Daily Courier*, December 22, 1865; Sidney Andrews, *The South Since the War*, 61; New Orleans *Times*, October 15, 1865; John G. Pratt, Speech at Opelousas, La., October 1, 1865, in Duncan Papers, LSU. Robert T. Hubard to Col. E. W. Hubard, May 26, 1866, in Hubard Family Papers; New Orleans *Times*, October 22, 1865. See also the 1864 and 1865 correspondence of Delta planters Andrew Hynes Gay, Stephen Duncan, and James G. Taliaferro, all LSU.

50. Macon *Daily Times*, November 1, 1865; Winnsboro *Tri-Weekly News*, n.d., quoted in Huntsville (Ala.) *Advocate*, October 22, 1865; Montgomery *Advertiser*, September 22, 1865.

of "innocent" Mississippians. The sponsor of the resolution, George Potter, did not make clear whether his definition of innocent Mississippians included all nonbelligerent slaveowners, or only those who were loyalists. The Potter proposal failed by a nine-to-one margin, and the Mississippians—like most other southern conventions—concluded that slavery, "having been destroyed," should not be reinstituted in the state. Only in South Carolina did the postwar constitution makers specifically attribute the death of slavery to the United States government, but the intent was always the same. The final vote accepting emancipation under state law was ninety-eight to eight in South Carolina, eighty-seven to eleven in Mississippi, twenty to fourteen in Florida, eighty-nine to three in Alabama, and without dissent in Georgia. The willingness of a substantial minority of southern politicians to vote against emancipation was hardly reassuring to Republican observers. Moreover, the Mississippi legislature—in direct contravention of Johnson's explicit requirement—refused to ratify the constitutional amendment abolishing slavery on the grounds that the second section giving Congress the power to enforce the amendment "by appropriate legislation" would open the door to federal legislation supervising political and racial relationships in the postwar South. These reactionary sceptics were right, of course. When Senator Lyman Trumbull introduced the Civil Rights Bill of 1866, he justified it constitutionally by explicit reference to the second section of the Thirteenth Amendment.[51]

Understandably, northern observers were not impressed with the rationale of the Mississippi legislature. As Sidney Andrews, the Boston journalist who covered four of the postwar constitutional conventions, viewed the first efforts at self-reconstruction by white southerners, he found the attitude of whites toward their former slaves the clearest warning that little had changed. Rather than welcoming emancipation, a disgusted Andrews observed, white southerners took the attitude that it was a disaster, because they considered the Negro an "animal; a higher sort of animal to be sure than the dog or horse, but after all, an animal."[52]

Even Whitelaw Reid, a more thoughtful observer than Andrews, was appalled at the attitude of white southerners toward emancipation. He realized the extent to which slavery had become a part of their thinking and was conscious of their inordinate pride. But Reid expected to find southerners to some degree conscious of the tragedy they had brought upon the nation. He found to his astonishment that most still regarded the federal

---

51. *Journal of the Constitutional Convention of Mississippi*, 140–65; Harris, *Presidential Reconstruction in Mississippi*, 141–42; *Congressional Globe*, 39th Cong., 1st Sess., 746.
52. Sidney Andrews, *The South Since the War*, 86–87.

government as the guilty party for waging a "wicked war" of subjugation. The majority might be "cowed" by the superior power of the federal government, but there was no consciousness of wrongdoing; they were as "full of the sentiments that made the rebellion as ever"—the "doctrine of secession, the rightfulness of slavery, the wrongs of the South." There was no evidence that the South was disloyal, concluded Henry Raymond of the New York *Times*. But it was "unloyal." Even the most conciliatory and moderate Republicans (and many northern Democrats) wanted some "outward signs of inner grace," as one Union army officer put it, or some evidence that the South was aware of its culpability in "sins" that had brought on the war.[53]

Not every American spoke with the vocabulary of evangelical Protestantism, but theological concepts of heresy, sin, grace, forgiveness, and punishment proved particularly adaptable to the postwar political debate. As the sectional gap between North and South widened from the 1830s onward, the national meetings of the major Protestant denominations became arenas for acrimonious exchanges over the relationship between God's word and the works of men. By 1860, southern church leaders had come to see the South as the defender of true religion, founded on the solid rock of biblical inerrancy and free from the contaminating influences of modernism and social experimentation. No one expressed this argument more cogently than the Reverend Benjamin M. Palmer, one of the most influential religious figures of the nineteenth century. In an 1860 Thanksgiving sermon, the New Orleans minister saw in the southern church a defense of the "cause of God and religion." The antislavery movement (which Palmer identified with the northern church) was "undeniably atheistic." The movement "wars against constitutions and laws and compacts, against Sabbaths and sanctuaries, against the family, the State and the church." Within a week of Palmer's sermon, more than thirty thousand copies had been printed and distributed in the form of a pamphlet, and one New Orleans unionist bitterly complained that Palmer had done more than "any other non-combatant in the South to promote rebellion."[54]

53. Whitelaw Reid, *After the War: A Southern Tour* (Cincinnati, 1866), 73–74; New York *Times*, August 18, 1865; Capt. Avery Williams to Maj. H. W. Smith, February 16, 1866, in BRFAL, South Carolina, Box 22.

54. Benjamin M. Palmer, "Thanksgiving Sermon, New Orleans, November 29, 1860," rpr. in *Fast Day Sermons; or, The Pulpit on the State of the Country* (New York, 1861), 61–62; Lewis M. Purifoy, Jr., "The Methodist Episcopal Church, South, and Slavery, 1844–1865" (Ph.D. dissertation, University of North Carolina, 1965), 222. For studies that describe the sometimes uneasy relationship of southern religious and secular thought before, during, and after the war, see Anne C. Loveland, *Southern Evangelicals and the Social Order, 1800–1860* (Baton Rouge, 1980); James W. Silver, *Confederate Morale and Church Propaganda* (Tuscaloosa, 1967); Willard E. Wight, "The Churches and the Confederate Cause," *CWH*, VI

By 1863 the great majority of southern church leaders had concluded that the South was engaged in a "holy war, and a righteous war, consecrated by God's Word and sanctified by His religion." James Henley Thornwell, editor of the *Southern Presbyterian Review*, put the matter most succinctly. The southern church represented the true faith; the northern church, heresy. The only solution to heresy was to separate oneself from its contamination. When peaceful separation was no longer possible, the struggle for southern independence became a holy war. "If the rescue of the holy sepulchre from the infidel Moslem induced three millions of men to lay their bones in the East," observed one Georgia minister in 1863, "shall we not willingly contend to snatch the word of God from the modern infidel?"[55]

At the end of the war, with their illusions shattered, southerners groped in the ruins of their sacred cause for some divine plan, but northern church leaders were confirmed in their sense of righteousness. Southern Christians had emphasized heresy; northern Christians employed the rhetoric of sin and the need for repentance. To the South's obstinate support for the evil institution of slavery had been added the guilt of plunging the nation into a needless war. As the Presbytery of Buffalo, New York, concluded early in the war, the revolt of the "so-called seceding States [is] a crime against God and the Church, no less than an offense against the Government," and there could be no reconciliation until "by repentence and public confession of their sin" southerners purged themselves of their offenses. Four years of war and the vindication of a righteous God only confirmed their conviction that sin had to be followed by repentance. Wisconsin Methodists unanimously rejected proposals for a postwar reunion at their fall, 1865, conference and declared that reconciliation was impossible until their southern brothers and sisters had confessed their sins and shown evidence of "penitence and reformation" on the moral issues of slavery and secession. A correspondent for the New York *Methodist Advocate* spoke for many members of his denomination when he insisted that he would not shake the "bloody unwashed hands" of southern Methodists.[56]

Cautious northern Presbyterians who had avoided division with their

---

(1960), 361–73; Charles Reagan Wilson, *Baptized in Blood: The Religion of the Lost Cause, 1865–1920* (Athens, 1980).

55. James Henley Thornwell, "The State of the Country," *SPR*, XIII (1861), 883–84; T. Bryan Conn, "The Churches in Georgia During the Civil War," *GHQ*, XXXIII (1949), 285.

56. New York *Methodist Advocate*, October 11, 1865; Ralph E. Morrow, *Northern Methodism and Reconstruction* (East Lansing, Mich., 1956), 17–18; William A. Russ, Jr., "The Influence of the Methodist Press upon Radical Reconstruction, 1865–1868," *SUS*, I (1937), 52.

southern brethren until after secession were as caught up in the demands for recantation as the Methodists. "Those who have sown the wind must expect to reap the whirlwind," insisted the church's 1865 general assembly. Recalling the critical role of southern clergymen, that same assembly resolved that no Presbyterian minister who had supported either slavery or secession should be allowed back into the church until he was willing to "confess and forsake his sin." Nor was the need for repentance restricted to men of the cloth. No southerner who had left the church preaching "heresy and treason" could be "restored to the bosom of the Church . . . until after recantation, confession and repentence." Such stern demands were justified by the punishment that God himself had brought upon these "wicked Southerners." Everywhere men could see the "darkness and desolation" that "broods over that region of our ecclesiastical territory within whose limits was nurtured into life a crime of unparalleled enormity against the government and free institutions of our government; a solemn stillness which tells of the just retribution and judgements of God." It was not a moment at which northern evangelicals were ready to turn the other cheek, a conclusion that may be supported by the election of R. L. Stanton as moderator of the church in 1865. Stanton had achieved some prominence by expressing confidence that he would meet "Benjamin Palmer in heaven," but he first expected to see him "hung on earth, and he would rejoice in that hanging."[57]

Politicians on both sides of the aisle and from both North and South were fond of quoting scriptures. And if white southerners were ready to cite chapter and verse on the tragedies of martyrdom, angry northerners were quick to respond with Old Testament demands for vengeance and New Testament requirements of repentance. Timid souls were anxious to avoid humbling and humiliating white southerners, sneered Thaddeus Stevens. But he insisted that they deserved humiliation and degradation because they "have not yet confessed their sins; and He who administers mercy and justice never forgives until the sinner confesses his sins and

57. Minutes of the General Assembly of the Presbyterian Church in the United States of America, 1865 (Philadelphia, 1865), XVII, 549–64; Christian Observer, April 19, 1865; "The General Assembly of 1865," SPR, XVII (1866), 78; Lewis G. Vander Velde, The Presbyterian Churches and the Federal Union, 1861–1869 (Cambridge, Mass., 1932), 221–22. James H. Moorehead has described the way in which southern slaveowners became symbols of the anti-Christ in his insightful study, American Apocalypse: Yankee Protestants and the Civil War, 1860–1869 (New Haven, 1978). Other historians of American religion have cautioned, however, that the desire for vengeance was not shared by all northern protestants and—in any case—the emotional vindictiveness common in 1865 soon began to fade. Donald G. Jones, The Sectional Crisis and Northern Methodism: A Study in Piety, Political Ethics, and Civil Religion (Metuchen, N.J., 1979), 92–95; Paul Clyde Brownlow, "The Northern Protestant Pulpit on Reconstruction, 1865–1877" (Ph.D. dissertation, Purdue University, 1970), 164–86.

humbles himself at His footstool." The Ohio congressman James A. Garfield often disagreed with Stevens, but he shared his political theology. "The burden of proof rests on each of them to show whether . . . [the South] is fit again to enter the Federal circle in full communion of privilege," he said on the floor of the House. Former rebels "must give us proof, strong as Holy Writ, that they have washed their hands and are worthy again to be trusted."[58]

One of the Philadelphia Union League's postwar pamphlets reflected the ease with which the language of the pulpit could be adapted to the political arena:

If they repent; if they turn for forgiveness to the Government whose ruin they madly sought; if they abjure the heresies which precipitated such miseries upon us all; if they frankly accept the situation, burn their false idols and resolve to be as energetic and persistent in upholding as they were in destroying; if they transfer their allegiance from the narrow boundaries of particular States to the wider claims of a glorious nationality; if they admit past errors; if they are willing to cultivate the kindly and fraternal feeling for us which are so confidently claimed of us for them—then we will joyfully bury the hatchet and welcome them back to their places in the capital of the nation.

The "haughty" and "insolent" absence of any sense of wrongdoing on the part of white southerners was a persistent theme in the *Report* of the Joint Committee on Reconstruction. For James Russell Lowell, writing in the influential *North American Review*, the absence of regional penitence was as important as any of the specific actions taken by individual southerners. As the New York *Tribune* warned in an editorial, white southerners might appear to acquiesce in the results of the war, but the "spirit" of each act had to be tested since the spirit of contrition was "quite as important as the act itself."[59]

The loss of the war *did* trigger a soul searching among religious southerners. They had convinced themselves during the early days of the Confederacy that, in the words of the Reverend Benjamin M. Palmer, their new

---

58. *Congressional Globe*, 39th Cong., 1st Sess., Pt. 3, pp. 2544, 2553. Other moderate Republicans shared Garfield's emphasis upon the need for repentance and ironclad guarantees of future conduct. See Allan Pesking, *Garfield* (Kent, Ohio, 1978), 258; Mark M. Krug, *Lyman Trumbull: Conservative Radical* (New York, 1965), 235–36; John Sherman's *Recollections of Forty Years: An Autobiography* (New York, 1895), 366–68.

59. *Congressional Globe*, 39th Cong., 1st Sess., Pt. 3, p. 2544; Board of Publications of the Union League of Philadelphia, *Loyalty and the Union* (Philadelphia, 1865), 4; *Report of the Joint Committee on Reconstruction*, I, xvii; James Russell Lowell, "The Seward-Johnson Reaction," *NAR*, CCXIII (1866), 536; New York *Tribune*, September 12, 1865.

nation was founded on the "immutable laws of God"; their revolution, on "the cause of God himself." Faced with defeat, southern Christians were often filled with despair. "I will try to be resigned, I will try to look beyond the blindness of earthly passion," wrote one southern woman as she chronicled the end of the Confederacy. "I know that I shall hereafter feel that he continually rules, but now, Oh God help me, it seems hard to bear." A few went so far as to renounce their faith. Louis Blanding of South Carolina listened to his brother's attempts to explain God's "inscrutable workings" and could only reply by rejecting the very notion of the existence of the Divine. Such explanations of defeat and such promises of "divine mercy" were "vague scholastic playthings, fit for the keen edge of discussion & of no earthly account."[60]

But there is no widespread evidence that southerners conceived themselves to be sinners because of their involvement with slavery or their endorsement of secession. The limits of southern repentance were reflected in the expulsion of John Henley Caldwell from his Newnan, Georgia, pulpit in the fall of 1865. Caldwell, who ultimately swung from secessionist to radical Republican back to conservative, had served as pastor of the small-town Methodist church through the last three years of the war. As late as January, 1865, he condemned as "infamous" the actions of Savannah residents in cooperating with Union officials, but at some point between January and May, Caldwell, like Paul, received a vision and was converted. On June 11, 1865, before a packed congregation, he began the first of two sermons entitled "Abuses of Slavery."

In language that Wendell Phillips or William Lloyd Garrison would have approved, Caldwell caustically described the effects of slavery upon the "moral and civil life" of the South. The peculiar institution had thwarted the law of God and made it subservient to the civil laws of slavery. "Hence, no marriage rite, no education, no emancipation could be allowed to the negro; hence slave marts and slave auctions, hence all discussion by the press, by the pulpit in legislative halls or elsewhere in which the right of the master to oppress his slave might be the topic was disallowed." To say that the South was fighting for liberty from 1861 to 1865 was a mockery, concluded Caldwell. "We have been enslaved ourselves! Our minds, our speech, our consciences, our press, our pulpit, all were in abject dependence upon the slave power."[61]

60. Silver, *Confederate Morale and Church Propaganda*, 31; Sarah Wadley Diary, SHC, May 13, 1865; Louis Blanding to James Douglas Blanding, July 7, 1866, in James Douglas Blanding Papers, SCL.
61. John Henley Caldwell, *Slavery and Methodism: Two Sermons Preached in the Methodist*

Caldwell was hardly the first southerner to criticize the abuses of some slaveowners, though his language was considerably more uncompromising than usual. As late as 1848, a group of Methodist ministers and laymen in Liberty County, Georgia, had scolded their fellow southerners for failing to treat slaves as "immortal and accountable beings . . . , heirs of the grace of life." And the members of the Association for the Religious Instruction of Negroes had piously insisted that owners promote the moral and religious well-being of their slaves. More concretely, they had condemned the break-up of slave families. Slaveowners should "not separate nor allow the separa-tion of husband and wife, unless for causes lawful before God." In 1863 when most southerners insisted on maintaining silence on such controver-sial issues, the *Southern Presbyterian Review* had published a lively debate between a proponent and an opponent of legislation that would guarantee minimal rights for slaves—including the right of families to be protected from forcible separation. That same year in a sermon delivered to the Georgia legislature, Methodist Bishop George Foster Pierce urged the re-peal of laws mandating slave illiteracy and encouraged the passage of mea-sures that would prohibit the separation of husband and wife.[62]

Such modest proposals were ignored during the war. Afterwards, south-ern churchmen spoke only in the vaguest language of the responsibilities of southern whites to the freedmen. And they certainly never crossed the di-viding line that Caldwell breached in the second of his sermons to his Georgia congregation. Going beyond the question of abuses under slavery, he argued that such evils were more than the deplorable by-products of the institution. Quoting Thomas Jefferson, he declared that slavery was "an evil, a sin per se." The awful destruction that southerners saw on every hand was God's judgment upon the region for its commitment to a "sinful" system. The "white race of this Southern clime" had committed itself to a "wicked institution," Caldwell told his sullen congregation. And God had

---

Church in Newnan, Georgia, by the Pastor, Rev. John H. Caldwell, A.M., of the Georgia Confer-ence (Newnan, 1865), 35–37. See Sidney Andrews, *The South Since the War*, 380. For infor-mation on the Caldwell incident, see Caldwell's brief account in his *Reminiscences of the Recon-struction of Church and State in Georgia* (Wilmington, Del., 1895), 5–6; Morrow, *Northern Methodism*, 102; *Minutes of the Georgia Annual Conference [Methodist Episcopal Church, South], 1865* (Macon, 1865). For Caldwell's January attack upon Savannah cooperationists see the Houston *Tri-Weekly Telegraph*, March 4, 1865.

62. *Thirteenth Annual Report of the Association for the Religious Instruction of Negroes in Liberty County, Georgia* (Savannah, 1848), 16–17; "Slavery and the Duties Growing Out of the Relation" and "A Slave Marriage Law," *SPR*, XVI (1863), 145–62; George Foster Pierce and B. M. Palmer, *Sermons of Bishop Pierce and Rev. B. M. Palmer, D.D., Delivered Before the General Assembly at Milledgeville, Georgia, on Fast Day, March 27, 1863* (Milledgeville, 1863), 11–18.

spoken "in the thunderous tones of a thousand battles and told us that we have sinned." There was hope "only if we repent."[63]

Five months later Caldwell was summoned before the Georgia Conference of the Methodist Episcopal Church, South. "Did you not say in these sermons," demanded South Georgia minister John B. McGehee, "that there were evils inherent to the institution of slavery?" No amount of hedging by Caldwell could satisfy the indignation of his fellow Georgia Methodists on this point. Under pressure from the conference and a resolution condemning his sermons, he resigned.[64]

White southerners were reconciled to the end of slavery; a few were even pleased with the death of the peculiar institution. But they simply were not willing to acknowledge any "sinfulness" in their antebellum connection with slavery. Fortunately, they found other convenient and more acceptable explanations for the cruel fate of the South. During the war, each military defeat had been excused as the merited judgment of a sinful people. These sins were usually politically safe: the "violation of the Sabbath, intemperance, demagoguery, corruption, luxury, impiety, murmuring, greed and lewdness, scepticism, 'Epicurean expediency,' private immorality . . . , profanity, a proud and haughty spirit, speculation, bribery, boastfulness"— even "illtreatment of slaves." Such lapses could also be employed to explain the final disaster of defeat. The Episcopal bishop of Arkansas could find the South's nemesis in its "arrogance and vanity." Louisianian Honoré Gayarré singled out his compatriots' dependence upon the excessive acquisition of "wealth and physical powers," while a South Carolina editor attributed the war's outcome to a "God-forgetting covetousness" that had "sapped the foundations of moral and religious principle." As one pious southerner concluded, "Southerners had strayed far and made void God's Law . . . and it was His own good pleasure to choose the worst of instruments to afflict, so that He might chasten us and bring us back from the wicked paths in which we were recklessly wandering." When slavery was seen as a factor in the South's woes, it was not because the institution itself was a sin, but because the South had failed to remove the "deficiencies and gross evils" that existed under slavery.[65]

63. Caldwell, *Slavery and Methodism*, 74–75.

64. *Minutes of the Georgia Annual Conference [Methodist Episcopal Church, South], 1865* (Macon, 1865), 16; Macon *Daily Telegraph*, November 16, 1865.

65. Silver, *Confederate Morale and Church Propaganda*, 31; "Good Friday Sermon, 1865," in Bishop Henry Champlin Lay Papers, SHC; Honoré Gayarré to Ruffin, October 1, 1865, W. M. Edwards to Ruffin, October 5, 1865, both in Ruffin Papers; Columbia (S.C.) *Phoenix*, April 29, 1865; Houston *Tri-Weekly Telegraph*, February 7, 1865. For an example of the fine line that Caldwell transgressed, his sermons should be compared with the "antislavery" comments of another Georgia minister at the end of the war. See notes of the "Sermon of the Rev. Mr. Davis," Sumter County, Ga., in Blackshear Diary, April 16, 1865.

The Presbyterian General Assembly, South, meeting in December of 1865, felt the issue important enough to circulate a special pastoral letter on the subject. While insisting that the church should be neither pro- nor antislavery, two essential facts remained. Dogma that asserted the "inherent sinfulness" of slavery was unscriptural and fanatical, "condemned not only by the word of God, but by the voice of the church in all ages." It was, said the Presbyterians, "one of the most pernicious heresies of modern times," and its "countenance" by any church was a "just cause of separation." Second, "whatever . . . we have to lament before God, either for neglect of duty towards our servants, or for actual wrong while the relation lasted, we are not called now that it has been abolished to bow the head in humiliation before men, or admit that the memory of many of our dead kindred is to be covered with shame."[66]

Had southerners been willing to cynically adopt the attitude of Alabama convention delegate William Stump Forward, the direction of Reconstruction might well have been quite different. Forward bluntly told his son: "We are sent here [to Montgomery] to amend our state constitution . . . or have all . . . we have got confiscated and ruled by a military force. Some might hesitate at such a choice. I will not."[67] White southerners were willing to advance their most conciliatory spokesmen and to compromise, if pressed, on many troublesome postwar issues, but they were not willing to accept Forward's ready pliancy. Unconsciously conditioned by a thousand antebellum speeches and arguments that had emphasized the importance of resisting degradation and second-class citizenship, they were unwilling to see themselves as a defeated people without any rights except those of endorsing the conqueror's terms.

Northern resentment of the tactless debates over emancipation and repudiation would soon dissipate, but the attitude and conduct of southern whites toward the three and a half million freed slaves of the South was to be a constant yardstick by which the reconstruction process could be measured. The sacrifices of the war had given a sense of moral rightness to emancipation that the abolitionist movement had never been able to achieve. The cause of freedom, however vaguely defined, was one of the great achievements of the war, a holy cause sanctified by the graves of hundreds of thousands of union soldiers, black and white. Most northerners, like Andrew Johnson, were reluctant to force southerners into endorsing politically sound and morally correct policies. After all, repentance was more

66. Atlanta *Daily Intelligencer*, December 23, 1865; "The General Assembly of 1865," 102–103.

67. William Stump Forward to Son, September 17, 1865, in William Stump Forward Papers, SHC.

effective when it came from the heart rather than the barrel of a gun. Under these circumstances, the persistent quibbling of white southerners over the victor's terms was always potentially disastrous. The lack of any sense of wrongdoing, of sinfulness, on their part was not the most critical factor in the growing suspicions of northern moderates and radicals, but the absence of these "outward signs of inner grace" so anxiously sought by Captain Avery Williams inevitably accentuated the divisions between North and South as the summer constitutional conventions gave way to the newly elected state governments in the early fall of 1865.

These elections, the second phase of self-reconstruction, reflected this growing division as southern political leaders followed the example of Andrew Johnson, talking more and more of the "constitutional rights" of the southern states and less and less of the necessity of pacifying suspicious elements in the Republican party. Mississippi Provisional Governor William L. Sharkey gave way to former Confederate General Benjamin G. Humphreys; James L. Orr, late of the Confederate Senate, replaced Benjamin Perry in South Carolina; and Jonathan Worth, the wartime treasurer of the North Carolina Confederate government, succeeded the mercurial W. W. Holden. Of the seven southern governors elected in the fall of 1865, only James Madison Wells of Louisiana could have taken the ironclad oath. And ironically, it was Wells who led the most reactionary trend in postwar southern politics as he put together a political coalition in the fall of 1865 led by many individuals who had been in the forefront of the secessionist movement of the late 1850s.[68]

On the other hand, none of the seven had supported secession. For the most part they were of the same sober, cautious, and whiggish background and outlook that had characterized the delegates to the constitutional conventions of 1865. Six, in fact, had been Whigs and three would ultimately join the Republican party. Whatever impression might be given by pointing to specific secessionists or "unrepentant rebels," the elections marked no decisive shift in the attitudes or voting behavior of white southerners.[69]

Despite its political failures, this conservative leadership had avoided disaster in the first efforts at self-reconstruction under the president's plan. However grudgingly, they had complied with Johnson's political demands while retaining the support of the great majority of white southerners. But their political skills were to be tested repeatedly as they began their first efforts at self-government. No one saw the challenge more clearly than the

68. Peyton McCrary, *Abraham Lincoln and Reconstruction: The Louisiana Experiment* (Princeton, 1978), 305–41; Joe Gray Taylor, *Louisiana Reconstruction, 1863–1877* (Baton Rouge, 1974), 58–62, 103–106.
69. See, for example, Breese, "Politics in the Lower South."

aging magazine editor, J. D. B. De Bow. The South's postwar political leaders, in the midst of economic chaos and social demoralization, would have to develop policies that could "revive the broken south, alleviate the concerns of Northerners and unite a fractious people."[70] Only through this delicate balancing act could southern conservatives cement their fragile position of leadership in the postwar South *and* bring the region back into the Union.

70. J. D. B. De Bow, "The State of the Country," *DR*, I (1866), 143.

IV / Uncertain Prophets in the Land of the Vanquished

A S THE postwar legislators traveled to their state capitals in the early fall of 1865, their journeys were a sobering reminder of the challenges of postwar reconstruction. Eleven miles from Savannah, the legislative delegation from Chatham County had to leave their train and climb into open wagons to travel the next forty miles along a crudely marked road that defied description. Most bridges and ferries had been burned or destroyed, and there were twenty-one creeks, streams, and large drainage ditches that therefore had to be forded; some had more than three feet of swiftly running water. After nine hours, the lead hackman, driving by the light of flickering pine faggots, misjudged the forest road and wedged his wagon between two trees. It had to be taken apart and then reassembled before the weary caravan could continue. "Surely nothing else can happen," wrote the Savannah *Republican*'s reporter in his diary.[1]

But just after dawn one of the mules fell dead after fording another creek, and the passengers had to wait three hours for a "spavined, one-eyed" replacement. At the end of twenty-four hours of jolting and "risking having one's brains knocked out" by low-hanging branches, the eleven delegates arrived at the breakfast house. For one dollar they received a cup of lukewarm coffee and some cold chicken, the veteran, claimed one surly traveler, "of a hundred cock fights." Another thirteen hours brought them to the temporary terminus of the Central Railroad at Halcyondale, where they learned they had missed the last train of the day by twenty minutes. Most of the delegation spent that night sheltered from a steady drizzle un-

1. Savannah *National Republican*, November 21, 1865.

der the wagons before rising the next morning to wait six hours for the train. The total distance from Savannah to Milledgeville was 97 miles; the traveling time: eighty-eight hours.

Every postwar national journalist who journeyed through the South in the summer of 1865 had his own horror story of the extraordinary hardships and difficulties of travel.[2] However exaggerated the depictions of northern journalists, who were likely to travel through the most devastated regions, and of a generation of sympathetic historians, who lumped slave value, land depreciation, and property losses in one indiscriminate estimation, the effects of war were apparent on every hand. But with time, buildings could be rebuilt, fences repaired, and draft animals replaced. Even the more expensive public works—railroads, canals, and levees—could be reconstructed. In their private correspondence and diaries, white southerners were remarkably philosophical about the devastation of war. They were far more concerned about what they perceived to be the obstacles to recovery. The land remained, but the intricate mechanisms of capital allocation and labor "management" had been shattered by war. Reconstruction was to be far more difficult than any but the most pessimistic had anticipated.[3]

The great majority of southern planters and businessmen faced the postwar period with minimal liquid assets. Their correspondence through the summer of 1865 was a litany of financial losses suffered in the late war. Some described their penury with pride, for it reflected the depth of their commitment to the Lost Cause. Shortly after he learned of the surrender of Joseph Johnston's army, Henry Ravenel of South Carolina sat down at his desk and itemized his losses: "$11,600 in Conf. 8 percent bonds; $6,500 in Confederate 8 percent stock; $2,000 in currency; $24,000 in Confederate

2. See, for example, Sidney Andrews' account of his near asphyxiation in a burning railroad car in the Chicago *Tribune*, October 26, 1865.

3. Walter Fleming, in *The Sequel of Appomattox* (New Haven, 1919), 87–89, was one of the first professional historians to emphasize the importance of the devastation of the war, but the image of the devastated South had already been fixed in the American mind by the poignant scenes from D. W. Griffith's film, *Birth of a Nation*. The broader issue of the long-range economic effects of the war have been discussed for more than twenty years. It is a debate first summarized in Ralph Andreano (ed.), *The Economic Impact of the Civil War* (Cambridge, Mass., 1964). More recently Claudia Golden and Frank Lewis on the one side and Peter Temin on the other have jousted with elegant mathematical equations in the *Journal of Economic History*. See Golden and Lewis, "The Economic Cost of the American Civil War, *JEH*, XXXV (1975), 299–326; Temin, "The Postbellum Recovery of the South and the Cost of the Civil War," *JEH*, XXXVI (1976), 898–907; Golden and Lewis, "The Postbellum Recovery of the South and the Cost of the Civil War: Comment," and Temin, "Reply to Golden and Lewis," *JEH*, XXXVIII (1978), 487–93. Roger L. Ransom and Richard Sutch have made clear their scepticism of the long-range effects of such wartime devastation in their chapter, "The Myth of the Prostrate South," *One Kind of Freedom: The Economic Consequences of Emancipation* (Cambridge, 1977).

securities." Although a portion of this had been purchased with depreciated currency, much of this worthless portfolio reflected investments made
early in the war. Even the loans he had made to his neighbors were generally without any value. Ravenel still had his small plantation but little else.
Another South Carolinian, Andrew McDowell of Aiken, was all the more
pathetic; unlike Ravenel, he did not even have the security of a full smoke-
house and a cellar full of sweet potatoes. By late summer of 1865 McDowell,
one of the wealthiest antebellum merchants in Edgefield and Aiken counties, was reduced to the humiliating expedient of pleading for loans every
few days from his equally impoverished neighbors.[4]

The experiences of Ravenel and McDowell were repeated thousands of
times across the region and descriptions of their fall from wealth to poverty
became staple items in accounts of the postwar South. No traveling newspaperman's dispatches were complete without melodramatic stories of
proud antebellum aristocrats reduced to draymen or woodcutters or of mis-
tresses of grand plantations forced to convert once hospitable mansions into
dreary boardinghouses. Such stories were rooted in reality, since the war
undoubtedly plunged many families into conditions of complete destitution. Many, like Margaret Mitchell's Ashley Wilkes, never quite adjusted
to the postwar world.

If the losses of the region's men of wealth and capital were enormous, for
those shrewd (and unpatriotic) enough to have invested in non-Confederate
securities and other forms of liquid capital, there were enormous opportunities for land acquisition and for quick profits if only cotton production
could be resumed before the unnaturally high wartime prices began to decline. Cotton prices had never been higher, wrote one Alabama planter. He
was ready to work and willing to experiment with free labor. "But where
can I get the capital to buy mules, seeds, furnishings and such for the coming year?" His frustration and despair were observed by everyone who
visited the South in the months after Appomattox. As Theodore Peters, a
Baltimore businessman, concluded after a trip through the region in the
summer of 1865, "The scarcity of capital . . . can only be comprehended by
one who has been through the country."[5]

Federal taxation policies exacerbated the difficulties of accumulating immediate capital. During the war, Congress had enacted a cotton tax of 3¢
per pound (later increased to 3.5¢) and a direct property tax of $20 million

4. Henry W. Ravenel Journal, SCL, May 22, 1865; Andrew McDowell to Rev. M. H.
Lance, August 26, 1865, in Read-Lance Family Papers, SCL.
5. Montgomery *Advertiser*, September 24, 1865; Theodore Peters, *A Report upon Conditions of the South with Regard to Its Need for a Cotton Crop and Its Financial Wants in Connection
Therewith as well as the Safety of Temporary Loans* (Baltimore, 1867), 7.

on each of the southern states. Although the Treasury Department collected little of the property tax after the collapse of the Confederacy, revenues from the cotton levy increased steadily from 1863 to 1867. By the time Congress repealed the measure in 1868, the former Confederate states had paid $68 million to the federal government, more than four times the amount the struggling provisional governments were able to raise by taxation between 1865 and 1867.[6]

The region's financial institutions, whose desperate plight had been a complicating factor in the convention debates over the repudiation of state war debts, had little to lend. Before 1860, the nation's banking system was nowhere stronger than in the Deep South. The five cotton states of South Carolina, Georgia, Alabama, Mississippi, and Louisiana outranked other regions of the United States in all important economic indices: invested capital, notes in circulation, and average level of deposits per bank. By the summer of 1865 commercial banking had almost ceased to exist. Before the war the Bank of New Orleans had been a source of credit for the city's business community and, through the many cotton factors of New Orleans, for the planters of the lower Delta. Although the officers only briefly closed the bank doors after federal occupation of the city, the Bank of New Orleans was crippled by Union General Benjamin Butler's requirement that deposits made in Confederate paper money be redeemed in United States currency. Unlike the majority of the city's thirteen banks, the Bank of New Orleans managed to limp along by curtailing its loans and moving from one expedient to another to stave off complete collapse. In January of 1865 it stopped paying depositors in hard currency as President W. T. Donnell desperately arranged short-term loans in an attempt to avoid total bankruptcy. Late in November, the bank began to issue promissory scrip to those customers who insisted on withdrawing their funds. By January of 1866 such scrip traded at fifteen cents on the dollar—by Donnell's own private acknowledgement, an inflated valuation.[7]

Other southern banks fared equally poorly. Stockholders and directors of the Bank of North Carolina had responded to the secession crisis with

6. James L. Watkins, *King Cotton: A Historical and Statistical Review, 1790–1908* (New York, 1908), *passim.* See also Milton M. McPherson, "The Federal Cotton Tax in the South, 1862–1868" (M.A. thesis, University of Alabama, 1959). Patrick J. Hearden has argued that the cotton tax was a blessing in disguise; because of its repeal, "agricultural diversification was discouraged and the South remained under the curse of a colonial economy." Hearden, *Independence and Empire: The New South's Cotton Mill Campaign, 1865–1901* (De Kalb, Ill., 1982). Although this may have been true in the long run, the immediate effect of the tax was to hinder the economic recovery of the region.

7. Stephen A. Caldwell, *A Banking History of Louisiana* (Baton Rouge, 1935), 90–96; Ransom and Stuch, *One Kind of Freedom*, 106–108; W. T. Donnell to Mary Shepard, November 25, 1865, January 1, 1866, both in Bryan Family Papers, DUL.

patriotic ardor, lending the state nearly $400,000 in specie. After 1862
bank officers had refused to accept payment in depreciated Confederate
currency, and as a result, more than half the loan was still outstanding at
the end of the war. This factor, coupled with the general losses suffered by
all bank institutions, left the Bank of North Carolina—once the most sol-
vent and reliable in the state—near bankruptcy. By the fall of 1865, bank
stock was worth less than twenty-five cents on the dollar. Most other banks
were even less fortunate. South Carolina's second largest financial institution, the Bank of Charleston, limped along less than three years before it
finally closed its doors for good. Even when bank officials like "Colonel"
Donald L. McKay of the People's Bank of Charleston were astute enough
to avoid any investments in the Confederacy or in the state's war effort, they
were scarcely better off. As McKay observed shortly after the war, railroad
stocks and bonds in which the bank had invested might eventually bring a
financial return, but the majority of the institution's outstanding loans were
worthless. Many loans had been made to cotton factors, who in turn had
transferred the funds directly and indirectly to low-country planters in a
chain of credit secured at its base by collateral of land and slaves. But by
1865 the slaves had been emancipated, and the value of the land had so
declined that it was seldom worth more than one-fourth its antebellum
value.[8]

The experience of Donald McKay was repeated again and again across
the South. Even when banks reopened their doors, there was no guarantee
of survival. And congressional legislation during the war further crippled
the region's banking industry. A 10 percent tax on the note issue of non-
national banks made it difficult to establish state-chartered banks. The National Banking Act of 1865, with its stringent minimum requirements for
paid-in capital and its restrictions on mortgage lending, made it almost impossible to establish national banks in the South. Between 1865 and 1868
only 20 of the 1,688 national banks chartered were in the Deep South, and
by 1869, 4 of them had closed their doors, in a failure rate six times the
national average. An Augusta newspaper editor accurately summarized the

8. Richard A. Zuber, *Jonathan Worth: A Biography of a Southern Unionist* (Chapel Hill, 1965), 144; Jonathan Worth to W. W. Holden, June 16, 1865, in North Carolina Governors' Papers, NCA; G. A. Kimberly (President of the Bank of Charleston) to James L. Orr, November 23, 1866, in James L. Orr Papers, SCA; Francis B. Simkins and Robert H. Woody, *South Carolina During Reconstruction* (Chapel Hill, 1932), 150; Donald McKay to Richard Lathers, June 7, 1865, in Alvan F. Sanborn (ed.), *Reminiscences of Richard Lathers* (New York, 1907), 245; Kemp Battle to William A. Graham, December 15, 1865, in James Gregoire de Roulhac Hamilton and Max R. Williams (eds.), *The Papers of William Alexander Graham* (6 vols. to date; Raleigh, 1957–), VI, 461–63. For a discussion of the banking situation in Alabama, see H. A. Schroeder (President of the Bank of Mobile) to Robert M. Patton, July 23, 1866, in Alabama Governors' Papers, AA.

financial crisis of his own city and of the South when he observed that Augusta's two banks remained open, but their assets (on paper) had been reduced to less than $500,000 and they had announced there would be no money available for loans for the city's merchants or for the five cotton factors in the up-country Georgia town.[9]

It is difficult to produce much sympathy for southern bankers like James Green Burr, president of the Bank of North Carolina, who continued to order specially made "linen underdrawers" from England and silk shirts from a Parisian tailor in New York even as he whined of the losses his bank had suffered during the war, but the collapse of the banking structure was to have profound immediate and long-range effects upon the recovery of the South. It was a situation made worse by the general paralysis of almost all large-scale financial transactions. The entire nexus of credit had been deeply disrupted less by the destruction of southern property than by the act of emancipation. It was not that the South as a region suffered direct financial losses by the emancipation process. As the Richmond magazine the *Farmer* observed at the time, the abolition of slavery had simply transferred the ownership of property from the slaveowner to the slave, with no net deficit for the region. The problem came instead from the disruption of the credit system, which in many instances had rested directly or indirectly upon the ownership of slave property. As one planter crudely but accurately observed, the South's slaves had been the linchpin in the precarious arrangements of an agricultural society.[10]

The destruction of slave assets was only one component of a complex credit machine crippled by the outcome of the war. As Robert Hubard of Virginia noted to a friend and neighbor, uncertainties paralyzed attempts to make plans for the future. What was the status of debts incurred for purchasing slaves? In 1863, after the Emancipation Proclamation, Henry Ravenel of South Carolina had lent two neighbors more than $7,000 in Confederate currency (worth about $2,500 in gold) to purchase slaves. A chivalrous Ravenel concluded at the end of the war: "If the negroes are emancipated I will return these bonds to them as their means of paying will be lost, & I would not wish to embarrass them with such a debt." Even for those of a less generous nature, there were paralyzing legal questions. Was

---

9. Ransom and Sutch, *One Kind of Freedom*, 106–25. Peters, *Report upon Conditions of the South*, 7; Augusta *Daily Press*, July 21, 1865; Macon *Daily Telegraph*, February 16, 1866; Atlanta *Daily Intelligencer*, January 27, February 11, March 29, 1866. For some of the problems of postwar southern banking, see especially Richard Sylla, "Federal Policy, Banking Market Structure, and Capital Mobilization in the United States, 1863–1913," *JEH*, XXIX (1969), 660–65.

10. *Fa*, I (1866), 169–70. See also T. P. Devereux to George W. Mordecai, June 1, 1865, in George W. Mordecai Papers, SHC.

a loan secured in collateral (slaves) that no longer legally existed binding?[11] When slaves were not involved, how was the value of wartime debts to be established? During the war, many southerners had contracted loans based upon highly deflated Confederate currency. Were these to be repaid at par or on the basis of the actual value in gold at the time of the loan? (Toward the end of the war, clauses indicating the value of the loan in gold specie were often inserted.) And what about state bonds issued during the war? Most southerners accepted the fact that Confederate securities were worthless, but the states' obligations remained, and not all expenditures had been for the "illegal" purpose of conducting the war. The uncertainty over the legitimacy of wartime state bonds also extended to those of the antebellum period, as W. B. Stipes of North Carolina discovered when he attempted to use prewar state bonds as collateral for supplies and furnishings for his Lewisville plantation. Northern merchants in particular were often doubtful that the southern states would recover enough to repay at par.[12]

Much of the story of the postwar credit adjustment was a tale of negotiation between debtor and creditor as each side sought a solution that would allow recovery without forcing bankruptcy. In this context, postwar debtors were in the stronger position because they were so common. In many ways, the value of open land was a reliable indicator of the economic condition of the southern agricultural system, and land values had plummeted at the end of the war. When Stephen Duncan, a wealthy Louisiana planter, ordered his attorney in Natchez, Mississippi, to begin collecting debts owed him by dozens of Delta planters, he faced an insoluble dilemma. He could foreclose on the property, but it was often worth far less than the amount of the mortgage. The logical solution was to adjust and to refinance the debt in order to furnish the debtor with enough capital to reestablish the productivity of the property. But capital from other sources was unavailable on such heavily mortgaged property, and Duncan was reluctant to throw good money after bad. Eventually, he evaluated those loans and refinanced those planters who seemed most likely to recover. In other cases, he

11. Robert T. Hubard to Willie J. Eppes, September 1, 1865, in Hubard Family Papers, SHC; Ravenel Journal, May 22, 1865; Zebulon Preston to Stephen Duncan, December 13, 1865, in Stephen Duncan Papers, LSU.
12. W. B. Stipes to Jonathan Worth, January 6, 1866, in Jonathan Worth Papers, NCA. The pages of New York's *Merchant's Magazine and Commercial Review*, edited by William P. Dana, were filled with detailed accounts of the status of the southern state debtors, particularly of the actions taken by the provisional governments. See esp. "Will the Old State Debts of the South Be Paid?" *MM*, LIII (1865), 409–12, and "The Rehabilitation of the South," *MM*, LIV (1866), 169–74. See also Paul Renard Migliore's "The Business of Union: The New Business Community and the Civil War" (Ph.D. dissertation, Columbia University, 1975).

foreclosed in the hope that land prices would eventually recover and his investment could be recouped.[13]

Duncan's solution was common throughout the postwar South. Although arrangements between debtors and creditors varied significantly, in the majority of cases, creditors waived the interest accrued during the war and reduced the principal to its value in gold at the time of the transaction. In a few cases, debtors were able to settle for as little as ten cents on the dollar; in most instances, they agreed to repay from 50 to 75 percent of the original loan. At every turn, however, the forbearance of creditors was undercut by the realization that others might not be so generous, and patience could easily be rewarded by the bankruptcy of a debtor (who often owed money to several individuals).[14]

In the background of these financial uncertainties was always the paralyzing fear of confiscation. Weekly, sometimes daily, the newspapers of the South reprinted the text of the federal wartime confiscation legislation. Men like William Pitt Ballinger of Texas, a federal judge before the war and a self-acknowledged pardon broker in the summer of 1865, were inundated with requests for advice and clarification by wealthy southerners. How explicit did one have to be in support of the Confederacy to become subject to the laws of confiscation? Was a showing of actual service necessary? Did acceptance amount to approval of the Confederacy? Was net worth to be computed on antebellum value or on the deflated prices of 1865? These and dozens of other related questions were proof of the deep uneasiness of his clients and their fear that the limited land confiscation of 1864 and 1865 was but the prelude to a massive redistribution. In the summer of 1865, panicky James Conner of South Carolina expressed the fear that "nearly all the property in the South would be lost"—confiscated and then sold "without any judiciary proceedings." David Swain, the former governor of North Carolina and a professor of law at the state university,

13. Duncan's correspondence, 1865–1868, reflects the difficulties of obtaining accurate information on the financial condition of those indebted to the Mississippi planter.

14. Pressley, Lord, and Inglesby to Dr. E. E. Ellis, October 24, 1865, in Ellis Family Papers, SCL; John I. Ingram to Thomas Boone Fraser, August 18, 1866, in Thomas Boone Fraser Papers, SCL; Preston to Duncan, December 28, 1865, in Duncan Papers; Robert T. Hubard to Eppes, September 1, 1865, William B. Harrison to Edmund Hubard, August 16, 1867, both in Hubard Family Papers; Thomas Richardson to Thomas Davis Smith McDowell, May 30, 1866, in Thomas McDowell Papers, SHC; Thomas C. Browne to Richard Manning, December 13, 1865, in Williams-Chestnut-Manning Papers, SCL. The Edward McCrady L'Engle Papers, SHC, offer unusual insights into the interrelationship between northern creditors and southern debtors after the war. L'Engle, a Jacksonville, Fla., attorney, made his living in 1865 and 1866 collecting antebellum debts for northern firms and arranging financing and silent partnerships between northern firms and southern merchants and planters.

accurately described the importance of this issue for wealthy southerners. It was, he argued, a "hovering cloud" that would give "additional impetus to that spirit of 'equalization' & 'agrarianism' which can not be limited by section or state lines." Perhaps the greatest testament to the fears of wealthy southerners may be found in the extraordinarily high fees they were willing to pay to pardon brokers like Ballinger.[15] And although most southerners soon regained some confidence and publicly insisted that confiscation was unwise and even illegal as a postwar policy, their scornful preoccupation with the issue reflected a continued uneasiness.

Yet in the midst of this uncertainty, self-doubt, and even despair, some southerners saw an opportunity for a revitalization of the region. "I am very frank to say that I do zealously favor reconstruction," wrote the president of North Carolina's Trinity College in July of 1865. He saw defeat, not as an end for the South, but as a "glorious beginning."[16]

It was a conclusion shared by other resilient southerners. "We should forget the past," one enthusiastic Mississippian wrote his wife six months after the war was over. "We must create language, literature and art; we must develop science." The South's antebellum life of ease and prosperity built upon slavery had been a curse that dulled the "sensibilities" of the region. The end of this false prosperity would be the dawn of a new era. It *would* be, argued a Georgia newspaper editor, if the people of the South accepted the necessity for a "radical change" in which their very "modes of thought and feeling" were revolutionized.[17]

The peculiar defensiveness of the region before 1860 had exaggerated the degree of unity within the South. The region had always been characterized by class divisions and wide differences in political, economic, educational, and religious ideas; and war and defeat shattered the façade of unanimity among white southerners. For one brief, almost euphoric period, white southerners spoke their minds bluntly and without the restraints that

15. William Pitt Ballinger Diary, UTA, July–November, 1865. Mrs. Y. B. Manning to Husband, September 4, 1865, in Williams-Chestnut-Manning Papers; David Swain to Paul Cameron, July 1, 1865, in Paul Cameron Papers, SHC; M. L. Bonham to Gerrit Smith, June 24, 1867, in Gerrit Smith Papers, SUL. Citations documenting the fear of confiscation by well-to-do southerners are so numerous, they would be impossible to cite in full, but see esp. Mollie L. Morris to William Pitt Ballinger, July 2, 1865, in William Pitt Ballinger Papers, UTA; Mordecai to Thomas Ruffin, August 4, 1865, in Thomas Ruffin papers, SHC; Julian Mitchell to Will Murray, December 2, 1865, in Jenkins Family Papers, SCL; Tod Caldwell to Paul Cameron, August 17, 1865, in Cameron Papers; R. M. Louis to Duncan, July 29, 1865, in Duncan Papers.

16. Braxton Craven to Bishop Edward Ames, July 24, 1865 (copy), in Braxton-Craven Family Manuscripts, DUL.

17. Charles Wallace to Wife, October 1, 1865, in John Clopton Collection, DUL; Macon *Daily Telegraph*, October 18, 1865.

had characterized southern debate since the days of Jefferson and Madison. "Talk to me about a 'freeman,'" sneered Provisional Governor Hamilton of Texas. Under slavery, "the meanest dog in the community could bring you before a vigilance committee." In a somewhat more tactful commentary on the antebellum South, Georgia's Provisional Governor James Johnson scolded his fellow Georgians for their history of repression. "We abused mankind when they differed with us," observed Johnson. The white South had carried its opposition to free thought "to such an extreme, that men among us who dared to differ . . . were arraigned, not by law or before a legal tribunal, but before vigilant [sic] societies personally abused." Civilization had been driven from the land, Johnson told the state's first postwar Fourth of July celebration, and "law and order was suppressed by lawless men." Under the title "Things Passing Away," the Raleigh, North Carolina, Standard compiled a staggering indictment against the "bigotry, terrorism and repression" of the prewar South and urged southerners to turn these practices forever aside. More sweeping indictments of the antebellum South could scarcely have been penned by William Lloyd Garrison.[18]

Six weeks after the arrival of Union troops in Richmond County, Georgia, H. W. Hilliard spoke to a public meeting of his fellow citizens on the "results of the late conflict between North and South." Hilliard, an attorney and owner of a modest plantation outside Augusta, expressed confidence that his fellow southerners would accept the results of the war. The doctrine of secession—however correct in theory—had been laid to rest by the sword, and slavery was dead. With these two exceptions, he argued, the Union could be restored "as it was" before 1860, and southerners could resume their lives as though the war had never happened.

O. A. Lochrane, a Macon judge and longtime friend of Joseph Brown, sat respectfully through the speech of his friend, but when his turn came to speak, he gently but firmly offered his dissent. Anyone who believed the South could return to its old ways had failed to grasp the revolutionary implications of the war, said Lochrane. He frankly admitted that he had defended the legality of secession and the institution of slavery as both practical necessities and moral rights. But the great war was to him a "chasm

18. Macon Daily Telegraph, July 16, 1865; Raleigh Standard, August 8, 1865; New York Times, August 13, 1865. Georgia's first postbellum historian, Isaac Avery, claimed that at the close of Johnson's speech "his hearers retired in sullen dissatisfaction." But contemporary newspaper accounts said that his remarks were "roundly cheered," and two Georgia newspapers and another in South Carolina reprinted and endorsed his blunt criticism of the antebellum South. See Avery, History of the State of Georgia (New York, 1881), 183–84; Macon Daily Telegraph, July 23, 1865; Milledgeville (Ga.) Federal Union, July 11, 1865; Yorkville (S.C.) Enquirer, July 28, 1865.

which separates the old South from the new." It was difficult for men to "shake down their convictions like apples from a tree," he admitted. "But the lessons of the past years are unmistakeable." Unless an "improved and enlightened civilization" emerged from the ashes of the South, unless the backward customs and attitudes of the region could be swept away, the South would blindly relive the mistakes of the past. "We must be men, not monuments. . . . Let not pride, prejudice, and folly blind us and lead us stumbling backward over a wilderness of graves." The South, he concluded, had to be "reconstructed in the enlightened spirit of the age."[19]

For many of the aging veterans of antebellum politics, the principles of the old Whig party offered at least the hope of a way out of the poverty and ruin of the postwar South. Antebellum southern Democrats and Whigs had shared a political culture that emphasized the defense of southern rights and the absolute protection of slavery. Nevertheless, there were critical differences between the two parties. At least during the 1840s, Whigs were much less likely to make states' rights a political fetish. Even as they protected themselves from Democratic attacks by attacking federal incursions on the privileges of the states, they accepted the notion that the state would play a critical role in shaping and directing economic development. While the Democratic heirs of Jefferson and Jackson railed against the dangers of government in all its forms and warned of the threat to liberty in the manipulation of the powers of the state by the wealthy, southern Whigs backed the chartering and financial subsidization of railroads, the state sponsorship of other internal improvements, the enactment of legislation to sustain a sound banking structure, and the adoption of a public schools system (for public education promoted the development of a conservative and "enlightened" citizenry).

Such men had hardly been industrialists or even "proto-industrialists"; most were tied to the agricultural staple-crop economy of the South. But they were far more likely to be involved in large-scale commercial activities and to see the desirability of developing a complementary industrial sector to strengthen the southern economy and enhance the wealth of the cotton culture. Most of the legislatures of the 1840s and 1850s were dominated by planters, but these same legislatures had enacted flexible general incorporation laws, particularly for mining and manufacturing businesses unlikely to become "monopolies." By the 1850s, four of the eleven southern states had adopted general incorporation legislation that explicitly granted to business promoters that most valued advantage: limitations on the liability of stock-

19. Macon *Daily Telegraph*, July 1, 1865. Lochrane's address was published privately as O. A. Lochrane, *The Present Condition of the Country: Our Duty and Prospects* (Macon, 1865).

holders. In five other states, general incorporation statutes implied such limited liability. Eight of the nine general incorporation measures were enacted under Whig leadership.[20]

The memories of these and other Whig policies undoubtedly played an important role in shaping the thinking of the postwar "self-recontructionists." They were often the same individuals—adventuresome planters, town merchants, and entrepreneurs on the make, anxious to broaden the region's commercial economy and intrigued by the possibility of industrial as well as agricultural profits to be made. But it would be a mistake to see these calls for reshaping the postwar South as nothing more than a replay of antebellum whiggery. There was an intangible but significant shift in the outlook and values of these self-reconstructionists. They continued to emphasize the rhetoric of conservatism, but they saw themselves as agents of "progress" and "enlightenment" (however vaguely defined). These men were hardly egalitarian, but they were inclined to be mildly critical of their society and to complain of the region's refusal to embrace "progress" and to open up the South's political and social system to meritorious young men.

Thus, Judge O. A. Lochrane was not a Whig and neither was his political patron and law partner, Joseph E. Brown. James L. Orr and Benjamin Perry of South Carolina were up-country Democrats. Collectively the rejection of earlier ingrained assumptions went broader and deeper. In ways they would never acknowledge, not even to themselves, white southerners had assimilated many of the arguments of the free-soil, free-labor critics of the backward South. Let discredited politicians argue the abstract right of secession or the virtues of days gone by, said one postwar businessman; their "fulminations should be of far less concern to our future of financing

20. The attitude of antebellum southerners toward industry has been much discussed and little researched in the past fifteen years. I am grateful to Stephen Goldfarb for sharing with me the results of his extensive research on general incorporation laws in the antebellum South. ("Working Paper: Laws Governing the Incorporation of Manufacturing Companies Passed by Southern State Legislatures Before the Civil War" [Unpublished paper in possession of the author]). In his study of antebellum southern politics, William J. Cooper, Jr., concludes that differences between Democrats and Whigs on economic issues were far less significant than their agreement on the slavery question. See Cooper, *The South and the Politics of Slavery, 1828–1856* (Baton Rouge, 1978). Nevertheless, there were important economic divisions between Whigs and Democrats in the 1840s and 1850s as Charles Grieg Grier Sellers, Jr., argued in his still useful article "Who Were the Southern Whigs," *AHR*, LIX (1954), 335–46. For recent state studies that describe these party differences, see J. Mills Thornton III, *Politics and Power in a Slave Society: Alabama, 1800–1860* (Baton Rouge, 1978); William H. Adams, *The Whig Party of Louisiana* (Lafayette, La., 1973); Herbert J. Doherty, Jr., *The Whigs of Florida, 1845–1854* (Gainesville, 1959); Paul Murray, *The Whig Party in Georgia, 1825–1853* (Chapel Hill, 1948); Marc W. Kruman, *Parties and Politics in North Carolina, 1836–1865* (Baton Rouge, 1983); Thomas E. Jeffrey, "National Issues, Local Interests, and the Transformation of Antebellum North Carolina Politics, *JSH*, L (1984), 43–74.

the next mile of railroad or attracting capital for the construction of a new cotton mill." For this influential minority among southern elites, the war itself and the defeat of the Confederacy had been the final, convincing proof of the archaic nature of southern society.

No man more aptly summarized the links between this postwar cast of mind and the cautious stirrings of antebellum modernization than J. D. B. De Bow. For a decade and a half before the war *De Bow's Review* had been a forum for that minority of southerners who supported a changing South. William Gregg, James Taylor, Joseph Henry Lumpkin, Richard F. Reynolds, A. H. Brisbane, and Daniel Pratt had filled the pages of the *Review* with arguments for economic diversification and industrialization in the South. There was no argument made by the "New South" spokesmen of the 1880s that was not developed at length by these men through the 1840s and 1850s. They pointed to the proximity of waterpower and raw materials, the existence of a temperate climate, and the presence of a growing pool of displaced poor white workers. The agricultural depression of the 1840s seemed to offer an even more compelling argument. While planters, faced with cotton prices of four and five cents a pound, fought to stave off bankruptcy, the region's fledgling manufacturers—particularly those in textiles—reported profits on their investments of 10 to 15 percent annually.[21]

The great majority of southern planters would hear nothing of these arguments. Even the southern commercial conventions of the 1850s did not endorse the contention that southern manufactures were essential for the future economic health of the region.[22] When cotton prices returned to their earlier levels in the late 1840s and 1850s and the South fell back into an increasingly militant defense of its peculiar institution, the planter class savagely attacked the "Trojan Horse" of southern industrialism. Industrialization would weaken the antitariff solidarity of the region; it would lead to the growth of the "filthy, crowded licentious factories" that already contaminated the North; above all, it would undermine and threaten the basis of southern civilization: plantation slavery.

---

21. Richard W. Griffin, "Antebellum Industrial Foundations of the (Alleged) 'New' South," *THR*, V (1964), 22–43; Thomas P. Martin, "The Advent of William Gregg and the Graniteville Company," *JSH*, X (1945), 389–423; Herbert Collins, "The Southern Industrial Gospel Before 1860," *JSH*, XII (1946), 386–402; Fabian Linden, "Repercussions of Manufacturing in the Antebellum South," *NCHR*, XVII (1940), 313–31. David Goldfield emphasizes the continuity between the old South and the new in his study *Urban Growth in the Age of Sectionalism: Virginia, 1847–1861* (Baton Rouge, 1977), 271–83, as does Patrick J. Hearden, from a different perspective, in *Independence and Empire*, 1–19.

22. See John G. Van Deusen's "The Antebellum Southern Commercial Conventions," *TrCHP*, XVI (1926), 7–111.

Under the brunt of these attacks, most southern industrial spokesmen gave ground, denouncing the inequities of a high tariff with the fervor of a Delta planter, increasingly couching their proposals in the context of a defense of the southern agricultural way of life, and accepting (at least publicly) a secondary role for industry within the region. The "necessaries" of life were to be produced in the South, concluded De Bow himself as the war began, but most southerners did not wish to become a "commercial or manufacturing people." We "would not be shopkeepers, common-carriers and cobblers for mankind. Agriculture is our natural and our favorite pursuit." Not every southern industrialist agreed. William Gregg bluntly argued in 1860 that the South should erect stiff tariffs to protect southern manufactures, and another South Carolina businessman scolded his fellow southerners for continuing to invest capital in land and slaves instead of manufactures.[23]

With some notable exceptions, however, antebellum entrepreneurs deferred to the planter class, muted their implicit criticisms of the plantation system (which could easily be transformed by opponents into an attack on slavery itself), and accepted a decidedly inferior position within the southern economy. Southern business leaders limited their proselytizing to insistence that the factory could be a healthy complement rather than a form of competition to the plantation. Throughout the 1850s De Bow argued that the planters had an irrational fear of the threat industrialization posed to southern plantation agriculture. All societies had to change and progress, he argued, and there was no reason why a slave economy could not evolve in such a way that the "plow, the loom, and the anvil shall be brought together in harmony and success." In the context of the 1840s and 1850s there were plausible arguments to support the notion that industry and agriculture were complementary rather than antagonistic. As late as 1860, the value and production of agricultural goods far exceeded those of manufacturing in such "industrial" states as New York, Massachusetts, and Pennsylvania. They were considered models of economic health precisely because they seemed to have achieved a proper balance between agricultural and industrial interests.[24]

23. J. D. B. De Bow, "The Perils of Peace," *DR*, XXXI (1861), 299–300; "Southern Patronage to Southern Imports," *ibid.*, XXIX (1860), 778; William Gregg, "Southern Patronage to Southern Imports and Domestic Industry," *ibid.*, 77; "Southern Imports," *ibid.*, 232; "Southern Patronage to Southern Industry," *SP*, XXI (1861), 160.

24. *DR*, II (1847), 199, VII (1849), 25. Despite the "logic" of modern historians who see an inevitable conflict between the planter class and a potentially threatening industrial-manufacturing class, the majority of antebellum southern planters seldom expressed systematic hostility to southern industrialization. Fred Bateman and Thomas Weiss concluded that planter-dominated legislatures in the antebellum South rarely fostered manufactures, but nei-

Although this was the position southern industrial promoters developed for public consumption, their comments immediately after the war cast some doubt on the sincerity of their arguments. There might have been ways for agriculture and industry to peacefully coexist, but both the planters and the would-be industrialists seemed instinctively to realize the potential for conflict between the static and inherently conservative slave plantation and the more dynamic and unsettling forms of urban industrialism.

The war itself first changed the ground rules for the issue. Few southerners were as emphatic as Alexander Featherman of Tennessee when he angrily attacked the "fatuous shibboleths of agrarianism," which had made the people of the South "vassals of Yankeedom for the very materials of first necessity." In 1862 he warned, "Lands and negroes and an abundance of undeveloped resources cannot make a nation prosperous and happy." But the events of 1863 and 1864 soon brought home to knowledgeable southerners the critical role that industrial production played in the strength of a nation. When defeat came, the gloomiest prophecies of southern industrial advocates had become reality, and the lessons were inescapable. "We were not prepared for war—lacking all its munitions—lacking work shops, foundries and almost every necessary agency," acknowledged the militantly southern *Phoenix* of Columbia, South Carolina. For years, scolded another southern editor, he and fellow supporters of industrialization had warned of the inherent weaknesses of a reliance upon King Cotton. When the war had finally come, the people of the South were utterly helpless in a world in which national strength was measured in the statistics of manufacturing and production.[25]

John A. Wagener, South Carolina's postwar commissioner of immigration and a contributor to *De Bow's Review*, tried but ultimately failed to stifle the understandable impulse to remind his fellow southerners that he had earlier warned of disaster if the region did not develop an industrial

---

ther did they prohibit them. They do argue that this may be because "antebellum southern industrialization had not proceeded far enough to encourage a political constraint." Bateman and Weiss, *A Deplorable Scarcity: The Failure of Industrialization in the Slave Economy* (Chapel Hill, 1981), 161–62. See also the article by Bateman, Weiss, and James Foust, "The Participation of Planters in Manufacturing in the Antebellum South," *AH*, XLVII (1974), 277–98.

25. Alexander Featherman, "The True Policy of the Confederate States," *DR*, XVIII (1862), 51; Columbia (S.C.) *Phoenix*, May 1, 1865; Augusta *Daily Press*, March 6, 1866. For a discussion of the belated efforts of southerners to develop wartime industries, see Lester J. Cappon's "Government and Private Industry in the Southern Confederacy," in *Humanistic Studies in Honor of John Calvin Metcalf* (Charlottesville, 1951), 151–89. For the argument that the war itself led southerners to reevaluate their agrarian biases, see Raimondo Luraghi, *The Rise and Fall of the Plantation South*, (New York, 1978); Emory Thomas, *The Confederacy as a Revolutionary Experience* (Englewood Cliffs, N.J., 1971).

base. Quite apart from the effect upon the South's fight for independence, noted the German-born Wagener, the prideful insistence that nonagricultural labor was degrading and "menial" had "impoverished the region" and made the effects of defeat even more melancholy. If only the advice of William Gregg and other industrial statesmen had been followed, he concluded, the "rivers would now resound with the busy hum and clatter of machinery." To men like Wagener, some of the bitterness of defeat was eased by the vindication of a lifetime of warnings.[26]

And if the war and the South's defeat had illustrated the military weakness of the cotton South, emancipation had removed the institution these men saw as the greatest obstacle to the revitalization of southern society. The alacrity with which many southerners accepted the end of slavery offers suggestive evidence that in subtle ways the antislavery argument had been unconsciously absorbed into their thinking. The *North Carolina Times* was a distinctly pro-Union newspaper published under the watchful eyes of Union forces in Wilmington. Perhaps it is not surprising that it excoriated the "retarding and depressing effects of the institution of slavery" and welcomed emancipation as the opening chapter of a "glorious future for this redeemed land." Under similar circumstances, the Savannah *Republican* argued that the South without slavery would soon be alive with the "hum of machinery, the clatter of busy drays along paved streets . . . the shrill whistle of locomotives as they speed along."[27]

Even such planter-oriented southern newspapers as the Macon *Daily Telegraph*, the Augusta *Chronicle and Sentinel*, and the Montgomery *Advertiser* welcomed the end of the South as it was before the war. The region had been blessed with a climate and soil equal to most of the northern states, said Macon editor John Dumble; nevertheless, there was a great disparity in the growth of wealth and economic prosperity. "We are forced

26. *Report of the Special Committee of the General Assembly of South Carolina, on the Subject of Encouraging Immigration* (Charleston, 1866), 14. See also John A. Wagener, "European Immigration," *DR*, 2nd ser., IV (1867), 94–104. For examples of the way in which southern newspapers and spokesmen for industrial development used the "lessons" of defeat, see Cartersville (Ga.) *Express*, July 21, 1866; Augusta *Chronicle and Sentinel*, December 21, 1865; Macon *Daily Telegraph*, October 18, 1865; Richmond *Whig*, May 18, 1865; (Jacksonville) *Florida Union*, September 15, 1865; Houston *Tri-Weekly Telegraph*, February 7, 1865; Richmond *Times*, December 18, 1865; Yorkville (S.C.) *Enquirer*, November 1, 1866; (New Bern) *North Carolina Times*, April 14, 1865; *Fa*, I (1866), 289–90.

27. (New Bern) *North Carolina Times*, April 14, 1865; Savannah *Republican*, August 8, 1865; Augusta *Chronicle and Sentinel*, June 28, 1865. The Savannah *Republican* was published by John Hayes during the Federal occupation of the city and after the war. Hayes, a former New York *Herald* reporter, assumed a strongly pro-Union position in 1865 and the beginning of 1866, but the prospect of widespread black suffrage led him back toward conservative positions in late 1866 and 1867.

to admit that, in aggregate wealth and improvement to the State, in internal enterprise and national progress, facts that are incontrovertible teach
us that slave labor was not conducive to the highest prosperity of the
country."[28]

With the "troublesome negro" no longer the preoccupation of the most
talented southerner, said one editor, "the din of manufactories will be heard
in the south and the mechanic arts will arise and flourish." There was no
reason why the South would not soon be dotted with factories and commercial centers. And with the "injurious effects" of slavery forever ended by
emancipation, corporations for mining, transportation, and manufacturing
would "spring up over the state," promised the Columbus Enquirer,
"bringing the happy fruits of the disappearance of the late 'peculiar institution.'" Samuel Reid of the Montgomery Advertiser, cautious in weighing
the overall effects of emancipation and particularly sensitive to the problems
of social and economic readjustment in Alabama's black belt, nevertheless
found a silver lining in the disruption of the antebellum economic system.
The way was at last open for the South to take its place as a land of "factories and workshops."[29]

The most enthusiastic response to emancipation came from many of the
surviving southern newspapers that had been associated with the Whig
party in the 1840s and 1850s. By the time of its collapse as a political party,
southern whiggery had become as defensive and sectionalist-minded as the
southern democracy, but there remained a substantial minority within the
party that supported manufacturing and commercial development, at least
as an adjunct to the plantation economy. Echoes of Henry Clay's American
system were apparent in the rhetoric and policy suggestions of these newspapers. After the war, they often simply elaborated upon the same proposals they had made in the antebellum period.

Still, there were differences. There was little talk of the factory as a support for the South's system of staple-crop production. The "plantation system, in connection with slave labor, is one principal reason why the South,
despite its advantage of soil and climate, is behind the other sections of the
union in population and in industrial enterprises," concluded the editor of
the Augusta Chronicle and Sentinel. With equal bluntness, William Ira
Smith of the Richmond Whig told his readers that the greatest blunder
southerners had ever made was to blindly cling to an "outmoded" social

28. Macon Daily Telegraph, August 18, 1865.
29. Columbus (Ga.) Enquirer, n.d., quoted in Macon Daily Telegraph, February 26, 1866;
Richmond Times, December 18, 1865; Montgomery Advertiser, September 29, 1865.

and economic system. For its own sake,, he concluded, "the South should have abandoned slavery long before 1865."[30] Such policies fit most comfortably with old-line Whig newspapermen, but they were also endorsed by such Democratic newspapers as the Richmond *Times*, the Augusta *Daily Press*, the Columbus *Enquirer*, and even the flagship of Alabama's planter class, the Montgomery *Advertiser*.

At times, southern journalists came perilously close to accepting and endorsing the most scathing criticisms of antebellum free-labor advocates. Slavery, more than any other factor, had acted as a deadweight on the antebellum South, concluded the editor of the Augusta *Chronicle and Sentinel*. Instead of advancing with the technology of the age, southerners had depended upon raw, physical black labor. When northerners faced a shortage of labor, they had responded by encouraging the development and sale of reapers, mowers, planting machines, and new and improved plows. The South had plodded along, investing its capital in slaves with hoes and axes, "scratching the earth's surfaces and never going deep enough for any practical good."[31]

Dumble's criticism of antebellum farming practices reflected another facet of this reappraisal of postwar society. Once slavery, the foundation of southern agriculture, was destroyed, a "radical reconstruction" of the system—as conservative North Carolina planter William Pell described it— was required. Such a complete overhaul was necessary, he concluded, because the "knell of African slavery in the South . . . doomed cotton as king." There was no evidence that cotton and other staple crops could be grown successfully with free labor, argued Pell. Inevitably, therefore, there would be a substantial decline in the production of cotton, rice, sugar, and to a lesser extent, tobacco. As a Virginia planter and longtime agricultural reformer insisted in a letter to the *Farmer*, no result of the war was more certain than the end of the South as a worldwide supplier of agricultural staples.[32]

Agricultural reform was hardly a product of the postwar South. From the time of Jefferson and Washington, southerners had condemned backward and inefficient agricultural practices that had destroyed the land and impoverished the people. John Binns and John Taylor of Caroline promoted the virtues of fertilization and crop rotation, and no individual agi-

30. Augusta *Chronicle and Sentinel*, June 28, 1865; Richmond *Whig*, May 1, 1865.
31. Augusta *Chronicle and Sentinel*, August 19, 1865.
32. Pell was editor of the Raleigh *Sentinel*, which had been the house organ of North Carolina's Whig party but after the war spoke for the Worth faction of North Carolina conservatives. *Sentinel*, January 24, 1866; *Fa*, I (1866), 322–33; Richmond *Whig*, July 13, 1866.

tated more actively for broad-scale agricultural reform than the southern nationalist, Edmund Ruffin. In that sense, the resurgence of interest in postwar agricultural reform was simply a continuation of the work carried on by individuals and agricultural societies in the half century before the Civil War.[33]

The predicted decline in the staple-crop production only intensified earlier pleas for crop diversification. In his resuscitated postwar magazine, J. D. B. De Bow shifted his emphasis on agricultural reform from the improvement of staple production to an emphasis upon diversification. Fruit production and particularly wheat farming and livestock raising were put forth as panaceas by agricultural journals and southern newspapers. The incessant concentration upon such money crops as cotton and tobacco gave the illusion of prosperity, said the Augusta *Chronicle and Sentinel*, but the ultimate result was to place the South in an economically disadvantageous position compared to the North. The region, forced to purchase not only manufactured goods but also livestock and even the wheat it consumed, remained impoverished, and the illusory profits were "consumed in the payment of Northern debts."[34]

A southern plantation owner of the 1850s would have felt quite at home with such reformist rhetoric. He would hardly have been pleased, however, with the blunt denunciations of plantation slavery, which held that the plantation system "in connection with slave labor is one reason why the South, despite its advantage of soil and climate, is behind the other sections of the union." It was a matter of the highest policy, said one editor, to abandon a form of agriculture that left the southern countryside in a state that compared unfavorably to the "worst cultivated districts of France and Spain." Such heresy was not an aberration; it was the refrain repeated by some of the most influential southerners after the war. As a committee of the first postwar legislature in South Carolina argued: There might remain a place in the South for some large-scale farming enterprises, "but there is an even greater place for the small farm." To the earlier calls for fertiliza-

33. Southern publicists promoting postwar agricultural modernization often emphasized the pioneering work of antebellum southerners. See particularly the postwar issues of *Field and Fireside* from November, 1865, to December, 1866, the *Southern Cultivator*, the *Southern Ruralist* and the *Farmer*. *De Bow's Review* continued its articles on agricultural reform with special emphasis on the effects of emancipation. The *Land We Love*, which began publication in 1866, also ran numerous articles on the necessity for southern agriculturalists to abandon the "archaic" practices used under slavery.

34. Otis Clark Skipper, *J. D. B. De Bow: Magazinist of the Old South* (Athens, 1958), 211; Augusta *Chronicle and Sentinel*, June 28, 1865; Newnan (Ga.) *Herald*, n.d., quoted in Atlanta *Daily Intelligencer*, February 19, 1867; Augusta *Daily Press*, October 13, 1866; Yorkville (S.C.) *Enquirer*, October 26, 1865.

tion, crop rotation, and mechanization was added a new and far more radical injunction: "divide, sub-divide and sub-divide again" the plantations of the region.[35] This argument appealed particularly to such up-country newspapers as the Yorkville, South Carolina, *Enquirer*, the Rome, Georgia, *Southerner*, the Huntsville, Alabama, *Independent*, and W. W. Holden's Raleigh *Standard*. What was astonishing, however, was that several black-belt dailies took a similar position, at least during the initial months after the war. The facts were "stern and incontrovertible," concluded the editor of the Macon *Daily Telegraph*. The plantation was "not conducive to the highest prosperity of the country." However unpleasant most southerners might find such conclusions, it was essential "to look at facts as they exist, instead of following in the path of past and exploded theories."[36]

Montgomery *Advertiser* editor Samuel G. Reid, the antebellum protégé of fire-eater William Lowndes Yancey, was less enthusiastic over the breakup of the plantation in his postwar editorials, but he was no less emphatic. Emancipation, he told his readers in a series of articles during the summer and fall of 1865, had changed the very foundations of southern agriculture. The old system of large plantations, worked by slave labor, was not without benefits. Economically it had made possible a high level of production in staple crops, and it had served as a method of solving the "social relationships" of a society in which blacks and whites had to coexist side by side. But this plantation style of farming was incompatible with a free-labor system in which it would be "difficult for any one farmer or planter to provide in advance for the cultivation of any great amount of land." The only means of survival for the planter was to sell portions of his landholdings, "not entire plantations, but portions for farms which would with a few years increase in population and constant labor . . . so enhance the value of what they retain as to make it a benefit to dispose of what they now consider a surplus." With the same flexibility that later led him into the Alabama Republican party, Reid insisted that "nothing is clearer than that—if

35. Augusta *Chronicle and Sentinel*, June 28, August 19, 1865; South Carolina Committee on Immigration, *South Carolina House of Representatives Special Committee on European Immigration, Report on the Subject of Encouraging European Immigration* (Charleston, 1866), 14–15; *FF*, December 16, 1865; *Fa*, I (1866), 322–24; J. L. Bernard to F. J. Blount, December 14, 1865, in Alabama Governors' Papers.

36. Yorkville (S.C.) *Enquirer*, October 18, 1865; Augusta *Daily Press*, March 13, October 13, 1866; Rome (Ga.) *Southerner*, March 12, 1866; Huntsville (Ala.) *Independent*, n.d., quoted in Yorkville *Enquirer*, October 25, 1866; (New Bern) *North Carolina Times*, April 14, 1865; Richmond *Whig*, May 18, 1865; Augusta *Daily Constitutionalist*, November 9, 1866; Columbus *Enquirer*, March 26, 1866. In general, the most scathing comments on the old plantation system came from newspapers outside the black belt.

we are to be prosperous in the future, farmers and farm-houses must dot every hill-side." The small farm was the hope of the future South.[37] The destruction of plantation agriculture in many respects represented the resurgence of the old Jeffersonian dream of a South of small yeoman farmers. For two generations, southerners had looked out upon vistas of increasingly shabby, run-down and dilapidated fields and outbuildings; a depressing contrast to the well-kept farms of the North. Within ten years, insisted the editor of the conservative Raleigh *Sentinel*, plantations with their centralized labor system would be replaced by "small, neat flourishing and improved farms." Georgia Provisional Governor James Johnson was even more rhapsodic. Instead of investing every penny in the purchase of overpriced slaves, this southern class of "respectable small farmers" would spend their money in "increasing the comforts of our homes, manuring our lands, planting orchards, [and] building fences." A well-tilled countryside would in turn spread prosperity throughout southern society rather than limit it to the hands of a few. "Our towns and villages, instead of going into decay, will improve and arts and sciences will flourish among us." Even Virginia's former governor Henry Wise, an uncompromising defender of the old regime, spoke approvingly of his state's future as a "land of yeoman farmers" instead of a commonwealth controlled by a few wealthy planters and their slaves.[38]

A South of small farms and factories required other changes in the society. Before the war, the southern rail system had been hampered by inadequate capitalization, by too many small and inefficient competing corporations, and by the multiplicity of track gauges, argued one Atlanta merchant, but its greatest handicap had been the fact that it was designed primarily as a conduit for staple agricultural goods. Southerners were linked far more closely with the "commercial entrepots of Liverpool and New York than their neighbors one hundred miles away." What was needed, agreed a South Carolina newspaper editor, was a rail system that would serve both the farmers and the manufactories that were certain to spring up in the future. Without such a transportation system the South would remain "backwards and impoverished." For a region that had just emerged from a devastating civil war, the South was remarkably alive with railroad development schemes in the summer and fall of 1865. And even though most promoters were most concerned with immediate economic benefits,

---

37. Montgomery *Advertiser*, September 28, 29, October 26, November 1, 14, 1865.
38. Raleigh *Sentinel*, October 27, 1865; Macon *Daily Telegraph*, July 16, 1865; Richmond *Enquirer and Sentinel*, January 4, 1867; Columbus (Ga.) *Enquirer*, March 25, 1866; Augusta *Constitutionalist*, November 9, 1866.

they always argued that railroads would promote industrial and business, as well as agricultural, development.[39] Equally critical was the creation of a postwar educational system that would avoid, in the words of one Louisiana editor, the antebellum "spirit of caste, growing out of our 'peculiar institution.'" Such postwar pleas for educational reform were sometimes expressed in vague and rhetorical exhortations. And occasionally a spokesman for the old regime insisted that southerners should return to the "scholastic education" that had trained its leaders in the traditional disciplines. Former Confederate general Daniel Harvey Hill would ultimately become defender of Old South values, but for the immediate postwar period at least, his attacks on the values of the plantation South were as scathing as those of any antebellum New England abolitionist. In his little magazine, the *Land We Love*, he scolded his own generation for its arrogance and pride in concentrating all its energies upon the defense of a backward and retrogressive social order. His most slashing attacks were reserved for an educational system—"such as it was"—that ignored geometry, chemistry, biology, engineering, and the "plain principles of practical science" for instruction in Cicero and Juvenal. What young southerners needed was not a mastery of Ovid but a stronger and coarser intellectual fabric that would lay the foundations for a regenerated South; such an educational system would ultimately "renovate and re-people our cities and villages—build railroads, dredge rivers and harbors and start the music of machinery and manufactures wherever a waterfall or pine forest will afford water and steam." For too long, Hill told his readers, the South had chased the elusive cotton boll while ignoring the real sources of prosperity.[40]

Even as they struggled to rebuild their state's government, South Carolina's Benjamin Perry and James L. Orr set aside several days for discussions with legislators on the reshaping of the traditional classical curriculum at South Carolina College. Perry, a longtime enemy of the college (it

39. Atlanta *Daily Intelligencer*, July 28, 1865; Columbia *South Carolinian*, October 12, 1866; Augusta *Daily News*, October 16, 1866. See also the voluminous "Railroad File—1865–1868" of Governors Louis Parsons and Robert Patton in Alabama Governors' Papers. John Stover describes the postwar adjustment and long-range changes in the region's railroad in *The Railroads of the South, 1865–1900: A Study in Finance and Control* (Chapel Hill, 1955). Almost every detailed study of the state politics in the Reconstruction era returns to this important issue.

40. Daniel Harvey Hill, "Education," *LL*, I (May, 1866), 8. For information on Hill's magazine, see Ray M. Atchison, "The *Land We Love*: A Southern Postbellum Magazine of Agriculture, Literature and Military History," *NCHR*, XXXVII (1960), 506–16. Macon *Daily Telegraph*, May 31, July 19, 1865; Mobile *Daily Tribune*, n.d., quoted in Savannah *Republican*, September 9, 1865.

fostered an "aristocratic ideal," he had complained in the 1840s), proposed a program of courses that would train a new generation of engineers, mechanics, skilled craftsmen, and agriculturalists. After a state legislator complained timidly of the impracticality of the college in the 1840s President James Henley Thornwell had replied scornfully that the institution was designed to prepare leaders, not to serve as a training school for "sappers, miners, apothecaries, doctors or farmers." In 1865, however, even William Gilmore Simms, a longtime defender of the old order, agreed that it would be disastrous to keep the "old fogey college system." When Orr, Perry's successor, urged the legislature to develop a university "in tune with the needs of the modern age," no one rose to defend Greek, Latin, and rhetoric. It was to be poverty, not ideology, that served as the main obstacle to educational change in 1865 and 1866.[41]

The *Farmer*, which continued to champion the principles of whiggery and Henry Clay, in 1865 agreed with Perry and Orr. In one of its first postwar issues, the editor suggested tactfully that the "planter's education" of the Old South was unsuitable for the new. The "dead languages, metaphysics, law and political economics should no longer be the sole, or even the chief studies of our children." What was needed was a "practical education" that would teach the natural and physical sciences and their practical application to agriculture, mechanics, and commerce. When a group of Georgia citizens suggested the creation of a polytechnic college in that state, the Savannah *Republican* noted that the necessity for such an institution was "too palpable to call for further elucidation." It would be two decades before these plans found their fruition in the creation of the Georgia Institute of Technology, but other more traditional southern institutions hurried to fill the need. Four former Confederate army officers reopened the Hillsboro, North Carolina, Military Academy in the fall of 1866, and the antebellum courses in the classics as well as those in ordnance, gunnery, infantry, and cavalry tactics were subordinated to a new curriculum designed to "fit the young men of the rising generation to develop the great natural and mineral wealth of the country, and to direct their attention to its agricultural improvements and its immense industrial resources."[42]

Nor was it simply a matter of reshaping the curriculum for the elite. The basic weakness of the antebellum educational system lay in elitism itself, claimed the editor of the New Orleans *Times*. The "wealthy planters were

41. Columbia (S.C.) *Daily Phoenix*, August 22, October 31, December 6, 1865; Lillian F. Kibler, *Benjamin F. Perry, South Carolina Unionist* (Durham, N.C., 1946), 306–308.
42. *Fa*, II (1867), 57–59; Savannah *Daily Republican*, February 6, 1868; Hillsboro Military Academy, Brochure, February 1, 1867, in John Lancaster Bailey Papers, SHC; James E. Brittain and Robert C. McMath, Jr., "Engineers and the New South Creed: The Formation and Early Development of Georgia Tech," *TC*, XVIII (1977), 172–201.

altogether too proud to send their children to free public schools, which they regarded as little better than pauper institutions." Without the support of influential community leaders, the public school system had foundered, hopelessly underfunded and backward. The South had too many "academies" for the few, agreed one Georgian. The region needed a free school system that would give every southern child a chance to acquire a good education. The land of New England was "sterile and rocky, the climate . . . cold and ungenial, but there is a plentiful crop of school houses and from these spring the educated men who make the land fertile and the whole country a hive of industry, energy and prosperity." Alabama's Samuel Reid was equally impressed by the "lesson taught by Massachusetts and her sisters" that universal education was the key to prosperity. How many men of science and industry had "lived and died poor in the South, who, under a different state of things would have taken their rank among the most distinguished?" In some Confederate units, admitted one southern editor, less than 25 percent of the Confederate soldiers were able to sign their names for the muster role. The "rich and powerful" may have prospered under the old regime, "but what of the poor and lowliest?" It was not true that the state could not afford to educate her children; it could "not afford to let them go uneducated."[43]

Such an educational reformation had to be part and parcel of a total transformation of the white southerners' attitude toward work and leisure. "No more fox-hounds!" said Virginia's former governor Henry Wise. "No more lazy morning hours!—No more segar [sic] and juleps!—No more card-parties an club-idleness! No more syren [sic] retreats in summer and city balls in winter!"[44]

But not all members of the planter class justified Henry Wise's condemnation of lazy morning slumbers, afternoon fox hunts, and evening card parties. Even the elite did not always live lives of sybaritic ease, and the majority of southerners were hardly members of that elite. They worked long, hard hours, particularly during the seasons when crops needed cultivation and harvesting.[45]

43. New Orleans *Times*, December 5, 1865; Augusta *Chronicle and Sentinel*, August 4, 1865; Augusta *Daily Press*, March 6, 1866; (Jacksonville) *Florida Union*, September 16, 1865; Montgomery *Advertiser*, August 6, October 27, 1865.

44. Richmond *Enquirer and Sentinel*, January 4, 1867; Atlanta *Daily Intelligencer*, January 31, 1866; *Fa*, I (1866), 289–90; Columbia (S.C.) *Phoenix*, October 28, 1865; Yorkville (S.C.) *Enquirer*, November 9, 1865; Huntsville (Ala.) *Independent*, October 24, 1865.

45. On this, as on so many subjects dealing with the economic history of the nineteenth-century South, historians have traded mathematical equations with inconclusive results. According to Forrest McDonald and Grady McWhiney, the southern "Celts" dominated antebellum southern society. These people, heirs to centuries of pastoral life that emphasized swine raising rather than cultivation, "were contemptuous of work and did as little as pos-

Moreover, many such outbursts of self-criticism, though cast in the rhetoric of the postwar crisis, reflected the tensions that had always existed between well-to-do fathers and sons. Few southern patriarchs were willing to acknowledge that their sons were adequately bearing the burdens and responsibilities of plantation management, particularly when such acknowledgment would imply that they should step aside. Members of the younger generation wanted to "get their bread by the results of head work," a North Carolina wholesale merchant told his good friend Paul Cameron. Few were willing to "take the plough handle or the adze or trowell." But when Alexander Kevan complained that the young were oblivious to the changed conditions of the postwar era ("We must teach the coming generation that honest labor is no degredation"), his primary audience was probably his two sons. And Cameron, the wealthiest antebellum planter in North Carolina, was more than sympathetic to such complaints. In the years following the war, as he repeatedly rescued his extended family from financial ruin, he remembered the expression of an old friend. "Paul, it does very well . . . when the children all suck the mammy but I tell you when they suck the daddy it is the devil!"[46]

Whatever its validity, the indictment of the lazy and traditional South represented an attempt on the part of postwar self-reconstructionists to set aside the values of the traditional planter-merchant elites of the region. When they scolded fellow southerners for "sneering at the Mechanical branches of industry" and for patronizing those southerners who were not planters or members of a related professional class—merchants, lawyers or doctors—self-reconstructionists never saw themselves as antisouthern. Their complaints were always accompanied by appeals to regional patriotism and warnings that, unless southerners cast off past "modes of

---

sible." But Stanley Engerman insists that the "crop-time method that Professors McDonald and McWhiney use for the South leads to a serious underestimation of the actual labor time in agriculture." I suspect we shall have to be content with the certainty that the majority of northerners (and a good number of southerners) *believed* in the lazy South. For a summary of the recent literature on the subject see Forrest McDonald and Grady McWhiney, "The South from Self-sufficiency to Peonage: An Interpretation," *AHR*, LXXXV (1980), 1095–1118; "*AHR* Forum: Antebellum North and South in Comparative Perspective: A Discussion by Thomas Alexander, Stanley Engerman, Forrest McDonald, Grady McWhiney, and Edward Pessen, *ibid.*, 1150–66. C. Vann Woodward commented perceptively on the ambivalent reaction that most Americans have had to the "lazy South" in "The Southern Ethic in a Puritan World," in Woodward, *American Counterpoint: Slavery and Racism in the North-South Dialogue* (Boston, 1971), 13–46.

46. Paul C. Cameron to Anne [Lin] Collins, January 22, 1886, in Cameron Papers; Michael P. Johnson, "Planters and Patriarchy: Charleston, 1800–1860," *JSH*, XLVI (1980), 58; Bertram Wyatt-Brown, *Southern Honor: A Study in Ethics and Behavior in the Antebellum South* (New York, 1982), 174–75; Drew Gilpin Faust, *James Henry Hammond and the Old South: A Design for Mastery* (Baton Rouge, 1982), 322–29.

thought and feeling, strangers will come and usurp the places which should be filled by native men." Atlanta, with its bustling activity and constant whirlwind of development and growth, was to be the model of a resurgent South; let Charleston languish with its 9 A.M. business openings, two-hour lunch breaks, and early closing. When the South was reborn, the North would once again respect the region's economic strength and power.[47]

Their apprehensions and warnings only highlighted their sense of optimism. The potential for wealth was there. It was simply a matter of combining capital, labor, and an enlightened and transformed southern leadership. Here again, the act of emancipation seemed to have removed one of the greatest obstacles to development. Of all the injurious effects of slavery, concluded the Columbus *Enquirer*, the greatest was the disposition of planters to invest all their surplus income in more slaves and new land. As a result, agreed the Richmond *Whig*, for generations the southern slaveholding class had invested enormous amounts of capital in unproductive land and useless slaves. Under this outmoded system, the plantation was not the productive beehive of activity depicted by its antebellum defenders, but a holding ground for dozens of slaves who performed no real economic function, but simply served as "superfluous ornaments for the old style."[48]

Although such an analysis had an appealing logic for postwar southerners anxious to find some silver lining in the nightmare of emancipation, there is no evidence that investment in excess lands and slaves created a capital shortage that retarded industrialization. In any case, just how could the remaining limited southern capital be mobilized and directed away from the unproductive plantation to mining, transportation, and industrial production? The Augusta *Chronicle and Sentinel* proposed the exemption of all manufacturing investment from taxation for a decade, and the Columbus *Enquirer* went one step further. "In our judgment, the legislatures [of the South] could issue bonds or appropriate money for no better purpose than to aid in the erection of manufacturing establishments—say, in the purchase of sites for them at least." At that point, entrepreneurs could be given a rent-free lease with an agreement to begin paying reasonable rents

47. Macon *Daily Telegraph*, October 18, 1865; Augusta *Daily Press*, March 6, 1866; Newnan (Ga.) *Herald*, January 10, 1867; *LL*, quoted in the Yorkville (S.C.) *Enquirer*, June 14, 1866; Raleigh *Standard*, August 1, 1865; Atlanta *Daily Intelligencer*, January 31, 1866; G. B. Littlejohn to E. W. Hubard, March 9, 1866, in Hubard Family Papers; Don H. Doyle, "Leadership and Decline in Postwar Charleston, 1865–1910," in Walker Fraser, Jr., and Winfred B. Moore, Jr. (eds.), *From the Old South to the New: Essays on the Transitional South* (Westport, Conn., 1981), 93–106.

48. Columbus *Enquirer*, n.d., quoted in Macon *Daily Telegraph*, February 26, 1866; Richmond *Whig*, May 1, 1865.

within the decade. The editor of the *Enquirer* acknowledged that there would be opposition to such state interference in "private enterprises," but he pointed to the aid that southern states had extended to the railroads in the 1850s. Given the desperate need for economic development in the South, what was the difference between giving assistance to a railroad and giving it to a factory that would employ hundreds of impoverished southerners? The reasoning was "precisely the same," claimed a contributor to *De Bow's Review*, "with this special and conclusive addition: The state must build a poor-house and a prison, or a cotton factory in every county or parish."[49]

Willoughby Newton, president of the Virginia State Agricultural Society and a prominent antebellum Whig, proposed an equally radical solution to the problem of capital shortage. Newton, who had studied the operation of the Bank of Scotland, suggested a system of state-backed banks throughout the state. These banks, buttressed by the financial strength of state support, would draw upon European capital by guaranteeing a return of 7 or 8 percent. Such funds could then be lent to Virginia farmers and entrepreneurs at a rate of 10 or 12 percent—a high rate by national standards but quite low in terms of prevailing postwar practices. The Raleigh *Sentinel*, press spokesman for conservative North Carolinians, suggested a variant scheme. The *Sentinel* supported the creation of a "North Carolina Land Loan Company" that would allow farmers to mortgage their land. With the state serving as a guarantor, the company would send agents to Europe to borrow the essential capital. And Duff Green, the irrepressible antebellum dreamer, outlined a hazy blueprint for state-supported agricultural credit agencies, which would channel needed capital to small farmers, who, freed from the pressing necessity of producing immediate cash crops, could make the investments essential for diversification and good agricultural management.[50]

Mark R. Cockrill, a Tennessee sheep-raiser and experimental farmer, had suggested as early as 1849 a scheme for mobilizing industrial capital for textile production. Under his plan, professionals, business leaders, and

49. Augusta *Chronicle and Sentinel*, September 25, 1866, November 1, 1866; Columbus (Ga.) *Enquirer*, n.d., quoted in Augusta *Daily Press*, October 31, 1866; Bateman and Weiss, *A Deplorable Scarcity*, 159–60; "Exodus," *DR*, V (1868), 983. All of the provisional governors and their elected replacements routinely answered correspondence regarding economic opportunities in the postwar South. Perry and Orr of South Carolina, Holden and Worth of North Carolina, and Parson and Patton of Alabama were particularly energetic in their promotional activities. See, for example, Patton's "The New Era of Manufactures," *DR*, 2nd ser., III (1867), 56–68.

50. Willoughby Newton to William MacFarland, July 24, 1866, rpr. in *Fa*, I (1866), 379–80; Raleigh *Sentinel*, February 22, 1866; Fletcher Green, "Duff Green: Industrial Promoter," *JSH*, II (1936), 29–42.

particularly planters would contribute capital to form a corporate community enterprise. Such pooled capital would be used to construct workshops
and to hire skilled managers and operatives who would in turn train local
whites for the mills. This scheme was revived in the months after the
war and gained the support of such up-country Piedmont newspapers as
the Yorkville *Enquirer*, the Rome *Courier*, and the Charlotte *Western
Democrat*.[51]

Mark Cockrill's plan suffered from one overwhelming disadvantage: the
absence of a reservoir of available capital. If there was inadequate private
capital, however, the first postwar legislators were quick to use the power of
the state to support development. Even as provisional governors and state
officials struggled to restore a semblance of normality to the functions of
government and as travelers and newspaper reporters described the chaotic
state of the region's economy, state legislators approved grandiose charters
for a hundred new enterprises, with the railroads leading the way. The
"whole Southern country appears to have taken a mania for railroads," concluded one Georgia newspaper correspondent after reviewing that state's
first postwar legislature. Legislative support for these future roads was
often the product of blatant self-interest on the part of legislators. Sixteen
Arkansas legislators, for example, were listed as chief stockholders or
officers of the postwar railroad companies they chartered and, in some
cases, directly subsidized, and the majority of governors were linked to the
industry. But enthusiasm was unfeigned. In the larger commercial centers
and in barely incorporated hamlets, local boosters convened their "mass
meetings" and then headed for state capitals to obtain charters with imaginary capitalization and promised benefits that would have challenged the
Union and Northern Pacific railroads.[52]

By the summer of 1866, tax collection in Augusta, Georgia, had col-

51. Yorkville (S.C.) *Enquirer*, November 1, 1866; Rome (Ga.) *Courier*, n.d., quoted in
Milledgeville (Ga.) *Federal Union*, September 26, 1865; Charlotte *Western Democrat*, December 12, 1865. Cockrill's proposal first appeared in *De Bow's Review*, VII (1899), 484–90,
under his son's name. It was later reprinted in southern newspapers in 1865 and 1866 and in
William J. Barbee's *The Cotton Question* (New York, 1866), 138–41. In a somewhat different
form this plan of community stock investment was used in many parts of the South in the
1880s and 1890s.

52. Atlanta *Daily Intelligencer*, July 7, 1866; Paige E. Mulhollan, "Arkansas General Assembly of 1866 and Its Effect on Reconstruction," *AHQ* (1961), 336–67. Mark Summers
notes the direct connection between the subsidy programs of the Johnson governments and the
Republicans that followed in "Radical Reconstruction and the Gospel of Prosperity: Railroad
Aid Under the Southern Republicans" (Ph.D. dissertation, University of California, 1980),
29–31. For an insight into the connections between some Virginia lawmakers directly involved
in railroad promotion and the legislation they sponsored, see David J. Burr to E. W. Hubard,
October 31, 1866; Robert T. Hubard to E. W. Hubard, August 14, 1867, F. B. Drapp to E. W.
Hubard, July 8, 1867, all in Hubard Family Papers.

lapsed and town fathers were paying 22 percent interest for short-term loans needed to maintain minimal fire and police services. In a November 20 advisory election, however, the Augusta taxpayers voted by a margin of six to one to support a $100,000 bond issue for the Augusta and Columbia Railroad. The Augusta *Daily Press* claimed that completion of the east-west road from Augusta to Columbia would mean that the "grain of the great west will come whirling into our midst . . . ; manufactories will grow apace . . . and wealth will flow into the coffers of the people." It was no time to listen to the timid few who warned of bankruptcy and counseled frugality. "We live in an age of enterprise and progress . . . ; we must move along with that spirit."[53]

Alabama, Arkansas, and North Carolina were most generous in granting state aid. Alabama's "act to establish a system of internal improvements" authorized state endorsement of first mortgage bonds up to $24,000 for each twenty miles of laid track. Aside from minimal restrictions on the subsidy (bonds were not to be sold for less than ninety cents on the dollar), any railroad company that laid the requisite twenty miles of track was eligible under the act. But the state legislature's generosity did not stop there. Time after time, the legislature passed bills empowering local governments to endorse railroad bonds, even when these municipalities were effectively bankrupt. And the legislators also excluded a number of lines from any state taxation. Arkansas's "act in the aid of railroad construction" was almost identical and was made even more valuable by a blanket five-year exemption from state taxes. Jonathan Worth's administration in North Carolina never granted that state's railroads the *carte blanche* railroads in Arkansas and Alabama received, but acting on an individual basis, the state guaranteed more than $3 million in railroad bonds in 1866 and 1867. Mississippi, the most cautious of the postwar state governments, refused to give direct aid to the state's roads, but the legislature did grant dozens of charters and in 1867 repealed the special tax on railroads that had been hastily levied in the fall of 1865.[54]

53. Charleston *Daily Courier*, October 12, 1866; Augusta *Constitutionalist*, November 15, 1866; Atlanta *Daily Intelligencer*, July 7, 1866; Augusta *Chronicle and Sentinel*, October 7, 1866; Augusta *Daily Press*, November 15, 20, 1866.

54. *Alabama Acts*, 1866–67, pp. 4–8, 23, 60, 359, 686–93; *Acts of Arkansas*, 1866–67, pp. 303–304, 333–34, 428–32; James Gregoire de Roulhac Hamilton, *Reconstruction in North Carolina* (New York, 1914), 427; Vicksburg *Herald*, January 23, 20, 1867; William C. Harris, *Presidential Reconstruction in Mississippi* (Baton Rouge, 1967), 214–16. As the conservative Alabama historian, A. B. Moore, observed nearly fifty years ago, the legislatures of the provisional government of that state passed legislation that "served as a basis for all of the state aid laws of the Carpetbag-Scalawag regime." The carpetbaggers, he observed, merely "adopted and extended policies already in place." Moore, "Railroad Building in Alabama During the Reconstruction Period," *JSH*, I (1935), 422.

Georgia's more established railroad companies, fearing that postwar subsidies would go primarily to new and competing firms, lobbied against additional state aid in the 1866 and 1867 legislative sessions. But even with the opposition of the most powerful railroad companies in the state, it took vigorous lobbying and the repeated vetoes of Governor Charles Jenkins to narrowly beat back measures that would have surpassed those of Alabama and Arkansas in the support of railroad construction.[55]

State subsidies and direct aid to the railroads of the region were not a postwar phenomenon; many of the most important lines were directly or indirectly owned by state governments. But the alacrity with which the impoverished legislatures of 1865 and 1866 laid plans for underwriting the region's railroad corporations reflected the strong continuity of postwar economic policy between the Johnson governments and the Republican regimes that followed. Had the provisional governments of 1865–1867 remained in power, they would undoubtedly have continued the ambitious programs of railroad subsidization that were to be associated with the Republican regimes of "Radical" Reconstruction. And there is little evidence that they would have been free from the excesses that plagued the biracial legislatures of the late 1860s and 1870s.

In at least one state the railroads themselves were to be the foundation of a broad program of state-supported capital investment. The Mississippi legislature established the "American Industrial Agency" with authority to invest in the stocks and bonds of "sound" railroad corporations. These stocks in turn were to be "held as the basis of credit, enabling the company to obtain money and credit upon such time and upon such terms as well enable them . . . to make loans and advances to Railroad companies, farmers, planters, manufacturers and others, upon terms more favorable than such loans are usually made by banks." What made this investment company unusual was that it was required to deposit its bonds with the state treasurer as security. Supposedly, this would give greater confidence and security to potential investors in the company.[56]

Although railroads led the way in the incorporation epidemic of 1865 and 1866, legislators seemed intent on dragging the South into the forefront of the modern industrial world by fiat. One delegate from the 1865 Alabama constitutional convention returned home late that year to form the Clarke County Petroleum and Manufacturing Company. The new corporation, Samuel Forward predicted, would soon exploit the vast petroleum reserves of Clarke County and make its stockholders rich beyond their imaginations. He seemed undeterred by the absence of any geological evidence that petroleum existed within fifteen hundred miles of his black-belt home.[57]

Other would-be entrepreneurs matched Forward's enthusiasm. A dozen Selma businessmen and planters laid plans for a corporately owned group of first-class hotels to be built across the devastated South. Within five years, the traveler would no longer have to endure the discomfort and misery of the "filthy and decrepit hostelries" that made up the majority of the region's accommodations. Forty miles south of Selma, three residents of Alabama's port city formed the Mobile Camel Company and announced their scheme to import the desert beasts into the South to make up for the shortage of mules. These agile beasts, claimed their promoters, would make the mule as obsolete as the ox.[58]

Alabama led the South in chartering new enterprises, incorporating during a six-week period seven mining firms, twenty manufacturing corporations, thirteen insurance companies, five new railroads, four savings and loan associations, and a dozen other miscellaneous corporations. Georgia was a close second, as the editor of the Columbus *Enquirer* noted in February of 1866. Readers examining the reports of the legislatures of those states might be surprised, he observed, but anyone who understood the "healthy effect" emancipation had had upon the South's "investment of capital" should have realized that these developments were "inevitable." During the three-month period, the Georgia legislature incorporated eighty-three manufacturing and mining companies for aspiring state capitalists spurred on by exaggerated reports of profits to be made from manufacturing or from the "staggering caches" of gold, oil, gas, iron, coal, copper, and other mineral deposits. North Carolina's England and American Wool and Vine Growing, Mining, Manufacturing and Agricultural Association in the United States needed only reference to a ferry crossing, savings and loan association, and railroad to make it a completely inclusive symbol for the dreams of postwar development.[59]

For the South's postwar political leadership, the granting of generous charters was an inexpensive way of promoting industrial development, but their ingenuity extended to the most unlikely avenues of the southern po-

57. Samuel Forward to William Stump Forward, May 22, 1866, in William Stump Forward Papers, SHC.
58. Montgomery *Advertiser*, February 21, 1866.
59. Columbus (Ga.) *Enquirer*, February 22, 1866. Here again it is tempting to overestimate the shift between antebellum and postbellum attitudes toward industrialization. As Stephen Goldfarb noted in his recent article, planter-dominated state legislatures often encouraged industry, passing limited liability laws and granting shareholders (in manufacturing corporations) limited liability. Stephen J. Goldfarb, "A Note on Limits of Growth of the Cotton-Textile Industry in the Old South," *JSH*, XLVIII (1982), 548.

litical economy. No aspect of government services was more affected by the war than the region's prison system. In the spring of 1865 only the Texas State Prison at Huntsville remained intact; the remaining pentitentiaries had been put to the torch by Union troops or, in three instances, by half-starved convicts abandoned by retreating Confederate soldiers. The destruction of the limited antebellum prison system, and the reluctance of politicians of all persuasions to appropriate additional funds were the primary factors in the history of postwar southern penology. As one North Carolina prisoner testified in 1872, he could find little difference in the conditions of prison life whether governed by Democrats or Republicans, federal troops or state officials. There was the same wretched food (enlivened by an occasional rat or cat that happened to stray into reach) and the same mortality rate of 10 to 20 percent a year.[60]

Racism played an even more important role. A number of postwar southerners were remarkably blunt in emphasizing their conviction that emancipation had dramatically altered the options available for controlling what was certain to be an "epidemic of crime" by the emancipated slaves. "The champions of the penitentiary seem to forget that our social system has been completely overturned," scolded the Macon *Daily Telegraph* when a Georgia legislator proposed the expansion of the state's prison. Under the circumstances, the majority of southerners would probably have preferred to return to the time-honored antebellum practices: execution for a broad range of "capital crimes," prison sentences for serious offenses, fines for minor crimes by respectable individuals, and the whipping post with the lashes "well laid on" for most freedmen and for those "white men who have sunk to that level." Efforts to return to the whipping post brought a quick response from army and Freedmen's Bureau officials. As General Daniel Sickles told South Carolina's James L. Orr, such a form of punishment simply could not be allowed. Rightly or wrongly, he said, it was a form of punishment "associated with the epoch of slavery" and totally unacceptable to northern public opinion.[61]

Somewhat suprisingly, a number of southerners agreed. One Milledge-ville, Georgia, resident scathingly condemned the whipping post and the antebellum branding iron as "barbaric instruments" no longer acceptable in an enlightened age. A grand jury in Fulton County, Georgia, argued

60. Dan T. Carter, "Prisons, Politics, and Business: The Convict Lease System in the Post–Civil War South" (M.A. thesis, University of Wisconsin, 1964), 35–61.

61. Natchez *Daily Courier*, October 18, 1865; A. B. Springs to Orr, October 22, 1866, Daniel Stickles to Orr, October 25, 1866; Francis Fickling to Orr, October 18, 1866, all in Orr Papers; Samuel Agnew diary, SHC, July 20, 1865; Raleigh *Tri-Weekly Standard*, April 14, 1866; Judge James S. Hook to Gov. James Johnson, August 22, 1865, in Georgia Governors' Papers, GA.

that such a relic of the past was "shocking to the finer sense of humanity."[62]
Alabama's penitentiary warden William G. Moore proposed a solution.
In a report to Governor Robert M. Patton he graphically described the destruction of the state prison at Wetumpka and the enormous costs that
would be required to restore the antebellum system. Fortunately, he concluded, the "changed conditions" of the postwar era offered new opportunities. Alabama was on the verge of considerable expansion in its manufacturing and mineral interests. Why, he asked rhetorically, could the state's
prison population not become a boon to this process? By placing the state's
convicts at work in the coal mines, railroads, canals, and roads, under the
control of enterprising businessmen, they could become a "lever" rather
than an "obstacle" to the development of these interests.[63]

Not the least of the advantages of the convict-lease system was the personal financial gain to be made from controlling the labor of thousands of
criminal workers. The ever resourceful Governor Patton of Alabama enthusiastically endorsed Warden Moore's proposal—first persuading the
legislature of Alabama to approve the leasing of all of that state's convicts to
a private company, then secretly collaborating with business associates to
form the convict-leasing company of Smith and McMillan. The new company, of which Patton was a silent partner, received control of over four
hundred convicts without restrictions, plus $15,000 as a payment for re-
lieving the state of the "burdensome expenses" of maintaining the state
prison at Wetumpka. At the county level, variations of the same practice
sprang up as black-belt planters assumed the fines of freedmen employees
who ran afoul of the law on the condition that the fines be "worked out"
under long-term contracts.[64]

Within months after the restoration of self-government in the South,
special commissions and legislative committees in five states had endorsed
the transfer of convicts to private businessmen and developers. Several
southern (as well as northern) states had leased prison labor to private entrepreneurs before 1860, but the convict-lease system of the postwar South
marked a radical departure in two respects. First, entrepreneurial lessees
were given the authority to employ convicts not simply within prison walls
but, in the words of the Alabama statute, "wherever the said lessee may

62. Atlanta *Daily Intelligencer*, February 21, July 29, 1866; Washington, D.C., *National Intelligencer*, January 13, 1866.
63. William G. Moore to Patton, January 17, 1866, in Alabama Governors' Papers.
64. See "Petitions for Pardons" and "Penitentiary Files" of Governors Lewis E. Parson and Robert K. Patton, Alabama Governors' Papers. The "Smith" of Smith and McMillan was William Smith, Alabama's first postwar Republican governor. See William Smith to Governor Robert M. Patton, May 12, 1866, Alabama Governors' Papers.

deem advantageous to their interests." Second, all discipline, control, and maintenance of the prisoners passed from the state to supervising businessmen.

In defending this new departure, a special Georgia committee appointed to recommend changes in the state's prisons concluded that the foremost priority of "civilized government" was the "development of the state's economic resources." The state's penitentiary ("an incubus at best upon the state") could be used in exploiting Georgia's great mineral resources and building new railroads to the benefit of all its citizens. One by one, the postwar southern legislatures authorized the leasing of prisoners to private entrepreneurs, each lease accompanied by pious assurances that the "health and well-being" of the prisoners would be safeguarded.[65]

A handful of southern veterans of the antebellum prison reform movement protested that the abrogation of state control would inevitably mean the "cruel and inhumane maltreatment of these helpless wards of the state" and the abandonment of any hope of "reforming and restoring these lost wretches to a life free from crime and degredation." But Moore's proposal was an idea whose time had come. Southerners had never had great faith in the notion of prison as a means of reformation. The idea was a "sham and delusion," said one former member of the Alabama legislature. Millions had been spent on the region's criminals without "ever having even approached reformation in a single instance."[66]

With few critics to defend the hapless, mostly black postwar prisoners, the convict-lease system reflected the fortuitous conjunction of self-interest and regional economic development in the postwar policies of the Johnson governments, the Republicans that followed, and the white supremacy "redeemer" regimes that in turn replaced the Republicans. The system would continue uninterrupted for the most part into the twentieth century—a legacy of the dreams of painless economic development filtered through postwar poverty, greed and racism.[67]

65. "Report of the Special Committee on the Penitentiary, November 2, 1866," in Descriptive Inventory No. 1, Records of the Georgia Prison Commission, 1817–1936, GA; Hendersonville (N.C.) *Pioneer*, n.d., quoted in Raleigh *Tri-Weekly Standard*, June 26, 1866; Macon *Daily Telegraph*, January 27, 1866; "Annual Report of the Board of Control for the Louisiana State Penitentiary, 1867," *Louisiana Legislative Documents*, 1867; Paul B. Foreman and Julien R. Tatum, "A Short History of Mississippi's State Penal System," *MLJ*, X (1938), 260; *Alabama Acts*, 1866–67, pp. 86–87, 183; *Acts of Arkansas*, 1866–67, pp. 76, 455.

66. S. D. Morgan to Patton, November 28, 1866, in Alabama Governors' Papers; Gladys Gessell King, "History of the Alabama Convict Department" (M.A. thesis, Alabama Polytechnic Institute, 1937), 72–75.

67. Mark Carleton, *Politics and Punishment: The History of the Louisiana State Penal System* (Baton Rouge, 1971).

It was all a beguiling prospect. The "newspaper editors keep promising that a 'Great Day' is coming and our farmland is going to become the Garden of Eden and every creek from Pensacola to Richmond will be turning the waterwheels of factories & c., & c.," observed Alexander Kirkman of South Carolina. "I am beginning to think that we won the war and the Yankees lost."[68]

Alexander Kirkman's scepticism was well taken, for many of the plans for self-reconstruction were moral exhortations rather than practical blueprints for postwar modernization. And they all rested upon the willingness of a militarily defeated, economically devastated, and politically embittered people to cast aside their historic misgivings and embark on an ambitious program of state-supported industrial development. The proponents of economic transformation had scarcely outlined their postwar scenario before their opponents had begun to fight back.

For a generation the more reactionary elements of the old planter class had stressed the link between northern radicalism and "corporation slavery," and in 1865 they resumed the arguments where they had left in 1861. The corporation was an efficient mechanism for combining capital and labor, conceded South Carolina's former governor Francis Pickens, but it remained a system even "more heartless and selfish and more grinding to the face of the poor" than the antebellum slave system. The corporation with its promises of wealth and prosperity was "full of professions of humanity; but under it, all are educated to hypocrisy, to flattery, to deceit and selfishness." Southern slavery was an "open system of undisguised force; the other [corporate slavery] is a system of disguised fraud." As the remnants of the old system of "patriarchal slavery" disappeared there would be a "new system of modern slavery . . . , whereby the whites and blacks shall both be owned by capitalists and associated wealth in the shape of corporations [protected] through the power of government." Corporations, "hedged around with peculiar privileges and exemptions," could "truly be said to possess no soul," warned the editor of the Augusta *Chronicle and Sentinel*.[69]

Although Pickens was not alone in his attacks upon corporate slavery (George Fitzhugh saw developments as the fruition of his gloomiest antebellum prophecies), such reactionary rhetoric was important because it

68. Alexander Kirkman to Orr, January 11, 1866, in South Carolina Governors' Papers, SCA.
69. *Letter of Hon. Francis W. Pickens. The Crops and Conditions of the Country. The Interests of Labor. Effects of Emancipation. The Different Races of Mankind. Written to a Gentleman of New Orleans* (Baltimore, 1866), 12; Augusta *Chronicle and Sentinel*, June 8, 1866. For similar expressions of anticorporate hostility from the perspective of the old planter class, see Richmond *Whig*, April 4, 1866.

rested upon the continuing suspicion of the great mass of southerners that corporations and state-supported economic development led only to monopolies, which enriched elites at the expense of the masses. A Louisiana Democrat had summarized the Jacksonian credo in 1852, "The Whigs want banks to steal the money of the people and . . . railroads to run away with it." Corporations of all kinds were by their very nature "engines of popular oppression," claimed Benjamin Yancey in 1839, "combinations . . . of wealth against labor, of the rich against the poor."[70]

The bitter sectional conflict of the 1850s, the breakup of the party system, and the passions of the war itself had blurred the memories of these antebellum fears, but the very poverty of postwar southerners acted as a catalyst for renewed denunciations of banks, railroads, and corporations of all kinds. By *corporations*, most critical southerners meant natural or potential monopolies that combined great economic influence with the direct or indirect power of the state. Thus, they were far more likely to denounce railroads, banks, and semipublic institutions than private businesses, which were rarely incorporated in any case. Even on this point, however, there was a common ground of suspicion and distrust among a substantial minority—perhaps a majority—of white southerners against the significant accumulation of nonagricultural power and wealth in any form.

When three hundred small farmers gathered in Yorkville, South Carolina, in the late summer of 1866 to petition their legislature for relief, they attacked banks and railroads for "thundering at the door of . . . [the] capital" for new charters and relief from the provisions of old ones. But they warned as well of the growth of new concentrations of power in private business, as well as banking and railroad construction, ventures intent upon obtaining favorable legislation and charters of incorporation that would "grind everyone who uses them to powder" and "make slaves of you!" In less flamboyant language the editor of the Richmond *Times* warned of the dangers in the state legislature's readiness to hand over for the asking "charters, monopolies and vast exclusive privileges." Whole counties were being handed over to incorporated companies with almost "unlimited privilege to dig, mine, build and do, in a word, anything and everything." The promises of business promoters were "presented in apples of gold, in pictures of silver," warned Josiah Parrott of Bartow County, Georgia, "but within, it is bitter and ashes."[71]

70. Roger W. Shugg, *Origins of the Class Struggle in Louisiana: A Social History of White Farmers and Laborers During Slavery and After, 1840–1875* (Baton Rouge, 1939), 137; Thornton, *Politics and Power*, 108–109.

71. Yorkville (S.C.) *Enquirer*, October 1, 25, 1866; Macon *Daily Telegraph*, November 4, 1865; Richmond *Times*, February 3, 6, 8, 1866.

On the surface, most southerners appeared eager to encourage northern investment in the southern economy. Even the most sceptical northern visitors commented upon white southerners' enthusiasm for northern capital. Still, there remained an undercurrent of hostility. Southerners talked endlessly of the advantages of northern capital and its promise of making the South rich and prosperous, warned a Virginia planter, but in this eagerness to obtain northern capital, there was always the danger that these economic organizations would become so powerful that they would "paralyze . . . the wants and sentiments of the people." As the editor of the Augusta *Chronicle and Sentinel* warned, corporations "hedged around with peculiar privileges and exemptions" were always a threat to the political system. When these were northern corporations with little interest in the southern people, the danger was even greater.[72]

For the proponents of economic self-reconstruction, there was also the danger that an aggressive promotion of large-scale business and corporate development would arouse the suspicions of the great mass of southerners. One Alabama business promoter and former Whig reminded Governor Robert M. Patton that the "old party" had been whipsawed between accusations of elitism and charges that southern whiggery was subservient to northern political and economic interests. And even though the events of the war had moved the region's conservative, traditional leadership into positions of power, the events of the war itself had also exacerbated class divisions.[73]

Antebellum southerners outside the plantation elite had often complained of an inequitable tax structure, which they believed unfairly benefited slaveowners. In North Carolina and Alabama, for example, spokesmen for these states' small farmers had persistently agitated for an *ad valorem* tax system that would have shifted the tax burden to the shoulders of the wealthy slaveowners. As the wartime tax burdens increased, old resentments of this allegedly inequitable revenue system grew—a resentment exacerbated by the fact that most southerners acknowledged that the war was "essentially a struggle for the rights of [slave] property," and yet the southerners who benefited most, the largest slaveowners, were legally exempted from combat. (In 1862 the Confederate Congress had exempted from the draft all landowners or overseers who supervised twenty or more slaves.)[74]

72. Richmond *Whig*, May 23, 1866; Augusta *Chronicle and Sentinel*, June 8, 1866; Richmond *Times*, February 12, 1866; Harrison to Edmund Hubard, July 16, 1867, Hubard Family Papers.
73. Daniel Pratt to Patton, November 23, 1865, in Alabama Governors' Papers.
74. George Anderson Mercer Diary, SHC, June 11, 1865.

In point of fact, the Confederate conscription legislation also exempted thousands of nonslaveholding southerners from miners to craftsmen, from railroad workers to the cowboys of Texas ("one male citizen for every five hundred head of cattle"). Nor is there any evidence that the proud "chivalry" of the region systematically avoided military service; social pressure alone forced most prominent slaveowners of military age to take up arms for the Confederacy.[75]

Moreover, despite well-publicized instances of hoarding, profiteering, and tax evasion by the South's traditional elite, the region's slaveowners paid a larger proportional share of taxes during the war than before. Although North Carolina's slaveholders successfully thwarted the taxation of their slaves at market value from 1835 to 1860, the state legislature overwhelmingly adopted *ad valorem* taxation as soon as the war began. Georgia legislators were even more determined to shift the tax burden to the state's wealthy citizens. The legislature combined an *ad valorem* tax, a progressive income tax, a manufacturing tax, and an inventory tax to tap the property of the rich. Finally the southern elite's investment in Confederate and state war bonds was equivalent to massive taxation upon the wealthy—or at least the patriotically wealthy. With repudiation, their investments became out-and-out contributions to the Lost Cause.[76]

What was important, however, was not the reality but the perception of large numbers of nonslaveholding southern whites. And this bitterness erupted in print from time to time, as when a Texas spokesman for that state's small farmers bitterly attacked the region's "Tory" leaders. They feigned comaraderie with the people, he sneered, but they could not conceal their "contempt for the people, the masses" who these "self-styled

75. *The Statutes at Large of the Confederate States of America, Passed at the Second Session of the First Congress, 1862* (Richmond, 1862), 78–79.

76. In one of the few attempts to examine the tax structure of the antebellum South, J. Mills Thornton III has argued that poorer whites were exempt from significant taxation, and the "wealthiest third of the citizenry of the Lower South paid at least two-thirds of its taxes." See Thornton's "Fiscal Policy and the Failure of Radical Reconstruction in the Lower South," in J. Morgan Kousser and James M. McPherson (eds.), *Region, Race, and Reconstruction: Essays in Honor of C. Vann Woodward* (New York, 1982), 349–94. Peter Wallenstein has countered that such an evaluation is based upon the assumption that proportional rather than progressive taxation "offers the most appropriate standard of fiscal fairness." Wallenstein does conclude that Georgia forced its wealthier citizens to carry a greater tax burden during the war. With emancipation, however, their taxes became proportionally even less than before the war, as yeoman whites were forced to pick up the slack when taxes shifted from slaves to land. Wallenstein, "Rich Man's War, Rich Man's Fight: The Civil War and the Transformation of Public Finance in Georgia," *JSH*, L (1984), 15–42. See also Wallenstein, "From Slave South to New South: Taxes and Spending in Georgia from 1850 Through Reconstruction," *JEH*, XXXVI (1976), 287–90. For an examination of this issue in North Carolina, see Donald Butts, "The 'Irrepressible Conflict': Slave Taxation and North Carolina's Gubernatorial Election of 1860," *NCHR*, LVIII (1981), 44–66.

aristocrats regarded as unfit to govern themselves." More often these resentments were expressed privately among friends. It was the "poor and
middling classes" who had borne the burdens of the war, concluded a
small-scale slaveowner in upstate South Carolina, but it was the rich who
had profited by hoarding meat and supplies, waiting for higher prices and
refusing to be paid in the "poor people's" currency (Confederate money).
They would not deny themselves even "one solitary comfort to satisfy the
hunger of the soldiers," concluded Robert Hemphill. "I am beginning to be
of the opinion of the Yankee, that this was the Rich Man's war but the *poor*
man's fight." As a bitter Sumter County, Georgia, soldier wrote in his
diary, "Demagogues wanted this war for want of sense; rich men wanted it
to save their slaves."[77]

Such a conclusion was hardly shared by that wealthy minority of southerners, who had never reconciled themselves to the democratization of the
white South. As the Confederacy collapsed, they railed against the "ignorant masses" and blamed them both for causing the war and for failing to
support the struggle for independence. It was the "mobocracy" that had
hysterically demanded the war and then abandoned the new nation, claimed
the southern novelist William Gilmore Simms. The existence of a "free and
equal suffrage" had been the basic weakness of the new nation, agreed
a bitter North Carolina planter. The "lower class" had abandoned the
struggle for independence once sacrifice was required, while "those elevated by birth or education . . . contended against fearful odds with a con-
stancy and heroism never surpassed." Unrestricted suffrage would continue
to furnish an opportunity for ambitious demagogues to exploit the "ignorance and unscrupulousness of the masses," who were as "great a threat as
the Yankees." Ultimately, their influence in shaping policies would "prostrate property and the material interest of the country in order to gratify a
morbid and false sentimentality." In an all too typical example of convenient
amnesia, South Carolina's former governor Pickens, a leading secessionist
in 1860, claimed that it had been the "fiery and uncalculating" small property holders and the landless who had provoked disunion.[78]

For a handful of frightened conservatives, these "unthinking masses"
posed an even greater danger in the unsettled conditions of the postwar

77. Houston *Tri-Weekly Telegraph*, January 30, February 1, 1865; R. N. Hemphill to Rev.
W. R. Hemphill, May 19, 1865, in Hemphill Collection, DUL; James Appleton Blackshear
Diary, EU, January 26, 1865.
78. William Newton Mercer Diary, LSU, June 11, 1865; David Schenck Diary, SHC,
December 12, 1864, February 19, 1865; *Letter of Francis Pickens*, 5–6; Columbia (S.C.) *Phoenix*, April 26, 1865. In his memoirs, Union General James H. Wilson observed that many
upper-class Georgia leaders took some solace that the "plebeian" Joseph E. Brown was in
worse trouble than they. Wilson, *Under the Old Flag* (New York, 1912), 250–56.

South, particularly when there was the nightmarish possibility that blacks might be given the vote. For many conservatives, the repudiation of the state war debts had been the first battle, and it had been lost. In the fall and winter of 1865, the second was joined as state legislators responded to the pleas of their constituents and introduced laws that would allow debtors to postpone repayment of their obligations. Although often ignored in the controversy over race and the differences between North and South, these proposed stay laws provoked more angry internal division among whites than any single issue in the postwar South.

To proponents of debt-relief legislation, the need for action seemed self-evident. Between September of 1865 and the end of 1866, northern and local creditors filed forty thousand lawsuits in South Carolina's courts. Mississippians in one black-belt county were served with more than four hundred lawsuits in one week as creditors scrambled to protect their interests against other litigants and to pressure debtors to settle outstanding obligations. As the Georgia legislature concluded in a joint resolution, the people of that state were in "great fear lest creditors should . . . seize the little property remaining since the disasters of the war." To conservatives, that fearfulness was ominously reflected in bitter recriminations and angry threats. "The sons of a certain character in Shakespeare's *Merchant of Venice* are abroad in the land seeking their pound of flesh," complained a Delta planter, while citizens in hundreds of rallies demanded that their elected leaders act decisively. We would "deprecate a resort to violent measures for the redress of . . . these grievances," insisted three South Carolina rallies, "but violence is inevitable unless our property is protected."[79]

As the pressure grew for state legislation delaying the repayment of debts, frantic doctrinaire conservatives responded with dire warnings of anarchy and economic chaos. Old-line Whigs were horrified at the prospect of any legislation that would modify the contractual obligation of debtor to creditor. In practical terms, argued several conservatives, this would place state residents at a decided disadvantage to out-of-state creditors (particularly northerners), who would be able to take their case directly to the federal courts to enforce their economic rights. But the real hostility toward such legislation was emotionally ideological. "Our life-long position on these questions—the very basis on which the old Whig Party was built—should not be regarded as a position properly to be abandoned now or at any

79. Simkins and Woody, *South Carolina During Reconstruction*, 46; Harris, *Presidential Reconstruction in Mississippi*, 178; Henri M. Freeman, "Some Aspects of Debtor Relief in Georgia During Reconstruction" (M.A. thesis, Emory University, 1951), 17; Newberry Citizens Meeting to Orr, July 3, 1866; Citizens Meeting of Abbeville, S.C., to Orr, July 16, 1866; Citizens Meeting of Edgefield, S.C., to Orr, July 16, 1866, all in Orr Papers.

other time." In a phrase that recurred among such conservatives, the old Virginia Whig R. T. Hubard scolded his vacillating brother with the warning that any tampering with contracts or debts was "immoral and unconstitutional," in the words of Benjamin Perry, a "violation of the sacred laws of political economics."[80]

The postponement of the collection of debts would only delay the state's recovery, Mississippi's first elected postwar governor told that state's legislature. The only way to restore the state's fortunes was through "patient industry, strict economy and 'long suffering,'" not through such unconstitutional measures as stay laws. "Temporary relief from debt often tends only to additional embarrassments," insisted Benjamin Humphreys. One Alabamian called such legislation "financial morphia which temporarily dulls the pain, but ultimately kills," and a special committee of the South Carolina house warned that northern capital would shun the South if this "disgraceful legislation" were enacted. Howell Cobb of Georgia went so far as to insist that the state and federal governments had no authority to modify contracts of debts unless their action "advocated the efficacy of collection contracts," a position described by one up-country editor as amounting to the notion that the "state can always act to forward the cause of the rich, but never that of the poor."[81]

Even though the stay laws for private debtors and the relief legislation for bank stockholders and officers were technically unrelated, they became barometers by which southern voters measured the responsiveness of their postwar leadership. And they created an agonizing political dilemma for many conservatives.

The banking industry's crisis was authentic. The repudiation of the southern states' wartime obligations had been the last in a series of crippling events. By the end of 1865, the president of the Planter's Bank of Georgia confronted a ledger book typical for most southern banks. He had significant numbers of worthless Confederate and state war bonds, as well as securities and mortgages on property worth only a fraction of the liabilities of stockholders and depositors. "It is a matter of the deepest mortification to me," reported the state's comptroller general, that the banks of Georgia were "hopelessly bankrupt." By January, 1868, every one of the

80. Harris, *Presidential Reconstruction in Mississippi*, 175; R. T. Hubard to Edmund Hubard, September 21, 1866, in Hubard Family Papers; Benjamin Perry to Father, December 15, 1865, in Benjamin Perry Manuscripts (Microfilm, 2 reels, SHC, 1967). Conservative critics were probably right in their assessment of the attitude of the federal courts. See, for example, *Shortridge v. Macon*, I Abbot U.S., 58.

81. New York *Times*, February 4, 1866; New Orleans *Picayune*, October 18, 1866; Atlanta *Daily Intelligencer*, June 20, 30, July 6, 1866; Huntsville (Ala.) *Advocate*, November 12, 1866; *Report of the Special Committee on Immigration*, 19.

state's twenty-five antebellum banks had declared bankruptcy and closed its doors.[82]

In the long run, financial recovery required the creation of a sound and profitable banking system; in the short run, there was the pressing problem for bank officers and stockholders that the restrictive charters issued in several southern states made investors personally liable for the debts incurred by the banks in which they had invested. Understandably, investors took the position that these dramatically increased liabilities existed through no fault of the banks but because of the unforeseen events of the war. Moreover, in at least three southern states, investors had purchased bank bonds in 1864 and 1865 with heavily depreciated Confederate currency, and bank stockholders understandably felt it unreasonable that the banks should have to repay at par. Lobbyists in Georgia, North Carolina, and South Carolina pleaded for relief measures that would absolve them of liability or, at the very least, allow adjustment of their investment to specie value on the date of purchase. Although the situation was probably hopeless, one sympathetic legislator concluded, such legislation would protect innocent investors, and it might stave off bankruptcy for a few banks. Even Joseph Brown of Georgia, that implacable antebellum foe of the banking establishment, reversed himself and lobbied for bank relief legislation, although his change of heart may have been encouraged by a confidential lobbying fee of five thousand dollars from four of Augusta's banks.[83]

Postwar conservative leaders also attacked the interest restrictions that existed in all but two of the antebellum southern states. Such usury legislation, which placed a legal ceiling of 6 or 7 percent on all loans, was realistic in the antebellum period, agreed one Mississippi planter (an old-line Whig), but it made no sense at a time when he was paying 2.5 percent per month. With considerable exaggeration, the Richmond *Times*, a strong opponent of the state's usury law, claimed that banks and capitalists—particularly those in the North—were "absolutely gorged with greenbacks," but the state's usury law made capital "shun Virginia as the cup of water evaded the fevered and eager grasp of Tantalus."[84]

However rational as a policy to lay the groundwork for postwar economic development, the disparity between the treatment for banks and the

82. *Annual Report of the Comptroller General of Georgia, 1866*, 88–89; *Report of Madison Bell, Comptroller General of Georgia, 1869*, 18–20.
83. Yorkville (S.C.) *Enquirer*, August 6, 1866; Atlanta *Daily Intelligencer*, February 11, 1866; Macon *Daily Telegraph*, March 18, 1866; A. A. Gilbert to T. B. Fraser, September 19, 1866, in Fraser Papers, SCL; Kimberly to Orr, November 23, 1866, in Orr Papers; Joseph Brown to Alfred Baker, January 22, 1866, in McLeod Collection, UGL.
84. See Richmond *Times*, January 3, 20, 1866; *Fa*, II (1867), 1011; Augusta *Daily Press*, October 25, 1866; Atlanta *Daily Intelligencer*, January 27, 1866.

treatment for private citizens angered impoverished southerners and divided southern conservative leadership. While the state banks were "thundering at the door of . . . the capital" for permission to "repudiate their just debts due to citizens," claimed one up-country South Carolina rally, they spurned the pleas of honest citizens for a brief postponement in the payment of their debts. "What more favorable claim have they [the banks] to such indulgence than any other man engaged in other businesses or avocations?" Even a proponent of bank-relief legislation acknowledged that, on the surface, it would be a "glaring and outrageous" example of legislative favoritism.[85]

The legislatures of six southern states voted on various forms of bank-relief legislation in 1865 and 1866. Georgia's legislature relieved bank stockholders and officers of criminal penalties since they were forced into bankruptcy. (The constitutional convention of 1865 had defeated a similar measure 132 to 125.) It took the combined efforts of Governor Jenkins and the skillful behind-the-scenes lobbying of Joseph Brown to push through this limited bill. The North Carolina legislature, with the help of a barrel of whiskey and some judicious lobbying, came within four votes of repaying banks for the depreciated value of two forced loans made to the state during the war. In every other instance, the postwar legislation rejected the pleas of banks for assistance by decisive margins. By mid-1866 there were only a handful of state-chartered banks functioning effectively in the entire region.[86]

In contrast to this unsympathetic attitude toward the region's banks, eight of the eleven postwar state governments responded to the pleas of their impoverished constituents and began drafting legislation that would allow debtors to postpone repayment of their financial obligations. Georgia's lawmakers led the way, first by adopting a "scaling ordinance," which required that all debts incurred during the war be converted from depreciated currency to their actual value in gold at the time of the transaction. At the same time, the state legislature adopted a timetable under which creditors would be repaid no later than January 1, 1870. The Virginia and Arkansas stay laws were the first adopted in the southern states after the

85. Yorkville (S.C.) *Enquirer*, August 6, October 1, 1866; Atlanta *Daily Intelligencer*, February 11, 1866; W. W. Cameron to James Green Burr, September 15, 1866; Gilbert to T. B. Fraser, September 19, 1866, in Fraser Papers.

86. Allen Daniel Candler, *The Confederate Records of the State of Georgia* (4 vols.; Atlanta, 1909–11), IV, 325–31; *Acts of the Georgia General Assembly*, 1865–66, p. 313; Atlanta *Daily Intelligencer*, February 11, 1866; Macon *Daily Telegraph*, March 18, 1866; William A. Wright to James Green Burr, June 3, 1866, in John MacRae Papers, SHC; Donnell to Shepard, November 25, 1865, in Bryan Family Papers; H. A. Schroeder to Patton, July 23, 1866, in Alabama Governors' Papers.

war, but they seem to have had little effect on the shape of legislation in the region. Georgia's law, on the other hand, was reprinted in newspapers throughout the region and, with a considerable number of modifications, was enacted in all of the southern states except Florida, Louisiana, and Tennessee.[87] Stay laws were not, of course, an innovation of the post–civil war years. During hard times, responsive antebellum southern legislatures had enacted similar legislation to give temporary relief in straitened circumstances.

Most creditors, whether in New York or Charleston, were well aware of the precarious financial situation of most southern planters and were willing to adjust antebellum and war debts downward, forgiving interest accrued during the war and often reducing the outstanding principal from 10 to 60 percent. John Ingram of Manning, South Carolina, had gone north to Philadelphia in the summer of 1866, filled with dread and apprehension over the necessity of facing his four major antebellum creditors. To his surprise he was greeted warmly and sympathetically; all agreed to reduce his outstanding debts by 50 percent and to waive interest accrued during the war. With relief, he reported to his good friend Thomas Fraser that he had "not the slightest difficulty in arranging my affairs with creditors."[88] Ingram's creditors seem to have been unusually generous, but such concessions were not uncommon. In the twenty-eight postwar settlements between southern planters and northern creditors from July, 1865, to January 1, 1866, that I examined, twenty-two creditors waived wartime interest, and the average reduction of the antebellum principal was 38 percent.

Not every creditor was so forgiving, however. In January of 1861, Thomas Harrold, co-owner of one of the largest mercantile establishments in south central Georgia, had frantically destroyed all records that showed his connections with northern businessmen, and he strictly warned his son against revealing the fact that he had a silent partnership with a northern backer. Should this be known, he observed, "the political excitement and unsettled condition of affairs in the South . . . may get worse and end in mobs and depredations." After the war he tried to resume his partnership and was chagrined to discover that his former associate wanted full restitution. After months of haggling, Harrold agreed to repay 80 percent of the antebellum debt with interest computed through the war at 6 percent.[89]

87. Kenneth Edson St. Clair, "Debtor Relief in North Carolina During Reconstruction," *NCHR*, XVIII (1941), 215–16; Freeman, "Debtor Relief in Georgia"; *Acts of the Georgia Assembly*, 1865–66, pp. 241–42, 256–57; *Acts of Arkansas*, 1864–65, p. 27–28; *Statutes of South Carolina*, 1865–66, p. 285–86; Harris, *Presidential Reconstruction in Mississippi*, 176.
88. Ingram to T. B. Fraser, August 18, 1866, in Fraser Papers.
89. Thomas Harrold to Thomas Wood, June 17, 1866, Wood to W. B. Harrold, June 26,

Understandably, southern planters and businessmen were most concerned over whether their creditors would try to extract "Shylock's last pound of flesh" or would act as "gentlemen, sympathetically mindful of havoc wrought by the war." Far more significant, however, was the growing importance of those "Northern connections" that had always existed between credit-dependent southerners and northern suppliers. E. H. Deas of Berkeley County, South Carolina, had occasionally arranged loans from northern investors during hard times in the 1840s and 1850s, but he was unprepared for the difficulties he encountered in the winter of 1865–1866. After making the rounds in New York City and calling upon every investor he knew and many he did not, Deas finally managed to borrow $2,500 from a New York businessman. In order to obtain the loan, he had to put up his plantation (worth $150,000 before the war) as collateral and to pay 28 percent interest. Other planters reported similar arrangements. The "easy credit ways" of the 1850s were gone, a bitter Henry Blanding told his brother. The only way southern planters could survive was to accept interest rates "heretofore regarded as ruinous" and to "mortgage their places to Yankees."[90]

Blanding and his fellow planters sometimes exaggerated this new reliance upon "Yankee capital"; northern businessmen had always played a critical role in funding the cotton economy. Nevertheless, they were correct in concluding that wartime devastation and emancipation had brought a revolution in the financial infrastructure of the region's economy. If the antebellum factorage credit system was ultimately doomed by a combination of circumstances unrelated to the war, such as changes in transportation and communications, the destruction of the southern banking structure and the near bankruptcy of many casual sources of local capital accelerated this demise and led to a desperate reliance upon northern sources of capital. As one Georgetown, South Carolina, factor frankly admitted to an old friend, without the support of New York investors, he and most of his fellow factors would be on the streets.[91]

1866, W. B. Harrold to R. R. Graves and Co., June 30, 1866, W. B. Harrold to George Williams, July 3, 1866, W. B. Harrold to Uriah B. Harrold, July 3, 8, 12, 1866, Uriah B. Harrold to Thomas Harrold, July 2, 1866, all in Harrold Brothers Papers, EU.

90. Articles of Agreement Between E. H. Deas and Edward L. Minot, April 18, 1866, in Elias H. Deas Papers, SCL; Henry Blanding to James Douglass Blanding, May 30, 1866, in James Douglas Blanding Papers, SCL.

91. Pressley, Lord, and Inglesby to Dr. E. E. Ellis, October 24, 1865, in Ellis Family Papers. See also J. G. Guignard to Adams and Frost, Cotton Brokers, October 8, 1866, in Guignard Family Papers, SCL; Samuel Fraser to T. B. Fraser, September 18, 1865, and J. Harby Moses to Samuel Fraser, October 27, 1865, both in Fraser Papers; Henry Blanding to James Douglass Blanding, April 27, 1866, in L'Engle Papers. The Gordon Family Papers,

As they confronted the uncertainties of the postwar economy with fresh memories of unpaid antebellum loans, northern business investors reacted predictably to the legislative proposals for the postponement of debt repayment in the region. Such legislation was "phase two of the civil war," claimed Henry Raymond of the New York *Times*, "odious to every principle of justice" and "actuated by feelings of revenge they hope to inflict upon the North." The editors of the Boston *Advertiser* could find no clearer evidence of the intimate connection between "high treason" and "financial immorality" than the efforts of postwar southerners to "cast off the sacred obligations of the financial obligations they have incurred, just as they cast off the sacred bonds of union in 1861." Henry Raymond of the *Times* was not surprised to see Mississippians and Georgians put forth such "dishonorable" legislation, "but that Virginia . . . should follow an example so bad is strange and inexplicable."[92]

Northern creditors at least had the comforting assurance that, as a last resort, they could depend upon the federal courts to protect their financial interests. Southern proponents of the stay laws were less fortunate. In the months after the enactment of such legislation, ideological conservatives and creditors fought back through the judiciary, the ultimate protector of public and financial morality. Frustrated by the state legislature, South Carolina's stay-law opponents obtained an injunction against the enforcement of the legislation from the state appeals court. Although the legislature temporarily thwarted the judiciary by suspending the terms of the courts of common pleas for six months, once the court reconvened in the spring of 1867, it declared South Carolina's stay law null and void. Mississippi's highest court, with the support of Governor Benjamin Humphreys, overturned that state's stay law in the spring of 1866. That same year, a special Military Supreme Court in Texas set aside that state's stay law with the support of soon-to-be Radical Republican Andrew Jackson Hamilton. The state supreme courts of Georgia and North Carolina took similar action.[93]

But penury was a far greater problem for creditors than stay laws. The

---

SHC; the Harrold Brothers Papers, EU; the John C. Burrus Papers, MSA; and the Golsan Brothers Collection and the Eli Capell Papers, LSU, contain significant materials on the reshaping of credit and financial arrangements in the postwar South.

92. New York *Times*, n.d., quoted in Richmond *Times*, January 1, 1866; Boston *Advertiser*, March 22, 1866; New York *Times*, February 24, 1866. See also, "The Rehabilitation of the South," 169–74.

93. Simkins and Woody, *South Carolina During Reconstruction*, 46–47; John L. Waller, *Colossal Hamilton of Texas: A Biography of Andrew Jackson Hamilton, Militant Unionist and Reconstruction Governor* (El Paso, Tex., 1968), 107; Harris, *Presidential Reconstruction in Mississippi*, 176–77; Freeman, "Debtor Relief in Georgia," 19–20.

extraordinary lengths to which creditors went to uncover concealed property reflected the desperate times. Edward L'Engle, a diehard Florida secessionist, had planned to abandon his law practice and emigrate to Brazil in 1865. He quickly discarded the notion when he discovered the rewards to be gained by serving as an investigator and collection agent for northern creditors. L'Engle and other southern attorneys soon developed lucrative practices, surreptitiously investigating debtors and quietly locating their assets before placing liens on their property—parts of which had often been transferred secretly to other family members. The problem, as L'Engle and other creditors soon learned, was that the value of assets—particularly land—had decreased to the point that it was often more advantageous in the long run to readjust old debts, arrange for a gradual repayment, and hope for the best. This economic reality, more than stay laws, forced creditors, north and south, to compromise.[94]

Stephen Duncan learned this, and he learned as well the pressures the postwar community could bring to bear in the fall and winter of 1865. Despite constant Confederate harassment and the problems of adjusting to free labor, the wealthy Natchez planter nearly doubled his vast fortune during the war. In 1863 alone he grossed $234,000 on less than fifteen hundred of his five thousand acres. After June of 1865, he moved quickly to collect antebellum debts from fellow planters who had borrowed heavily in the late 1850s. Nothing enraged him more than the prospect of any form of stay laws. When he ordered his attorney, Zebulon Preston, to begin immediate collection procedures, however, Preston tactfully but firmly dismissed Duncan's complaints of "financial immorality." If southern planters and farmers were forced to settle their accounts immediately there would be chaos and bloodshed that would make the war pale in comparison, insisted Preston. All decent men of any compassion—not just debtors—accepted the necessity of some form of legislation that would prevent the wholesale transfer of property in the postwar South, he argued.[95]

One by one, most southern newspapers either endorsed or accepted the inevitability of some form of forced postponement of the repayment of private debts as an unavoidable consequence of the collapse of the southern economy. The Raleigh newspapers that supported Jonathan Worth first

94. L'Engle's correspondence, especially for the years 1865 and 1866, gives a particularly good insight into the frantic scramblings of postwar southerners to protect their property. In his study of the Natchez District, Michael Wayne describes a similar pattern of deception, whereby indebted planters used a variety of extralegal measures to shield their property from creditors. See Wayne, *The Reshaping of Plantation Society: The Natchez District, 1860–1880* (Baton Rouge, 1983), 91–95.

95. Preston to Duncan, December 13, December 28, 1865, in Duncan Papers.

opposed and then reluctantly endorsed such legislation. Though "we are in favor of holding every man to the performance of his contracts," insisted the editor of the *Sentinel*, "the conviction is forced upon us that if, at the present time, our people are forced to pay their individual debts, two-thirds of the real estate in the State must be forced onto the market." Changed circumstances changed men's minds, admitted one Georgia planter who had always scorned any modification of the "sacred bonds" of the contract between debtor and creditor. Linking the crisis of emancipation and the suffering of the returning Confederate veteran to the justice of that state's stay laws he asked rhetorically: Would it be "right to strip him of what land he owns before he has a reasonable time to test the virtues of the free labor system . . . ? Is it right, is it just, is it fair, is it honest to turn him out of house and home before the reverberation of the cannon has died away?" Although southern conservatives often voiced their private discomfiture over the dangerous precedent of this legislation, others were quick to warn that any attempt to force the issue would lead to "dissatisfaction among the masses" and an entering wedge for propositions of even more "radical and destructive kinds." North Carolina State Senator Leander Gash opposed stay laws throughout 1865 and into 1866. When he talked to his constituents, however, and learned of increasingly frequent incidents of organized resistance to bankruptcy sales, he reluctantly endorsed a strong measure. If something were not done, he told his wife, "the whole state would be in a mob before corn planting time." A former Georgia Whig agreed. The demands for immediate repayment would inevitably produce a "spirit of discontent, despondency and revolution."[96]

Stay laws helped as well to prevent the wholesale transfer of property away from the South's antebellum elites. It was true that land values declined precipitously in the aftermath of the war, but the purchase or lease of a plantation still required substantial capital, sums well beyond the reach of

---

96. Raleigh *Daily Sentinel*, January 30, 1866; W. T. Napier, *A Speech on the Stay Law and the State of the Country* (Macon, Ga., 1867), 6; James H. Rion to T. B. Fraser, September 29, 1866, in Fraser Papers; Ravenel Journal, September 11, 1865; Benjamin H. Wilson to Orr, June 22, 1866, in Orr Papers; W. W. Cabell to E. W. Hubard, December 18, 1866, in Hubard Family Papers. Benjamin Perry to Father, September 16, 1866, in Perry Manuscripts; Leander Gash to Wife, February 9, 1867, in Leander Gash papers, NCA. J. D. Mathews to Alexander H. Stephens, August 2, 1866, in Alexander Stephens Papers, EU. Of the twenty-three southern newspapers I examined for the postwar period, only the Charleston *Daily Courier*, the New Orleans *Picayune*, and the Mobile *Advertiser and Register* opposed *all* stay legislation. The popularity of stay legislation among the southern conservatives convinced a few Republicans that it was a conspiracy of former Confederate planters ("envenomed copperhead . . . landowners"), who saw it as a "sure retreat behind which they can safely intimidate Republicans, keep their own poor men in line and bid defiance to creditors." St. Clair, "Debtor Relief in North Carolina," 234.

most southern whites and the overwhelming majority of former slaves. Northern investors did increase their role in the postwar South to such an extent that one army general predicted northerners would soon own "every railroad, every steamboat, every large mercantile establishment, and everything which requires capital to carry it on." But however plausible this scenario may have appeared in the immediate aftermath of the war, there was no flood of northern takeovers in the troubled aftermath of the war. Several thousand northern investors did try their hand at cotton cultivation—particularly in the Delta—but two years of army worms, droughts, floods, and declining cotton prices ended this experiment. The South's old elites, particularly the planters, suffered a decline in their standard of living, but war and emancipation did not lead to their displacement as an economic and social class.[97]

These class antagonisms unquestionably continued to exist throughout the months after Appomattox. The danger of a coalition between poor white and poorer blacks was particularly on the minds of apprehensive conservatives. In 1867 Benjamin Perry, by no means an uncritical mouthpiece for the propertied interests in South Carolina, would argue against Congressional Reconstruction plans by warning that the blacks, if given the vote, would unite with poorer whites and parcel out the lands of the state. On the other hand, he had insisted in 1865 that black suffrage would give the planter class a "most undue influence in all elections. He would be able to march to the polls with his two or three hundred 'freedmen' voters," and poorer whites, Perry had warned, would have far less influence in politics. Which of these theories did Perry really believe? It is difficult to say, but

97. George Fort Milton, *The Age of Hate: Andrew Johnson and the Radicals* (New York, 1930), 244. The literature of "planter persistence" is large and growing. Although Charles and Mary Beard (*The Rise of American Civilization* [2 vols.; New York, 1927], II, 269) early popularized the notion that there had been a shift from plantations to small farms in the South after the war, Roger Shugg pointed out as early as 1937 that such an interpretation was based upon a misreading of the agricultural census. See Shugg, "Survival of the Plantation," *JSH*, III (1937), 234–73, 311–25. More recently, historians have insisted that the same antebellum planters as well as their antebellum plantations survived. As Jonathan Wiener argued, Alabama planters were as "highly persistent . . . or more than eastern urban elites of which we have knowledge." Wiener, *Social Origins of the New South: Alabama, 1860–1885* (Baton Rouge, 1978), 3–35, 229–39. Although the degree of planter persistence varied, most historians find little difference between the antebellum and postwar levels of change. See Wayne, *Reshaping of Plantation Society*, 86–91; Dwight B. Billings, Jr., *Planters and the Making of a "New South": Class, Politics, and Development in North Carolina, 1865–1900* (Chapel Hill, 1979), 70–75; Kenneth S. Greenberg, "The Civil War and the Redistribution of Land: Adams County, Mississippi, 1860–1870," *AH*, LII (1978), 292–307; C. A. Haulman, "Changes in the Economic Power Structure of Duval County, Florida, During the Civil War and Reconstruction," *FHQ*, LII (1973), 175–84; Frank Jackson Huffman, Jr., "Old South, New South: Continuity and Change in a Georgia County, 1850–1880" (Ph.D. dissertation, Yale University, 1974), 220–23.

there is suggestive evidence that Perry, like most white southerners, was willing to use any rhetorical weapon, including class, to unite white southerners in opposition to black suffrage. The base line opposition was always race. As he confided to a friend in the spring of 1867, most whites were influenced by their "fears rather than by their honor," and by pointing to the danger of black domination, he had successfully united most whites in opposition to Congressional Reconstruction. The "fire," he said, had "worked admirably."[98]

Stay laws, for example, did not reflect widespread support for out-and-out repudiation and other "agrarian" schemes, as the most timid conservatives feared. Instead, such measures reflected the economic desperation of a region of impoverished agricultural debtors—planters and yeoman farmers alike. None of the postwar legislatures in 1865 and 1866, for example, seriously considered "homestead" legislation that would have aided smaller property owners by exempting no more than two thousand dollars' worth of land or property from foreclosure. (Such legislation would have been meaningless to large-scale planters whose property was worth far more.)

There were economic interests at stake in the postwar era, and the lines between these interests would ultimately become more sharply drawn. But there simply is no widespread evidence that either the elite or the yeoman class manipulated class differences on a substantial scale; many of the political and economic issues of the postwar era were extraordinarily resistant to compartmentalization in rigid class categories. In the short run, those class differences were far less important in shaping events than a combination of defensive pride among whites centered around the experiences of the war and the heritage of regional grievances, fear of black domination, and an overwhelming spirit of defeatism and inertia.

The committed group of self-reconstructionists within the postwar Johnson governments wielded disproportionate rhetorical weight in the first months of the postwar era. But the postwar subscription list to *De Bow's Review* reflected the narrow base from which they operated. By the end of 1866, there were still only 624 subscribers to the magazine that most enthusiastically reflected the gospel of postwar development and self-

98. Charleston *Daily Courier*, May 4, 1867, September 16, 1865; Benjamin Perry to F. Marion Nye, May 25, 1866 (copy) in Perry Manuscripts. Armstead L. Robinson, "Beyond the Realm of Social Consensus: New Meanings of Reconstruction for American History," *JAH*, LXVIII (1981), 287, cites Perry's warnings of a proletarian biracial coalition, though not his comments about the dangers of upper-class manipulation of the black vote. I believe when we have considered the interaction of class and race we will still conclude that, in the immediate aftermath of slavery at least, racial considerations were most important. For an eloquently argued counter point of view see Barbara Field, "Ideology and Race in American History," in Kousser and McPherson (eds.), *Region, Race, and Reconstruction*, 151.

reconstruction. The addresses of these subscribers were as revealing as their small number. More than 200 issues went to New York City; another 265 were mailed to Nashville, Baltimore, and the southern port cities of Charleston, Savannah, New Orleans, and Mobile. The remaining 124 copies were scattered across the small agricultural market towns of the black-belt South, to Camden, Augusta, Selma, and Columbus and only occasionally to a rural community or up-country post office.[99] It was, to some degree, the same committed minority that had ineffectually challenged the antebellum plantation South, the same handful of urban newspaper editors and southern businessmen with one foot in the commercial stirrups of the Old South and the other reaching uncertainly for the South that might be, but was yet unborn.

Even the irrepressibly optimistic J. D. B. De Bow himself occasionally acknowledged the breadth of the problems of the postwar South and the inability of most of his fellow southerners to respond with what he believed was the flexibility of true conservatism. Eighteen months after the war had ended, he confided his fears to his good friend, former Alabama governor A. B. Moore. Too many southerners remained obstinately committed to the past, concluded De Bow, a past that had no meaning in the changed setting of the postwar South. And Moore agreed. When would these men of the "Bourbon school" understand that "conservatism to be powerful must now be progressive"? There was no hope for the South, concluded Moore, unless the "spirit of ongoing change can be successfully provoked."[100]

The ease with which the postwar southern leaders appropriated the slogans and rhetoric of New South economic development, even as they carefully weighed their own potential gains and losses, amounted to a dress rehearsal for the New South movement of the 1870s. The men who shaped southern postwar politics had learned a great deal from the war and from their own defeat. But they lacked the luxury of a decade of northern weariness with the southern question. Above all, they were fatally compromised by their own fears and their own illusions. If a case can be made that this conservative leadership saw, at least dimly, the need for economic and social change and the political necessity of conciliation and compromise, an even stronger case can be made that they were as shortsighted as all their fellow southerners on that most critical issue of all: the future of the freed men and women in their midst.

99. Subscription List to *De Bow's Review*, April 24, 1866, in J. D. B. De Bow Papers, DUL.
100. A. B. Moore to J. D. B. De Bow, January 25, 1867, in De Bow Papers. For a discussion of Moore's role in antebellum Alabama politics, see Thornton, *Politics and Power*, 406–407, 432–39.

V / The Proslavery Argument in a World Without Slavery

SOUTHERN whites were obsessed with race in the months after Appomattox. "Everybody talks about the negro at all hours of the day, and under all circumstances," reported a Boston journalist as he traveled through the South. "Let conversation begin where it will, it ends with Sambo." As an Ohio school teacher, arriving in Mississippi in late 1865 also discovered, in the hotels, railroads, and riverboats, wherever whites gathered, "the nigger is the everlasting theme & the general complaint is they won't work."[1]

The public pronouncements of white southerners were usually sober calls for a good faith attempt to work with free labor, coupled with warnings that the success of such an "experiment" was entirely dependent upon the leeway given to white southerners in working through this difficult period of readjustment. Privately, the observations of white southerners, particularly those tied to the old slave plantation economy, was a melange of fear, uncertainty, and deep pessimism, leavened only occasionally by a grudging and guarded optimism.

Underlying the assumptions of white southerners was their all-pervasive

1. Sidney Andrews, *The South Since the War as Shown by Fourteen Weeks of Travel and Observation in Georgia and the Carolinas* (Boston, 1866), 22; J. P. Bardwell to Rev. M. F. Strieby, November 20, 1865, in AMA, Mississippi, Reel 1. A number of historians have attempted to weigh the complex and ambivalent response of whites to the emancipated slave, notably James L. Roark in *Masters Without Slaves: Southern Planters in the Civil War and Reconstruction* (New York, 1977). Leon Litwack, while attempting to shift the focus from white to black, also has much to say about the way in which whites responded to emancipation. See Litwack, *Been in the Storm So Long: The Aftermath of Slavery* (New York, 1979).

belief in the fixed and immutable racial inferiority of blacks. Few whites in the region felt the necessity of elaborating upon these racial convictions; they were simply accepted like the weather or the existence of God. Faced with the necessity of educating occupiers whom they believed hopelessly naïve, however, southern journalists and political leaders returned again to the well-worn antebellum "evidence" that had buttressed their proslavery arguments. Only now it was black subservience rather than outright slavery that was to be justified with religious rhetoric ("So long as the Scriptures remain true and God's word immutable, so long must the sons of Ham serve the sons of Japeth"); with pseudoscientific evidence ("The cerebral formation of the negro is shown by chemical analysis to be inferior in every respect to that of the white man"), and the "manifest lessons of history" ("The negro and other inferior races have never, not even under the most favorable circumstances, been capable of self-government or of mastering the most primitive forces of civilization").[2]

When General O. O. Howard gave a lengthy speech to a gathering of freedmen in a New Orleans theater in November of 1865, he warned of the hard times ahead, but he held out the ultimate promise of "racial advancement and development" through hard work, education, and the "moral uplift" of supportive whites. To this Josiah Nott replied with scorn in an article excerpted in more than twenty southern newspapers. Howard's faith in education and self-improvement was a "phantasmagoria," claimed the Mobile physician, "ethnologist," and prewar exponent of scientific racism. The cranial capacity of the Negro was "nine cubic inches less than that of the white man," argued Nott, and the implications were obvious. To talk about "improving the race" was "manifestly absurd." Under any conditions—well paid or ill paid, coddled or abused—the results were inevitable. The Negro could perform only the simplest, most basic physical tasks. What was equally critical, he had "no ambition of bettering his condition. He only cares to provide for his momentary wants." Shiftless, improvident, unreliable, he could not be made to observe the validity of a written or moral contract "further than is compatable with momentary caprice." What was perhaps most depressing was the fact that the intellectual capacity of the race was "fixed and immutable, having been the same for the past 5,000 years." To talk about "improving the race" was a logical contradiction.[3]

2. New Orleans *Times*, November 7, 1865; Josiah Nott, "The Problem of the Black Races," DR, 2nd ser., (1866), 281–82.
3. New Orleans *Times*, November 7, 1865. See also Theodore Brantner Wilson's chapter, "Slavery and the Free Negro: The Emergence of an Institution," in his *The Black Codes of the South* (University, Ala., 1965), 12–41.

Nott attempted to maintain a tone of lofty detachment in his public pronouncements; his anger was directed mostly against foolish and ignorant white "negrophiles" from the North. Privately, the racial observations of Nott and his followers were marked by hysteria and bitterness. No "Yankee villainy and ingenuity" could even make that "race which has *always* governed the world subservient to a stinking deformed race, cousin of Chimpanzee and Orangotan [*sic*]," Ethelred Philips told his brother. Privately echoing Nott's controversial contention that blacks were a separate creation, the Florida physician insisted that the Negro was a "creation as distinct from the Caucasian as the Gorilla which he resembles more than he does that race to which the creator gave . . . superiority." Only the "sectarian, ignorant and intolerant notions" of the church had blinded whites to reality.[4]

Philips, like Josiah Nott, considered himself an expert on the influence of race on the long history of mankind. But the editor of the Richmond *Times* pointed to far more recent experiences. There had been an ample opportunity to test the "usefulness" of free Negroes, for there had been 130,000 living in the antebellum South in 1860, with nearly 50,000 in Virginia alone. With rare exceptions, said the *Times*, their "laziness and depravity" had made them despised by all, even by slaves. What was worse, "it has always been found impossible to get from them any regular and continued labor."[5]

That notion that the freedman was inherently lazy was the most striking aspect of the revised proslavery argument. To antebellum northern visitors who had looked out upon a vista of slaves working dawn to dusk while whites refined the practice of leisure to an art form, it seemed an absurdity. But southern whites believed only the carefully controlled use of force could keep the slave at work, maintain the economic viability of southern agriculture, and incidentally, return a profit as well. As David Christy had

4. Ethelred Philips to James J. Philips, December 1, 1867, in James John Philips Papers, SHC. Antiblack racialism appears in the writings of almost every white southerner and ranges from gentle condescension to a bloodthirsty, almost incoherent rage. For some of the more extended discussions of what were considered the innate characteristics and capabilities of the freedmen, see the Augusta *Daily Press*, October 19, 1865, April 5, 1866; Atlanta *Daily Intelligencer*, September 14, 1865; (Jacksonville) *Florida Union*, August 26, October 28, 1865; Macon *Daily Telegraph*, October 28, 1865; Raleigh *Daily Standard*, September 9, 1865; Lynchburg (Va.) *Republican*, November 30, 1865; Louisville (Ky.) *Daily Democrat*, June 16, 1865; Raleigh *Sentinel*, January 23, 1866; George Fitzhugh, "What's to Be Done with the Negroes," *DR*, 2nd ser., I (1866), 578; J. D. B. De Bow, "The State of the Country," *ibid.*, 141; W. W. Boyce, "President Johnson's Plan of Reconstruction," *ibid.*, 14; Selma *Daily Messenger*, July 30, 1865; Wilmington (N.C.) *Daily Herald*, December 7, 1865; Richmond *Times*, November 25, 1865; New Orleans *Times*, November 30, 1865.

5. Richmond *Times*, October 24, 1865. See also Wilson, *Black Codes of the South*, 13–41.

observed, "Every piece of evidence pointed to the inescapable conclusions: that blacks could survive the tropical heat of the cotton culture, but only by coercion would they work."[6]

Equally if not more persuasive evidence of the disastrous economic consequences of emancipation could be found in the results of wartime experiments with free labor. The history of free labor, particularly in the Mississippi Delta, was seen as a confirmation of the gloomiest implications of antebellum free labor. Most white southern planters were aware, well before the war had ended, of federal wartime experiments with free labor in the Delta. Under the command of General Nathaniel Banks, federal officials had approved a contract-labor system in 1863. There had been considerable uncertainty at the outset over the approach to be taken by federal authorities. Doctrinaire abolitionists generally favored complete and unconditional emancipation without government regulations (except those that would protect the freedmen). Other, more cautious reformers, endorsed General Nathaniel Banks's contract-labor system adopted in 1863 as a halfway house between slavery and freedom under which a paternalistic (though often ineffective) federal government sought to guarantee wages for slaves while requiring them to remain as plantation laborers, often under the supervision of their old masters.[7] For the most part, those who inspected the plantations praised the results of the experiment in freedom, particularly when the freedmen were treated fairly and humanely. The freedmen were "more willing to work, and more patient than any set of human beings I ever saw," insisted James McKaye, who inspected the Delta plantations on behalf of the Freedman's Inquiry Commission. The few instances of discontented, rebellious, or unproductive free workers were attributed to the refusal of the old plantation aristocracy to accept "any terms short of absolute slavery, with the sacred right of unlimited power to starve, imprison and flog."[8]

6. David Christy, *Cotton Is King; or, The Culture of Cotton and Its Relation to Agriculture, Manufactures, and Commerce; the Free Colored People; and to Those Who Hold That Slavery Is in Itself Sinful* (Cincinnati, 1855), 187–91.

7. During the past decade, there have been at least a half dozen works describing the Louisiana wartime experiments in plantation management. C. Peter Ripley's *Slaves and Freedmen in Civil War Louisiana* (Baton Rouge, 1976) is the most thorough. Louis S. Gerteis' *From Contraband to Freedmen: Federal Policy Toward Southern Blacks, 1861–1865* (Westport, Conn., 1973), has a lengthy section on Louisiana (65–115), but he relies almost entirely upon army sources. William F. Messner highlights the ideological dimensions of the issue in *Freedmen and the Ideology of Free Labor: Louisiana, 1862–1865* (Lafayette, La., 1978), while Peyton McCrary relates these developments to the complex wartime and postwar politics of Louisiana in *Abraham Lincoln and Reconstruction: The Louisiana Experiment* (Princeton, 1978), 66–158.

8. James McKaye, *The Mastership and Its Fruits: The Emancipated Slave Face to Face with His Old Master: A Supplementary Report to the Honorable Edwin M. Stanton, Secretary of War* (New York, 1864), 17; McCrary, *Abraham Lincoln and Reconstruction*, 135–37.

Northern journalists, missionaries, and at least some army and Freedmen's Bureau officials were well aware of the shortcomings of the blacks
they encouraged. The idealistic evangelicals, in particular, often recoiled
with horror from their first encounters with the freedmen. "As I looked
down upon them in their filth and rags," reported one missionary to his
superior, "I could hardly repress a feeling of disgust." The Reverend J. P.
Bardwell managed to go on only by remembering that, "notwithstanding
their filth & degredation," they are "beings for whom Christ died." Of
course the freedmen were "backward and depraved," concluded the head of
Nashville's Fisk School. Moreover they were "exceedingly low both in morals and intellect." But how could it be otherwise, noted John Ogden. "I
never realized the deep and damning effects of human slavery until I was
brought in close and daily contact with these people." There was, agreed a
fellow missionary, "no stronger proof of the 'evil wickedness of slavery' than
the condition of the ex-slave."[9]

It was comforting to believe that the resistance of the freedmen to "regular and sustained labor" was "as much the effects of the institution of slavery
as of the fault in the individual." Few of these northern missionaries were
confident that blacks would ever equal whites. What they did believe was
that blacks, with help and guidance from sympathetic whites, could develop whatever capabilities they possessed more fully in a free-labor economy. And thus, by the end of the war most northerners believed that the
moral and economic supremacy of free labor over slavery had been established. As the New York *Times* concluded as early as 1863, "Thank God,
[free labor] is no longer an experiment; it has been tried and found to be the
better system."[10]

The outlook depended, however, upon the perspective of the reporter.
Contemporaries and historians have insisted that local federal officials allowed themselves to be seduced by southern planters into siding against the
freedmen in disputes over wages and working conditions. But northern investors who tried their hand, no matter how idealistic they were at the outset, soon had a tendency to parrot the most jaundiced views of white southerners. In February of 1864, Isaac Shoemaker had assumed management of

9. Bardwell to Rev. M. E. Strieby, December 24, 1864, April 2, 1866, Rev. S. G. Wright
to Rev. George Whipple, March 28, 1865, both in Mississippi, Reel 1, John Ogden to Rev.
E. P. Smith, May 8, 1867, Rev. E. O. Jade to Strieby, February 6, 1866, Rev. E. M. Craveth to
Strieby, February 13, 1866, all in Tennessee, Reel 1, E. A. Young to Rev. C. H. Fowler, February 4, 1864, in Arkansas, Reel 1, F. Ayer to Rev. Sam Hunt, June 2, 1866, in Georgia, Reel 2,
all in AMA.
10. Lt. Col. Allan Rutherford to Capt. J. T. Chur, October 29, 1866, in BRFAL, North
Carolina, Box 13; Eric Foner, *Free Soil, Free Labor, Free Men: The Ideology of the Republican
Party Before the Civil War* (New York, 1970), 260–300.

a cotton plantation outside Warrenton, Mississippi. Within weeks he was confronted with workers who abandoned their tasks without explanation, ignored his orders, and stole every item of portable property that was unsecured. Shoemaker at least had a ready explanation: Slavery had turned blacks into "careless children," and it would take time and patience before they could become self-reliant workers. Shoemaker's conclusions were all too often echoed by other northern would-be planters.[11]

The more optimistic planters initially tended to blame this lack of productivity upon the unsettled conditions throughout much of the Delta. During 1863 and 1864, areas nominally under the control of the federal government were subjected to persistent raids by Confederate forces. Wilmer Shields, who tried to manage Dr. William Newton Mercer's plantations on the Mississippi from 1863 to 1865, reported a common situation in late 1863. "All is anarchy and confusion here—everything going to destruction," he told Mercer, with both Union and Confederate troops carrying off supplies. Even more frightening were the occasions when bands of former slaves, sometimes accompanied by white jayhawkers, terrorized isolated rural areas of southern Louisiana. Little wonder that sugar planter William Minor concluded in late 1863 that a "man had as well be in pergatory [sic] as attempt to work a Sugar Plantation under existing circumstances."[12]

A handful of southerners urged patience on the part of planters with arguments that sounded suspiciously similar to those of antebellum northern abolitionists. In the 1865 South Carolina constitutional convention, Judge Edward Frost of Charleston readily acknowledged the shortcomings of the freedmen, but he insisted that this was the fault of white southerners. "Did he [the freedman] make himself ignorant?" asked Frost of his fellow delegates. "Did he ever have a chance to choose his station in life?" Was it not an "act of insubordination" for him to even attempt to learn to read and write? "We may as well admit it first as last," insisted Frost: "slavery made him what he is." The special committee of the North Carolina legislature made the same argument in recommending legislation for the postwar

11. See scattered entries, February through April, 1864, in the Isaac Shoemaker Diary, DUL. One need not accept the white southerners' racism to acknowledge the accuracy of their argument that free men and women did not labor as consistently as slaves. See John Richard Dennett, *The South As It Is*, ed. Henry M. Christman (New York, 1965), 200–15; Edward S. Philbrick to Charles Preston Ware, October 9, 1865, in Elizabeth Ware Pearson (ed.), *Letters from Port Royal, 1862–1868* (Boston, 1906), 315–23; Lawrence N. Powell, *New Masters: Northern Planters During the Civil War and Reconstruction* (New Haven, 1980), 106–109.

12. Wilmer Shields to Dr. William Newton Mercer, December 11, 1863, January 25, 1864, June 10, 1865, all in William Newton Mercer Papers, LSU; Messner, *Freedmen and the Ideology of Free Labor*, 86; William F. Messner, "Black Violence and White Response: Louisiana, 1862," *JSH*, XLI (1975), 19–38.

South. The "vices" of the freed population were a "natural offspring of their recent slavery and degredation."[13]

The overwhelming majority of white planters, however, had nothing but contempt for such arguments. Neither the "heritage of slavery" nor the disorder of the war and immediate postwar period could explain the "laziness and impertinence" of the freedmen, insisted one sugar planter after two disastrous seasons with free labor. The "nature of the negro" could not be changed by the usual inducements. All "he desires is to eat, drink and sleep and perform the least possible amount of labor." As a delegation of Louisiana planters told the federal authorities in 1864, their once "faithful and obedient" servants had become so indolent and insubordinate that the economic future of the region was in grave jeopardy. These planters expressed "grave and serious doubts" that the freedmen would continue to work without some method of "compelling them to labor diligently in the fields." General Nathaniel Banks might blame the problems on the "theories, prejudices & opinions . . . [of] the old system," but the planters had one compelling argument that overshadowed any theoretical explanations. The rich sugar and cotton economy of the Delta was collapsing under the free-labor system.[14]

One South Louisiana sugar planter described the effects of free labor upon agricultural production in Terrebonne Parish. In 1861 he had produced 600 hogsheads of sugar on his plantation alone. In 1863, the first year of his experiment with free labor, production had declined to 260 hogsheads. When he tried to reassert some form of discipline, however, the freedmen rebelled, and he produced fewer than 90 hogsheads. Total production that year in the entire parish was only 625 hogsheads. Nor was his experience unusual. Of the 177 hands on William Newton Mercer's Laurel Hill Plantation in 1864, 133 had abandoned the plantation—and their work—without explanation for periods of three days or more by June of that year. Whatever the reasons, the results were clear. Between 1861 and 1864 sugar production in the sixteen parishes of the Gulf Department declined from nearly 400,000 hogsheads of sugar to less than 7,000 hogs-

13. Sidney Andrews, *The South Since the War*, 73–74; "Report of the [North Carolina] Committee on the Subject of the Freedmen, January 22, 1866," rpr. in Raleigh *Standard*, January 31, 1866.

14. Sergeant Gardner to A. Franklin Pugh, September 6, 1864, Pugh to Provost Marshal, November 1, 1864, (copy), both in Pugh Family Papers, UTA; J. Carlyle Sitterson, *Sugar Country: The Cane Sugar Industry in the South, 1753–1950* (Lexington, Ky., 1953), 214; New Orleans *Times*, October 21, 1864; *Senate Report on the Condition of the South*, 39th Cong., 1st Sess., Vol. I (Serial 1237), 84–88; J. Carlyle Sitterson, "The Transition from Slave to Free Economy on the William Minor Plantations," *AH*, XVIII (1943), 220; Barnes F. Lathrop, "The Pugh Plantation, 1860–1865: A Study of Life in Lower Louisiana" (Ph.D. dissertation, University of Texas, 1945), *passim*.

heads. These figures—widely reported in the press—were hardly likely to promote optimism on the part of southern planters.[15] And there were other examples, not quite so close at hand, that seemed to point toward the disastrous economic and social consequences of emancipation. Throughout their history, southerners, like northern abolitionists, had looked to emancipation in the Caribbean as a testing ground for black freedom. In his poetic defense of a slave society, William Grayson had summed up white southerners' antebellum perceptions of the results of this bleak experiment in freedom.

> The Bright Antilles, with each closing year,
> See harvests fail, and fortunes disappear;
> The cane no more its golden treasure yields;
> Unsightly weeds deform the fertile fields;
> The negro freedman, thrifty while a slave,
> Loosed from restraint, becomes a drone or knave;
> Each effort to improve his nature foils,
> Begs, steals, or sleeps and starves, but never toils;
> For savage sloth mistakes the freedom won,
> And ends the mere barbarian he begun.

In the first issue published after emancipation, the Georgia farm magazine *Southern Cultivator* morosely described the economic disintegration that had followed emancipation in the Caribbean. Citing articles from the British press and the authoritative *Encyclopaedia Britannica*, white southerners concluded that the essential problem was the innate tendency of blacks once freed from slavery to withdraw from the tiresome labor required for staple-crop production and to retreat into the limited economy of subsistence agriculture. The freed black population was satisfied with the new economic order, said one southern planter who visited the Caribbean in the 1850s. "Indolent and improvident," lacking any "taste for the artificial comforts and luxuries which are the chief incentives to steady industry," the free population was satisfied with the new economic order. The result was disaster for the overall economy of the islands. Under slavery, the Caribbean

15. New Orleans *Times*, n.d., rpr. in Houston *Tri-Weekly Telegraph*, June 7, 1865; *DR*, I (1866), 201; Messner, *Freedmen and the Ideology of Free Labor*, 83; "List of Workers," June 10, 1864, Mercer Papers; Samuel Agnew Diary, SHC, April 11, 1865; David Schenck Diary, SHC, January 6, 1865; Yorkville (S.C.) *Enquirer*, September 28, 1864; James L. Lobdell to E. J. Gay, January 16, 1863, in Gay Papers, LSU; Report to Planters of the Parish of St. Mary, February 17, 1864, in William T. Palfrey Papers, LSU. The New Orleans *Times* specialized in nightmarish stories of the unproductivity of free labor. See especially issues in October and November of 1864.

island had been a "fairy land of perpetual beauty, astonishing fertility and enormous riches," claimed J. D. B. De Bow. But in the wake of emancipation, land values had declined 80 percent, the currency had become worthless, plantations were abandoned, and in Jamaica alone exports declined 300 percent from 1809 to 1854.[16]

William MacFarland of the *Farmer* magazine was one of the small band of white southerners who rejected the prevailing notion that blacks would not work except as slaves. Throughout the months after the war, he scolded his fellow southerners for their gloomy prognosis. And in a revealing review of William Sewell's study of emancipation in the West Indies, the aging Whig editor insisted that the economic decline in the sugar islands had little relevance to the southern economy since it was well underway by the time of emancipation in the 1830s. James L. Reynolds, professor of English literature at South Carolina College, agreed and insisted in an article in *De Bow's Review* that emancipation had played an insignificant role in the decline of the West Indies. The economic collapse had come when the British government embraced free trade and "thus exposed the planters to the competition of Brazil and Cuba whilst the protective measures of France and Belgium and other continental countries in favor of their beet sugar excluded cane sugar from the market and caused a disastrous surplus in England." MacFarland and Reynolds also argued that the attempt of "greedy British landowners" to substitute a repressive and coercive apprenticeship system had been equally contributory to the economic decline. Several of the islands were already staging a modest economic comeback

---

16. William J. Grayson, *The Hireling and the Slave, Chicora, and Other Poems* (Charleston, 1856), 34; *SCu*, XXIII (1865), 70; De Bow, "State of the Country," 144–48. As Eric Foner has noted, the consequences of emancipation in the Caribbean had played a "small but noteworthy part in antebellum discussions of slavery." Foner, *Nothing but Freedom: Emancipation and Its Legacy* (Baton Rouge, 1983), 40–43. Joe B. Wilkins, Jr., describes these southern perceptions in "Window on Freedom: The South's Response to the Emancipation of the Slaves in the British West Indies, 1833–1861" (Ph.D. dissertation, University of South Carolina, 1977). Once emancipation actually came, most white southerners were even more fixated on the Caribbean experience as they groped for some understanding of what they were about to face. See, for example, (Jacksonville) *Florida Union*, October 28, 1865; Selma *Daily Messenger*, July 30, 1865; Natchez *Daily Courier*, November 2, 1865; Augusta *Daily Press*, April 5, 1866; Nott, "The Problem of the Black Races," 281–82; Lynchburg (Va.) *Republican*, November 30, 1865; Augusta *Chronicle and Sentinel*, December 4, 1865; Boyce, "President Johnson's Plan of Reconstruction," 21; A. Bretton, "West India Emancipation—Its Practical Workers," *DR*, 2nd ser., I (1866), 596–600; Louisville (Ky.) *Daily Democrat*, June 4, 1865; Atlanta *Daily Intelligencer*, July 28, 1865; Charles M. Wallace to Wife, May 15, 1865, in John Clopton Collection, DUL. Literate southerners were quite aware that many leading English liberals had adopted a gloomy assessment of West Indian emancipation. (See, for example, Thomas Carlyle, "Fifteen Years After Emancipation in the West Indies," *Old Guard*, IV (1866), 239–44, 308–11, 372–77.) Such pessimistic accounts were excerpted in most of the postwar southern journals and newspapers.

under far less favorable circumstances than existed in the postwar South. Under the "mild and patriarchal character of the slave system in the Southern states," the freedmen of the region had "socially and mentally progressed much further than the barbaric West Indian slave." If white southerners would only practice "fairness and honesty" in their dealings with the freedmen and appeal to their common economic self-interest, rather than trying to coerce them into laboring arrangements, there was ample reason to hope for a resurgent agricultural South.[17]

Most white southerners had no more sympathy for the arguments of MacFarland and Reynolds than for the notion that the inadequacies of the freedmen were a product of slavery. On every side, they insisted, could be seen the evidence of black demoralization, particularly in the tendency of the freedmen to gather in the villages, towns, and cities of the South, away from the labor-starved plantations of the countryside. In the contemporary literature of southerners, in the writings of later historians, and even in the works of novelists the theme of the exodus became a powerful element of the drama of emancipation.[18]

There had indeed been an increase in the number of blacks in the South's few urban and semiurban centers. During the war itself, slaves fleeing for freedom had congregated in the only place they could find freedom and safety—the centers of population where military headquarters were usually established. At the same time, the repeated sweeps of opposing forces in many contested areas of the South often drove blacks and whites from unprotected areas in the countryside. Thus, the greatest influx of blacks into urban areas was along the east coast, where Federals had made landings and in the Delta and upper Mississippi regions where Union troops made their first deep advances into the Confederacy.[19]

As the Union armies had spread south from Tennessee, each new post or

17. *Fa*, II (1867), 109–12; James L. Reynolds, "The South: Its Duty and Destiny," *DR*, I (1866), 73. See W. L. Mathieson, *British Slavery and Its Abolition, 1823–1838* (London, 1926), 283–86; William Lawrence Burn, *Emancipation and Apprenticeship in the British West Indies* (London, 1937); William A. Green, *British Slave Emancipation: The Sugar Colonies and the Great Experiment* (Oxford, 1976); James M. McPherson, "Was West Indian Emancipation a Success: The Abolitionist Argument During the American Civil War," *CS*, IV (1964), 26–35.

18. Thomas C. Holt has offered a provocative assessment of the complex impact emancipation had upon blacks and whites in the Caribbean, England, and the United States and the way the response to emancipation was interwoven with nineteenth-century liberal democratic assumptions. See "'An Empire over the Mind': Emancipation, Race, and Ideology in the British West Indies and the American South," in J. Morgan Kousser and James M. McPherson (eds.), *Region, Race, and Reconstruction: Essays in Honor of C. Vann Woodward* (New York, 1982), 283–313.

19. James Welch Patton, *Unionism and Reconstruction in Tennessee, 1860–1869* (Chapel Hill, 1934), 145–46.

garrison became a magnet that drew the former slaves from the surrounding countryside, particularly after the 1863 Emancipation Proclamation. Asa Lawrence Fisher, superintendent of contrabands at Memphis, Tennessee, noted a dramatic influx into the army lines beginning in the winter of 1863. By mid-March, his successor, John Eaton, had completed a survey of army posts down the Mississippi. Everywhere he saw pathetic, crowded shantytowns of freed men, women, and children. In the eleven towns and posts he visited from Cairo, Illinois, south to the Federal forces besieging Vicksburg, he counted more than twenty thousand homeless and jobless contrabands—nearly five thousand in Memphis alone. Although the number fluctuated, it increased steadily until February of 1864 when Federal troops began shipping out blacks to newly leased plantations along the Mississippi.[20]

Even when the war had ended, much of the black population seemed to be on the move. Of the former slaves interviewed during the WPA slave narrative project of the 1930s, 25 percent left their home plantations during the war or during the first month after emancipation. Another 15 percent were gone within the year.[21] Most of those interviewed during the 1930s were under twenty years of age at the time of emancipation and thus were likely to be more mobile than the general black population, but the extraordinarily high percentage of individuals who moved tends to reinforce the earlier stereotypes of a black population in turmoil. If this sample accurately reflected the population as a whole, for example, more than 1.5 million former slaves took to the roads and byways of the South—on the move and testing the limits of freedom.

To white southerners, most of these former slaves seemed to have settled in the urban communities of the South. Poor blacks were "now in huddles

20. Northern missionaries and schoolteachers sent to minister to the freedmen responded ambivalently to their tendency to gather at the military posts and in towns. Only in the urban and semiurban settings could the northern evangelists protect the blacks against white southerners. But town life led to "physical and moral corruption" and by 1865 their views had begun to shift. See D. T. Allen to Fowler, January 1, 1864, in Arkansas, Reel 1, John Eaton to Prof. Henry Cowles, March 13, 1863, Asa Lawrence Fisher to Eaton, March 13, 1863, both in Tennessee, Reel 1, William Thirds to Mrs. Smith, October 8, 1863, Joel Grant to Cowles, April 10, 1863, Rev. A. A. Olds to Whipple, February 10, 1864, Rev. E. R. Pierce to Rev. S. S. Jocelyn, April 29, 1863, Wright to Whipple, April 1, 4, 1864, all in Mississippi, Reel 1, Rev. H. B. Greely to Whipple, January 4, 1866, in Florida, Reel 1, Dr. Lucius Mills to Whipple, July 27, 1865, in Louisiana, Reel 1, all in AMA.

21. In *Slavery Remembered: A Record of Twentieth Century Slave Narratives* (Chapel Hill, 1979), 137, Paul Escott arrived at slightly different statistics from those I tabulated using the WPA narratives perhaps because I used the supplemental narratives published by Greenwood Press, which were not available when Escott completed most of his research. On the other hand, the statistical variation is relatively small and tends to support Escott's view that the information in the supplemental narratives does not alter his basic findings.

all about the cities," said one Alabama former slaveowner after he had traveled to Montgomery, Selma, and Mobile. They "swamps [*sic*] the street daily," complained William Forward, "the most of them idle and constantly shouting." Genteel Lucy Walton of Richmond was horrified at the city streets of Virginia's capital. It was a "sea of black," said the disdainful Miss Walton, with "piles of negro goods and noisy chatter everywhere" as blacks set off on their way to some "fancied Elysian fields of Freedom."[22]

Occasionally travelers or a convened grand jury complained of the threat this black population posed to the persons and property of law-abiding citizens. But the greatest apprehension was caused by the appearance of idleness and vagrancy at a time when the South faced agricultural prostration. More than "two hundred idle negroes in the prime of vigorous manhood" had congregated with their families in Rome, Georgia, complained one planter, "and this in the face of a desperate shortage of agricultural labor." A Georgia girl complained that while her family sought workers every vacant house and shanty in Augusta was filled with such idle blacks. With freedmen and their families crowding into towns, said one Louisiana sugar planter, "the country is lost for the time [being]." If the freedmen continued to vanish into the nearby towns and villages whenever the whim occurred to them, said another sugar planter. "it would be far better [and] . . . cheaper to abandon our lands, however productive in former times." Something of the importance of this issue to planters may be measured by the fact that more than 40 percent of the first contracts signed during 1865 attempted to place limits on the "town visits" of freedmen.[23]

There was an increase in black population in the few cities and small towns of the South. Between 1860 and 1870, the black population in Deep South communities of more than ten thousand increased 68 percent—eight times that of the white increase. But such statistical figures are misleading because so few blacks were urban dwellers in 1860. The notion of an urban

22. Samuel Forward to William Stump Forward, September 17, 24, December 22, 1865, all in William Stump Forward Papers, SHC; Lucy Walton Diary, DUL, April 25, 1865. For complaints of the urban congregation of freedmen see Elias Henry Deas to Daughter, May 5, July 15, August 15, 1865, all in Elias H. Deas Papers, SCL; Robert Battey to Mary Battey, July 19, 1865, in Robert Battey Papers, EU; James Appleton Blackshear Diary, EU, May 11, 1865; Minnie Cameron to Cousin Maggie Cameron, July 15, 1865, in Paul Cameron Papers, SHC; B. F. Moore to Thomas Ruffin, September 22, 1865, in Thomas Ruffin papers, SHC; Gov. John Letcher to Col. George W. Munford, August 30, 1865, in Munford-Ellis Family Papers, DUL; Joseph Davis Smith to Son, September 2, 1865, Nan Bridges to Charles Bridges, July 24, 1865, both in Charles E. Bridges Correspondence, DUL.

23. Robert Battey to Mary Battey, July 19, 1865, in Battey Papers; Eliza Andrews, *The Wartime Journal of a Georgia Girl, 1864–1865*, ed. Spencer Bidwell King (Atlanta, 1976), 253, 314; Houston *Tri-Weekly Telegraph*, June 7, 1865; "Report of the Special [Charleston, S.C.] Coroner's Jury," July 5, 1866, in James L. Orr Papers, SCA.

exodus reflected less the actual increase in black population than the heightened visibility of freedmen in a few urban locations. Before 1865, there were relatively few free blacks in the towns and smaller cities of the South. Slaves went into town only on errands and specific assignments. As a result, for most white southerners, the sight of any significant number of blacks in the small towns of the region was unusual. And in many areas, it would have been considered dangerous and threatening. After the war, the right to move about freely was one of the most cherished fruits of freedom, and the freedmen exercised that right by repeated trips to the small towns and cities of the region. But by 1870 at least, less than 5 percent of black southerners lived in urban communities of more than ten thousand.[24]

Occasionally a white southerner questioned the almost universal assumption that blacks left their homes to avoid work. Freedmen, concluded a Louisiana planter, "have intelligence enough to know that they must labor to subsist and [most] feel a desire to accumulate something more than their bare subsistence." There were many factors that led black southerners to move about in the first months after emancipation: a desire to be reunited with family members separated under slavery, the personal freedom from supervision and dependence that was almost unattainable on the plantation, and the security from physical violence guaranteed by the presence of a town military garrison. But ironically, it was the ambition to better themselves—in Robert Battey's words, to "accumulate something"—that led most former slaves to risk the uncertainties and hardships of leaving their old homes, which, however unpleasant, at least offered the security of the known.[25]

Most writers had little sympathy with such explanations. Sometimes out of spiteful maliciousness, more often out of genuine ignorance and fear, southern whites attributed the most reprehensible motives to the vast movement of black people across the region. If they misinterpreted the motivations of southern blacks, however, whites instinctively grasped the significance of this democratic upheaval. In the cities and towns of the South white authority as it had existed in the era of slavery slipped away. Even in

24. Approximately 40 percent of the 1865 contracts that I examined required explicit permission for the freedmen to visit local towns. See, for example, the model contract proposed by the Richmond *Times* as late as January, 1866. Richmond *Times*, January 4, 9, 1866. By 1866 such restrictions were relatively uncommon.

25. The slave narratives themselves, despite some obvious limitations, offer revealing insights into the motivating factors behind the tendency to move about immediately after emancipation. See also Litwack, *Been in the Storm So Long*, 292–335; Escott, *Slavery Remembered*, 119–42; Peter Kolchin, *First Freedom: The Response of Alabama's Blacks to Emancipation and Reconstruction* (Westport, Conn., 1972), 3–29; Joel Williamson, *After Slavery: The Negro in South Carolina During Reconstruction, 1861–1877* (Chapel Hill, 1965), 32–46.

the rural areas, it was far more difficult to maintain control over "strange negroes," as one white said, than to continue their hold over a people conditioned by a lifetime of obedience.

Interwoven with these bleak assessments was the trauma of emancipation itself and the destruction of a system of racial control that whites had deceived themselves into believing was based upon free will rather than coercion. For a few southerners, like Mary Boykin Chesnut, the wartime diarist, the postwar return to the old plantation was a warm homecoming with the former slaves hard at work pledging in their "furious, emotional way," their lifelong devotion. For others, however, the end of such illusions had quickly come in the first hours of freedom. George Trenholm, one of South Carolina's wealthiest antebellum slaveowners, was confused and perplexed. Spurned at every turn by his former bondsmen, who refused to return to his plantation, he seemed bewildered by their "sullen ingratitude." The gentle Trenholm maintained his confidence that, if whites continued to "befriend the negro," this temporary rupture between masters and their former servants might yet be repaired.[26]

Many of his contemporaries had little interest in restoring any such relationship. There were tears and anger when the house servants had left at the first news of emancipation, recalled a South Carolina teenager in her diary, but since then the "breaking of ties has excited little feeling; both parties are very indifferent and the most that is felt is a polite and gentle interest in the affairs of each other." In a revealing thumbnail summary of the conditional nature of antebellum paternalism Grace Elmore casually observed that the "ties of affection" had always been conditioned upon the legal obligations of slavery.[27]

During the war, slaveowners subject to the visits of Federal troops had quickly come to understand the shallow roots of such loyalty. Robert and Rebecca Hunter, an aging South Carolina couple north of Columbia, had conscientiously attended to the religious needs of their twenty-one slaves. Each Sunday the Hunters made certain that their slaves were present in the gallery of the Concord Baptist Church to receive instruction in the Christian faith. And by the testimony of at least one former slave they were neither brutal nor unfair owners. As Sherman's army moved through South Carolina in the winter and early spring of 1865, Hunter selected several of his most faithful slaves to hide their personal effects and most valuable belongings. But when the army detachment arrived at the Fairfield County

26. C. Vann Woodward (ed.), *Mary Chesnut's Civil War* (New Haven, 1981), 821; George A. Trenholm to Son, September 1, 1865, in George Alfred Trenholm Papers, SCL.

27. Grace Brown Elmore Diary (Typewritten copy in SCL), June 25, 1865, p. 92.

plantation, the very men who had helped Hunter led the soldiers to the hiding places, and told them: "Here is de stuff, hid here, 'cause us put it dere." As one of his former slaves recalled, "It sho' set old marster down." At age sixty-seven he had lost everything—including the belief that he knew and understood his "people."[28]

Before 1860 Paul Cameron of North Carolina recalled that he and his family had owned seven hundred slaves "all descended by inheritance from our father—only two having been purchased & and then only to bring man & wife together." Despite what he insisted was his "mild & humane care & control of the family of negroes," as the war progressed, they had spurned his offers of friendship and had become increasingly sullen and hostile.[29]

All too many southerners responded to this "betrayal" with neither the indifference of Grace Elmore nor the resentment of Paul Cameron, but with a burning rage. When whites had warned against the possibility of freedmen escaping to Union lines toward the end of the war, a Mississippi overseer talked with his "servants." They insisted, he plaintively recalled, that they wanted "no truck" with the Yankees. Then, as soon as the Union soldiers drew near, the slaves drifted away at nightfall to the northern lines. "Let me again repeat that but very, very few are faithful," Wilmer Shields told his employer. "And some of those who remain are worse than those who have gone."[30]

Dr. Elias Henry Deas, a rice planter on the Cooper River near Charleston and a prominent physician, had also dismissed his neighbors' wartime warning that his faithful slaves could not be trusted and should be removed from the coast. He had remained at his home, but when the Federals arrived, his former slaves had scattered like the rest. Bitterly, he told his daughter of their flight. The younger ones he could accept, he said, "but the old ones in a great many instances are no better than the young." They had all acted with "diabolic perfidiousness." All his life, said Augustin Taveau of Charleston, he had believed that the slaves who spoke to him with their cheery "howdies" were "content, happy and attached to their masters." But the events of the spring of 1865 had shattered his comfortable assumptions. "Good master and bad master, all alike shared the same fate." The freedmen had acted with duplicity and treachery. "We have all been laboring under a delusion." And anger over thievery and dishonesty

28. George G. Rawick (ed.), *The American Slave: A Composite Autobiography*, Original ser. (19 vols.; Westport, Conn., 1972), II, South Carolina Narratives, Pt. 1; *Eighth Census, 1860: South Carolina*, Schedule 22, p. 104.

29. Paul Cameron to Jonathan Worth, December [?], 1865, (copy) in Cameron Papers.

30. Shields to Mercer, January 25, 1864, and see December 11, 1863, both in Mercer Papers.

compounded that sense of betrayal. "You can not yet fully conceive the an-
noyance we have from the miserable conduct of the negroes," stormed a
Sidney, Alabama, planter. "They steal everything they can secrete." Whenever an implement, a tool, or livestock vanished, said Josi Borden, he was
quick to question his hands, but "*nobody ever knows anything about it.*" To
her cousin, a South Carolina teenager complained "there is so much stealing going on down here you never saw the equal to it." Hogs and cows had
to be kept in the yard and articles of clothing left on the line became "involuntary donations." In one night twenty gallons of molasses and all of the
family's salted meat disappeared. Another South Carolina planter reported
that he had lost "forty of my bacon hogs since the negroes were set free."
Though most of the thefts took place under cover of darkness, W. D. Berry,
a Mississippi overseer, reported to his employer a series of brazen thefts in
which cotton was removed from the storage houses in broad daylight. In
one case he had ridden up as two wagons were being loaded—by "seven or
eight of our own people," he said with disgust—and he was forced to put
all the cotton in a shelter immediately adjacent to the house. "I have had
more trouble in the last three months than I have had in all my Oversee-
ing," he concluded. A discouraged Charleston factor told his clients in September, 1865, that he could not conscientiously recommend selling rice at
the existing depressed prices, but the choice seemed to be between selling
low or having it stolen from storage. Thievery had reached "epidemic pro-
portions," wrote one North Carolina attorney, who argued that this "involuntary confiscation" amounted to a transfer of ownership second in importance only to emancipation.[31]

31. Elias H. Deas to Daughter, May 5, July 15, August 15, 1865, all in Deas Papers;
Augustin Taveau to William Aiken, April 24, 1865, in Taveau Papers, DUL; Josi Borden to
Doctor [?], October 2, 1865, in Reconstruction Miscellany, Folder No. 46, EU; D. to Cousin,
September 10, 1865, in Hemphill Collection, DUL; N. B. Sparm to T. B. Fraser, Septem-
ber 30, 1865, in Fraser Papers; Thurston and Holmes to J. Harleston Read, September 6,
1866, in Read-Lance Family Papers, SCL; W. D. Berry to Paul Cameron, November 7, 1865,
in Cameron Papers; Moore to Thomas Ruffin, September 22, 1865, in Ruffin Papers; E. J.
Thompson to Benjamin Hedrick, March 17, 1866, in Benjamin Hedrick Papers, DUL. Even
Mary Boykin Chesnut, who praised the conduct of her former slaves, commented on the disil-
lusionment that had often come to her friends, neighbors, and family. Woodward (ed.), *Mary
Chesnut's Civil War*, 233–36, 415. For the anger that came at what Eugene Genovese has
called the "terrible moment of truth," see Frank G. Ruffin to Thomas Ruffin, May 23, 1865, in
Ruffin Papers; Sarah Wadley Diary, SHC, September 26, 1865; C. B. Kerville to J. D. B. De
Bow, August 15, 1865, in J. D. B. De Bow Papers, DUL; H. M. Polk to Maj. John H. Bills,
December 6, 1865, in Horace M. Polk Letters, LSU; Wade Hampton to Andrew Johnson,
August 25, 1866, in Andrew Johnson Papers, LC; Samuel Agnew Diary, April 11, 1865;
Robert Manson Meyers (ed.), *Children of Pride: A True Story of Georgia and the Civil War*
(New Haven, 1972), 729; Arney R. Robinson (ed.), *The Private Journal of Henry William
Ravenel, 1859–1887* (Columbia, S.C., 1947), 244–45. For some of the most virulent denun-
ciations of "black thievery," see Emma Hopkins to English Hopkins, July 30, 1865, in

For northern missionaries, teachers, and planters, this persisting "vice of slavery" was equally infuriating. Charles Stearns, the northern philanthropist and postwar planter, claimed that it went far beyond the implications of the term *vice*. It was, he said, "wholesale robbery of everything in their power to help themselves to, except articles of whose values they are ignorant." While all items were subject to disappearance the freedmen were most likely to steal cotton and food.[32]

Occasionally, white southerners denied that the freedmen were responsible for all the petty thievery that swept the South in the months after the war. "The whites are as much to be dreaded now as the blacks," the wife of an Orangeburg, South Carolina, farmer concluded. And there is even some evidence that whites occasionally played upon widespread assumptions that the freedmen alone were responsible for thefts. Two years after the war, Samuel Agnew of northeastern Mississippi reported a wave of neighborhood thefts apparently carried out by a lone black man. But when a neighbor surprised the thief in his home, he was close enough to see that the apparent black man was in fact a white man with corked face.[33]

Nevertheless, there was no question that the majority of thefts were carried out by blacks. A Pike County, Mississippi, slave recalled the days after emancipation. The black man, he acknowledged, "wud steal cattle an' hogs." They had nothing, he said succinctly, "an' dat is whut made de black man steal." Occasionally sympathetic whites acknowledged as much and even justified petty thefts of food as a "necessity for survival." But the more common response was to complain bitterly that such actions proved that blacks were a "curse to the earth . . . , a miserable and degraded people" becoming "every day more corrupt."[34]

Thievery — corruption — indolence — ingratitude — the words soon blurred together in a torrent of obsessive racial rhetoric. After reading and listening to this din of racial excoriation, little wonder that John Dennett,

Hopkins Family Papers, SCL; Zebulon Preston to Stephen Duncan, December 28, 1865, in Stephen Duncan Papers, LSU; Joseph Davis Smith to Son, April 15, 1866, in Joseph Davis Smith Papers, LSU; Munford to Charles Ellis, January 9, 1866, in Munford-Ellis Papers; Thomas Affleck to Editor, New Orleans *Picayune*, September 14, 1865 (copy), in Thomas Affleck Papers, UTA; Frank G. Ruffin to Thomas Ruffin, May 23, 1865, in Ruffin Papers; Kerville to De Bow, August 15, 1865, in De Bow Papers.

32. Charles Stearns, *The Black Man of the South and the Rebels* (Boston, 1872), 54–56; Pearson (ed.), *Letters from Port Royal*, 322–23; Powell, *New Masters*, 104–106.

33. Anna R. Salley to Aunt, November 13, 1865, in Bruce-Jones-Murchison Family Papers, SCL; Samuel Agnew Diary, May 5, 1867. For other incidents of whites disguising themselves as blacks in robberies, see George R. Walbridge to L. J. Featherston, October 17, 1866, in Lucius H. Featherston Manuscripts, EU; Montgomery *Advertiser*, December 17, 1865.

34. Rawick (ed.), *The American Slave*, Supplementary Ser. 1 (12 vols.; Westport, Conn., 1977), I, Mississippi Narratives, Pt. 2, p. 605; Joseph Davis Smith to Son, April 15, 1866, Joseph Davis Smith Papers.

the traveling correspondent for the *Nation*, concluded: "So far as I have seen, all native Southerners, the poorest and the most degraded equally with the rich, and people of the most undoubted Unionism as well as secessionists, unaffectedly and heartily hate the negroes. Truly they are a despised race."[35]

Complaints of insubordination and thievery were expressed by the great majority of southern whites, but it was the issue of labor that lay at the core of much of the anger of white landowners who were dependent upon their former slaves. At times, the private correspondence and the personal diaries of southern landowners seem little more than a litany of complaints about the disastrous qualities of the freedman as laborer. "The negroes you hire work about one half their time and are idle the balance," recorded David Schenck in his diary in June of 1865. As a class they are "idle, improvident and roguish." "Our negroes" did as they pleased, complained Samuel Agnew of Tipton County, Mississippi, going off in the afternoon "and not giving their master's concerns any attention." Yet complaints of indolence and laziness had been standard throughout the antebellum period, too. And the slaveowner who boasted of the work habits of his property was exceptional. Deprived of ultimate authority and facing economic deprivation and bankruptcy in many instances, white southerners' concern over the alleged shiftlessness of their free labor became a raging anger. "The newspapers inform him [the freedman] that he cannot be maintained in idleness," said a Rome, Georgia, planter, but freedmen scarcely paid attention to what some southern white newspaper said. "The provost marshall tells him that he has to labor," but every black soldier he saw assured him this was not the case," and his daily observation proves to him that the soldier is the wiser of the men." Although it is unlikely he actually expected a response to his notice in the Athens, Georgia, *Southern Cultivator*, one Georgia planter accurately summarized the attitude of most such southerners when he offered a fifty-dollar reward for information that "will enable me to make a living . . . on my farm by the use of negro labor." He had tried without success, he said, and had finally "exhausted all my theories and those of my neighbors."[36]

Northerners who indicted slavery for its failure to incorporate 3.5 million blacks into the larger national economy might insist (sometimes ap-

---

35. Dennett, *The South As It Is*, 119.
36. David Schenck Diary, June 14, 1865; Samuel Agnew Diary, July 24, 1865; Robert Battey to Mary Battey, July 19, 1865, in Battey papers; *SCu*, XXVI (1868), 207. Complaints of idleness and poor work habits are so numerous it would be impossible to list the citations for the postwar period. Statistically, for each landowner who expressed satisfaction with free labor during the first two years after the war, there were forty complaints, many of them expressed with unrepressed fury. See also Roark, *Masters Without Slaves*, 11–55.

prehensively) that black southerners were as anxious to buy, sell, and accumulate as whites and that this alone would drive them to work harder
under freedom. But southern whites (and a good number of northerners)
knew that there was an undercurrent of resistance to the strict regimen of
the postwar workplace. When federal agent R. B. Avery scolded a former
slave for raising dogs rather than hogs, Samuel Maxwell replied with irrefutable logic: "A pig won't help us catch coons and rabbits." Avery found
this a detestable form of laziness and attributed it to the debilitating legacy
of slavery. A hundred years later, however, the South Carolina author
William Price Fox had one of his poor white characters respond with
equally irrefutable logic to his wife's complaint that he had traded the family's last hog for still another red-tick hound. "Emma Louise," replied
Coley Moke scornfully, "I traded that hog and got me a dog for the plain
and simple reason that I can't go running no fox with no hog."[37] Large
numbers of black and white southerners may not have been "lazy," but they
always acted on the assumption that there was a rational trade-off between
the uncertain returns of long hours in the hot sun and the immediate rural
pleasures of hunting, fishing, and socializing.

Respectable southern whites might respond with bemused and tolerant
scorn when they encountered those "shiftless" whites who existed on the
margins of society, but they were convinced that their future survival—let
alone their prosperity—was threatened by emancipation. In the absence of
those controls that whites believed made the biracial society possible, eight
to ten thousand southerners fled the region in futile attempts to re-create
their old life in Central and South America. Most of these emigrants fared
disastrously and returned to the United States as soon as they were finan-
cially able. News of their desperate plight deterred other potential travelers
after 1866.[38] Well before the disastrous results of emigration were known to

37. R. B. Avery, Report, n.d., Samuel Maxwell, Claim, June 8, 1878, both in Liberty
County, Ga., Case Files, Southern Claims Commission, RG 217, NA; William Price Fox,
Southern Fried Plus Six (St. Simons Island, Ga., 1974), 165–66. In questioning of witnesses,
members of the Joint Committee on Reconstruction continuously sought reassurance from observers and visitors to the postwar South that the freed men and women were motivated by the
same acquisitive instincts that they believed drove whites to labor. Eric Foner, like a number of
other recent historians, has argued that former slaves resisted the regimen of the marketplace.
Foner, "Reconstruction and the Crisis of Free Labor," in his *Politics and Ideology in the Age of
the Civil War* (New York, 1980), 98–101. It is a point with which I certainly agree, although
historians should always be cautious in equating a reluctance to work long hours for minimal
returns with ideological resistance to work discipline.

38. Lawrence F. Hill, "The Confederate Exodus to Latin America," *SwHQ*, XXXIX
(1935), 100–34, 161–99, 309–26; Douglas A. Grier, "Confederate Emigration to Brazil,
1865–1870" (Ph.D. dissertation, University of Michigan, 1968); Andrew F. Rolle, *The Lost
Cause: The Confederate Exodus to Mexico* (Norman, Okla., 1965); Blanche Henry Clark
Weaver, "Confederate Emigration to Brazil, 1865–1870," *JSH*, XXVII (1961), 333–53;

whites, however, most had acknowledged the impossibility of re-creating the Old South—though it is extraordinary how many spoke longingly of migration from the land of their birth. They also dreamed of a South in which blacks simply disappeared. And such dreams made possible the brief flowering of the interrelated delusions of the "vanishing Negro" and the prospect of massive white immigration into the region.

Like other postwar illusions the myth of the vanishing Negro had its origins in the antebellum proslavery argument. Without the care and control of kindly masters, southerners had argued, blacks inevitably would perish from hunger and disease. Nor was this idea restricted to southerners. In an 1843 lecture, the New York anatomist and surgeon John Augustine Smith sadly concluded that emancipation would lead to the annihilation of the "weaker race" as "sure as the sun is to rise." Pointing to the "well-known facts of ethnologists," the former governor of South Carolina predicted in the summer of 1865 that the "negro race will now run out." And Episcopal Bishop Stephen Elliott of Georgia agreed. He insisted that he had only the "highest interests" of the freedmen at heart, but the facts were inescapable and the racial consequences of emancipation inevitable. "Avarice and cupidity and ignorance will do for their extinction what they have always done for an unprotected inferior race. Poverty, disease, and intemperance will follow in their train and do the rest." There was in all predictions of racial suicide a sonorous ring of certainty as ethnography, history, and "common sense" were summoned to document the obvious. The "mulattoes as an inferior hybrid race will be the first to go, claimed the racist New York *World*, but the pure-blooded blacks will soon sink to the same state of barbarism and savagery."[39]

Again and again, white southerners pointed to the fate of the Indian. Only the careful and close supervision of southern slaveowners had kept their bondsmen from the fate of Latin American slaves who were never able to replenish their numbers through natural reproduction. But with that supervision forever gone, "like the red man of the forest, the freedmen will follow the tide of destiny to utter extinction." In fact, the Negro was even more unsuited for self-survival than the Indian. The native American at least had a history of self-reliance and self-sufficiency. The North American Indians had been massacred piecemeal by the whites who claimed their

New York *Herald*, January 2, 1866; Montgomery *Advertiser*, July 17, 1866. Even in Brazil, where slavery still existed, southerners hardly found it possible to re-create the Old South. See "The Brazilian Diary of Andrew McCullon [1865]," Andrew McCullon Collection, SHC.

39. William Stanton, *The Leopard's Spots: Scientific Attitudes Toward Race in America, 1815–1859* (Chicago, 1960), 313; New York *World*, n.d., quoted in Atlanta *Daily Intelligencer*, July 15, 1865.

hunting grounds, observed the London *Herald* viewing the evolving events in the postwar South. "The negro is now a rival of the white man instead of his servant and he will disappear more rapidly than his copper-colored predecessor." While the editor of the Selma *Daily Messenger* denied that southern whites would harm their former freedmen ("unless they rise against the whites"), he agreed with the London *Herald* that fifty years hence the "genuine Southern born and bred negro, as he exists now, will prove then as great a rarity as the Indians are at this time." With a more savage swipe at blacks and their northern supporters, a Georgia journalist predicted that the "day will come when a Yankee will exhibit among the 'Cowikees' a bush negro as a curiosity, charging 25 cents admission fee."[40]

Not surprisingly, many whites claimed to see evidence on every side of the impending racial extinction of the freedmen. "They are dying by hundreds with starvation and sickness," wrote Francis Warrington Dawson from Richmond in the fall of 1865. And he added in a savage footnote, "I can only hope . . . that the whole negro race will soon become extinct." For a number of planters, who depended upon black labor, however, there was little reason to rejoice. A committee of Calhoun, South Carolina, planters expressed grave concern over the future of their agricultural interests since the freedmen were "diminishing at a fearful rate."[41]

Southern writers soon filled their diaries and conversations with accounts of blacks concentrated in overcrowded and unsanitary conditions, "dying of disease and want," their fate sealed by their refusal to attend to each other. "They will often see a fellow-laborer and even a near relative die for want of a cup of gruel or of water, rather than lose a few hours' sleep in watching," insisted an Alabama doctor. One Georgia planter claimed in his diary that three hundred of the five hundred former slaves who had once

40. The voluminous prophetic literature of extinction in the postwar era is equally apparent in the private and the public record, although it was more common among well-educated southerners familiar with the writings of such proslavery ethnologists as Josiah Nott. See Raleigh *Standard*, January 19, 1866; Macon *Daily Telegraph*, June 22, 1865; *Fa*, II (1867), 36–37; South Carolina Committee on Immigration, *South Carolina House of Representatives Special Committee on European Immigration, Report on the Subject of Encouraging European Immigration* (Charleston, 1866), 3–8; Richmond *Times*, January 4, 1866; London *Herald*, June 26, 1865, quoted in Selma *Daily Messenger*, July 30, 1865; New Orleans *Times*, October 22, 1865; *Letter of Hon. Francis W. Pickens. The Crops and Conditions of the Country. The Interests of Labor. Effects of Emancipation. The Different Races of Mankind. Written to a Gentleman of New Orleans* (Baltimore, 1866), 6–7; Affleck to Alexander Hannay, July 14, 1865, in Affleck Papers; George Anderson Mercer Diary, SHC, June 11, 1865; David Schenck Diary, Jun 18, 1866. After the war, Nott reaffirmed his antebellum prediction of race extinction in two articles, "Climates of the South in Their Relations to White Labor, *DR*, 2nd ser., I (1866), 166, and "The Problem of the Black Races," 269, 281.

41. Francis Warrington Dawson to Father, October 4, 1865, in Dawson Papers, DUL; Committee of Calhoun Citizens, "The Future of South Carolina," *DR*, II (1866), 41.

belonged to a nearby planter had died in the two months after the war. The rate of black mortality in Savannah, claimed George Mercer, was a thousand a month. (It was in reality less than a hundred a month.) The normally level-headed Robert Patton of Alabama predicted a 25 percent decline in the black population of the southern states during the first five years after emancipation, a conclusion endorsed by Georgia's most prominent Baptist church leader. Even such federal agencies as the wartime Sanitary Commission called attention to what it claimed was the "great mortality of colored troops under similar circumstances of diet and exposure with white troops." This "inherent" racial weakness had grave implications for the future of the freed Negro, claimed a commission physician, and should be "soberly considered by physiologists and philanthropists."[42]

Spurred by the bleak stories of the impending extinction of the freedmen, colonization—a scheme discredited for most antebellum southerners by its association with the antislavery movement—underwent a desultory revival. J. D. B. De Bow, a consistent antebellum opponent of colonization, opened the pages of his magazine to colonization advocates and outlined a fifty-year program of black emigration, complete with cost projections and proposed colonization sites. As Lincoln had done before his death, De Bow insisted that Africa was "too remote and pestilential" and suggested instead several locations in Central and South America where the United States might establish a black protectorate complete with educational and medical facilities and full opportunities for black self-government. In a critical caveat, however, De Bow revealed what may well have been his primary motive in suggesting such an outlandish proposal. If such a colony succeeded, "all humanity would rejoice." If it failed, said De Bow (with the unstated conviction that this was likely) "it would be but another link to the chain of facts proving that the black race cannot maintain itself when left alone."[43]

42. George Anderson Mercer Diary, June 11, 1865; Robert M. Patton, "The New Era of Manufactures," *DR*, 2nd ser., III (1867), 58; Macon *Daily Telegraph*, February 18, 1866; Nott, "The Problem of the Black Races," 281; *SCB*, I (1864), 743; Josph C. G. Kennedy to James R. Doolittle, March 9, 1866, *PSHA*, VIII (1904), 369–70; Dr. Erasmus Darwin P. Fenner, "[Postwar] Mortality of Negroes in America," *NOC*, XII (1867), 312–15. Statistics on early postwar mortality are notoriously inaccurate. The 1866 censuses taken by Georgia and Alabama, which purported to show a massive decline in black population, were soon shown to be inaccurate. There is some evidence that black mortality tended to be higher in urban areas as a result of communicable diseases caused by poverty and overcrowded and unsanitary conditions, but there is nothing to indicate a dramatic increase in the death rate. See, for example, the death statistics of Charleston, Montgomery, Savannah, and New Orleans for the first postwar months. Charleston *Daily Courier*, April 6, 1867; Augusta *Transcript*, n.d., quoted in Charleston *Daily Courier*, January 21, 1866; Montgomery *Advertiser*, March 17, 1866; *NOC*, XII (1867), 588–89.

43. De Bow, "The State of the Country," 144–45. De Bow's scheme was patterned very closely after that of Hinton Rowan Helper's in *The Impending Crisis* (New York, 1859),

The widespread myth of the vanishing freedman gave an extra induce-
ment to the development of an equally bizarre aspect of postwar southern
thought: the belief that the end of slavery would lead to a floodtide of white
immigration into the postwar South. Southern proponents of economic
self-reconstruction had found in this illusion a comfortable and appealing
solution to many of the dilemmas their grandiose plans seemed destined to
encounter. They had expressed little confidence in the ability of former
slaves to function either as independent agricultural laborers or as the
sturdy mechanics and operatives of an industrializing South. In almost all
of the literature supporting postwar economic self-reconstruction, there
were enthusiastic references to the inevitable tide of European and northern immigration. These whites would come into the South, not to replace
the freedmen in the cotton fields, but to act as agents of agricultural and
industrial revitalization. As one reflection of this interest in immigration,
there were more than one hundred immigration companies established in
the South during the first two years after the war.

The majority of northern whites also believed that the end of slavery
would dramatically increase white emigration into the region, but they
gave, for the most part, little attention to the apocalyptic theories of race
suicide. They were far more attracted to the notion that the integration of
faithful unionists in the former Confederacy would lay the foundation for a
truly loyal South by revitalizing the region's decadent economic and political system. Far from presiding over the extinction of the freedmen, northerners would start the former slave on the road to self-improvement by introducing the panaceas of education and free labor.[44]

Obviously, this was not what southern whites had in mind. "If I can't
manage the negroes," declared Joseph Smith of Solitude Plantation in the
Louisiana Delta, "I will import, Germans, Swedes or some other race."
Many landowners were so desperate for "controllable" labor they were willing to consider the most bizarre expedients. One group of Georgia planters
seriously contemplated the creation of a "deputation of intelligent planters"
to visit the West Indies and Cuba to investigate the "Coolie system" and
arrange for its transplantation to the South. Fellow planters in South Carolina agreed. "I, with many others similar situated, am anxious to substitute

---

49–156. In view of most white southerners' hostility toward antislavery Helper, De Bow understandably did not emphasize the connection. For other support for the colonization movement, see Rev. Isaac Henderson, "The Future of the Negro Population," *DR*, I (1866), 58;
Augusta *Daily Press*, July 26, 1866; Atlanta *Daily Intelligencer*, April 11, 1866.

44. See, for example, Lawrence Powell's discussion of the assumptions of northern planters
in *New Masters*, 1–34. Powell describes one of the most important promoters of northern landowning in the South in "The American Land Company and Agency," *CWH*, XXI (1975),
293–308.

coolie or Asiatic labor," wrote a large landowner in the summer of 1865. "We are encouraged to make the experiment here by the success which has attended it in California." And one state senator worked for legislative appropriations that would subsidize their immigration. The Chinese were "active, hardy and willing operatives," he said. For the production of cotton, "no foreign labor will likely succeed so well as the Coolie."[45]

Smith and his fellow planters wanted docile, manageable labor. But other postwar southerners were more interested in immigration as a method of modernizing and reshaping the region's economy. To these proponents of southern self-reconstruction, the European or northern immigrant would not come South to replace the freedman in the cotton field but to substitute "small, neat, flourishing and improved small farms." The northern and European immigrant, unlike the freedman, would promote not only small farming but "diversified industrial pursuits." These immigrants, repeating the pattern of America's colonial forebears, would become the sturdy yeoman of Thomas Jefferson's dream.[46]

The irreconcilable aims of planters, southern self-reconstructionists, and the immigrants themselves were soon apparent. Thomas Affleck of Glenblythe, Texas, a longtime planter, outlined an ambitious plan in June and July of 1865 for "rejuvenating the South through immigration." Affleck, who was familiar with previous German immigration movements into Texas, believed that to undertake such a program required careful planning, widespread publicity, and ample capital. His plan called for dividing his plantation and those of his neighbors into sections that could be easily farmed by one family, but the groups would be congregated into villages rather than isolated as in previous attempts. He would then travel to Scotland and sign up Scottish cottars to come as colonists. They would pay their own transportation costs and sign a five-year contract. He would furnish land, teams, and implements, and would advance their first year's food. In return they would receive one-third of the crop. If they furnished teams and implements, they would receive half of the crop. Throughout the fall and winter of 1865, Affleck gathered support for his project, writing

45. Joseph Davis Smith to Son, September 22, 1865, in Joseph Davis Smith Papers; Houston *Tri-Weekly Telegraph*, July 13, 1865; Macon *Daily Telegraph*, August 9, 1865; Yorkville (S.C.) *Enquirer*, October 28, 1865; Bennettsville (S.C.) *Journal*, n.d., quoted in Yorkville *Enquirer*, August 2, 1866. For a discussion of the issue in Alabama during early Reconstruction, see Sylvia Krebs, "The Chinese Labor Question: A Note on the Attitudes of Two Alabama Republicans," *AHQ*, XXXVIII (1976), 214–17.

46. *SCu*, XXIII (1865), 188; Raleigh *Daily Standard*, August 2, 1865; Augusta *Chronicle and Sentinel*, June 28, 1865; Raleigh *Sentinel*, July 28, October 27, 1865; Augusta *Daily Press*, March 13, 1866; Rome (Ga.) *Southerner*, n.d., quoted in the Augusta *Daily Press*, March 16, 1866; Richmond *Whig*, May 18, 1865; Macon *Daily Telegraph*, October 8, 1865; South Carolina Committee, *Report on Immigration*, 11–12; *Fa*, I (1866), 44–45, 91.

letters, arranging finances, and publicizing the project. In the spring of 1866, with the support of several friends, he incorporated the Texas Emigration Aid & Loan Improvement Company. The prospectus spoke vaguely of a capital of a million dollars; in reality it was less than ten thousand dollars. In late May he sailed from Galveston to New York and from there to Scotland with applications for immigrants from dozens of individuals and with high hopes.[47]

One year after he left, Affleck wrote bitterly from London of his "complete and utter failure." Although he ascribed the failure to the unsettled political situation of the South, it is obvious that he had found the Scottish cottars remarkably unresponsive to his glowing promises of a "pretty village" (the former slave quarters) or the nearby "Kirk" that would be available (a church he had formerly kept for his slaves). Clearly, the needs of southern planters and the ambitions of land-hungry European immigrants did not always coincide.[48]

Even when southerners succeeded in bringing groups of immigrants to settle in the South, their experiments were almost uniformly disastrous. J. Floyd King, the son of wealthy Georgia planter Thomas Butler King, came out of the war with little more than his good name and a record of service in the Confederacy. He went north in the summer of 1865 with plans to start a sawmill on his old family plantation. Unable to find a financial backer, he became an agent of the American Emigrant Company. His background in planting and his distinguished southern connections made him the ideal choice for a major experiment in immigrant labor. And in the fall of 1865 he sailed from New York with 213 Dutch, Danish, and German immigrants and a commitment to lease a twenty-two-thousand-acre Louisiana Delta plantation.[49]

King started with high hopes but quickly realized that he had inherited a nightmare. When he landed in New Orleans he almost lost his entire contingent when a local planter offered them jobs at more than the AEC had promised them. With help from local parish officials, he managed to get them upriver to the plantation near Natchez, Mississippi, where they had been promised comfortable housing and ample food. When the immigrants saw the dilapidated slave shacks and tasted the fatback and cornbread, they sat down and refused to work. Even when King frantically began repairing the cabins and promised beef and bacon every day, he had little success. By

47. Houston *Tri-Weekly Telegraph*, July 22, 1865; Affleck to Hannay, July 14, 1865 (copy), and see Affleck Letterbooks, 1865, 1866, in Affleck Papers.

48. Affleck to Charles S. Sawyer, May 14, 1866, in Affleck Papers.

49. J. Floyd King to Anne [Lin], December 24, 29, 1865, in Thomas Butler King Papers, SHC.

the end of January he had lost over half his labor force. The experiment was a disaster.[50] Something of the interest of southerners in the immigration question can be judged from the fact that at least thirty-seven firms advertised in southern newspapers in 1865 and 1866, promising to import white labor from the North or from overseas.[51] Official efforts to encourage immigration also continued halfheartedly through the next two years, as most of the southern states created immigration bureaus, immigration agencies, or boards of immigration; gave them gradiose charters; and then failed to appropriate any funds. John Wagener, immigration commissioner for South Carolina, drew up a detailed plan for placing state agents in every country of Western Europe, advertising in all major European publications, and stationing bilingual state representatives in South Carolina communities near proposed settlements of Europeans. The Virginia and Alabama immigration boards drew up similarly ambitious plans, which were endorsed by J. D. B. De Bow in the *Review*. But in none of the states did the legislature appropriate more than a pittance; in most, nothing at all.[52]

The immigration movement was a charade that reflected the fantasies of white southerners rather than a genuine possibility for change. Quite apart from the fact that the immigrants' hunger for land collided head-on with the landowners' desire for cheap, docile wage labor, white southerners were never able to agree on the value of the new arrivals or to put aside their fears and prejudices about outsiders. Some argued that Europeans were preferable to northern whites. "The Yankee goes forth carrying his own character with him," argued a South Carolina legislative committee, while the "Europeans come among us [and] adopt our habits and ideas." On the other hand, there were southerners who were even more suspicious of Europeans than of Yankees. "Immigrants from Europe are usually low-minded agrarians who settle to themselves in large bodies and preserve . . . their national peculiarities," insisted George Fitzhugh. And there were still others who were quick to point out that the importation of Asians would simply repeat

50. King to John Mallery, January 18, 1866, in Thomas Butler King Papers.
51. Unfortunately the papers of most of these immigration companies did not survive, but there are two collections that have significant materials—that of Theodore Boinest, South Carolina Agent of the American Emigrant Company from 1865 to 1866 (DUL), and the papers of Thomas Affleck.
52. John A. Wagener to James L. Orr, February 22, 1867, in Orr Papers; *Fa*, I (1866), 294–95; *Alabama Acts*, 1866–67, No. 314, adopted February 6, 1867, copy in Alabama Governors' Papers, AA; (Jacksonville) *Florida Union*, October 14, 1865; J. D. B. De Bow, "Future of the U.S.," *DR*, 2nd ser., I (1866), 10–12. For surveys of the quite different black and white attitudes toward immigration, see Rowland T. Berthoff, "Southern Attitudes Toward Immigration, 1865–1914," *JSH*, XVII (1951), 328–39, and David J. Hellwig, "Black Attitudes Toward Immigration Labor in the South, 1865–1910," *FCHQ*, LIV (1980), 151–68.

their forebears' folly of introducing a "hostile" race into the region. For all "ethnological experts" quoted in the southern press agreed that the Chinese were "licentious; extremely loose in morals; [and] possessed by the most disgusting and demoralizing practices." When the Republican Reconstruction regimes replaced the Johnsonian governments, they were understandably reluctant to underwrite programs openly designed to replace the freedmen.[53] By the end of the century, there were pockets of Asians scattered throughout the Delta as visible symbols of the desperate search of white southerners for alternatives to emancipated labor. But the region was to remain untouched by the waves of immigration that would transform the nation in the late nineteenth and early twentieth century.

There were opportunities for immigrants in the postwar South, but few were willing to forgo the known challenges and opportunities of the American North and West for a war-torn and backward region. Like many southern political leaders, Alabama Governor Robert M. Patton issued a public invitation to northern and foreign immigrants in late 1865 and urged them to seek their fortune in the South rather than the West. In an article in *De Bow's Review* he described the remarkable opportunities that awaited new arrivals in the industrial Eldorado that Alabama was certain to become in the 1860s and 1870s. But when confronted by a lengthy and precise questionnaire from the German society of New York ("What are current monthly salaries for laborers . . . ? What resources are available to finance land purchases . . . ? Are there *well-funded* public schools and churches in the districts in which laborers are required?"), he could only respond with the hackneyed assurance that German immigrants would be a "welcome addition" to the economy of the state.[54]

During the first full year after the war, a quarter of a million immigrants entered the United States. Although more than a third (ninety-seven thou-

53. South Carolina Committee, *Report on Immigration*, 12; Edward Conigland to Thomas Ruffin, December 4, 1865, in Ruffin Papers; George Fitzhugh, "Cam Lee and the Freedmen's Bureau," *DR*, II (1866), 355; Yorkville (S.C.) *Enquirer*, October 28, 1865, August 2, 1866; Houston *Tri-Weekly Telegraph*, July 7, 1865; Louis Agassiz to Samuel Gridley Howe, August 9, 10, 1863, in E. C. Agassiz, *Louis Agassiz: His Life and Correspondence* (2 vols.; Boston, 1866); Joseph Davis Smith to Son, April 15, 1865, in Smith Papers; Natchez *Daily Courier*, November 10, 1865; Augusta *Daily Press*, February 22, March 4, 1866; R. Dozier to Rev. Theodore S. Boinest, October 9, 1868, John M. Mathis to Boinest, June 28, 1868, both in Boinest Collection; *Fa*, II (1867), 35–36; New Orleans *Times*, November 12, 1865; Richmond *Enquirer*, July 18, 1868; Macon *Daily Telegraph*, July 24, 1866. Particularly revealing are the sceptical letters from the heads of immigrant groups to southern political leaders. See Willy Wallach to Gov. Robert M. Patton, January 22, 1860; W. H. Quincy to Lewis Parsons, October 16, 1865, all in Alabama Governors' Papers; J. E. Orr to Gov. James Orr, August 18, 1866, in Orr Papers.

54. German Society of New York to Patton, January 30, 1866, Patton to Wallach, February 21, 1866 (copy), both in Alabama Governors' Papers.

sand) settled in New York City, there was significant movement directly into the nation's agricultural states. Illinois received twenty-two thousand immigrants; Wisconsin, nine thousand; and Ohio, thirteen thousand. More than eight thousand settled in the rural areas of Pennsylvania. In contrast, the entire South received fewer than three thousand immigrants, with the great majority settling in Virginia and Tennessee. Such statistics hardly supported the notion that the South—once slavery had disappeared— would become a mecca for white immigration.[55]

H. D. Boozer, a Newberry, South Carolina, planter, would later give his bitter assessment of the "immigration craze," as he called it. After paying the passage from Germany for seven men, one woman, and two children, he had had their services for less than three months before they quietly slipped away one evening in the midst of the growing season. Without laborers, without money, he angrily declared: "I am four hundred dollars and sixty-five cents out to the Immigrants—they have nearly broke me. I have never in all my life lost as much money on one Enterprise as on this Immigration business."[56]

A poorer (but he thought wiser) Floyd King had also concluded very early after the war that it was foolish to attempt to import Europeans to replace the freedmen in the production of the staple crops of the South. These foreigners were ignorant of the "simplest principles of cotton production," said King, and they cared little about learning more on the subject. Moreover, they demanded "expensive" food and lodging, and they were even more unreliable than the freedmen in keeping to signed contracts. He could sympathize with desperate southern whites, King told his friend John Mallery, but the facts were indisputable. "Where the negro will work, he is by far the most profitable laborer." John Mallery could only agree. "I fed them better than ever I thought of feeding my hands," he said of his German workers, who insisted on beef, coffee, and sauerkraut, "when what should they do but demand butter for their bread and milk for their coffee." Mallery balked at this last "outrageous demand," and the entire work crew left in the middle of the growing season.[57]

More than he realized, Floyd King's chastened summary of the failed immigration enterprises of the postwar South reflected the shadowy substance of reformers' illusions and the seemingly inexorable drift of southern economic life. It was soothing for men to talk of a prosperous and racially homogeneous South revitalized through industrialization and agricultural

55. "Emigration at New York and the Emigration Board," *MM*, LVII (1867), 191.
56. H. D. Boozer to Boinest, June 16, 1868, in Boinest Collection.
57. (Jacksonville) *Florida Union*, December 30, 1865; King to Mallery, January 18, 1866, in Thomas Butler King Papers; Columbus (Ga.) *Enquirer*, June 10, 1866.

diversification. But where were the money to build and the skilled operatives to man the factories everyone prattled about? asked an Americus, Georgia, merchant. Even the dreams of ending the region's obsession with King Cotton seemed unreachable. Men might hold up the model of the North and complain of the problems of cotton, acknowledged Thomas Harrold, but the South's traditional staple crop required no "expensive cultivators, straw and hay cutters, corn shellers, reapers, self-discharging hay and grain rakes, corn planters, threshers and separators, force pumps, cider mills, churns, grain drills, mowers and the like." The South was beginning an uncertain and doubtful future with scarcely enough money to avoid starvation, Wilmer Shields told his employer. Few southerners, insisted the Mississippi overseer, had the resources to chase the tantalizing dreams of wealth through "feed crops, viticulture or Ramie production." It "seems to me very unwise to incur any great risque [*sic*]. Cotton is the answer." And Floyd King, despite all his talk of a changing South, essentially agreed. For he, after all, had brought those fair-skinned Europeans to the South to substitute them for the region's former slaves, not to transform the economic and social fabric of the Delta's cotton culture.[58]

For most white southerners, particularly those dependent upon the agricultural labor of the freed slaves, the comfortable catechisms of the proslavery argument were sufficient justification for inertia and resistance. Each step away from slavery would be taken grudgingly and reluctantly. Even those with ambitious plans for reshaping the postwar South soon concluded, however, that economic and social self-reconstruction could not be undertaken until the southern economy was stabilized and revived. And given the alternatives that existed in 1865 and 1866, this seemed to mean the resuscitation of the traditional plantation economy. Whatever alternatives they might consider for the distant future, the white southern leadership of 1865 had to return to the interlocking future of the freedmen and the plantation. And in that process, the proslavery argument—shaken but unbroken by emancipation—drew the overwhelming majority of whites into the same web of crippling assumptions.

58. Columbus (Ga.) *Enquirer*, January 12, 1866; Shields to Mercer, December 13, 1865, in Mercer Papers.

VI / Self-Reconstruction: The Final Act

HITE conservatives were fully aware of the pitfalls involved in the enactment of any legislation that affected the region's black population. As early as July, 1865, a close adviser of Alabama Provisional Governor Lewis Parsons warned that any laws perceived as "intemperate and unfair" would arouse the suspicions of moderate and conservative northerners and strengthen the arguments of Republicans who opposed the South's reentry into the Union. The editor of the Jackson *Clarion* echoed his words. The postwar legislatures had to enact "wholesome legislation to protect the white and black people of the South" even as they satisfied "the most sceptical Northerners that our law affords . . . [the freedmen] every protection and security." At the same time E. G. Richards was convinced that a failure to enact measures to regulate and control the behavior of the freedmen would lead to the inevitable collapse of the southern economy. At best, the South would "lapse into a primeval forest, like Haiti, Jamaica or any other of the West Indies." At worst there would be a racial holocaust far more gory and barbaric than the civil war through which the nation had just passed. Establishing this new relationship between black and white would require the "wisdom of Solomon" argued a politically sensitive South Carolina journalist. And he gloomily acknowledged that he had encountered very few men like Solomon in the months after the war.[1]

1. E. G. Richards to Lewis Parsons, July 21, 1865, in Alabama Governors' Papers, AA; Charleston *Daily Courier*, October 11, 1865; Jackson *Clarion*, October 11, November 12, 1865.

Julius Fleming was right. On no other issue did the postwar southern leadership fail so completely. A half century later, the Mississippi historian and politician J. H. Jones was still incredulous at the "stupidity" and "monumental folly" of his predecessors. They seemed to have slept through the Civil War like Rip Van Winkles, declared Jones, then awakened in the fall of 1865 to begin enacting legislation as though nothing had happened between Fort Sumter and Appomattox.[2]

That harsh judgment has echoed across a century and with good reason. The repressive racial legislation of 1865 and early 1866—half symbol and half cause of the Johnson government's downfall—was a product of political ineptitude. But it also reflected the deeply ingrained intellectual, ideological, and racial assumptions that continued to dominate the thinking of white southerners in the critical first months of white self-government in the region. Above all else, it was a chilling object lesson in the restraints that these notions placed upon any prospect for self-generated change in the region.

To most northerners who traveled through the defeated Confederacy in the months after the war, the difficulties southerners professed to see in incorporating the freedmen into southern society seemed irrational. In matters of equity and legal justice, insisted Whitelaw Reid, southerners should erect a judicial system blind to color and caste. To Reid and many fellow northerners, the only problem was the archaic and unreasoning attitudes of white southerners. "I have conversed with dozens of planters," said Reid as he neared the end of his travels, and their "talk all runs the same channel. They have no sort of conception of free labor." In legal and economic matters, agreed John Townsend Trowbridge, there was no hope for the recovery of the South until whites learned that "natural laws compel him [the freedmen]: we need no others." When a group of southern planters sullenly asked northern writer Edmund Kirke what he would do with four million emancipated blacks, the antebellum abolitionist responded, "Set them at work and pay them." And if they did not work, he cheerfully added, "they will starve."[3]

In practice, the issue was far more complex than either Reid or Trow-

2. J. H. Jones, "Reconstruction in Wilkinson County," *PMHS*, VIII (1904), 156.

3. Whitelaw Reid, *After the War: A Southern Tour* (Cincinnati, 1866), 417; John Townsend Trowbridge, *The South: A Tour of Its Battle-fields and Ruined Cities* (Hartford, 1866), 575; John Richard Dennett, *The South As It Is*, ed. Henry M. Christman (New York, 1965), 365–68; Sidney Andrews, *The South Since the War as Shown by Fourteen Weeks of Travel and Observation in Georgia and the Carolinas* (Boston, 1866), 398; John William De Forest, *A Union Officer in the Reconstruction*, ed. James H. Croushore and David M. Potter (New Haven, 1948), 28–29; Edmund Kirke, *Down in Tennessee and Back by Way of Richmond* (London, 1864), 26.

bridge acknowledged. It was true that most northerners were theoretically committed to a free-labor society governed by the natural laws of competition. The "talisman power" of free labor would ultimately remove the poverty and ignorance of the former slaves and "replace them with wealth, knowledge and happiness," insisted the head of the Georgia Freedmen's Bureau. But this ideological commitment was undercut by the existence of overtly discriminatory economic and political legislation in a dozen northern states and, even more important, by the precedents federal officials had established during and immediately after the war in dealing with black southerners.[4]

During the war itself, federal policy toward slaves in the liberated territories had evolved in stops and starts, the product of conflicting crosscurrents of idealism, political expediency, and military necessity. As Union forces pushed southward down the Mississippi toward Vicksburg and northward from New Orleans in 1863 and 1864, Louisiana's richest sugar-producing region came under federal control. With the economy in shambles (production in 1862 declined to less than 20 percent of the 1861 crop) and thousands of fleeing slaves crowding military posts, first General Benjamin Butler and later General Nathaniel P. Banks deliberately forced blacks back to the plantations. For their own well-being, argued Banks, the freedmen had to be made to work as wage laborers or sharecroppers, for only in this way could they be "preserved from vagrancy and idle, vicious habits." While Banks recognized the possibility that planters might mistreat and exploit their former slaves, he placed great faith in the formulation of written contracts spelling out the duties and obligations of landlord and tenant. A handful of abolitionist Republicans condemned Banks's policies as a re-institution of slavery, but he gained the support of centrist Republicans and the president.[5]

Although conditions changed rapidly after the war as a degree of stability returned to southern society, most military officials remained convinced that the freedmen had an inflated and unrealistic view of the consequences of emancipation. On the basis of "data carefully and conscientiously col-

4. Paul A. Cimbala, "'The Talisman Power': Davis Tillson, the Freedmen's Bureau, and Free Labor in Reconstruction Georgia, 1865–1866," *CWH*, XXVIII (1982), 154. For a general discussion of the way in which antebellum notions of free labor were affected by postwar events, see Eric Foner's "Reconstruction and the Crisis of Free Labor," in his *Politics and Ideology in the Age of the Civil War* (New York, 1980), 97–127.

5. U.S. Department of War, *Compendium of the General Orders of the United States Army, 1863, Department of the Gulf* (Washington, D.C., 1864), General Order No. 6, January 10, 1863. See also General Orders No. 12, 1863, *OR*, XV, 666–67. For a particularly critical analysis of Federal wartime policy, see Louis S. Gerteis, *From Contraband to Freedman: Federal Policy Toward Southern Blacks, 1861–1865* (Westport, Conn., 1973).

lected by my agents," concluded General Davis Tillson in Georgia, it was "obvious" that the freedmen were lazy, inclined to "shirk their work," and "great liars and most skillful thieves . . . breaking into smoke-houses throughout the country and . . . stealing and killing animals to an extent that jeopardizes the future prosperity of the State."[6]

Army officers and Freedmen's Bureau officials found themselves torn between a duty to protect the rights of the freedmen and frantic commitment to reviving the southern economy. "I am clean worn out with their wan and haggard beggary," complained a cavalry officer in Okolona, Mississippi, in the early summer of 1865. "I would rather face an old-fashioned wartime skirmish line anytime than the inevitable morning eruption of lean and hungry supplicants." Each day Lieutenant Colonel H. C. Forbes confronted unmistakable evidence of the "cruelty and heartlessness" of planters who made a mockery of their oft-expressed love of "their people." But Forbes was also a good nineteenth-century liberal who believed that progress for the former freedmen was possible only if they practiced hard work, temperance, punctuality, and honesty in their labors. After two months in the field, he was convinced that "demoralization" had overtaken the freedmen. A "large portion of the able-bodied are already become vagrants and more are daily become so." The slightest disagreement with their former masters sent them into "vagabondism," claimed Forbes, and as soon as they ceased to work, "they subsist by stealing." As Federal soldiers, "we can neither recognize slavery nor its equivalent," argued the dispirited Forbes, but how could the former planters be expected to clothe and to feed the dependent freedmen when they lacked "control of the labor needful to provide the means?" Politicians sat at a distance free to "spin very fine theories for the regulation of the labor question," concluded Forbes, but he had discovered the uselessness of all theories in the face of the chaos he encountered.[7]

Forbes, like many of his fellow army officers, was unable to understand that the flight of freed slaves from their former masters was often an attempt to avoid painful and potentially dangerous confrontations. A minority of freed men and women accepted the inevitablity of conflict and bluntly demanded their rights, inevitably infuriating and frightening whites unaccustomed to such behavior. But most continued to use the same methods of indirection and passive resistance that had been effective under the old regime. After the war the decision to leave, to simply walk away, was itself a nonviolent assertion of independence.

6. Savannah *National Republican*, November 7, 1865.
7. Lt. Col. H. C. Forbes, undated report quoted in Edward Hatch to Brig. Gen. W. D. Whipple, June 22, 1865, *OR*, Vol. XLIX, Pt. 2, pp. 1024–25.

Occasionally army and Freedmen's Bureau officials recognized this by blaming landlords and planters for the refusal of the freed blacks to remain under their former masters. In the first weeks after Appomattox, however, most federal officials single-mindedly concentrated upon resurrecting the southern economy. And this meant, in their view, returning the freed men and women to the same fields where they had worked all their lives. During that early summer of 1865, therefore, local army officers adopted stringent and sometimes draconian measures. In mid-June the provost marshal of Lynchburg, Virginia, announced that "hereafter all negroes employed within the limits of the city will be required to have passes from their employers stating that they are in their employ and all found without such passes will be arrested." One hundred and fifty miles to the east, a Smithfield provost marshal sent letters throughout his district assuring planters that they still had the right to restrict the movement of their former slaves and to exercise "wholesome restraint" in cases of impudence and misconduct.[8]

After a northern missionary complained, Provost Marshal William Bullard withdrew his endorsement of corporal punishment and reluctantly informed white Virginians that they could not restrict the movements of the freedmen. But he assured planters that there would be no collapse of discipline in his district; he would "severely punish insolence and misconduct or vagrancy" by the freedmen. Under direct orders from Secretary of War Stanton, the Freedmen's Bureau and the army explicitly outlawed a pass system in late June of 1865 because it smacked of the old slave pass system, but the tendency of officers in the first few weeks after Appomattox to require such documents is understandable since it had been federal policy as late as the spring of 1865. Even after the army had disavowed restrictions on the movements of the freedmen, Peter J. Osterhaus, commander of the Department of the Gulf, struck a common note in June of 1865 when he sternly warned the freedmen under his jurisdiction to remain on their old plantations unless they were abused or maltreated.[9]

The common outlook that sometimes bound army officers and white southerners together was nowhere better illustrated than in the black-belt Georgia community of Macon. There, in June of 1865, the commander of

8. William Bullard to R. H. Riddick, June 13, 17, 1865, in J. R. Kilby Papers, DUL; Lynchburg (Va.) *Republican*, June 3, 1865.
9. Donald Nieman, "To Set the Law in Motion: The Freedmen's Bureau and the Legal Rights of Blacks, 1865–1868" (Ph.D. dissertation, Rice University, 1975), 120–22; Houston *Tri-Weekly Telegraph*, June 23, 1865; Columbus (Ga.) *Enquirer*, July 6, 1865; *Flake's Bulletin* (Galveston, Tex.), June 17, 1865; Meridian (Miss.) *Clarion*, August 9, 1865. Osterhaus' General Orders No. 57, dated May 27, 1865, was repeatedly reprinted in the Meridian *Clarion* and the other Mississippi newspapers during June, July, and August of 1865.

the local garrison sat down with the city fathers to assist them in preparing a series of ordinances that would restore order to their community. "Whereas the relationship of master and slave" had ceased to exist, began the legislation, "be it ordained by the Mayor and Council of the City of Macon . . . , that all idle, mischievous and disorderly negroes found in the city, be taken up by the police and confined in the guardhouse, preparatory to trial before the mayor." The mayor was to have the power to inflict "such penalties as ball and chain, bread and water, work on the streets, public works, confinement in the guardhouse and stocks." The Macon code was the first of several that would be adopted during the summer of 1865. Although military officials were seldom so directly involved in writing these urban black codes, the town councils of Galveston, Texas; Opelousas, Louisiana; and Lynchburg, Virginia, passed similar ordinances at the request of local provost marshals.[10]

Quite apart from their overtly discriminatory provisions, such local legislation invited abuse by white authorities. Although Macon's mayor insisted that whites as well as freedmen were subject to arrest for such offenses as "public idleness" or the "use of obscene language on the streets," freed men and women were disproportionately represented on the city court docket under these charges. The mayor alleged that this was simply a reflection of the "demoralization" of the city's black population, but it was considerably more difficult for him to justify the racially disparate sentences he daily administered. In early July a white townsman charged with drawing a knife and threatening a local merchant in a dispute over prices received a five-dollar fine. At the same session, a black laborer convicted of using obscene language (he cursed a white resident who had pushed him off the sidewalk) was given the ball and chain for twenty days' work on the streets. By August the mayor's court had established what would become a venerable tradition in the postwar South. The majority of blacks convicted in the court were released into the custody of their landlords and forced to work out their fines for their employers.[11]

When they encountered such a sympathetic attitude from federal of-

10. Macon *Daily Telegraph*, June 15, 1865; Atlanta *Daily Intelligencer*, July 15, 1865; Houston *Daily Telegraph*, June 17, 1865; Howard Ashley White, *The Freedmen's Bureau in Louisiana* (Baton Rouge, 1970), 20–21; Columbia (S.C.) *Phoenix*, May 3, 1865; Selma *Daily Messenger*, July 30, 1865. Other accounts of such black codes may be found in Freedmen's Bureau and army records and state archives. See, for example, G. Wilson (town intendant) to Colonel Thomas, June 24, 1865, Brig. Gen. Wager Swayne to Parsons, July 31, 1865, both in Alabama Governors' Papers; *OR*, Vol. XLVIII, Pt. 2, pp. 854–55, Vol. XLIX, Pt. 2, pp. 728, 916, 1043–44.

11. See reports of the mayor's courts in the Macon *Daily Telegraph* for June, July, August, and September, 1865.

ficials, white southerners initially responded with surprise and gratitude. A month after Union soldiers arrived in Raleigh, Ann Battle reported to her brother that several freedmen had gone to the state capital with complaints of ill treatment. The local provost marshal, after questioning black workers on the Battle plantation, dismissed the charges and warned the freedmen that such "frivolous complaints" would result in stern punishment by the army. "Whenever the complaint of the negro is investigated and proved to be in fault," reported Battle, the commander of the local garrison allowed the former master to "correct them or have it done themselves."[12]

By midsummer, almost every southern newspaper had recounted stories of freedmen who were rudely disabused of their assumption that Federal army officers would take their side against their former masters. The Atlanta *Journal* gleefully told its readers of one freedman who had wandered into the city's military commissary and requested an issue of rations. He was "tired of working" the *Journal* claimed, and he had decided to leave his plantation. The officer on duty instructed him to go behind the commissary building. There two soldiers "first divested him of the few dirty rags he wore . . . and then buckled him down and administered to his broad ebony back rations that he hadn't counted on." The *Journal* editor concluded proudly, "We think it probable that he went to work after that, and will be willing to *work* for his rations in the future."[13]

In several localities army favoritism toward former slaveowners became so pronounced that paternalistic planters were placed in the anomalous position of criticizing their "Yankee overlords" for being unsympathetic to the freedmen. "A large number of farmers, finding they are making nothing, put off to Chester [South Carolina] with some frivolous complaint to the Provost Court & have their hands discharged," complained R. N. Hemphill from his Blackstone plantation. His brother agreed. The army officers' insensitive attitude toward the freedmen would lead to "great suffering on the part of blacks," concluded James Hemphill. The federal officers were simply "too obliging in listening to the complaints of whites." The son of a Savannah planter agreed. The "Yankee officers" showed the blacks "no kindness, no friendliness, no justice," he complained to his fiancée. Worst of all, they closed their eyes to the ways in which southern and northern whites "cheat the negro out of all he earns."[14]

As the control of freedmen's affairs passed into the hands of agents of the

12. Ann Battle to Kemp Battle, June 12, 1865, in Battle Family Papers, SHC.
13. Atlanta *Journal*, n.d., quoted in the Macon *Daily Telegraph*, June 1, 1865.
14. R. N. Hemphill to Rev. W. R. Hemphill, August 11, 1865, James Hemphill to Rev. W. R. Hemphill, August 27, 1865, both in Hemphill Collection, DUL; J. Floyd King to "Lin," January 1, 1866, in Thomas Butler King Papers, SHC.

newly created Freedmen's Bureau, emphasis shifted from maintaining order to protecting the freedmen's rights, but there remained considerable
continuity in the attitudes of the personnel of both federal agencies. When
the Louisiana Freedmen's Bureau commissioner was unable to find a suitable applicant to serve as a local agent for the bureau, he simply delegated
the duties to the nearest provost marshal. Even those local agents who were
ostensibly "civilians" had often developed notions of proper procedure from
a tour in the United States Army, for the majority were veterans. Joseph
Fullerton spoke as civilian head of the Louisiana Freedmen's Bureau *and* as
an army general when he warned black plantation workers that it was "not
the intention of the Bureau to nurse and pamper you, to feed and clothe
you, or to give you any privileges that others do not enjoy."[15]

Most Union officials saw their actions as temporary measures required
by the need to protect blacks from the oppression of whites and to ease
them through the first stages of the transition from slavery to freedom. And
few northerners saw any similarity between the federal government's be-
nevolent guardianship over the freedmen and the much heralded paternalism of white southern planters. Nevertheless, a national policy that had
veered erratically between laissez-faire and federal paternalism furnished
something less than a clearcut example of consistency on the subject of
legislation for the freedmen.[16]

The notion that whites (southern whites, that is) should serve as "protectors" of the South's freedmen struck a responsive chord among many postwar conservatives. The paternalism of the old regime, revised in light of the
changed condition of the postwar era (and sometimes presented in disarm-
ingly compassionate language) would often serve as the ideological basis
for the adoption of the postwar black codes. Public interests were always
paramount over private interests, argued the editor of the Richmond *Farmer*.
All men—and all groups—were bound to submit to restraints for the "gen-

15. J. Thomas May, "Continuity and Change in the Labor Program of the Union Army
and the Freedmen's Bureau," *CWH*, XVII (1971), 251. Almost every historical account of the
Freedmen's Bureau has commented upon the close ties between the military and the bureau.
See especially White, *Freedmen's Bureau in Louisiana*, 33; Clifton L. Ganus, Jr., "The Freedmen's Bureau in Mississippi" (Ph.D. dissertation, Tulane University, 1953), 54–58. For discussions in the secondary literature of the support that both the army and the bureau gave to
strict vagrancy laws, see James E. Sefton, *The United States Army and Reconstruction, 1865–
1877* (Baton Rouge, 1967), 42–43; Theodore Brantner Wilson, *The Black Codes of the South*
(University, Ala., 1965), 55–59. As a justification for the codes most of the state studies by
early twentieth-century historians emphasized the connection between the bureau policy on
vagrancy and that of white southerners.

16. Herman Belz has described the process by which the conflict between paternalistic supervision and laissez-faire policies was resolved by an emphasis upon full equality with the temporary guardianship of the Freedmen's Bureau. *Emancipation and Equal Rights: Politics and
Constitutionalism in the Civil War Era* (New York, 1978), 47–74.

184 / When the War Was Over

eral welfare" of society. In such a "harmonious and organic society" individuals had different talents and received different rewards, but all had general obligations to the society as a whole. In the South, where two "distinct races" were involved, one superior and the other inferior, it was essential that blacks remain in a "healthy subordination" so that they could be protected from their own failures and inadequacies. Under such conditions it was essential to adopt a legal code that sternly punished vagrants and required labor from the former slave, "not only for the peace, order and safety of the society but for the happiness of the freedman and his prosperity." In defense of his state's rigid vagrancy laws, a Virginia planter insisted they were designed not to punish "but to protect the freedman by safeguarding him from his natural dispositions." As Joel Williamson has noted, to northerners, legal protection for the freedman implied "protection in his natural and occasionally, in his civil and political rights." For southerners, however, protection for the Negro meant protection from his own inadequacies.[17]

Again and again former slaveholders returned to the comfortable rhetoric of paternalism to insist that they alone had the best interest of the freedmen at heart. George Fitzhugh urged his fellow southerners in 1865 and 1866 to accept the end of legal slavery, but he warned of the dangers inherent in abandoning a social structure that had regulated the "mutual duties and obligations" of black and white. There was every reason to believe it might be replaced by a more grinding despotism in which it would be—in Fitzhugh's phrase—"every man for himself and the devil take the hindmost." A competitive society was to replace slavery, and no one would be able to succeed in the oncoming "war of the wits" who was not "selfish, unfair in dealing, penurious and rapacious." Blacks would soon become helpless pawns, ruthlessly exploited by the wealthy on the one hand and physically attacked by resentful poor whites on the other. The "old system of patriarchal slavery has been changed," agreed a gloomy Francis Pickens, and laissez-faire capitalism—"the new modern system of slavery"—would soon be instituted.[18]

J. Floyd King professed to see this social and economic revolution months after the end of the war. There was nothing more depressing, he

17. *Fa,* I (1866), 242–43, 91; Joel Williamson, *After Slavery: The Negro in South Carolina During Reconstruction, 1861–1877* (Chapel Hill, 1965), 73.
18. *Letter of Hon. Francis W. Pickens. The Crops and Conditions of the Country. The Interests of Labor. Effects of Emancipation. The Different Races of Mankind. Written to a Gentleman of New Orleans* (Baltimore, 1866), 12. For similar statements by representatives and ideologues of the old planter class, see George Fitzhugh, "John Stuart Mill on Political Economy," *DR,* 2nd ser., III (1867), 53; Fitzhugh, "What's to Be Done with the Negroes," *ibid.,* I (1866), 578; J. D. B. De Bow, "Justice to the Freedmen," *ibid.,* II (1866), 91–92; *FF,* December 16, 1865, February 13, April 28, 1866; *Fa,* I (1866), 44–45.

wrote in the fall of 1865 from the Natchez plantation he managed, than to see the "physical abuse of blacks by lower class whites" and by the blustering nouveaux riches planters of the Delta. They blamed every petty theft on the freedmen and then "find in their inflamed heart no mercy for the offenders." If only the "old planter class" could regain control of the relationships between black and white.[19]

A minority of white conservatives went so far as to support the development of black education as an integral part of the new order. It was an "undeniable truth," insisted a Vicksburg planter writing in De Bow's Review, that the "best slaves were the educated. The most useful were the well-informed." It was simply not safe, agreed a Franklin, Tennessee, lawyer, "now that slavery is destroyed, to have the freedmen uneducated amongst us. The prosperity of this place as well as the entire South depends upon the educated laborer." Most southerners who encouraged black education believed that whites from the region (particularly upper-class whites) alone possessed that combination of patience and understanding of the abilities and limitations of the freedmen that would allow an education of the proper sort. The educational efforts of the Freedmen's Bureau and northern schoolmarms, on the other hand, seemed only to result in "increased dissatisfaction, impudence and worthlessness." But a handful of white southerners were so anxious to see the development of black education they were willing to accept schoolteachers of any background—local or northern blacks, even regular "Down Easters." Florida Provisional Governor William Marvin, for one, insisted that white southerners should welcome northern teachers. Some of them had their peculiarities, he admitted, but their talents in keeping the freedmen from becoming the "veriest vagabonds and . . . an incubus upon the country" far outweighed any faults. The Charleston Courier's correspondent in Sumter, South Carolina, was particularly distressed at fellow southerners' "daily fling at the 'Boston Schoolmarms.'" Popular education lessened crime and pauperism, insisted Julius Fleming, and it mattered not who supplied the "three r's."[20]

19. J. Floyd King to "Lin," January 1, 1866, in Thomas Butler King Papers.

20. (Jacksonville) Florida Union, July 29, 1865; John Hammond Moore (ed.), The Juhl Letters to the Charleston "Courier" (Athens, 1974), 120–21; Col. George W. Giles to Lt. Col. H. W. Smith, May 22, 1865, in BRFAL, South Carolina, Box 23; C. K. Marshall, "Education of the Freedmen," DR, 2nd ser., III (1867), 311–12; E. H. Freeman to Rev. Samuel Hunt, June 28, 1866, in AMA, Tennessee, Reel 1; "Education for Whites and Blacks," Fa, II (1867), 57–59; David Schenck Diary, SHC, March 13, 1866; Wilmer Shields to Dr. William Newton Mercer, December 1, 1866, in William Newton Mercer Papers, LSU; J. R. Siler to Robert M. Patton, March 23, 1867, in Alabama Governors' Papers; Journal of the Protestant Episcopal Church, Diocese of Alabama, 1867 (Mobile, 1867), 13. For a particularly fascinating view of the work of one prominent South Carolinian in this regard, see G. A. Trenholm's lengthy report to Gov. James L. Orr, October 12, 1866, in James L. Orr Papers, SCA. For a summary of the

The emphasis white southerners placed on black education was minimal at best. Continuing antebellum suspicions of black education were not easily abandoned, and many whites frankly preferred that blacks remain illiterate and uneducated. It was difficult to arouse much enthusiasm for public expenditures for black education at a time when most white schools remained closed. Nevertheless, there were whites who dissented. In part, they were convinced that education might help in the process of creating internal self-discipline within the black population since slavery no longer existed. To a lesser extent, there was a consciousness that an illiterate and ignorant population would act as a bar to economic development within the region.

But there was little support for education as a means of developing a self-reliant and independent black population. At base these paternal notions implied simply a shift from slavery to a modified form of legal serfdom. Fitzhugh, the veteran antebellum apologist for slavery, had a ready solution. Reaching back into classical antiquity, he compared the situation of the freedmen with that of the Roman freedmen who possessed limited civil but not political rights. The greatest protection of the Roman freedmen was not the vagary of the law but their wisdom in choosing "patrons" who served as sponsors and protectors, defending them from oppression and acting in their behalf in civil and legal matters. The future of the freedmen and the planters were "inextricably intertwined," agreed a Virginia publisher and planter. It was in the interest of the laborer to accept his subordination and the landowner in turn to exercise the obligations of noblesse oblige in protecting him.[21]

Fitzhugh's proposal for a form of legal paternalism modeled on Roman law had an appealing ring to a handful of southerners educated in the classics. A young army colonel traveling through Mississippi in the summer of 1865 was bewildered to overhear two planters trading historical references on the subject from their old Roman texts. The head of Georgia's special commission on the freedmen began his preparation for writing postwar legislation by reading and reflecting upon the "Ulpian and Papinian freedmen's code." Even the normally level-headed J. D. B. De Bow pointed approvingly to Roman law that made it possible for freedmen to "secure patrons . . . among the Patricians," who thought it no disgrace. The "negroes would profit by their example," said De Bow.[22]

mixed southern white response to black education, based primarily upon northern sources, see William Preston Vaughan, *Schools for All: The Blacks and Public Education in the South, 1865–1877* (Lexington, Ky., 1974).

21. Fitzhugh, "What's to Be Done with the Negroes," 579; *Fa*, I (1866), 243.

22. Col. J. L. Haynes to Capt. B. Filler, July 8, 1865, in BRFAL, Mississippi, Reel 10;

However elegantly quotations from Livy or Virgil might adorn their comments on the momentous postwar issues of race and law, practical men did not seriously consider the adoption of Roman law in the postwar South. Such comments instead reflected their attempts to find some legal stopping point between slavery and freedom that would satisfy the demands of the victorious Union but preserve and codify the subservient relationship of blacks to whites.

The story of the adoption of the black codes is filled with many ironies. Not the least is the fact that Andrew Johnson's provisional governors had sought to avoid what one privately called the "clamor of the unthinking masses" by placing this issue in the hands of carefully chosen commissions and legislative committees. Collectively, the men who framed postwar legislation affecting racial relations in the South constituted some of the most capable, cautious, and politically prudent individuals among the leaders who dominated the region's first postwar governments. Of the fourteen special commissioners or legislative committee members who authored the infamous black codes, eleven had been antebellum Whigs; and ten had been prominent attorneys or judges before the war. David Wardlaw of South Carolina and R. S. Donnell of North Carolina had served as superior court judges in the 1850s; Ebenezer Starnes, chairman of the special Georgia Committee on the Freedmen, sat on the Georgia Supreme Court during that same period. Horatio F. Simrall, chairman of the Mississippi committee, had been a professor of law at the University of Louisville before the war, and Armistead Burt of South Carolina and Bartholomew Figures Moore of North Carolina were widely acknowledged as among the most respected and eminent constitutional lawyers of the South. Something of their political moderation and flexibility may be judged by the fact that three of these men would ultimately become Republican appointees to their states' supreme courts in the late 1860s.[23]

Postwar racial legislation was a barometer of postwar public opinion in-

---

Washington, D.C., *National Intelligencer*, January 13, 1866, quoted in the Raleigh *Standard*, January 17, 1866.

23. Legislation touching upon the freedmen originated randomly from the Virginia, Louisiana, Texas, and Alabama legislatures, but it was under reasonably tight control in the North and South Carolina, Georgia, Florida, and Mississippi legislatures. The recommendations of the special Georgia committee were published in full in the Macon *Daily Telegraph*, January 9, 10, 11, 1866; the North Carolina committee, in the Raleigh *Daily Standard*, January 31, 1866; the Florida committee, in the *Florida House Journal*, 1865–66, pp. 56–59; and the South Carolina special commission, in a pamphlet, *Report of the South Carolina Commission on the Code* (Columbia, 1865). In Mississippi, the Joint Committee on the Freedmen did not issue a formal report, but the heart of the black code as it was adopted reflected the committee's point of view. See *Laws of the State of Mississippi*, October, November, and December, 1865, pp. 82–86.

creasingly tempered by white southerners' awareness of northern suspicion. The most politically sensitive proposal, however, would ultimately come from the North Carolina Commission on the Freedmen under the leadership of Bartholomew Moore. Moore, respected throughout American legal circles for his work as author of the 1854 Revised Code of North Carolina, had received national attention as early as 1834 for his successful defense of a North Carolina slave who had killed his overseer. Moore's legal brief in *State* v. *Will*, which affirmed the right of the slave to protect himself by force from unlawful violence, was one of the most subtle attempts by an antebellum southerner to reconcile the humanity of the slave with his status as "property." And much of the rationale of that 1834 argument foreshadowed Moore's postwar views.

A North Carolina court had sentenced "negro slave Will" to death for fatally stabbing his overseer. In a fit of rage, the overseer had made an unprovoked attack upon the slave who had first tried to flee and then fought back only when cornered. In his appeal, Moore had sought to find some middle ground between radical southerners' insistence on absolute power over their slaves and the equal-rights dogma of the antislavery movement. He believed he had found it in the legal relationship of the master to his apprentice. Although there were important differences in the two institutional arrangements, there was one essential similarity: the master had the right to control the labor of both, even to the point of using corporal punishment, but he did not have the right to unrestricted and abusive authority.

"Absolute power is irresponsible power, circumscribed by no limits save its own imbecility," argued Moore before the North Carolina Supreme Court. If anything, the slave should be allowed greater latitude and lenience than whites under the law. In an argument astonishing for its potential condemnation of slavery, Moore insisted that the "relation of master and slave may repress all the noble energies and manly sentiments of the soul, and may degrade the moral being into a brute condition." When that happened, said Moore, "we shall not be astonished to see the moral brute exhibiting the instinct natural to brute condition." He insisted that he supported the institution of slavery but that violence against the slave produced not harmony but "open conflicts and secret assassinations." What was necessary, argued Moore two and a half decades before the Civil War, was to use the law to improve the condition of this "unfortunate race of men" who were "advancing from the depths of slavery and wretchedness to a higher ground." Nor was the creation of a just legal system that protected the slave simply a matter of Christian benevolence. "Rome had no servile wars," Moore had warned his fellow North Carolinians, till her masters had outraged every feeling of justice and benevolence and made their slaves drink the cup of unmitigated cruelty to its last drop." The reference to the recently suppressed Nat Turner insurrection was unmistakable.[24]

Long before the crisis of the 1850s, the war, and emancipation, Moore had endorsed limitations on the powers of the slaveowners that could potentially subvert the institution of slavery. And to this outlook Moore added a relatively consistent history of conservative unionism. He had not overtly opposed the Confederacy, but he had withdrawn from the practice of law in 1861 when he learned that he would have to take an oath of allegiance to the new government. Yet despite his opposition to secession and his role in the North Carolina peace movement, Moore remained on good terms with North Carolina Confederates. More than anything else, he was a political realist. Unlike the majority of white southerners, he corresponded with northerners (including Republicans), and he seldom allowed wishful thinking to cloud his political judgments.

Two months after the war had ended, Moore publicly called upon his fellow North Carolinians to grant "every right to the freemen short of the suffrage." The black man "must be allowed to walk the streets when he pleases, as freely as we do; he shall not be insulted or imposed upon by anybody; he shall choose his own employers and exercise the privilege of working or not at the wages offered; he shall have full and complete redress at the hand of the authorities for all wrongs done him; he shall buy and sell and get gains as freely as any . . . ; he shall have schools and churches and the privilege of attending them; he may attend public meetings or may have public meetings among his own race."[25]

Privately, Moore saw a bleak outlook for the future of blacks in the postwar South. Slavery was a curse, he confided to Benjamin Hedrick, "but I would to God that the slaves and I had two separate Countries—they will not work with industry, neither can any man depend on his hirelings— Energy is paralyzed. . . . I feel utterly unsafe." Despite these fears, he realized the practical drawbacks of any attempts at legal coercion. Thus, Moore and his fellow commissioners recommended that all reference to color be repealed from the North Carolina Code with the exception of those sections pertaining to the suffrage, the right to serve on juries, and the right to marry across racial lines. And they proposed adding an apprenticeship section giving former masters priority to apprenticing former slaves. The committee did refer to what it called the "demoralized" freedmen's ten-

24. "The State v. Negro Will," in Thomas P. Devereux and William H. Battle (eds.), *Reports of Cases at Law Argued and Determined in the Supreme Court of North Carolina, 1834–1836* (Raleigh, 1837), 145.
25. Wilmington (N.C.) *Daily Herald*, July 11, 1865.

dency to engage in petty thievery and vagrancy ("a condition in which they are often joined by whites"), but they recommended that the freedmen be subject to the same antebellum vagrancy code that had existed for whites. After a bitter debate in the North Carolina House of Commons, the legislature generally adopted the Moore committee's recommendations with a number of significant modifications. North Carolina lawmakers restricted black testimony to cases involving "persons of color," and they passed another law that established capital punishment for blacks convicted of raping white women.[26]

A vocal and articulate minority of white southern conservatives shared the "liberal" views of the Moore committee. "We must not only acknowledge the freedom of the slave," a Macon judge told his fellow Georgians in the summer of 1865; "we must recognize his right to acquire property—the right to testify in courts for his protection, and . . . [we must] place criminal and police regulations upon a common principle of legislation. We cannot have distinctions of class or race in crimes—all violators of law must stand equal before the law." After a public speaker at a Wilmington, North Carolina, rally suggested that blacks had no rights "except those which whites choose to grant," the editor of the local newspaper agreed that "whites only may vote and hold office," and thus remained the "governing race," but editor Thomas M. Cook rejected the notion that the freed population had only those "privileges" that whites might be willing to confer. The war had given the southern black population a whole range of "inalienable rights" short of the suffrage.[27]

When Provisional Governor Lewis Parsons of Alabama read in the Montgomery *Advertiser* some of the repressive proposals of state legislators, he attacked such "class legislation." "The idea," he scornfully told the legislature, "of requiring a freedman to carry a pass at any time . . . , that he shall not be at liberty to hire himself for a less period than a month and that he shall not be permitted to have a *light* in his dwelling after any

26. B. F. Moore to Benjamin Hedrick, July 4, 1865, in Benjamin Hedrick Papers, DUL; James B. Browning, "The North Carolina Black Code," *JNH*, XV (1930), 461–73. After bitter debate in which the legislature restricted black testimony to cases involving "persons of color," the legislature generally adopted the Moore Committee's recommendations, adding, however, a measure that gave former masters priority in apprenticing younger former slaves and another that established capital punishment for blacks convicted of raping white women. *North Carolina Ordinances*, 1865–66, pp. 21, 37; *North Carolina Public Laws*, 1866–67, p. 6.

27. Atlanta *Daily Intelligencer*, August 18, 1865; Wilmington *Herald*, July 21, 1865, quoted in Raleigh *Daily Standard*, July 24, 1865. Cook, it should be noted, was a "Yankee" and a former correspondent for the New York *Herald*, but his views seemed to reflect those of his partner, Wilmington merchant and longtime publisher H. H. Munson. See William McKee Evans, *Ballots and Fence Rails: Reconstruction on the Lower Cape Fear* (Chapel Hill, 1967), 41, 46–48.

given hour is not only inconsistent with our American notions of freedom, it is utterly at war with them." True liberty and the curfew were incompatible, he warned the legislature. The South should do nothing except to adopt vagrancy codes—preferably modeled after that of Massachusetts—and then pass an act declaring that the freedmen should have the same measure of protection as the state's nonvoting white population. In the constitutional conventions of 1865, the people of the South had "forever prohibited slavery—in doing so, they have forever established liberty! Let us," he told his fellow Alabamians, "boldly, watchfully and with unfaltering purpose, pursue this grand ideal."[28]

With the exception of South Carolina's Benjamin Perry, all of Johnson's provisional appointees insisted that blacks should be given most civil rights short of the suffrage. Privately, North Carolina's W. W. Holden insisted that the president did not absolutely require blacks be admitted to the witness box ("the concession will be a pandering to Sumner & co."), but publicly he gave grudging approval to this if it proved to be indispensable to the restoration of the Union. Some indication of the attitude of southern conservatives may be gauged from the correspondence of Lewis Parsons of Alabama. In the early fall of 1865, Parsons had written four dozen prominent Alabamians asking for advice on whether or not blacks should be allowed to testify. Though a handful argued for caution on the issue, the overwhelming majority of his respondents insisted that there should be, in the words of E. S. Dargan, "absolutely no shirking insofar as civil rights for the blacks are concerned." Privately and often publicly, these advocates of civil rights for the freedmen emphasized the importance of satisfying a generation of sceptical northerners that the South would "do justice" to the freedmen.[29]

But overshadowing both paternalistic compassion and political expediency was an undercurrent of irrational fears shared by whites of all classes and political persuasions. In the three decades before the war proslavery spokesmen had resolutely insisted that freedom for their slaves was incompatible with social stability. Former South Carolina governor James Henry Hammond was not the first white southerner to describe the frightening chain of events that would follow emancipation, but his predicted scenario was among the more vivid. Released from slavery, he predicted, the newly

28. Montgomery *Advertiser*, November 23, 1865.
29. Raleigh *Standard*, February 9, 1866; R. H. Battle to Benjamin Hedrick, March 5, 1866, in Hedrick Papers; G. P. Dargan to Parsons, August 29, 1865, in Alabama Governors' Papers. For the response of prominent Alabamians to Parsons letter see his correspondence for the months of September and October, 1866. As most of these conservatives pointed out, without such a concession, the courts would never be turned over to white southerners.

freed blacks would refuse to work, would leave their plantation homes and settle in "squalid groups" on the outskirts of southern villages and towns. After expulsion by angry whites, they would begin stealing and robbing; "finally our scattered dwellings would be plundered . . . and the inmates murdered." Hammond could offer only the limited reassurance that the better-organized whites would ultimately crush this racial rebellion after the death of thousands and the economic devastation of much of the region.[30]

It was a gloomy prediction that many southerners remembered in the months after Appomattox. By the time the Reverend Mansfield French made a six-week tour of south and central Georgia in July of 1865, rumors of black insurrectionary plans were spreading through the region. French, a Boston-born abolitionist and veteran of the Port Royal experiment, had undertaken his trip as a representative of the Freedmen's Bureau with the avowed goal of easing the fears and misunderstandings on the part of both blacks and whites. He had been stunned to find that many whites had a "fearful apprehension that the freedmen have a deep laid plot for an insurrection and slaughter." Throughout central Georgia, whites recounted threats of retribution by sullen freedmen and stories of former slaves sarcastically promising to "pay white families for some of their furniture [and] silver" after the black takeover. Everywhere there were vivid secondhand accounts of armed blacks drilling in nightly conclaves, waiting only for the signal that would trigger a coordinated massacre sometime during the Christmas holidays.[31]

The reports baffled and disturbed French. He listened patiently to the stories of whites in the area and interviewed and questioned dozens of freedmen on the plantations he visited. He found not a shred of evidence to substantiate the rumors. Moreover, common sense indicated (to French at least) that emancipation had removed the main impetus for insurrection. Why should blacks revolt when they had finally received their freedom? And yet the hysteria of whites seemed unfeigned. In several predominantly black rural counties white women and children had been evacuated to "secure" areas as distraught planters waited for the first hint of the dreaded "rising."[32]

30. Columbus (Ga.) *Enquirer*, quoted in Richmond *Times*, November 8, 1865. For a discussion of antebellum fears of emancipation see Steven A. Channing, *Crisis of Fear: Secession in South Carolina* (New York, 1970), 58–70.

31. Rev. Mansfield French to Gen. James Blair Steedman, September 5, 1865, in AMA, Georgia, Reel 1.

32. Amy Stephens to Charles Bridges, September 7, 1865, and see John Bridges to Charles Bridges, September 7, 1865, both in Charles E. Bridges Correspondence, DUL; Macon *Daily Telegraph*, July 16, 1865; French to Steedman, September 5, 1865, in AMA, Georgia, Reel 1.

Even as French filed his report with Georgia Freedmen's Bureau officials, gloomy predictions of an impending race war came from other areas of the South. In North Carolina the panic began at approximately the same time when a Wilmington army hospital steward described a conspiracy by blacks to "murder the white race [and] the old slave owners, to get their land and houses" after federal troops withdrew. C. C. Emerson, a native of Indiana, claimed he had been told of the plot by one of the participants. His report panicked Wilmington–New Hanover whites who begged Provisional Governor William Woods Holden for one hundred Spencer rifles and navy revolvers to arm the police and to form a *posse comitatus* of other white citizens.[33]

Major Samuel C. Oliver of the Second Massachusetts Artillery spent a week in early August questioning whites and blacks in the area and found nothing to support Emerson's fears. The few altercations that had occurred between blacks and whites were inconsequential, minor incidents that would be dismissed from any magistrate's court in New England. Oliver's report failed to reassure officials or citizens in the area. Two months later Wilmington whites continued to assert that Negroes were "armed, [and] drilling at night" and daily exhibiting "insolence and insubordination" toward whites.[34]

A correspondent for the *Nation* traveling through middle and lower South Carolina during late October found the fear of insurrection nearly universal. In Kingstree, whites appealed to federal officials for army protection against the "imminent rising." The arrival of two northern schoolteachers and an increase in night religious services by blacks seem to have triggered the panic in the little community. By the time an investigating officer arrived form Charleston a "citizens' committee" had whipped more than a dozen freedmen in the area. The vigilantes also expelled the alien teachers, even though local whites admitted the two men had counseled moderation and forbearance within the black community. The army officer who investigated the wild allegations questioned more than a dozen of the alleged plotters and found nothing to indicate that the former slaves were planning illegal actions. His final report was a scathing attack on the mayor and council for acting like "frightened old women" and unnecessarily alarming the whites of the area. Even after the investigation ended, whites

33. C. C. Emerson, Untitled MS, June 3, 1865, in Governor William Woods Holden Papers, NCA. Although Emerson's manuscript was dated June 3, it was not sent to Holden until early July. See Mayor and Commissioners to Gov. W. W. Holden, July 3, 12, 1865, Holden to Mayor and Commissioners, July 15, 1865, both *ibid*.,; Wilmington (N.C.) *Journal*, August 16, 1865; Wilmington (N.C.) *Daily Dispatch*, August 27, 1865.

34. Maj. Samuel C. Oliver to Capt. E. C. Latimer, August 26, 1865 (copy), in Holden Papers.

were reluctant to admit their fears were groundless. In late November two white men from a neighboring community visited blacks around Kingstree pretending to represent the Freedmen's Bureau. They encouraged freedmen to express their grievances and promised to investigate complaints. The litany of grievances passed on to local whites was enough to raise the specter of insurrection once more. Sixteen of the most vocal blacks were chased down, accused of planning mass murder, and beaten.[35]

By November rumors of an impending insurrection had spread to more than sixty counties and half a dozen parishes throughout the eleven states of the former Confederacy. The apprehension seemed greatest in the areas heavily populated by blacks that stretched in an arc from the coast of the two Carolinas westward through the heart of Georgia, Alabama, Mississippi, Louisiana, and East Texas. There, in the cradle of a hundred antebellum slave-uprising scares, reports of the alleged insurrection sprouted spontaneously throughout the late summer and early fall.[36] Noxubee County, Mississippi, whites described an elaborate plot that heavily armed freedmen had supposedly concocted at a series of midnight meetings. Former slaves, led by blacks discharged from the Union army, were said to have formed rifle companies throughout the Deep South. During the Christmas holidays they would strike with coordinated skill, slaughtering or expelling whites from Alabama, Mississippi, Louisiana, and East Texas. Unidentified whites, it was alleged, had laid down the timetable for the massacre.[37]

In southern Alabama a fifty-eight-year-old farmer with an inventive imagination reported that the freedmen had stolen hundreds of Spencer rifles from a lightly guarded army depot in preparation for the insurrection. (There was no such depot, according to army officials, and no cache of arms was reported missing anywhere in the state.) A Macon County farmer even claimed to have seen former slaves "assembling in a secluded spot in the woods and drilling at night." (After an extended interrogation

---

35. *Nation*, November 23, 1865, p. 651. Brig. Gen. Giles to Col. H. W. Smith, August 29, 1865, in BRFAL, South Carolina, Box 23; G. Pillsbury to Col. Smith, December 11, 1865, in BRFAL, South Carolina, Box 25. The following year still another rumor of black insurrection swept the area. See W. J. B. Cooper, David W. McGill, and S. J. Bradley to Gov. James Orr, December 11, 1866, Cooper to "Jim" [Orr], December 11, 1866, both in South Carolina Governors' Papers, SCA.

36. Nearly two hundred accounts or references to the danger of insurrection were found in secondary sources, the diaries and private correspondence of white southerners, the records of the Freedmen's Bureau, the American Missionary Association Archives, southern and northern newspapers, and the governors' correspondence of North and South Carolina, Georgia, Alabama, Mississippi, and Texas.

37. For a brief description of the panic as it spread through Mississippi, see William C. Harris, *Presidential Reconstruction in Mississippi* (Baton Rouge, 1967), 89–92.

by an army officer, he acknowledged that he was some distance from the group; it was "possible" they were simply conducting a prayer meeting as they later claimed.) Even in northern Alabama, where blacks were in the minority, white citizens requested a military garrison to protect them against the threat of racial upheaval.[38]

There was a bitter humor to some of the lurid accounts. In Lauderdale Springs, a few miles northeast of Meridian, Mississippi, whites became convinced that a "horrifying conspiracy of freedmen" had murdered a local planter, William B. Wilkinson. Wilkinson sold his cotton in Meridian on November 1 and left the bank with a thousand dollars in gold. When he failed to appear at his home, the story spread through the area that Wilkinson's former slaves had planned to sell the cotton after taking over the plantation in a December uprising. They were, according to the rumor, so angered at his precipitous sale of "their" cotton that they had killed Wilkinson, stolen his money, and secretly buried him in some remote part of the plantation.[39]

A vigilante group led by the most prominent members of the community searched the freedmen's quarters behind Wilkinson's home and found a knife with dried blood and a shovel which appeared to have been recently used. For nearly six hours the group beat and tortured three freedmen in an unsuccessful attempt to coerce a confession. The blacks denied having killed Wilkinson and insisted they had no knowledge of the apprehended insurrection, but they were rescued from lynching only by the arrival of soldiers from Meridian. The next day the military provost marshal found Wilkinson in a Meridian brothel, quite alive, though somewhat disheveled by the two days he had spent celebrating his cotton sale.[40]

As accounts of the alleged plot spread through the South, similarities to earlier episodes emerged. The typical antebellum slave scare arose in a setting of emotionalism and uncertainty that might be related to national affairs or to purely local circumstances. The hysteria that swept the South in 1856 was linked to the national political campaign of that year. The well-known Mississippi uprising panic of 1835 seems to have been more related to local affairs. An uneasy and apprehensive community might go un-

38. John A. Winston to Parsons, August 1, 1865, B. C. Fine [?] to Cooper, September 23, 1865. Lawrence County Citizens' Delegation to Parsons, September 26, 1865, Militia Questionnaire, September 24, 1865, E. G. Richards to Parsons, October 19, 1865, Report of the Adjutant and Inspector General of Alabama, November 5, 1866, all in Alabama Governors' Papers.
39. Mobile *Daily Tribune*, November 6, 1865; Natchez *Daily Courier*, November 10, 1865.
40. S. G. Wright to M. E. Strieby, November 4, 1865, in AMA, Mississippi, Reel 1; Lt. O. B. Foster to Maj. T. S. Free, November 15, 1865, in BRFAL, M-826, roll 30.

scathed, but too often an incident (or series of incidents) as ominous as an unexplained series of fires or as inconsequential as the furtive whispering of two recalcitrant slaves would ignite the tinderbox of fear and foreboding.[41]

Once alerted, frightened whites would hastily assemble a vigilance committee, free to act swiftly and decisively without the restraints of legal technicalities. In such a setting the "investigation" that followed became a frightening exercise in uncontrolled hysteria as the vigilantes confronted the alleged conspirators with a horrible dilemma. If they denied the existence of the "plot" they would be speedily hanged; if they furnished details (and the names of other "participants") they might be spared. Quite understandably, most of the accused elected to implicate others in the nonexistent conspiracy. The mob quickly and conveniently discovered that the originators of these infamous schemes were their traditional enemies: abolitionists and assorted Yankees, nonconformist white southerners, and free blacks. The persistent insistence that whites or free-black "degenerates" initiated such plots allowed slaveowners the luxury of continuing to insist that their bondsmen were docile and submissive unless misled and deceived.

In the most extreme cases these episodes were climaxed by executions— public events that dramatized the necessity for eternal vigilance and unity by white southerners while warning blacks against any act that might arouse the whites with whom they lived.[42]

A few southern whites had used the insurrection myth as a warning against "outside interference" with their peculiar institution. Abolitionist publications, claimed white southerners, were "firebrands hurled by fanatics into peaceful and unoffending communities to encourage servile insurrection." Northern opponents of emancipation echoed this warning that the talk of abolition would lead "to discord and civil war with all its kindred horrors of rape, sack and slaughter." Although the antislavery spokesmen denied the charge, the repeated accusation did force conservative abolitionists onto the defensive and led them to repeatedly emphasize their commitment to pacific emancipation.[43] Nevertheless, most southerners avoided the subject. Too much discussion implied the instability of slavery and

41. This general description is based upon a reading of the extensive historical literature on antebellum slave insurrections. See especially Edwin A. Miles, "The Mississippi Slave Insurrection Scare of 1835," *JNH*, XLII (1957), 49–62.

42. Bertram Wyatt-Brown discusses some of the factors underlying such behavior in *Southern Honor: A Study of Ethics and Behavior in the Antebellum South* (New York, 1982), 402–35.

43. Clement Eaton, *The Freedom-of-Thought Struggle in the Old South* (New York, 1964), 119; Benjamin Quarles, *Black Abolitionists* (New York, 1969), 224; Bertram Wyatt-Brown, *Lewis Tappan and the Evangelical War Against Slavery* (Cleveland, 1969), 153. For a useful discussion of this issue, see Robert H. Abzug, "The Influence of Garrisonian Abolitionists' Fears of Slave Violence on the Antislavery Argument, 1829–40," *JNH*, LV (1970), 15–28.

raised an issue most whites thought impolitic to discuss in the public arena. There was far more talk of slave insurrection in William Lloyd Garrison's *Liberator* than in all the southern press combined. Whatever its value as a defense of the slave South, the recurrent pattern of panic, community mobilization, and mock trial functioned primarily as a secular ritual—an elaborate psychodrama that temporarily resolved the tensions of a perilously unstable society.

In many respects, the insurrection panic of 1865 was a recapitulation of those that had taken place during the antebellum period. There was the same preoccupation with "outsiders," with nonconformist white southerners, and with assertive blacks. And there was the same ambivalent response of most white southerners: assertions that they had nothing to fear from the blacks they personally knew and yet terror of the great mass of former slaves.

But in 1865 there could be no vigilance committees to unmask the threatening holocaust, no state and local government with all its force in reserve. Symbolic of the change was the presence of thousands of armed and trained black soldiers, ostensibly under the control of the federal government but subject (in the words of one Alabama legislator) to the same "barbaric impulses" that had always characterized people of color. When Martin Delany, the outspoken black nationalist and Freedmen's Bureau officer, appeared before five hundred freedmen on St. Helena Island, South Carolina, in the summer of 1865, he reminded his listeners that there were "200,000 of our men well drilled in arms and used to warfare." It is unlikely that his listeners needed that reminder; certainly white southerners did not.[44]

The fighting had scarcely subsided in the spring of 1865 before President Johnson began to receive a stream of bitter letters from white southerners complaining of the dangers posed by black soldiers. The imaginative Eliza Andrews, whose father had told her often of the Indian mutinies at Lucknow and Cawnpore, felt sure that white southerners were "standing on a volcano that may burst forth any day." And when that happened, she confided to her diary, the drilled and trained black soldiers would "act the part of the Sepoys in India, thanks to Northern teaching." The Sepoys, she recalled, after raping the English women of Cawnpore, had killed them alongside their children and husbands.[45]

44. In this case, federal officials were equally horrified. See Lt. Edward Stoeber to Bvt. Maj. Frank Taylor, July 24, 1865, "Memorandum of Extracts from Speech of Major Delany, African, at the Brick Church, St. Helena Island, South Carolina, July 23, 1865," both in Records of the Assistant Commissioners, Incoming Correspondence, BRFAL, South Carolina.

45. Eliza Andrews, *The Wartime Journal of a Georgia Girl, 1864–1865*, ed. Spencer Bidwell King (Atlanta, 1976), 314–15. It would be impossible to cite the hundreds of letters,

The editor of the Natchez *Daily Courier*, on the other hand, seemed unable to decide whether the presence of black soldiers was more humiliating or frightening. Southerners were accustomed to seeing blacks, whether slave or free, only as "respectful servants," he complained. They were "mortified, pained and shocked to encounter them . . . wearing the federal uniform and bearing bright muskets and gleaming bayonets." It was not simply that they offended whites; they were a "constant source of discord and dissatisfaction, fruitful in idleness and vice among the negroes not armed, and harbingers of insurrection." Unless the black troops were withdrawn, a former Confederate army officer wrote from Wilmington, North Carolina, their presence would "inevitably result in a *massacre*." Even before the first black soldier arrived in Sumter County, Alabama, industrialist and planter John Anthony Winston warned that black soldiers would lead to "insurrection and race war within six months." Charles Wallace, a Mississippi businessman traveling through the region in the fall of 1865, was more insightful than most of his southern colleagues. The real problem was not black military discipline, he said. "I have not seen a drunken black soldier in my way from Richmond to Jackson." Their real offense was that their presence was "galling to the feelings of the White population." [46]

Nor was the fear of agitators and incendiaries limited to black soldiers. The newspapers of the South, particularly in the more remote regions, repeatedly warned of the dangers posed by "bad white men," who were inciting the confused and unstable freed black population. "Why these mid-

petitions, and complaints from whites that poured into the offices of the provisional governors and the White House and appeared on the pages of the resuscitated postwar southern newspapers. For some representative examples see R. Dozier *et al.* to Gov. James Orr, November 3, 1865, in South Carolina Governors' Papers; Mayor and Commissioners of Wilmington, N.C., to Holden, July 12, 1865, in Holden Papers; Holden to Andrew Johnson, August 10, 1865, in Andrew Johnson Papers, LC; Citizens of Monroe, La., to Gov. J. Madison Wells, Petition, October 26, 1865 (copy), in Incoming Correspondence, BRFAL, South Carolina; Citizens Delegation to Parsons, September 26, 1865, Tuscaloosa Citizens to Parsons, October 6, 1865, Demopolis Delegation Petitioners to Parsons, October 18, 1865, all in Alabama Governors' Papers; Atlanta *Daily Intelligencer*, February 17, 1866; Savannah *Daily Republican*, September 4, 1865; Richmond *Whig*, August 4, 1865.

46. Natchez *Daily Courier*, November 18, 1865; A. M. Waddell to Holden, June 18, 1865, in Holden Papers; John Anthony Winston to Parsons, August 1, 1865, in Alabama Governors' Papers; Charles Montriou Wallace to Wife, September 7, 1865, in Clopton Family Papers, DUL. The hostility toward Negro troops was a near obsession among white southerners, who used every opportunity to vilify and condemn the black troops. James E. Sefton concluded that the black troops "were less well trained and disciplined than the white volunteer units," citing the cases of mutiny that occurred in several black regiments. Sefton also noted, however, that whites were far more sensitive to misconduct by blacks, inflating trivial or nonexistent incidents into episodes of wanton brutality. In all too many instances reports of infractions by black troops were vague and nonspecific, and rigorous investigations often revealed that charges of "insolence," "impudence," or "misconduct" were unfounded. Sefton, *Army and Reconstruction*, 51; Harris, *Presidential Reconstruction in Mississippi*, 70–71.

night assemblages of negroes in some of our neighboring parishes?" asked the Franklin, Louisiana, *Planters' Banner*. In some cases there were a hundred blacks ("a thousand in one instance") and always goaded on and advised by "renegade white men." Only a fool could close his eyes to the "deep, secret, damnable rascality" afoot among this "unfortunate and misguided race." Such "wretched *white* men" should be tried and executed without delay, warned the Vicksburg *Herald*, lest the South be "consumed in the flames of race war."[47]

By implication, such threats were to be directed against suspicious arrivals and individuals lacking status in the community. But no one was exempt from the threat of reprisal. In the late summer of 1865 a Summerton, South Carolina, vigilance committee agreed to disarm the freedmen of the area because of the danger of insurrection. At the vigilance meeting, however, conservative planter Warren Manning challenged the plan to disarm the blacks. He recalled that some of his slaves carried weapons for the protection of the plantation before the war, and now these men had been "made free and therefore had a right to carry arms." More practically, he noted that any attempt to disarm the freedmen would lead to swift retaliation by the nearby army garrison. Within a week he found himself accused of favoring "negro suffrage." He had to publish a denial in the local newspaper, and he learned to temper his defense of the freedmen's rights.[48]

Few accounts more clearly captured the dynamics of such insurrection panics than the official Freedmen's Bureau report of an incident near Watkinsville, Georgia. Throughout the fall of 1865, Lieutenant Colonel Homer B. Sprague, the Freedmen's Bureau agent in Augusta, Georgia, was inundated by reports of "suspicious activities" among the freedmen. In early December a delegation of citizens from nearby Watkinsville arrived in Augusta and urged Sprague to bring a detachment of troops back to their homes. They had uncovered a "dangerous conspiracy of the negroes to rise in insurrection and murder all the white inhabitants." Although the white instigators of the movement had successfully escaped, the fifteen freedmen most prominent in this "diabolical plot" had been captured in their homes and confined under guard in a makeshift jail.

When Sprague arrived in Watkinsville, he separated the three "ringleaders" and interrogated them for nearly six hours. On the evening of De-

47. Franklin (La.) *Planters' Banner*, November 28, 1865; Vicksburg *Daily Herald*, November 7, 1865; see also Natchez *Daily Courier*, November 24, 1865; Hazelhurst (Miss.) *Copiahan*, December 8, 1865; Louisville (Ky.) *Daily Democrat*, December 1, 1865; R. M. Smith to Stephen Duncan, December 3, 1865, in Stephen Duncan Papers, LSU; Grace Brown Elmore Diary (Typewritten copy in SCL), October 1, 4, 1865.
48. Mrs. Y. B. Manning to Husband, September 4, 1865, Williams-Chesnut-Manning Papers, Box 8, SCL.

cember 2, Sprague learned, a group of white vigilantes had seized the fifteen men after receiving their names from a "faithful old darky," who had
described the plot after questioning by his former owner. The heavily
armed whites roped the men together and dragged and pulled them a half
mile to the banks of a deep stream. Blindfolded and forced to kneel on the
brink, the men were "made to kiss the bible and swear a solemn oath to tell
all they knew about the risings." For the next two hours the mob fired their
pistols and rifles in the air and threatened repeatedly to kill those who lied.

The first witness told Sprague he was so alarmed he thought the "only
chance of saving his life was to say what the white men evidently wanted
him to say and so he said 'yes' to their questions because they would not
take 'no' for an answer." The other two freedmen told the same story. When
one found it was useless to tell the truth, he "made a lie up 'out of whole
cloth,' to use his own expression," reported Sprague. "Never," he concluded, "have I seen such a capacity for being humbugged, such astound-
ing gullibility as men otherwise intelligent and sensible have exhibited in
reference to negro insurrections."[49]

Events in the Caribbean in late October subtly reinforced these misgivings. By the first week in November, southern newspapers had begun to
reprint garbled and lurid accounts of an uprising of blacks in the British
West Indies. The insurrection had erupted when angry blacks Jamaicans
killed thirteen whites and seized the Morant Bay courthouse to protest
drastic new taxation policies. As such affairs went, the Morant Bay insurrection was relatively minor. It was most distinguished by the ferocity with
which Governor Edward John Eyre crushed the outbreak. Obviously, it
was not a direct consequence of emancipation, since slavery had ended in
Jamaica between 1833 and 1838. Nevertheless, white southerners depicted it as a "wholly unprovoked" rebellion replete with "unparalleled
atrocities" that showed the "instincts of the uncurbed Africans." In Ocala,
Florida, a former Confederate colonel wrote that the reports from Jamaica
had led many of his neighbors to fear that the "horrible scenes there . . .
may be re-enacted in this country." For one North Carolina planter it was a
"rehearsal for the South's Armageddon." The American correspondent of
the London *Times* believed the Jamaican insurrection was the single most
important factor in alarming southerners in the fall of 1865.[50]

Throughout the months of November and December, the stories con-

49. Lt. Col. Homer B. Sprague to Brig. Gen. Davis Tillson, January 10, 1866, in
BRFAL, Microcopy 752, Roll 24.
50. R. Bullock to E. M. L'Engle, December 5, 1865, in Edward McCrady L'Engle Papers, SHC; Wilmington, (N.C.) *Daily Herald*, November 7, 1865; London *Times*, January 13,
1866.

tinued, with almost every newspaper in the South giving extensive and, for the most part, bizarrely inaccurate accounts of the insurrection. In language seldom used in polite conversation, southern newspapers described how the bodies of white men were "mutilated in shocking manner" and the women—deprived of their white protectors—were forced to "subserve the lustful pleasures of the disgusting murderers." (Not one of these statements, it should be noted, was true.) Articles from the London *Daily Telegraph* and the *Times* emphasizing the "pernicious effects" of full citizenship to the Jamaican freedmen appeared regularly in the region's press and for white southerners constituted one more piece of evidence that untrammeled freedom for their former slaves would lead to chaos.[51]

There were additional reasons to be concerned as the Christmas holidays approached. Christmas had often been a time of uneasy celebration as slaveowners briefly loosed the bonds of servitude and relaxed traditional discipline. While the yule log burned, the bondsmen might frolic, be merry, drink corn whiskey, and even "fun" their masters a bit. During these holidays, slaves often overstepped the bounds of decorum carefully observed during the rest of the year, and southern officials repeatedly warned of the opportunities the slaves had at their dances, balls, and parties to concoct sinister plans. At least two southern legislatures unsuccessfully tried to limit such black gatherings in the 1850s and nearly one-third of the rumors of antebellum uprisings focused upon the Christmas holidays. South Carolina Provisional Governor James Lawrence Orr reached back to these memories in a December letter to the Union commander in his state. During "Christmas week, which has always been a holiday for the negroes, they will congregate in large numbers at the villages and towns where they will get liquor," he warned, "and while under its influence I fear that collisions will occur between them and the whites." When these confrontations began, warned Orr, "no one can tell where the conflict will end."[52]

51. Richmond *Times*, January 23, 1866; Yorkville (S.C.) *Enquirer*, November 16, 1865. Christine Bolt assesses the impact of the Morant Bay insurrection on English public opinion in *Victorian Attitudes to Race* (Toronto, 1971), 75–108.

52. Orr to Gen. Daniel Sickles, December 13, 1865 (copy), in South Carolina Governors' Papers. Almost every state and regional study of slavery has commented upon the importance of Christmas as a holiday from the cares of slavery and a time of potential disorder among blacks. See Charles S. Sydnor, *Slavery in Mississippi* (Baton Rouge, 1966), 21–22; Charles G. Sellers, *Slavery in Alabama* (University, Ala., 1950), 123–26 (quotation on p. 123); Joseph C. Carroll, *Slave Insurrections in the United States, 1800–1865* (New York, 1938), 176, 192, 207; Orville W. Taylor, *Negro Slavery in Arkansas* (Durham, 1953), 206–208; Joe Gray Taylor, *Negro Slavery in Louisiana* (Baton Rouge, 1963), 128–31. Ralph B. Flanders specifically noted the heightened fear of uprisings that came at Christmas in his *Plantation Slavery in Georgia* (Chapel Hill, 1933), 275, as did Herbert Aptheker in *American Negro Slave Revolts* (New York, 1943), 348, and Williamson in *After Slavery*, 250.

White southerners were not alone in associating the laxity of discipline surrounding the holidays with the danger of escalating race war. A Tory member of Parliament insisted in early December of 1865 that the Morant Bay insurrection was simply the first act of a much larger plot in which Jamaican blacks had "organized for next Christmas Day the massacre of every white inhabitant upon the island."[53]

As the editor of the Atlanta *Daily Intelligencer* reminded his readers, between December 24 and January 2 they would "witness what has never before transpired in this state." Southerners would see "thousands of negroes turned loose as freedmen and freedwomen with no homes and no disposition to secure homes." It might begin as a frolic, but it could easily become a riot. "It is the nature of the negro race to be self-indulgent and to be extravagant and reckless in it." Emboldened by liquor, encouraged by "bad white men," they could be "easily persuaded to . . . commit outrage and violence." Such was the chilling prospect of the first Christmas after slavery.[54]

White southerners claimed to see evidence of this "retreat into barbarism" in the changed behavior of the freedmen. During the summer and fall, bewildered army and Freedmen's Bureau officials received from whites a stream of complaints that charged their former slaves with "disrespectful and impudent language" or "conduct unbecoming their humble station." Captain Garrett Nagle, a South Carolina Freedmen's Bureau agent, initially could detect no signs of the impertinence local whites professed to see at every turn. Gradually, however, he came to understand the importance of the etiquette of subservience—the tipping of the hat, the elaborately deferential greeting, the averted eyes in the presence of the whites. As a perceptive northern traveler observed, southern whites "perceive insolence in a tone, a glance, a gesture, a failure to yield enough by two or three inches in meeting on the sidewalk."[55]

Even before the war had ended, the growing "impudence" of their slaves had unnerved white southerners. In early 1865 the Houston *Tri-Weekly Telegraph* had felt it essential to publish a lengthy description of the "proper distinction" essential to safeguard the relationship between the "superior and inferior population." Whenever blacks failed to observe these outward signs of subservience, they meant it to be "a self assertion, or . . . tacit insolence," said the *Telegraph*. "This is the handful of soil from the bank that

53. Bernard Semmel, *Jamaican Blood and Victorian Conscience: The Governor Eyre Controversy* (London, 1962), 231.

54. Atlanta *Daily Intelligencer*, December 21, 1865.

55. Capt. Garrett Nagle to Colonel H. W. Smith, September 31 [*sic*], 1865, in BRFAL, South Carolina, Box 23; Philadelphia *Inquirer*, August 9, 1865.

may lead to a flood." And after the war had ended, model contracts published by southern planters placed extreme emphasis upon the importance of overt deference and politeness by freed men and women. Such contracts were often more detailed in their descriptions of proper racial etiquette than in their enumeration of working conditions.[56]

Indeed, once he had become familiar with these subtle signals Nagle realized that a change had taken place. Some blacks had come to regard these former signs of obsequiousness as a "badge of servitude and they made clear their independence in word and manner." The whites, on the other hand, "are quite indignant if they are not treated with the same deference that they were accustomed to receive from these people before their emancipation." Nagle might think the refusal of blacks to bow and scrape a sign of "simple manliness"; white southerners saw it as a dangerous portent of the future.[57]

In this tension-filled setting, white southern landowners—most for the first time—began the process of negotiating the new relationship between former master and former slave. The distress of whites was strengthened by the fact that they believed they were being forced to choose, as one argued, between the "horrible" and the "disastrous." E. W. Hubard of Buckingham County, Virginia, rented to a few favored former slaves, hired others on a monthly wage, and arranged to farm the rest of the plantation on shares. After two years of experimentation, he concluded that some form of "share farming" worked as well as any other system, but it was at best the lesser of a variety of evils. "What are you doing or what do you *propose* to do with the freedmen in your section?" S. F. Patterson asked his good friend Paul Cameron. "In my section everybody is acting . . . according to their own notions of what is best," he said. As a result there was a crazy quilt of arrangements. "I am greatly puzzled to know what to do for their benefit as well as my own," he concluded plaintively. It was symbolic that a planters' convention, attended by more than a hundred landowners in the black belt of Alabama, met in Montgomery for two days in an attempt to

---

56. Houston *Tri-Weekly Telegraph*, January 25, 1865; Macon *Daily Telegraph*, July 18, 1865; Richmond *Times*, January 4, 1866. See, for example, Elias H. Deas, Labor Contract, March 3, 1866, in Elias H. Deas Papers; Dr. E. E. Ellis, Memorandum, August 10, 1867, in Ellis Family Papers, SCL; Memorandum of contracts, December, 1865–February, 1866, in Hubard Family Papers, SHC; William Newton Mercer Diary, LSU, December 29, 1865; Gustavus J. Orr and Freedmen, Contract, August 14, 1865, Orr Family Papers, EU; George W. Mitchell and Freedmen, Contract, January 1, 1866, Miscellaneous Papers, GA.

57. Nagle to Col. H. W. Smith, September 31 [sic], 1865, in BRFAL, South Carolina, Box 23. Few historians have shown more insight in dealing with the question of the etiquette of race relations in the postslavery south than William McKee Evans in *Ballots and Fence Rails*, 76–79.

reach some consensus on whether wages, land rental, or some form of sharecropping was most desirable. After thirteen hours of sometimes angry disagreement, they adjourned without any recommendations.[58]

Certainly most white landowners were hostile to the notion of black landownership or even of rental to their former slaves. There were exceptions scattered throughout the region. In January of 1866, Emma Hopkins of Richland County, South Carolina, rented 260 acres to three of her former slaves ("good and faithful servants") for $350. John Bratton of York County, South Carolina, made special arrangements with a former slave to lease him a prime tract, advance him funds to purchase a team of mules, lend him money for living expenses for the first year, and guarantee the right to purchase the land within three years. But most freedmen did not have the special relationship Lewis Bratton had with his former master, John Bratton, and the more common reaction of whites was refusal to sell land to the freedmen. When Theodore Brown, a South Carolina planter, agreed to sell a small farm to one of his favorite former slaves, a local "vigilance committee" warned him to withdraw the offer since the possibility of land ownership incited "insubordination and unrest" among the freedmen. It seldom required the blunt action of neighbors and friends to act as a barrier against land sales; social pressure was usually enough. Yet even in the absence of such white hostility, the shortage of large amounts of capital doomed most freedmen to some form of dependency upon white landowners.[59]

After the collapse of the wartime confiscation program there had been occasional efforts by northern officials to promote rentals or even share farming as a halfway house to land ownership by the freedmen. But most northern military officers and Freedmen's Bureau officials, reflecting a national consensus, had come to emphasize the free-labor system as a panacea

58. Robert T. Hubard to Edmund Wilcox Hubard, November 2, 1865, December 2, 1867, both in Hubard Family Papers, SHC; S. F. Patterson to Paul C. Cameron, December 21, 1863, in Paul Cameron Papers, SHC; Montgomery *Advertiser*, November 26, 27, 1865.

59. Land Rental Memorandum, January 1, 1866, in Hopkins Family Papers, SCL; John Bratton and Lewis Bratton (Freedman), Articles of Agreement, January 1, 1866, in Bratton Family papers, SCL; Joseph Hennings and R. W. Hubard, Rental Contract, December 2, 1865, in Hubard Family papers; Mrs. Y. B. Manning to Husband, September 4, 1865, in Williams-Chesnut-Manning Papers, Box 8; Percival Moses Thomas, "Plantations in Transition: A Study of Four Virginia Plantations, 1860–1870" (Ph.D. dissertation, University of Virginia, 1979), 563–64; Roger L. Ransom and Richard Sutch, *One Kind of Freedom: The Economic Consequences of Emancipation* (Cambridge, 1977), 81; Jay Mandle, *The Roots of Black Poverty: The Southern Plantation Economy After the Civil War* (Durham, 1968), 23–24. As late as 1880 black southerners rented less than 4 percent of the land in the cotton south. Roger Ransom and Richard Sutch, "The Ex-slave in the Postbellum South: A Study of the Economic Impact of Racism in a Market Environment," *JEH*, XXXIII (1973), 137.

for the southern economy. That free-labor system, however, encompassed an extraordinarily wide range of variations; from a monthly wage system ("the same as hired laborers of the North") to elaborate and detailed year-long contracts that spelled out complicated compensation packages including shares of the crops, garden rights, and even secondary benefits such as medical care, rations, clothing, and housing.[60]

From the standpoint of southern white landowners, there were a number of critical objections to the wage system. Certainly most believed that it was impractical in its purest form because of the continuing absence of capital. James H. Simon, a Charleston lawyer and planter, preferred a wage system for his freedmen, but he soon became convinced that such a system could never be implemented throughout the region. A few of the better-financed planters might be able to raise the necessary cash; most would not. A reasonably large plantation would require a monthly cash payroll of one to two thousand dollars, he concluded, and most individuals he knew were scarcely able to obtain enough credit for seed and "bare furnishings." The editor of the *Southern Cultivator*, along with Willoughby Newton, president of the Virginia State Agricultural Society, reached the same conclusions. The wage system was theoretically a "far better system than any other" but, they gloomily concluded, impractical. Most landowners were so impoverished they were "fortunate if they can furnish teams, implements and food."[61]

Contrary to widely accepted notions, the absence of capital was not a fatal obstacle to the creation of some form of wage system. Most planters required large sums of credit whatever the system they employed. More critical was the lack of control that a straightforward monthly cash system implied. For planters there was always the danger that laborers who were paid a monthly wage would walk off the job while the crops were at a critical stage of production. "What can be done with an irresponsible laborer who throws down his spade and walks off?" asked George Trenholm, the former Confederate secretary of the treasury. At cultivation or harvest time, a walkout of the work force would be devastating, as Louisiana sugar planter E. J. Gay discovered on the eve of his first full cane harvest after the war. Two days after paying workers their December wage, in the midst of the critical pressing of the cane, his workers threatened to leave because of

60. These observations are made on the basis of examining approximately four hundred postwar contracts for 1865, 1866, 1867, and 1868 in the manuscript collections of southern landowners and in the Freedmen's Bureau papers. Of course, I have benefitted from the rich historical literature on the development of postwar economic arrangements.

61. James H. Simon to J. Harleston Read, December 20, 1866, in Read-Lance Family Papers, SCL; "Contracts with Laborers," *SCu* XXIII (1865), 180–81; *Fa*, I (1866), 379–80.

the lack of whiskey on the plantation. Overseer John Murphy blustered and threatened, but in the end he frantically (and angrily) wrote Gay: "Please . . . get me 1/2 bbl of whiskey. Otherwise they will leave me, which would injure both you and me materally [*sic*]." Although most bureau agents and federal officers denied this was a serious problem, there were occasional reports of strikes and threatened walkouts at crucial stages of the harvest. No southern landowner wanted to give his workers this kind of leverage.[62]

Lewis Ayer, a South Carolina low-country planter, clearly saw this problem. Despite all the protestations of the freedmen that they were willing to work, their "actions speak more truly than their words on this subject," he insisted. Though they might work "tolerably well" for a few weeks, he declared, when they accumulated eight or ten dollars, "then they quit work and visit from place to place until their last dollar is spent." The solution was to withhold substantial portions of the laborers' wages and to arrange an agreement for forfeiture if the yearlong contract was not fulfilled. Under this arrangement, the wage system would have the overwhelming advantage of allowing for the continued supervision of the landowner or his overseer. Corporal punishment could no longer be applied, but the threat of hunger and starvation might yet allow the plantation to function, albeit at a more inefficient level than before the war. And thus, on many of the larger plantations of the Deep South freedmen continued to work much as they had before the war in labor gangs, closely supervised by foremen, drivers, and overseers, receiving a monthly wage and sometimes a small share of the crops.[63]

62. John Murphy to Andrew Hynes Gay, January 3, 1866, in Andrew Hynes Gay Family Papers, LSU. Eric Foner describes one center of black resistance in the coastal rice plantations of South Carolina in *Nothing but Freedom: Emancipation and Its Legacy* (Baton Rouge, 1983), 74–88.

63. Lewis Malone Ayer, Jr., to D. H. Jacques, December 26, 1865, in Lewis Malone Ayer Papers, DUL. Almost all of the recent works dealing with the wartime and postwar economy of the South have described the economic transition from slavery to the various landlord-labor relationships: renting, sharecropping, leasing, sales, and a hundred variations. Harold Woodman describes two distinct land tenure arrangements that, he argues, ultimately predominated particularly in the postwar plantation South. Under the arrangement preferred by most tenants, they paid the landlord either in cash or with a share of the crop and retained relatively complete control over the land they farmed. Under the second system, which was almost unique to the postwar South and was more common, the sharecropper received a proportional share of the harvest, but he had no control over the land he farmed and was, in essence, a wage laborer. See Woodman, "Post–Civil War Southern Agriculture and the Law," *AH*, LIII (1979), 319–25. Jay Mandle, citing field studies made during the 1930s, concludes that this is not a significant distinction. Mandle, *Roots of Black Poverty*, 45. Ronald Davis reviews the extensive literature on land-labor arrangements in the first chapter of his *Good and Faithful Labor: From Slavery to Sharecropping in the Natchez District, 1860–1890* (Westport, Conn., 1982).

Nor was the attempt of landowners to maintain closely supervised gang labor restricted to the use of the wage system. In dozens of contracts drawn up in the first three years after the war planters laboriously divided their workers into classes of hands much as they had done under the antebellum system. Collectively, the workers would receive one-half, in some cases one-third or less of the crop. Commonly the freedmen's portion was to be divided on the basis of "shares of the half," with able-bodied adult males receiving a "full share." Other black workers, depending upon their age, sex and physical condition, were downgraded as second-class and third-class hands, and they received proportionally smaller shares of the total harvest. In still other instances, planters contracted with black individuals who agreed to work portions of large plantations in "squads" for shares of the harvest. These squads were often extended families or groups of families. Whatever the precise arrangement, it was an extraordinarily complicated division of labor that had one overriding advantage from the standpoint of landowners. It allowed a continuation of the labor patterns of the old regime.[64]

But the freedmen would have none of this. If there was anything on which white southerners agreed in observing postwar conditions, it was the universal opposition of the freedmen to a renewal of gang labor. In interviewing dozens of potential hands, a Memphis overseer was unable to find a single worker who was willing to work under the supervision of overseers in gangs as before the war. They preferred to own or rent, he reported, but since that was not possible they had developed a "mania for

64. Ralph Shlomowitz has categorized the enormous variety of financial arrangements that existed. Using labor contracts in South Carolina in the Freedmen's Bureau records, he concludes that the transition from large-scale gang labor to family sharecropping and other forms of tenancy was "effected by an intermediate stage which was called by contemporaries 'the squad system.'" Such squads were "semiautonomous worker peer groups" that maintained "scale economies," while giving the freedmen much more independence. See Shlomowitz, "The Squad System on Postbellum Cotton Plantations," in Robert McMath and Orville Vernon Burton (eds.), *Toward a New South: Studies in Post Civil War Southern Communities* (Westport, Conn., 1982), 265–80; Shlomowitz, "The Origins of Southern Sharecropping," *AH*, LIII (1979), 557–75. I found examples of such squad arrangements, but in examining the contracts sequentially for 1865, 1866, and 1867, I was struck by the speed with which landowners began dealing with the black nuclear family as the main unit of production and the equal rapidity with which the classical sharecropping arrangements emerged. What is equally clear is that the various contracts and agreements signed between landowners and the freedmen were often vague in describing the precise working arrangements of laborers. See also John David Smith, "More Than Slaves, Less Than Freedmen: The Share Wages' Labor System During Reconstruction," *CWH*, XXVI (1980), 256–66. Philip Morgan and Thomas Armstrong concentrate on what they believe to be a neglected component of postwar labor arrangements, the task system. Morgan, "Work and Culture: The Task System and the World of Lowcountry Blacks, 1700 to 1880," *WMQ*, XXXIX (1982), 563–99; Armstrong, "From Task Labor to Free Labor: The Transition Along Georgia's Rice Coast, 1820–1880," *GHQ*, LXIV (1980), 432–47.

farming on shares." They wanted their own house, he reported, their own garden, and their own plot of land. As he began the first full year after emancipation, Kemp Battle of Raleigh, North Carolina, offered his first-class hands fifteen dollars a month—considerably more than the average wage for the area. But his former slaves refused it. "My most sensible men say that they have no other desire than to cultivate their own land [on shares]," reported Battle. Thomas Watson of Louisa County, Virginia, much preferred the wage system in the first year and a half after the war, despite the problems of meeting his monthly payroll, but he was constantly pressed by several of his wage hands, each of whom wanted to rent a section of the plantation. By 1867 Watson had reluctantly concluded that he would have to compromise. "The darkies have the long end of the pole!" However much planters might rail against such arrangements and complain that the freedmen lacked the ambition, skills, and intelligence to work without the close supervision of whites, the trend was clear. As the editor of the Augusta *Chronicle and Sentinel* gloomily concluded, "We must give up the old gang system."[65]

The persistence and resourcefulness of the emancipated slaves were a daily rebuke to the myths of docility and dependency that had sustained white southerners, but they hardly saw black behavior in such a light. White landowners professed little confidence that the labor contracts recommended by the Freedmen's Bureau—whether they called for share farming, wage labor, or some other variation—would be observed by the freedmen. Still, they were anxious to have the agreements signed as early as possible. In the months of uncertainty in the fall of 1865, such labor con-

65. Kemp Battle to Benjamin Hedrick, January 20, 1866, in Hedrick Papers; Thomas Watson to Mrs. J. H. Robertson, June 7, 1867, Watson to Robertson, October 14, 1867, both in Thomas S. Watson Papers, UVa; T. P. Devereux to George W. Mordecai, June 1, 1865, in George W. Mordecai Papers, SHC; A. P. Cotter to Paul Cameron, December 31, 1865, W. O. Berry to Paul C. Cameron, July 1, 1865, both in Cameron Papers; Francis W. Pickens to Orr, February 9, 1866, in Orr papers; Wilmer Shields to William Newton Mercer, December 19, 1865, in Mercer Papers; E. H. Deas to Daughter, October 20, 1866, in Deas papers; Thomas C. Browne to Richard Manning, September 17, 1867, in Williams-Chesnut-Manning Papers; Robert T. Hubard to Edmund Wilcox Hubard, November 7, 1865, in Hubard Family Papers; Ethelred Philips to J. J. Philips, October 24, 1865, in James John Philips Papers, SHC; Augusta *Chronicle and Sentinel*, January 4, 1866; Charleston *Daily Courier*, October 3, 1865; *SCu*, XXIII (1865), 180. The slave narratives, though hardly conclusive, indicate that sharecropping of one form or another emerged in 1866 and 1867. Of the 2,000 former slaves interviewed in the 1930s under the WPA program, some 159 commented specifically on the subject. In this small sample, 8 percent rented or leased farms within three years of the war; 8 percent became small landowners; 9 percent worked as nonagricultural wage earners; 40 percent farmed on shares; and 34 percent worked for fixed wages immediately after the war. Among the interviewees from the Deep South, the proportion of sharecropping was more than 50 percent. Unfortunately few of the interviewers were sensitive enough to probe the precise nature of postwar working and economic arrangements.

tracts, witnessed and approved by the local provost marshal or Freed-men's Bureau agent, became a tenuous promise of stability in a sea of uncertainty.[66]

The majority of freedmen, on the other hand, wished to postpone the approval of contracts as long as possible. The dream of landownership was already beginning to fade in the summer and fall of 1865 under the re-lentless attacks of southern whites and most army and Freedmen's Bureau officials, but there was always the possibility that land might yet be made available. Under the circumstances, few of the freedmen wanted to ac-quiesce in postwar arrangements with detailed limitations and descriptions of duties and obligations. It all bore a disconcerting similarity to the old regime.

In those regions where the freed population made up a significant ma-jority, particularly when the planters were desperate for labor, freed men and women dropped any semblance of deference and bluntly rejected the new arrangements. On his plantations, Paul Cameron piously reported to North Carolina Governor Jonathan Worth, he had decided to treat his for-mer slaves "magnanimously and with generosity" after the war. After as-sessing their "capabilities" as first-, second-, and third-class hands, he agreed to distribute his crops equally between himself and the freedmen even down to the milk from the cows. His freedmen had angrily rejected the arrangement and demanded complete control of the stock. When one of his overseers reprimanded them, said Cameron, twenty of his former slaves armed themselves with clubs and cudgels and went "so far as to order the overseer from the field." In other cases they had "threatened the life of the overseer without the least provocation." Only a small minority of planters recounted such stories from firsthand knowledge, but there were enough examples of open defiance to satisfy the worst misgivings of whites. Such open and violent resistance existed throughout the South, but it was particularly common in the Sea Islands and low country of South Carolina, where former slaves were bitter over the failure of the federal government to continue the limited land confiscation program begun during the war. Throughout the fall of 1865, southern newspapers recounted stories of rioters and strikers who occupied the land of their former owners, casually torching outbuildings and "seizing quadrapeds of all kinds—particularly the porcine variety."[67]

Whites, while professing horror at these examples of black violence,

---

66. "Contracts with Laborers," *SCu*, XXIII (1865), 180–81.

67. Paul C. Cameron to Gov. Jonathan Worth, December [?], 1865, in Cameron Papers; Edward Magdol, *A Right to the Land: Essays on the Freedmen's Community* (Greenwood, Conn., 1967), 164–67.

often seemed to welcome the confrontation they promised. When one Richmond journalist described the escalating incidence of blacks' refusal to return to their old deferential state, it was with as much relief as apprehension. Soon there would be a "war of the races," he told his mother, in
which whites from North and South would unite and the "blacks will be
exterminated."[68]

Far more frustrating were those prosaic forms of indirection, passive resistance and "impudence," which black men and women used in carefully
calibrated doses. As free blacks soon learned, the shortage of labor in most
areas of the South and the freedom to leave might be limited tools, but
when they were tied to the skills mastered in a lifetime of bondage, they
could make a freedman by no means helpless in his dealings with his former masters.

Planters often feigned indifference in their first postwar negotiations
with the men and women who had been their slaves, but privately they
agonized and raged over the nerve-wracking minuet of offers and counter-
offers. Samuel Agnew, the Mississippi minister and planter who meticu-
lously described these postwar negotiations, had been relieved in the summer of 1865 when a neighbor ("Aunt Rilla") had worked out an agreement
with her former slaves giving them food and clothing and a tenth of the
crop. Within twenty-four hours Agnew and his neighbors had drawn up
similar arrangements. When time came for the fall negotiations, however,
his hands first agreed to terms of $150 per full hand and food and clothing
for the year and then within a week announced that these were inadequate.
One of his former hands "now demands 200 dollars and [to be] fed and
clothed," a furious Agnew recorded in his diary. Because of the circumstances, he declared, "he could get more and he took advantage of the circumstances." Zebulon Preston, a longtime Delta planter, expressed little
apprehension over his physical safety in the months after the war. It was
instead the "thousand and one annoyances" of having to negotiate every
action with his former slaves in a free-labor society. You cannot imagine
how "dreadfully humiliating & disgusting it is to be placed among them,"
Preston told his old friend Stephen Duncan. Their "insults" and "impudent demands" meant that it was a "perfect dogs life to live here & manage
free negroes." After two weeks of negotiating with his hands, Stephen F.
Duncan, Jr., decided that trying to reach agreements was "like Old Mr.

68. Francis Warrington Dawson to Mother, July 28, 1866, in Francis Warrington Dawson
Papers, DUL. As Bertram Wyatt-Brown pointed out, by creating and stage-managing violent
confrontation, southerners could relieve the frustration they felt over subtle, ambiguous manifestations of black "impudence." Wyatt-Brown, *Southern Honor*, 431–32.

Suggs notion of horse racing—... 'mighty onsartn.'" At the very least, he said, it required a great deal of "Machiavellian diplomacy" and patience.[69] Few white southerners were willing to engage in such diplomacy or to wait until the next year. Instead, they began to outline a nightmarish scenario that linked the freedmen's refusal to sign contracts with the danger of insurrection. Jabez L. M. Curry, president of Alabama's Howard College, issued a grim warning as early as September, 1865. Because of the rumors spread by "wicked and desperate men," blacks had become convinced that "all the plantations in the country are to be divided out among them, together with the stock, provisions &c. after Christmas." Deluded by this misconception, they were already refusing to accept contracts for the coming year. When they discovered that no such division would take place, said Curry, "under their great disappointment [they] will be in a favorable position to inaugurate an insurrection." By the middle of November the connection between the land question and the danger of black violence was a constant theme in the insurrection hysteria. "We are living in such times," said Ann B. Salley of Orangeburg, South Carolina, "worst than all I dread a general uprising of the blacks in January when they find no land is for them."[70]

Such apprehensions had distinct political advantages. By persistently drawing a direct connection between the talk of land distribution and the danger of violence and economic dislocation, white southerners forced the army and Freedmen's Bureau officials onto the defensive. When General Oliver Otis Howard visited the Deep South in late 1865 he felt certain

69. Samuel Agnew Diary, SHC, July 31, August 1, November 2, 3, December 25, 1865, January 3, 1863; Zebulon Preston to Stephen Duncan, December 3, 1865, Stephen F. Duncan, Jr., to Father, December 23, 1863, both in Duncan Papers. For examples of the tension created by contract negotiations, see S. C. Card to Paul C. Cameron, July 5, 1865, Cotter to Paul C. Cameron, December 31, 1865, both in Cameron Family Papers; Robert T. Hubard to Edmund Wilcox Hubard, November 7, 1865, in Hubard Family Papers; George W. Munford to Charles Ellis, January 9, 1866, in Munford-Ellis Family papers, DUL; Sergeant Gardner to A. Franklin Pugh, September 6, 1864, Pugh to Gardner, November 1, 1864, both in Pugh Family Papers, UTA; Amelia Montgomery to Joseph Addison Montgomery, September 5, 1865, in Joseph Addison Montgomery Papers, LSU; John Murphy to E. J. Gay, in Gay Papers; *Fa*, I (1866), 421–22.

70. Jabez L. M. Curry to Parsons, September 29, 1865, Alabama Governors' Papers; Ann B. Salley to aunt, November 13, 1865, in Bruce-Jones-Murchison Family Papers, SCL. Almost every published comment on the danger of insurrection mentioned it in connection with the question of land distribution. See Houston *Tri-Weekly Telegraph*, November 22, 1865; Macon *Daily Telegraph*, August 18, 1865; Natchez *Daily Courier*, November 24, 1865; Franklin (La.) *Planters' Banner*, November 28, 1865; Louisville (Ky.) *Daily Democrat*, December 1, 1865; New Orleans *Times*, October 21, 1865; Baton Rouge *Weekly Advocate*, n.d., quoted in Louisville *Daily Democrat*, November 24, 1865; Mobile *Daily Tribune*, n.d., quoted in Natchez *Daily Courier*, November 10, 1865; Jacksonville *Florida Tri-Weekly Union*, December 2, 1865.

there was little or no danger of such black violence. Yet there was always the agonizing possibility that some unexpected flare-up of violence by the freedmen would discredit the work of the bureau and lead to bloody reprisals by whites. Moreover, Howard had abandoned any hope for significant land distribution among the South's freedmen, and he was anxious to minimize any further disruption of the southern economy. On November 11, therefore, he issued a stern circular to the freedmen of the South. There were continuous rumors of land distribution, he observed. This "wherever it exists is wrong." He ordered Freedmen's Bureau agents to remove this "erroneous and injurious impression." Bureau agents throughout the region were to inform the freedmen there would be "no division of lands, that nothing is going to happen at Christmas, that . . . [you] must go to work . . . [and] make contracts for next year and . . . insurrection will lead to nothing but . . . [your] destruction."[71]

In spite of army and bureau sensitivity to the fears of white southerners, the insurrection scare was one of a number of factors that heightened hostility on both sides. At a superficial level, white southerners were prone to ridicule the efforts of white northerners to "manage" the freedmen. What was needed, insisted one Delta planter, was "firmness, fairness and above all else, *consistency*" in the handling of free Negroes. The shifting personnel and administrative changes of the army and the Freedmen's Bureau made this impossible. In late August, an up-country planter described, with malevolent amusement, the confusing changes in personnel and policies in his district. The original local garrison commander was an Ohio abolitionist, Captain Marcus Brown, who "held the ultra Northern doctrine that 'white man is as good as a negro if he behaves himself.'" After three weeks he was replaced by a Dutch-born officer ("his name is beyond my orthography"), who took precisely the opposite view. His remedy for all the "improprieties" of the freedmen was to pick up a "trace chain" and lay open a sec-

71. Freedmen's Bureau circular, quoted in New Orleans *Times*, December 10, 1865. William S. McFeely discusses Howard's changing position on the land issue in *Yankee Stepfather: General O. O. Howard and the Freedmen* (New Haven, 1968), 130–89. Throughout November and December, Freedmen's Bureau agents sought to deflate the rumors of land distribution. See Col. Samuel Thomas to O. O. Howard, November 2, 1865, in BRFAL, Microcopy 826, Roll 1. Similar orders went out in all the southern states. See report to Howard, November 6, 1865, BRFAL, Microcopy 809, Roll 1; Jacksonville *Florida Tri-Weekly Union*, October 7, December 30, 1865; New Orleans *Daily True Delta*, November 18, 1865; Richmond *Times*, November 6, 1865; Sickles to Orr, November 6, 1865, in South Carolina Governors' Papers; Houston *Tri-Weekly Telegraph*, November 20, 1865; Savannah *Daily Republican*, September 5, 1865; New Orleans *Times*, October 21, 1865; Montgomery *Advertiser*, October 10, 1865; Fayette (Miss.) *Chronicle*, n.d., quoted in the Vicksburg *Herald*, October 28, 1865; Charleston *Daily Courier*, December 16, 1865; W. W. Deane to W. Woodruff, November 6, 1865, in BRFAL, M-798, Reel 1.

tion of the miscreant's scalp. As a result of his example, "a good many men who had got behind in the matter of punishing their negroes during Captain Brown's administration, went home and brought up their average immediately." Within ten days, however, the Dutchman had been replaced by another harassed officer who in turn served less than three weeks before his own replacement in late August. The Louisiana bureau, in similar fashion, was headed successively by Thomas Conway, Joseph Fullerton, Absalom Baird, Philip Sheridan, and Joseph Mower in the first sixteen months of its existence.[72]

Republican radicals sensitive to the problems of the freedmen persistently complained that first army and then Freedmen's Bureau officials were not forceful enough in protecting the rights of the former slave. In December of 1865, the Republican customs collector for the port of New Orleans concluded that the "worst enemies the negro has are the agents of the [Freedmen's] bureau." Most had no real sympathy for the freedmen, claimed J. W. Shaffer, and those who did soon abandoned their scruples over the "wines and dinners" of the great planters they were supposed to regulate.[73]

It was a charge made repeatedly and with some justification. On numerous occasions—particularly under the Butler-Banks military regime in the Delta region from 1863 to 1865—there was collusion between federal agents and planters. But the first six months after the war amounted to a practical seminar on southern race relations for most bureau officials, who found the facts constantly contradicting the insistence of southern whites that they would deal fairly with the freedmen. Their letters and reports reflected a growing anger and frustration over the obstinancy of southern whites and their callous abuse of their former slaves.[74]

It was not simply the level of day-to-day violence with which helpless

72. Natchez *Daily Courier*, September 4, 1865; Yorkville (S.C.) *Enquirer*, August 24, 1865; White, *Freedmen's Bureau in Louisiana*, 17–28.

73. Col. J. W. Shaffer to Gen. Benjamin F. Butler, December 11, 1865, in Butler, *Private and Official Correspondence of Gen. Benjamin F. Butler During the Period of the Civil War* (5 vols.; Norwood, Mass., 1917), V, 688–89. For a particularly critical contemporary report of the army's relationship with planters, see James McKaye, *The Mastership and Its Fruits: The Emancipated Slave Face to Face with His Old Master: A Supplementary Report to the Honorable Edwin M. Stanton, Secretary of War* (New York, 1864), 21. Historians William McFeely, in *Yankee Stepfather*, 158–60, and Jonathan Wiener, in *Social Origins of the New South: Alabama, 1860–1865* (Baton Rouge, 1978), 53–58, have echoed such criticisms.

74. In this respect, it is instructive to read in chronological order the letters and reports of subagents who reported on white violence directed against blacks. See, for example, the extensive "Report . . . in Regard to the Outrages in the Southern States Committed by Whites upon Blacks and Vice-Versa," in Letters Received by the Adjutant General, 1866, Microcopy 619, RG 94, Roll 508, NA.

freedmen were victimized by their former masters; it was the contempt with which whites dismissed the most basic rights of their former slaves. Robert P. Dick of North Carolina, later to become a mainstay of that state's Republican party, put the matter delicately in 1865 when he supported the pardon of a white man convicted of murdering an "insubordinate" former slave. Whites had "lived a long life under a social system which would not tolerate insolence in a slave," said Dick. The change in the system was so abrupt that the people found it difficult to "accommodate." Freedmen's Bureau officers were less circumspect in their evaluations. "There is simply *no way* that the freedmen can be protected from the abuse and mistreatment of whites," concluded one officer. The "majority [of whites] will admit privately that this is the case, but few are willing to publicly defend the rights of the freedmen." The free-labor ideology that shaped the actions and policies of the Freedmen's Bureau officials may have blinded them to the long-term interests of the freedmen. But they were never pawns in the hands of the planter class, and their failure to protect the rights of the freedmen was far more complicated than the acceptance of invitations to deer hunts and plantation dinners.[75]

It was a brief period of time between April and December of 1865, but during those eight months there was a dramatic shift in the attitude of white southerners toward the bureau as well. Initially the army had been preferred to anarchy, but Anna Sherrard of Richmond unconsciously captured white southerners' ambivalence with her observation that the "blue coats preserved the peace by their hateful presence." The gradual restoration of state and local government offered a far more attractive alternative. White southerners, without any sense of inconsistency, continued to demand that the bureau protect white landowning interests even as they increasingly denounced the "Yankee Bureau" as an "expensive humbug and a crying nuisance." Occasionally white southerners bragged over their success in hoodwinking or manipulating agents. A few others might praise the moderation of the federal agents, but by the late fall of 1865 even these cautious voices of praise had ceased and South Carolina's Wade Hampton, in a suitably erudite summation of southern white sentiment, declared that "nothing on the face of the earth" equaled the "deformity and depravity" of those "monstrum horrendum, informe ingens."[76]

75. Robert P. Dick to Holden, August 22, 1865, Holden Papers; Lt. Col. Dexter E. Clapp to Lt. Fred H. Bucher, November 7, 1865, in BRFAL, North Carolina, Box 13.
76. Anna R. Sherrard to Elizabeth T. Munford, April 7, 1866, in Munford-Ellis Papers; Macon *Daily Telegraph*, February 4, 1866. Wade Hampton II to Andrew Johnson, August 25, 1866, in Charles Edward Cauthen (ed.), *Family Letters of the Three Wade Hamptons, 1782–1901* (Columbia, S.C., 1953), 130. Compare, for example, the June and December articles on

On the other hand, federal officials and watchful Republicans were increasingly convinced that the white southerners' continued allegations of nonexistent black "insurrections" was a callous ploy to neutralize the federal government or even to force it to intervene against the freedmen. Republican congressman Timothy Howe of Wisconsin followed the accounts of the so-called "Christmas Day Insurrection," and he warned his fellow Republicans with more insight than he realized that these "tales of conspiracies" were contrived by whites in order to provoke violence by the freedmen that would force the army to intervene on their side. In Mississippi, General Peter J. Osterhaus sarcastically called attention to the "remarkable and inexplicable coincidence" that white officials were never able to uncover a "trace of this great conspiracy." Like an equally sceptical Thomas Conway in Louisiana, Osterhaus found no "black conspiracy." Had there been one piece of concrete evidence to document these rumors, he said, he might have been more likely to give some credence to the much advertised insurrectionary plan "which everybody seems to fear, *or for obvious reasons affects to fear.*" Without equivocation, one Tennessee agent charged that the whole insurrection panic had been concocted "as a pretext so that the whites may disarm the colored population and thus control and manage them without danger of resistance." It was an accusation repeated by other federal officials who encountered this imaginary plot. No federal official was more scathing than James Matthews, subcommissioner of freedmen in Magnolia, Mississippi. A more "ingeniously devised pretext for oppressing a people was never conceived by man" than the insurrection hoax, claimed Matthews. It was nothing more than a subterfuge that white southerners used to justify the most "foul and bloody murders known to any people."[77]

Matthews may have been right, but it was far more than a cynical tactical maneuver. White southerners believed in the danger of insurrection

the Freedmen's Bureau in the New Bern (N.C.) *Daily Times*, the Macon *Daily Telegraph*, the Montgomery *Advertiser*, the Raleigh *Sentinel*, and the Houston *Tri-Weekly Telegraph*.

77. *Congressional Globe*, 37th Cong., 1st Sess., pp. 167–68; Maj. Gen. Peter J. Osterhaus to Bvt. Maj. Gen. M. F. Force, November 9, 1865, Osterhaus to Bvt. Maj. Gen. John A. Rawlins, November 11, 1865, both Microcopy 826, Roll 1, Swayne to James M. Smith, December 22, 1865, *ibid.*, Vol. I, p. 137, all in BRFAL; *Report of the Joint Committee on Reconstruction*. For other sceptical appraisals of the insurrection scare by Freedmen's Bureau officials and northern missionaries, see S. H. Melcher to Bvt. Maj. Gen. Clinton Fisk, December 12, 1865, in BRFAL, Tennessee, Registered Letters Received, Box 2. See also Freedmen of St. James Parish, Petition, December 25, 1865, in BRFAL, Louisiana, Registered Letters Received; Col. Samuel Thomas to Howard, November 13, 1865, Microcopy 826, Roll 1, Foster to Free, December 15, 1865, *ibid.*, Roll 30, all in BRFAL; George Almy to George Clavis, December 8, 1865, in Box 13, M. D. Hardie, Executive Order to Commanding Officer, Goldsboro, N.C., January 6, 1866, in Box 14, both in BRFAL, North Carolina; Rev. S. A. Wright to Rev. George Whipple, December 4, 1865, in AMA, Mississippi, Roll 1.

just as they had believed that such violent upheavals were imminent in the hundreds of nonexistent slave panics of the 1840s and 1850s. In mid-December of 1865, Major General Daniel Sickles, military commander of the district of South Carolina, assured whites in that state that there was no danger of revolutionary action by the freedmen. "Emancipation," Sickles told Governor Orr, had removed "whatever provocation may have existed to incite the colored people." For whites, however, the continued threat of a violent black upheaval was essential, for it justified the kind of rigid controls that alone could guide the freedmen and protect them and society from—in Josiah Nott's words—"their savage and unbridled instincts."[78]

The fear of racial apocalypse, yoked to self-interest, was a powerful force in uniting white southerners in 1865 as it had been for generations before. And so, blindly they pushed forward with plans for "special" legislation, unable to grasp the absolute political expediency (if not the justice) of embracing equality under the law. Throughout the fall of 1865, debate over legislation involving the freedmen was over details and emphasis. Only a handful of white southerners questioned the basic assumptions underlying what would come to be called the black codes.

For James Hambleton of Atlanta, an unsuccessful Democratic candidate for Congress in 1865, there was no question what should be done. The "entire African population now within the limits of the several Southern states . . . should, by state legislation, be made the same as that of the free-Negro before the civil war; nothing less, nothing more." Edward Yerger, the fiery Mississippi editor of the Jackson *News*, endorsed this "painless solution" by declaring that there was no need for any additional legislation, there were ample laws already on the books of the southern states for regulating the free Negro and the "freedman and the free negro must stand on the same footing."[79]

The absurdity of governing blacks under the same legal code as whites was obvious to every southern white man, argued the editor of the Macon *Daily Telegraph*. "There is such a radical difference in the mental and moral constitution of the white and the black race, that it would be impossible to secure order in a mixed community by the same legal sanction." A short confinement in jail as punishment for petty theft might deter a white man, "but not a black." The stocks or "hiring out for labor" were the only punishments that could possibly keep the penitentiary from being inundated. To make policy on the basis of "absurd theoretical notions of legal equality would be to abandon common sense and self-respect and admin-

---

78. Sickles to Orr, December 17, 1865, in Orr Papers.
79. Atlanta *Daily Intelligencer*, October 24, 1865; Jackson *News*, November 14, 1865.

ister our internal affairs on the fanatical notions of Thaddeus Stevens and Charles Sumner."[80]

A return to the antebellum black codes would have restored slavery in all but name, for such state legislation had restricted educational opportunities for free blacks, barred them from a number of occupations, restricted their mobility and prohibited them from testifying against whites in every slave state except Delaware. In Virginia free blacks suffered more severe restrictions than slaves in some respects. Slaveowners, for example, were not prohibited from teaching their slaves to read and write, but "free blacks or mulattoes were prohibited from learning to read and write under any circumstances." White southerners in most states were not politically insensitive enough to enact such sweepingly discriminatory laws.[81]

Instead, the legislation that emerged in the fall of 1865 was a melange of paternalism and repression, a fitful attempt to accommodate the wishes of northerners and the prejudices and fears of southern whites. Between November of 1865, when Mississippi passed the comprehensive legislation, and the fall of 1867, when the authority of the Johnson governments passed to the new regimes created by Congress, the postwar southern legislatures enacted hundreds of pieces of legislation touching directly and indirectly upon the relationship of blacks to whites and of the freedmen to the state. In several of the Deep South states, there was a conscious attempt to systematically rewrite state law; in the border states, the revisions proceeded on an *ad hoc* basis with little thought for thoroughness or consistency.[82]

In the minds of the framers of this legislation, their handiwork undoubtedly seemed a product of magnanimity and fairness. The legislation did mark a dramatic revolution in the region's legal codes when compared to the laws of the Old South. With some glaring exceptions, postwar legislation guaranteed the right of former slaves, in the words of the South Carolina Black Code Commission, to "acquire, own and dispose of property; to make contracts; to enjoy the fruits of their labor; to sue and be sued; and to receive protection under the law in their persons and property."[83]

80. Macon *Daily Telegraph*, February 22, 1866; Atlanta *Daily Intelligencer*, October 24, 1865.

81. Ira Berlin, *Slaves Without Masters: The Free Negro in the Antebellum South* (New York, 1974), 60–65, 90, 94–100, 122, 268, 304–306, 316–17; John Codman Hurd, *The Law of Freedom and Bondage in the United States* (2 vols.; Boston, 1862), II, 9.

82. Theodore Wilson's study of the black codes remains the best single compilation of postwar racial legislation, but even Wilson did not unearth all of the enactments scattered through the legislative journals of the Johnsonian governments. And many acts that did not specifically refer to race were clearly written in response to emancipation.

83. *Report of the South Carolina Commission on the Code*, 3. This preface was incorporated without change in the final legislation. *Statutes at Large of South Carolina*, 1865, p. 10.

Often overlooked in the reaction to the legislation were the attempts of the framers to protect the freedmen from overt repression and extralegal exploitation. The Georgia committee proposed special antivigilante legislation that would have required fines and imprisonment for "any band, association or combination formed without authority of law, for the purpose of injuring persons of color in their persons or property, whether under pretense of punishing crime or otherwise." The language and emphasis of the Georgia measure is so close to those of the South Carolina legislation adopted in December, 1865, that it seems quite likely that the Georgia committee used the South Carolina legislation as their guide. In four states, postwar legislative codes gave contracting laborers a first lien on the property of the landlord for payment of wages, and South Carolina's code, in addition to spelling out working hours and conditions, even defined exceptions. For example, servants could not be required to work during rain, sleet, or snow, and the code specifically prohibited landlords from expelling old or homeless former slaves from their property.[84]

The codes adopted by South Carolina and Mississippi and recommended by the Georgia commission were at times laundry lists of the "mutal obligations and duties of the servant and master." Thus, in the proposed Georgia code, servants were to be "honest, truthful, sober, civil and diligent" and to obey "all lawful orders of the master." But when there was some question of whether or not a command was reasonable, "the burden of proving it reasonable shall be on the master." Servants could be discharged for a range of offenses from "habitual negligence or indolence" to "drunkeness or lewdness" or "repeated or prolonged absence from the premises" —even for "gross disrespect or habitiual incivility to himself [the master], guests or agents." On the other hand, the servant could legally terminate his contract at any time if the master failed to live up to its terms, if he made any attempt at "debauching his [the servant's] wife or daughter," or if the master showed "violent and menacing conduct even though short of battery."[85]

At its core, however, the postwar legislation of the Johnson governments was unequivocally discriminatory and designed to keep blacks in a subordinate economic and social relationship to whites. It was the southerners' response to the prophecies of a generation of proslavery apologists as well as the chaotic events of 1865. And here, as elsewhere, the history of the Caribbean served as a warning and a convenient rationale for their repressive acts. The two most influential London newspapers, the *Times* and the *Daily Telegraph*, had both urged white southerners to carefully con-

84. Macon *Daily Telegraph*, January 9, 10, 11, 1866.
85. *Ibid.*

sider the lessons of emancipation in the West Indies. In the first eight years after emancipation, observed the *Times*, more than half of the Jamaican labor force left the plantations and dispersed onto small subsistence plots as freeholders or "squatters." As one former southern planter living in Kingston advised his southern counterparts in a letter published in several southern newspapers, the most important thing was to "avoid the dispersion of the blacks onto small separate plots."[86]

However much northern abolitionists and English liberals might attempt to dispute the gloomy assessment of West Indian emancipation or to offer differing explanations for the economic decline, southerners seized upon the "Jamaican fiasco" (as one newspaper editor called it) as justification for firm measures. As in Jamaica, the southern climate rendered subsistence possible with little labor, warned the editor of the *Florida Union*. Moreover, "the freedmen have not much taste for the artifical comforts and luxuries which are the chief incentives to steady industry; and land is abundant and cheap." With small capital, the freedmen could "purchase or lease a few acres, put up a cabin . . . get a truck patch and then exist without contributing anything to the community and in fact stealing in all directions like the residents of the West Indies after emancipation."[87]

White southerners needed little encouragement. The legislation adopted in the fall of 1865 went beyond such specific, individual acts as the barring of blacks from the ownership of weapons in Mississippi or the differential punishment for minor criminal acts in South Carolina. The heart of the postwar codes was an interlocking body of law that made vagrancy a crime and the breaking of contracts a serious offense against the state. On its face, such legislation might not even mention race. Louisiana legislators simply adopted the Massachusetts vagrancy act. But the purpose was always the same: to force the great majority of the freedmen to sign agricultural contracts for the coming year and to make them hold to these contracts under severe criminal penalties.

They were equally committed to the use of the state to maintain the same complete control they had held over 3.5 million former slaves. The same political and regional leaders who spoke gravely of the need for fairness toward the freedmen were equally adamant in demanding a strengthening of the police powers that had existed in the antebellum South. In

<hr/>

86. London *Times*, November 18, 1865; Bolt, *Victorian Attitudes to Race*, 78–79; Atlanta *Daily Intelligencer*, July 28, 1865; (Jacksonville) *Florida Union*, October 28, 1865; Yorkville (S.C.) *Enquirer*, November 25, 1865; Montgomery *Advertiser*, August 2, 1865.
87. (Jacksonville) *Florida Union*, October 28, 1865; Natchez *Daily Courier*, November 2, 1865; Macon *Daily Telegraph*, May 17, 1865; Lynchburg (Va.) *Republican*, November 30, 1865; Selma *Daily Messenger*, July 30, 1865.

every state of the Deep South one of the first legislative goals was the re-creation of a well-organized state militia. Although political leaders gave lip service to the supremacy of the federal government and the United States Army garrisons that were scattered across the South, they correctly sur-mised that such units, once in operation, would be able to act with consid-erable latitude. North Carolina's D. D. Ferebee, chairman of the State Sen-ate Committee on Military Affairs, petitioned General Thomas Ruger for arms and ammunition "with a view of enabling the newly formed militia of the state to more effectually suppress any insurrectionary movement on the part of the free negroes." As one elected militia officer bluntly told the Ala-bama governor in requesting more modern equipment, "It is feared that the negroes will be troublesome about Christmas unless there is some organi-zation that can keep them in subjection."[88]

On September 24, 1865, Alabama Governor Lewis Parsons sent a ques-tionnaire to the delegates at that state's constitutional convention asking them how many companies of militia they thought would be needed for the "peace and protection" of their counties. The response was extraordinarily revealing. Despite the fact that there had been considerable disorder and crime reported in the mountainous region of the state, the overwhelming requests for assistance came from the heavily black regions. By the middle of 1866, there were 2,624 men under arms. Of this number 2,496 were in counties where blacks made up more than 50 percent of the population. Most mountain and wiregrass counties did not even bother to request the formation of militia companies.[89]

In dozens of instances throughout the Deep South, local whites did not wait for the formation of official militia units; they simply organized them-selves into companies, elected officers, and then began systematically search-ing the homes of black residents and confiscating any firearms they discov-ered. While these search and confiscate missions sometimes degenerated into unruly and moblike plunderings of the homes of former freedmen, they were usually led by the most respectable and conservative members of the community. When one Eufaula, Alabama, militia company was joined by federal soldiers in searching black homes and confiscating arms, Mayor C. J. Pope was angered to learn that the U.S. soldiers had treated the freed-men "most discourteously," smashed their furniture, and stolen personal

88. Wilmington (N.C.) *Daily Herald*, November 30, December 25, 1865; "Col." John S. Garvin to Parsons, October 7, 1865, E. G. Richards to Parsons, October 19, 1865, both in Alabama Governors' Papers.

89. See responses from the Alabama convention delegations in late September and early October, 1865, in the Alabama Governors' Papers. For a report on the units actually formed, see Report of the Adjutant and Inspector General of Alabama.

items. He promised Governor Parsons that he would personally compensate the victims for any damage, despite the fact that it was done by federal troops. And officials in Alabama, Mississippi, Georgia, South Carolina, and North Carolina made little attempt to conceal their actions; indeed, on several occasions they informed state and federal officials in advance of what they intended to do, and they were often stunned to discover that their actions were regarded by federal officials as criminal. As one Shelby County "colonel" plaintively reported to Governor Parsons, he and his fellow militia men had simply been trying to prevent the freedmen's "depredations upon private stock" and to restrain their "growing impudence." If he had overstepped his authority, he told Parsons, "please communicate at your earliest convenience as I do not wish to do anything but what is right."[90]

But the assurance that white southerners would soon have ultimate police and judicial control did not alleviate the fears of many white southerners. The black codes, regarded as a return to slavery by northern Republicans, were seen as a departure too radical for white southerners still absorbing the effects of emancipation. In this respect, nothing aroused more controversy than the recommendation of the various state commissions that the freed black be allowed to testify in cases involving blacks and whites (though not whites alone). A precedent already existed in the Freedmen's Bureau and military courts where blacks had given testimony without restrictions, and it was there that white southerners first confronted the issue. When Charleston planter William Ravenel reported the theft of twenty bales of cotton by several former slaves, he was incredulous when the provost marshal refused to accept his account of the incident. It was "intolerable," an angry Ravenel reported, that his word as a gentleman should be subject to contradiction by a "passel of ignorant field hands." Ravenel was relatively philosophical in his responses to the new state of affairs; other white southerners were not. After being summoned before a bureau agent in early June of 1865 to answer the complaint of one of his

90. Fisk to R. C. Scott, December 13, 1865, in BRFAL, Tennessee, Letters Sent, Vol. 3; Hazlehurst (Miss.) Copiahan, December 9, 1865; Mrs. Y. B. Manning to Husband, September 4, 1865, in Williams-Chesnut-Manning Papers; Shields to William N. Mercer, July 10, 1866, in Mercer Papers; Foster to Free, December 15, 1865, in BRFAL, Mississippi, Reel 30; "Petition of Freedmen of Parish of St. James, Louisiana, December 25, 1865," in BRFAL, Louisiana, Incoming Correspondence; "Extract from Order of Hyde County, North Carolina Court, August 15, 1865," in David Miller Carter Papers, SHC; L. L. Clements to Worth, August 8, 1866, in Jonathan Worth Papers, SCA; Swayne to Lt. Spencer Smith, December 11, 1865, Swayne to Commanding Officer, Lowndes County, Alabama, Militia, December 13, 1865, both in BRFAL, Alabama, Reel 1, Vol. I; Lt. Spencer Smith to Col. C. Cadle, Jr., December 9, 1865, in BRFAL, Alabama, Reel 18; Mayor C. J. Pope to Parsons, December 11, 1865, W. A. McClure to Parsons, December 11, 1865, John Barnes and E. F. Boher to Patton, December 17, 1865, all in Alabama Governors' Papers.

former slaves, David Schenck of Lincolnton, North Carolina, seemed near apoplexy by the time he recorded the event in his diary. The "absolute disgrace" of having to answer a Negro's charge before a Yankee commander with "no more dignity or respect than is shown the negro" was, to Schenck, more intolerable to a southern gentleman than "war or famine." "It is literally turning the slave into the master and the master, slave," he fumed.[91]

Beyond the humiliation was the effect it would ultimately have on both the freedmen and their deluded northern radical supporters. In newspaper debates, public speeches, and private correspondence, opponents of the rights of blacks to testify insisted that it would inevitably lead to "bloodshed and violence" since the freedmen, already "intoxicated . . . with the idea of freedom," would be emboldened to commit acts they would never think of undertaking. And it was, argued one North Carolina senator, simply the opening wedge which would lead to full equality between blacks and whites. If you "admit a negro to testify," insisted the editor of the Montgomery *Mail*, "you will next propose to put him in the jury box or to let him vote."[92]

And no argument of opponents of black testimony was more effective than the citation of discriminatory northern laws absolutely prohibiting black testimony or sharply circumscribing the legal rights of blacks in the courtroom. William A. Jenkins of Warren County, North Carolina, always began his speeches against black testimony by citing the legal codes of Indiana, Iowa, Ohio, Illinois, and California, all of which barred blacks from testifying against whites. In a speech given in September of 1865, Indiana Republican Governor Oliver P. Morton had sadly acknowledged the disgraceful limitations of black rights in his state. Not only were blacks excluded from voting, he observed, they were barred from testifying in court, forbidden to attend the public schools, and incapable of making a valid contract or acquiring a piece of land. Morton's speech was gleefully quoted by Jenkins and reprinted in several southern newspapers. How much greater was the problem of black insubordination, said Jenkins, in the South where blacks often made up a majority.[93]

91. Mrs. Y. B. Manning to Husband, September 4, 1865, in Williams-Chesnut-Manning Papers. In fairness to Ravenel, he seemed far more infuriated by what he considered to be the credulity and stupidity of the investigating army officer than by the fact that blacks were allowed to testify; David Schenck Diary, June 14, 1865; Eliza Andrews, *Wartime Journal*, 364.

92. Raleigh *Daily Sentinel*, September 26, October 2, 1865, March 22, 1866; Jason Niles Diary, SHC, August 15–19, 1865; A. B. Cooper to Parsons, September 29, 1865, in Alabama Governors' Papers; Raleigh *Standard*, February 9, 1866; Montgomery *Mail*, n.d., quoted in the Montgomery *Advertiser*, February 25, 1866; W. N. H. Smith to Thomas David Smith McDowell, February 2, 1866; Natchez *Daily Courier*, October 5, 1865; New York *Times*, October 10, 1865.

93. Raleigh *Daily Sentinel*, March 22, 1866; Montgomery *Mail*, November 21, 1865;

Conservative proponents of the right of blacks to testify answered argument for argument, none more sarcastically than the old Whig-unionist editor of the Natchez *Daily Courier*. The notion that the reception of the black man's testimony in a court of law made him the equal of a white was as absurd as the argument that the "keeper of a brothel was made the equal of a Bishop because the law permits the testimony of each to be taken," claimed Giles Hillyer.[94]

In an argument remarkable for its condemnation of slavery, the North Carolina special commission agreed that blacks were not always trustworthy in their testimony ("We are fully aware of a lamentable prevalence of this vice among the race"). But Benjamin Moore's committee insisted this was simply one of the many unfortunate consequences of the institution of slavery. Forced into an existence of involuntary servitude from which they could hope to receive few rewards "it was natural that they were lazy." When faced with the whip slaves had lied, but this was expected for the "vice of lying is, and ever has been common to all people in slavery." The solution was not to bar blacks from the courtroom, but to begin the process of "uplifting this unfortunate race" by introducing them to as many of the duties and responsibilities of citizenship as possible—short of the ballot, of course.[95]

Florida Provisional Governor William Marvin even rejected the assumption of whites that the freedmen were more dishonest than whites as witnesses. Such statements, insisted Marvin, were a "slander upon both God and man." Experience had taught him, he said, that the "slave had often told the truth, whilst the master has lied." And from whence came the notion that only those who told the truth should stand in the witness box? "Who does not know that every courtroom is the theatre of more or less false swearing?" he asked one sceptical audience in Quincy, Florida. The only hope was that from this perjurous "hissing of tongues," with the aid of reason and a thousand surrounding circumstances, juries might reach the truth. But if the freedman were kept out of the court, "what chance has he for justice? Just none at all." Samuel F. Phillips, the North Carolina conservative who later turned Republican, sought to implement the Moore Committee recommendations by reminding his fellow representatives of the political implications of their actions. "How can we say [to a suspicious

---

Vicksburg *Herald*, November 28, 1865. For Morton's speech, see William Dudley Foulke, *Life of O. P. Morton, Including His Important Speeches* (2 vols.; Indianapolis, 1899), I, 448–50.

94. Natchez *Daily Courier*, October 5, 1865. For a similar argument, see Mississippi planter James Lusk Alcorn to Amelia Alcorn, August 26, 1865, in James Lusk Alcorn Papers, SHC.

95. Raleigh *Daily Standard*, January 31, 1866; *North Carolina Public Laws*, 1866, 98–104.

North], leave the freedmen to us, we will do him justice," he asked, "refusing in the same breath to allow him to tell his tale before a jury of white
men and white judges?"[96]

Conservatives—particularly the larger planters—had other practical arguments in favor of unrestricted black testimony. In the months after the
war, planters were obsessed with thievery, particularly the practice whereby former slaves secretly sold seed cotton to local merchants or "mercenary
whites." Even when planters were able to apprehend such thieves, however, they were often powerless to act against the whites whom they considered most guilty. "I know of a number of instances," insisted Walker
Brooke of Vicksburg, Mississippi, "where blacks were the only witnesses
to acts of wrongdoing by whites. The denial of the opportunity to testify
can only lead to miscarriages of justice." Mobile attorney E. S. Dargan
pointed out that the bar to black testimony was an invitation for criminal
whites to use the freedmen as a "catspaw" for illegal purposes, comfortable
in the knowledge that they were free from incrimination.[97]

Despite the support of influential southerners for the critical black testimony legislation, opposition existed throughout the region. A. B. Cooper,
a former slaveowner of considerable wealth and a delegate to the Alabama
constitutional convention, was quick to blame whites from the up-country
and those areas of the state where there had been few blacks before the war.
With some notable exceptions, Cooper may have been correct in his self-
serving assessment of the politics of the issue of black testimony.[98]

In Mississippi the question of black testimony was a bitterly divisive issue from the outset of Presidential Reconstruction. According to one of the
delegates at the 1865 constitutional convention, James Shannon, editor of
the Jackson *Clarion*, failed in his bid for the presidency of the convention
when he endorsed the right of freedmen to testify in all cases. Even after the
architects of the state's black code insisted to delegates that some form of
black testimony would have to be approved, a provision guaranteeing that
right lost in the house fifty to forty, despite the fact that Governor Sharkey
had already issued a proclamation directing the state courts to accept the
testimony of all without regard to race. And the vote on this issue showed a
strong correlation with the racial composition of the representatives' con-

96. (Jacksonville) *Florida Union*, September 15, 1865, Vicksburg *Herald*, November 17,
1865; Montgomery *Advertiser*, September 29, 1865; Samuel F. Phillips to Kemp Battle, September 5, 1865, in Battle Papers; Raleigh *Standard*, February 7, 1866.
97. Vicksburg *Herald*, November 10, 17, 1865; E. S. Dargan to Parsons, August 29,
1865, in Alabama Governors' Papers.
98. A. B. Cooper to Governor Louis Parsons, September 29, 1865, in Alabama Governors' Papers.

stituencies. Only one delegate from the six most heavily black counties (more than 80 percent) opposed black testimony. Within each delegation from the majority-black counties, from 60 to 80 percent of the representatives favored the testimony provisions. In contrast, of the eighteen counties with less than 40 percent black population, thirteen delegations unanimously opposed allowing blacks to testify.[99]

When a North Carolina delegate introduced a measure in early 1866 to reduce North Carolina freedmen to the status of antebellum free blacks without the right to testify in court under *any* circumstances, the proposal lost by a three-to-two majority, but the overwhelming support for this repressive bill came from the predominantly white counties of the state. The average black population of the counties whose delegates supported the measure was 29 percent. The average black population of the counties opposing this reactionary measure was 53 percent. The vote showed an even higher correlation with the Worth-Holden factions and constituted an ominous warning of the problems inherent in creating a coalition between blacks and the unionist faction led by Holden. Delegates from counties that had supported Holden were twice as likely to back this resolution as those from the counties where Jonathan Worth had won a majority.[100]

In Alabama, the black testimony issue never specifically came to a vote, but on a broader question, a similar pattern emerged. A group of black-belt senators introduced a broad measure that would have repealed all discriminatory laws except those involving suffrage, the right to serve on juries, and the "distinction which has existed since the days of Japeth and the curse of Ham"—intermarriage. The civil rights bill failed in the senate sixteen to eleven because of the opposition of those areas of the state with the fewest blacks—the wiregrass and piney woods regions and the Tennessee Valley and North Alabama counties. What was striking was the strong support through the heavily black counties of Montgomery, Lowndes, Autauga, Dallas, Wilcox, Marengo, and Greene.[101]

99. *Mississippi House Journal*, 1865, pp. 212–13; Jason Niles Diary, August 15, 1865.
100. *North Carolina House Journal*, 1866, pp. 151, 174–75; John L. Cheney, Jr. (ed.), *North Carolina Government, 1585–1974: A Narrative and Statistical History* (Raleigh, 1975), 1390–91. Like any legislative vote touching on complex issues, these can be misinterpreted. One state senator noted, for example, that a handful of western unionists voted against the bill allowing blacks to testify in the "hope that the state will be remanded back to a Territorial condition." Leander Gash to Wife, March 4, 1866, in Leander Gash Papers, NCA. And not every representative of the black belt favored the bill. Opposition to black testimony was led by Representative William A. Jenkins who represented a county with a 70 percent black population.
101. The bill was introduced by Frances W. Sykes from Lawrence County, the county in the Tennessee Valley with the largest black population in the area of the state. Sykes ultimately joined the Republican party. *Alabama Senate Journal*, 1865, pp. 140–41; Montgomery *Adver-*

Given the internal hostility toward far-reaching changes in southern law, proponents of the postwar black codes were quick to argue that they had gone as far as public opinion would allow. One cautious South Carolina conservative had voted against the black codes on the grounds that "our Northern brethren will rightly regard the codes as too much of a white man's law." But James Hemphill was frank to acknowledge that little more could be expected given the uncertainties of the postwar era. The most common response to the enactment of the first racial legislation was self-congratulation. With unintended irony, the editor of the Charleston *Daily Courier* called upon northerners to retract their baseless assaults upon the motives and intentions of white southerners in view of the "conservative and humane legislation recently enacted by the state's legislature."[102]

Even before the final votes, however, moderate and Republican newspapers had begun to publish angry attacks on the proposed racial legislation. Conservative southerners were quick to argue that northern Republicans often exaggerated the repressive aspects of the codes. The New York *Daily Tribune*, the Chicago *Tribune*, the Springfield *Republican*, and the Cleveland *Leader*, for example, systematically misrepresented provisions of postwar legislation and—in the case of the New York *Daily Tribune* at least—continued these misrepresentations after copies of the actual laws and pleas for correction had been mailed by white conservatives. But however they may have misrepresented their specifics, northerners had instinctively and accurately grasped the ideological underpinnings of the Johnson governments' postwar legislation.[103]

The revolution that had occurred in the thinking of white southerners was quite different from that envisioned by white northerners. They had assumed that the notions of free labor would sweep aside the detritus of the proslavery argument or that the southern whites would defer to their northern occupiers in matters of race relations. But southern whites, whatever their differences, were not willing to abandon the assumptions of generations. At their worst they wanted to reintroduce slavery without the name; at their best they wished to introduce an indefinite transitional status for the freedmen in which the state with some significant new departures would assume ultimate responsibility for the supervision and control of the freedmen.

---

tiser, December 5, 16; Sarah Woolfolk Wiggins, *The Scalawag in Alabama Politics, 1865–1881* (University, Ala., 1977), 62.

102. James Hemphill to W. R. Hemphill, November 7, December 1, 1865, in Hemphill Collection; A. A. Gilbert to Thomas Boone Fraser, November 4, 1865, in Thomas Boone Fraser Papers; Charleston *Daily Courier*, December 2, 1865.

103. See especially the New York *Tribune*, October 2, 3, 1865, and the complaints of the editor of the Charleston *Daily Courier*, November 29, 1865.

If the Republican majority had had any confidence in the good intentions of white southerners, they might have tolerated such a halfway house to freedom. In the initial constitutional conventions, however, northern observers had first glimpsed the southern man's ideas about what was to be done with the freedmen, and they were, for the most part, horrified. As delegate after delegate rose to demand that the freedmen be forced to work, northern observers were convinced that they were witnessing the first attempts to reinstitute slavery in all but name. And when they heard the casually brutal threats made off the record ("I would shoot one just as soon as I would a dog") and saw firsthand the readiness with which southerners lashed out against their former servants, they were not likely to be lulled by verbal assurances of fair and equitable treatment. The South Carolina constitutional convention passed few measures dealing specifically with the former slaves, reported a Boston journalist, but in their comments on the floor they dismissed the freedman "like an animal whose presence is endured but is in no way desirable." With some notable exceptions, concluded Sidney Andrews, whites' "prevailing sentiment" toward the South's black population was "blind, baffled, revengeful hatred." As one planter angrily exclaimed, "D——n their black souls, they're the things that caused the best blood of our sons to flow." [104]

Nothing had happened in the months that followed to change these perceptions. For that minority of the Republican party that had scorned the southern rebels and favored black suffrage from the outset, the events of the summer and fall of 1865 were simply confirmation of the assumptions and convictions they held. The more significant impact was upon the majority of Republicans who were hesitant and uncertain over what should be done with the defeated South. For these Republicans (and a handful of northern Democrats as well) each step taken by the postwar Johnson governments—when viewed in the context of journalistic and official reports of whites' mistreatment of the freedmen—reinforced their misgivings. Connecticut Republican Congressman Henry Deming, a self-styled moderate, was willing to acknowledge that the Johnson governments had *acquiesced* in the end of slavery, that the rebels had in "equivocal and guarded language" repealed the secession ordinances and repudiated the rebel debt. But even these limited concessions had been made only because of the president's threat of political exclusion. By January of 1866, Deming's dis-

---

104. Sidney Andrews, *The South Since the War*, 86–87; Reid, *After the War*, 417. "So far as I have seen, all native Southerners, the poorest and the most degraded, equally with the rich; and people of the most undoubted Unionism as well as secessionists, unaffectedly and heartily despise the negroes," concluded one correspondent. "Truly they are a despised race." Dennett, *The South As It Is*, 19.

illusionment was complete and his worst fears realized. These southerners had lied when they broke their oaths of allegiance in 1860 and 1861, concluded a bitter Deming, and they lied when they claimed to have accepted the requirements of a victorious and compassionate Union. Deming, like many of his fellow Republicans, considered the black code to be concrete evidence of his worst suspicions. This "generation of vipers," despite all its protestations of loyalty, would turn back the clock once it had regained self-rule. Lovers of the Union should look at these deeds, rather than their words, argued Deming. "I am told," he warned, "that Italian brigands are never so devout in kneelings, crossings, and paternosters as when they are about to plunge afresh into crimes."[105]

Reports of the infamous black codes had an even greater impact because they were published in the midst of the congressional elections held under the Johnson governments in October and November of 1865. And by the time the southern delegations had begun to gather in Washington, the pages of the mainline Republican newspapers—the New York *Tribune*, the Boston *Advertiser*, the Chicago *Tribune*, the Springfield *Republican*, and the Cleveland *Leader*—were filled with descriptions of the southern senators and would-be representatives as unrepentant secessionists standing, in the vivid words of the *Leader*, with "dagger in hand ready to strike down the Goddess of Liberty." For the Newark *Daily Advertiser*, the election of such former Confederates as Alexander Stephens proved that the "reptile spirit of secession is still alive . . . and ready to display its fangs at any moment." Horace Greeley's New York *Tribune* printed extensive tables and charts on the southern delegations, purporting to show that the men who presented their credentials to the Congress were "without an exception . . . disloyal men . . . , unrepentant secessionists." The Joint Committee on Reconstruction was only slightly less emphatic. The southern voters had "placed in power leading rebels, unrepentant and unpardoned" and had elected ("with very few exceptions") active secessionists with no love for the Union.[106]

Even Whitelaw Reid, usually cautious and careful in his reporting, was carried away with the emotions of the moment. The southern delegations, he insisted, reflected the views of such secessionists as James Mason, William Lowndes Yancey, Jefferson Davis, and Robert A. Toombs. These traitors had led the nation into a "sea of blood," but white southerners "be-

105. See *Congressional Globe*, 39th Cong., 1st Sess., 1866, Pt. 1, pp. 74–75, 145, 165–67, 294–95, 331–32.
106. J. Michael Quill, *Prelude to the Radicals: The North and Reconstruction During 1865* (Washington, 1980), 130–31; New York *Tribune*, November 30, 1865; Cleveland *Leader*, December 3, 1865; *Report of the Joint Committee on Reconstruction*, II, xvii.

lieved in them still." Although not as unequivocal as the writer for the *Tribune*, Reid insisted that most of the southern states had sent "not a single representative who could take the iron-clad oath of loyalty without perjury." In fact, of the eleven southern states, only three (South Carolina, Georgia, and Mississippi) sent delegations entirely consisting of individuals who could not have taken the ironclad oath, and in three states (Virginia, Tennessee and Arkansas), the overwhelming majority of senators and representatives could have taken such an oath.[107]

But these accusations were made with such vehement certitude that few modern historians have challenged their essential accuracy. A half century ago, the distinguished black historian W. E. B. Du Bois vividly summarized this view of the congressional delegation of 1865. It consisted, he said, of the vice-president of the Confederacy, "four Confederate generals, five Confederate colonels, six Confederate cabinet officers and fifty-eight Confederate Congressmen, none of whom was able to take the oath of allegiance." With some variations, the overwhelming majority of later scholars would accept Du Bois' assertion without challenges.[108]

In reality, Du Bois had underestimated the number of military figures. Ten had been generals, and another five had served at lesser ranks. But it could hardly be said that these men were unreconstructed secessionists. Of the eighty senators and representatives who unsuccessfully presented their credentials to the Congress in 1865, seventy-seven had taken a position on secession in 1860 and 1861. Only seven had been secessionists. Seventy had opposed disunion until the election of Abraham Lincoln; forty-four remained opposed to secession until their states had voted to leave the Union.[109]

107. Reid, *After the War*, 367, 437.

108. W. E. B. Du Bois, *Black Reconstruction in America, 1860–1880* (New York, 1935), 260–61. See also Fawn M. Brodie, *Thaddeus Stevens, Scourge of the South* (New York, 1959), 229–30; John Hope Franklin, *Reconstruction: After the Civil War* (Chicago, 1961), 43; Kenneth Stampp, *The Era of Reconstruction, 1865–1877* (New York, 1965), 67; Michael Perman, *Reunion Without Compromise: The South and Reconstruction, 1865–1868* (Cambridge, 1973), 164; George Fredrickson (ed.), *A Nation Divided: Problems and Issues of the Civil War and Reconstruction* (Minneapolis, 1975), 120. These figures have also appeared in a number of textbooks—most recently Allen Weinstein and R. Jackson Wilson, *Freedom and Crisis: An American History* (2 vols.; New York, 1974), II, 424; Peter d'Arcy Jones, *The U.S.A.: A History of Its People and Society Since 1865* (Homewood, Ill., 1976), 353; Forrest McDonald, *A Constitutional History of the United States* (New York, 1982), 133; and Idus Newby, *The South: A History* (New York, 1978), 256. I should add that this erroneous statement also appeared in my lectures for more than a decade.

109. These statistics and those that follow have been compiled from newspapers, county histories, state biographical dictionaries, obituaries, and other fugitive sources. I would like to acknowledge the invaluable assistance of Barton Shaw who assisted me in collecting biographical information on southern leaders elected in the summer and fall of 1865. The only published analysis of the 1865 congressional leadership based upon research rather than assertion is Alan B.

The majority of the southern congressional delegation of 1865 had supported the Confederacy. In addition to the fifteen who served in military
positions, sixteen senators and representatives served in minor civil and
judicial posts or were avowed public supporters of the Confederacy. And
nine would-be United States senators and congressmen had served in the
Confederate Congress. Thus, it would be a fair judgment to describe the
group, as a whole, as former Confederates—though certainly not former
secessionists.

But the wartime record of the nine former Confederate congressmen in
some ways reflects the difficulty of making glib judgments about the delegation of 1865. Five of the nine had been elected as peace candidates in
1863 and 1864 on platforms that, despite their circumlocutory wordings,
came perilously close to treason insofar as the Confederacy was concerned.
Moreover, what is almost completely overlooked is the fact that, of the remaining thirty-one individuals whose antebellum and wartime political
positions can be followed, fifteen were active and consistent unionists, supporting the United States government without equivocation. Another sixteen were outspokenly neutral during the war.

The refusal of white southerners to turn to the minority of consistent
unionists in the region, therefore, was evidence of a remarkable obtuseness
and stubbornness on the part of southerners as well as a continuing mis-
judgment of national public opinion, but it hardly reflected disloyalty or
the judgment of a secessionist electorate. Of the eight southern governors
elected by white voters in 1865, only three—James L. Orr, Benjamin
Humphreys, and Jonathan Worth—had been prominent Confederates, and
none had advocated secession. Seven of them had been Whigs at some time
during their political careers. Equally striking is the fact that four of the
eight would ultimately join the Republican party.

As evidence of their indignation grew, the same white conservatives
who had praised the statesmanlike actions of their political leadership frantically condemned their shortsightedness. William Henry Trescot, the man
who represented South Carolina's interests in Washington throughout late
1865 and much of 1866, originally pleaded with the state legislature to
take action to ensure the "control of labor," for it underlay "every other
question of State interest." After assessing northern response, however, he
urged James L. Orr to convene the legislature "for the express purpose of

Bromberg's excellent article, "The Virginia Congressional Elections of 1865: A Test of Southern Loyalty," *VMHB*, LXXXIV (1976), 75–98. Edward R. Morawetz, Jr., also shared with
me the results of his research in "The Decision for Exclusion: The Southern Senators-Elect to
the Thirty-ninth Congress and the Definition of Loyalty" (Unpublished seminar paper, 1976,
in possession of the author).

repealing that unfortunate code which Perry left as a fitting legacy of the Provisional Government."[110]

If a belated sense of political expediency underlay second thoughts on the part of white southerners, it was made possible because some of the near hysteria that had characterized their thinking in the late summer and early fall of 1865 had begun to subside. But the damage was done.

In dealing with this, the most politically sensitive issue of the postwar South, the region had been guided by its cautious and conservative leaders. The black codes and the accompanying legislation were their best effort to steer the white South through this political mine field. But the disastrously hostile response to their "moderate" handiwork reflected the enormous ideological and emotional chasm between northerners and southerners. White southerners, moderate and radical, unionist and unrepentant rebel, were willing to accept the end of legal slavery, the supremacy of the federal government, and the temporarily diminished political role for the region. But they were unwilling to accept the legal equality of the freedmen or even (as in the case of many of their more cynically astute leaders) to feign such acceptance. And that stubborn unwillingness to yield, when placed beside the other events of 1865, led the majority of northerners to agree with Horace Greeley's bleak assessment of the southern experiment in self-reconstruction. "The first fruits of reconstruction promise a most deplorable harvest," he declared, "and the sooner we gather the tares, plow the ground again and sow new seed, the better."[111]

110. William Henry Trescot to Orr, January 1, February 28, March 4, 6, 31, April 15, 20, May 6, 13, 1866, all in Orr Papers. Orr himself originally praised the code, then backpedaled frantically when he too realized the political implications of their passage. Unwilling to antagonize South Carolinians, the wily Orr quietly persuaded General Daniel E. Sickles to set aside the code. See Orr to Sickles, December 13, 1865 (copy), in Orr Papers; Orr to Sickles (telegram), January 4, 1866, in Daniel E. Sickles Papers, DUL. For similar turnabouts by other white southerners, see the Charleston *Daily Courier*, November 4, 1865, January 7, 1866; Harris, *Presidential Reconstruction in Mississippi*, 144–46.

111. New York *Tribune*, November 15, 1865.

VII / Political Alternatives in the Land of Fog and Confusion

B
Y JANUARY of 1866, Republican notions of southern perfidy and political unreliability were firmly established, and moderates within the party turned their efforts toward educating the public and convincing the president that his lenient policies had failed. Had the South's postwar conservative leadership been politically shrewd enough to grant the freedmen civil rights (short of the suffrage), accept the president's moderate demands without quibbling, and feign repentance for their past transgressions, Republicans would have been hard pressed to justify the continued exclusion of the South except on the partisan grounds that the future supremacy of the Republican party would be jeopardized. Fortunately for Republicans, white southerners—led by a blundering and insensitive president—had spared them the dilemma of choosing between political self-interest and moral altruism. After December of 1865, white southerners would play a role in the growing confrontation between president and Congress, but it was that of a Greek chorus rather than of central players.

Such may be seen from hindsight. For those moderate and conservative white southerners who had shaped the Johnsonian program of self-reconstruction, however, the new year began on a note of cautious optimism. Despite the failure of the Congress to seat the southern congressional delegation, the president seemed to retain widespread support in the North. And there was always the comforting belief that the Republican "radicals" with their extremist talk of Negro suffrage would overreach themselves. The sages of New England could try to construct their "free fabric of negro suffrage," acknowledged a Mississippi planter as the old year ended and the new year began. But the great majority of northerners would never accept such a "monstrosity." When the question of Negro suffrage was put before the Wisconsin and Connecticut legislatures in the fall of 1865, he noted with some satisfaction, these northerners had refused to "allow Mr. Nigger to vote." As long as President Johnson was at the helm of the national government and local whites continued to increase their control over local and state government, concluded North Carolina's Kemp Battle, "I think our people are . . . rather indifferent as to whether they get representation in Congress or not."[1]

At the same time, while the economic turmoil of 1865 and early 1866 could hardly be described with optimism, white southerners could (and did) take heart from the fact that the predicted apocalypse failed to arrive. J. Norman Jackson, a New Orleans cotton factor, feared the worst in the first months after the end of the war, but after a three-week tour of Louisiana plantations in early 1866, Jackson reported that most planters "speak very well of the negroes." With only a few exceptions, the freedmen were "working very well and the chief obstacle to the planters' success at present is want of money."[2] If few whites were as optimistic as Jackson, there was a widespread retreat from the rhetoric of catastrophe. Sometimes with surprise, sometimes with grudging admiration, whites acknowledged that the new system might stave off the complete collapse of the southern economy.

But that shadow of stability was itself a powerful factor in undercutting the counsels of caution and compromise. By the winter of 1865 and 1866, most white southerners were willing to stake everything on the president's political success. If the president had become a captive of his southern support, the relationship was reciprocal. As the chorus of praise by white southerners continued through the winter and early spring of 1866, it seemed impossible to believe that only a year before defeated Confederates had railed against his "despotic Majesty Andy Johnson," in the words of one North Carolina planter, a "bastard renegade, demagogue and drunkard."[3] By early 1866 it was almost impossible to find a southerner of any political persuasion who was willing to publicly condemn the Tennessean in the White House.

With only a handful of exceptions, most white southerners had no understanding of, and less appreciation for, the slow but relentless process by which the center of the Republican party was edging toward black suffrage.

1. Henry Garrett Diary, Claiborne Manuscripts, LC, January 2, 1866; Kemp Battle to Benjamin Hedrick, January 20, 1866, in Benjamin Hedrick Papers, DUL.
2. J. Norman Jackson to Stephen Duncan, March 22, 1866, in Stephen Duncan Papers, LSU.
3. David Schenck Diary, SHC, June 14, 1865.

It was true that more than two-thirds of the Republican congressional delegation had given theoretical support to black suffrage as early as 1864. (The bill involved the question of black suffrage in the proposed state of Montana.) Requiring Negro suffrage in a region where newly emancipated slaves often made up a majority was a far more weighty matter, particularly when there seemed little public support for such a measure. Most Republicans were reluctant to make it a political issue dividing the Republicans and Democrats. As late as February of 1866, the cautious Republican centrist Lyman Trumbull of Illinois had sarcastically dismissed black suffrage as the "most sovereign remedy . . . since the days of Townsend's Sasparilla."[4] The hostility of the president to the idea and his continued popularity in the nation seemed security enough.

Thus, when Johnson confronted the Republican party on February 19 by vetoing a measure that would continue the Freedmen's Bureau, five of the southern state legislatures passed resolutions praising the president for his "courageous defense of constitutional principles." Johnson's intemperate and vitriolic speech attacking Republican "radicals" three days later brought an equally enthusiastic flurry of congratulatory editorials from southern newspapers. The president had brought "joy and confidence. . . . Bright faces were seen and buoyant spirits exchanged congratulations," claimed one Georgian. The president's veto was "another thrilling sound of the tocsin," said one newspaper editor, "rallying together the conservative men of the Republic in support of the Young Hickory of Tennessee."[5]

White southerners' increasing boldness in resisting federal "intervention" did not begin in 1866. In August and September of 1865, Provisional Governor William Sharkey of Mississippi had announced plans to organize militia units and, when challenged by military authorities, successfully called upon the president for support. In that crisis, Sharkey soon drew back from confrontation, fearing the effect it would have on northern public opinion. When the president directly challenged the Republican congressional majority, however, southerners inclined to reassert traditional states' rights were further emboldened. Judge James Hook of Sandersville, Georgia, initially had acknowledged the authority of the military to try all cases involving blacks. In the wake of the president's adamant insistence

4. *Congressional Globe*, 39th Cong., 1st Sess., 746.
5. Michael Les Benedict, *A Compromise of Principle: Congressional Republicans and Reconstruction, 1863–1869* (New York, 1974), 164–67; LaWanda Cox and John Cox, *Politics, Principle, and Prejudice, 1865–1866: Dilemma of Reconstruction America* (Glencoe, Ill., 1963), 200–202; Eric McKitrick, *Andrew Johnson and Reconstruction* (Chicago, 1960), 310–17; W. R. Brock, *An American Crisis: Congress and Reconstruction, 1865–1867* (New York, 1963), 138–47.

that Reconstruction had ended, he decided to force a confrontation with military authorities by insisting on trying every case—whether involving blacks or whites—as it came to his docket. The president was now "steadily doing his study, fearless of personal consequences, so must I do mine."[6]

South Carolina Judge A. P. Aldrich, one of that state's eight convention delegates who refused to vote for an emancipation clause in the state's convention, initially acquiesced in the military trials of cases involving blacks. Three days after the Johnson veto of the Freedmen's Bureau extension bill, he openly sought a confrontation with General Daniel Sickles by sentencing a white defendant to six months in jail and thirty-nine lashes. (Sickles had forbade whipping as a judicial punishment in cases involving blacks.) When Sickles set aside the sentence on the grounds that it would be unfair to inflict such a "barbarous" punishment on whites when it was barred for blacks, Aldrich demanded that the president sustain the court of South Carolina. Either the courts were independent or not, he argued. If they were subject to review by the military, "then the reopening of the courts and the administration of the laws is a mere mockery." In a letter to the governor, he argued that the president had met the issue "fairly and squarely by vetoing the Freedmen's Bureau Bill," and he added, "I am inclined to think he will welcome any conflict like the present, in order to make the break more distinct." Although Aldrich lost on this particular issue and Johnson did not contravene the military decision, the South Carolina judge's belief that the president welcomed confrontation seemed borne out by Johnson's public statements on the "dangers of radical intervention in Southern affairs." In that respect, there was ample merit to the argument of angry Republicans that the president's actions emboldened southerners to directly challenge federal authority.[7]

Such complete reliance upon Andrew Johnson was a gamble made by all but a small minority of southern whites, and it might well have succeeded had it not been for the fatal miscalculation of the president in dealing with Republican moderates. On January 5, 1866, Senator Trumbull had introduced a cautious and conservative civil rights bill designed to set

6. James S. Hook to Gov. James Johnson, August 25, 1865, Hook to Gov. Charles Jones Jenkins, June 10, 1866, both in Georgia Governors' Papers, GA. As William Harris points out, it was Johnson's assurances that Sharkey had the power to enroll militia units that precipitated the crisis. William C. Harris, *Presidential Reconstruction in Mississippi* (Baton Rouge, 1967), 73–75.

7. For a review of the Aldrich-Sickles confrontation see "Report of Judge A. P. Aldrich to Governor Orr," February 22, 1866, A. P. Aldrich to James L. Orr, February 24, 1866, both in South Carolina Governors' Papers, SCA; James E. Sefton, *The United States Army and Reconstruction, 1865–1877* (Baton Rouge, 1967), 162.

aside the black codes and codify the basic notion of equal rights under the law. The measure contained no provisions for black suffrage, but it did empower the federal government to guarantee the newly emancipated slave the right to make and enforce contracts, to sue and give evidence in court, to inherit, hold, and sell real estate—in short to have the "full and equal benefit of all laws and proceedings . . . as is enjoyed by white citizens." As moderates within the Republican party pointed out, all the states had to do to avoid federal enforcement of the bill was to end legal discrimination in their own state laws. Clearly, the civil rights measure represented the minimum the Republican party would expect from the defeated South in dealing with the freedmen. The bill passed in the Senate on February 2 by a vote of 33 to 12 and in the House on March 13 by the margin of 111 to 38. Despite the fact that the president had earlier (February 19) vetoed the legislative extension of the Freedmen's Bureau, most conservative and moderate Republicans assumed he would approve this bill.[8]

For all the participants in the first year after the war, it was recognized as a decisive moment in the future of Congressional Reconstruction. In early February, one of Senator Lyman Trumbull's constituents had pointed out the importance of Johnson's action. Should Johnson sign the civil rights bill, concluded Charles Ray, the Republican party would have little ground to confront the president. The vast majority of the northern electorate believed that the civil rights bill was adequate protection, warned Ray; the freedman had to earn his right to vote "by giving evidence of his fitness."[9]

Just as the South had played out its part flawlessly in the summer and fall of 1865, however, so did Andrew Johnson. Eleven days after the final passage of the bill, he returned the measure accompanied by a veto that, if sustained, would have marked the end of any federally imposed postwar reconstruction of the South. Any such bill, he told the Congress, was an "unconstitutional invasion of states' rights," another "strike towards centralization, and the concentration of all legislative powers in the national government." Had the Congress accepted the president's veto, Reconstruction would have been over. But on April 6, the Republican-controlled Senate, by the narrowest of margins, overrode the president. Three days later, the House rejected the president's veto by an even wider margin. The issue was joined; the break between Andrew Johnson and the great majority of the Republican party was complete.[10]

8. Les Benedict, *A Compromise of Principle*, 164–67; Cox and Cox, *Politics, Principle, and Prejudice*, 200–202; McKitrick, *Johnson and Reconstruction*, 310–17.
9. Charles Ray, quoted in Patrick Riddleberger, *1866: The Critical Year Revisited* (Carbondale, Ill., 1979), 89.
10. James D. Richardson (comp.), *A Compilation of the Messages and Papers of the Presidents, 1789–1897* (Washington, D.C., 1896–99), VI, 405–13.

After the president's actions in the spring of 1866, it was apparent that he had embarked upon an ambitious attempt to reshape postwar politics by creating either a new political party or, at the very least, a coalition or movement that would support his policies in dealing with the southern question. Even before his overt break, Secretary of State William H. Seward had outlined the president's strategy in a series of private meetings with South Carolina's shrewd unofficial lobbyist, William Henry Trescot. The president, Seward confided to Trescot, planned to deliberately provoke the radicals into openly opposing him. Once they were no longer able to hide behind their hypocritical claims of support for the president, an aroused public opinion and a judicious use of the patronage power by the president would isolate them from the party. "In discarding the extremists," Seward told the South Carolinian, "the majority of the party, or a very large minority, will form a new party with the President." Initially, this new party would consist of moderate and conservative Republicans and supportive union Democrats, but before many months had passed, the "Southern reserve will be needed and sent for." [11]

Throughout the spring of 1866, as Johnson and the Congress repeatedly clashed over the issues of Reconstruction, the president and his closest advisers began their plans for the formation of a coalition of conservative Republicans and Democrats who supported his policies. Although Henry Raymond, editor of the New York *Times* and congressman from New York, was one of the prime initial movers behind the strategy, the final call for an organizing convention to meet in Philadelphia was the product of the advice of a number of the president's advisers under his close direction. It was published on June 25 over the signature of Senator James Doolittle, the conservative Wisconsin Republican who would defend the president until the last. The framers of the convention movement cautiously limited their statement of principles to those already accepted by the southern constitutional conventions of 1865: the end of slavery, the assertion of national supremacy, and the sanctity of the national debt. At the same time, they had made concessions to southern sensibilities by agreeing that the suffrage issue should be left to the states. On the critical issue of the relationship of the southern states to the Union, Doolittle and his cosigners had insisted that

11. William Henry Trescot to Orr, February 28, 1866, in James L. Orr Papers, SCA. Seward and his political alter ego, Thurlow Weed, were most hopeful of establishing southern support from whiggish conservatives like Trescot. As John and LaWanda Cox noted, Seward's vision of a postwar conservative party was similar to that of the shapers of the Compromise of 1877. Cox and Cox, *Politics, Principle, and Prejudice*, 47; Thomas Wagstaff, "Andrew Johnson and the National Union Movement, 1865–1866" (Ph.D. dissertation, University of Wisconsin, 1967), 255–60.

the southern states, having accepted and fulfilled Johnson's requirements, were entitled to "full representation in Congress."[12]

The National Union party's dependence upon the southern conservative elites that dominated the region after the war was enough to arouse the suspicions of estranged unionists like John Pool of North Carolina. The newspapers of the region were increasingly filled with "diehard bluster," warned Pool, one of W. W. Holden's closest political associates. And much of this could be attributed to the false hopes that Johnson's new party had aroused. The president's policies would "keep us out for some time to come & will compel us to submit to conditions that would never had been thought of, if a more prudent & wise course had been adopted." No one could foresee the disasters to come if white southerners did not wake up to the fact that "the President is not able to control Congress." Benjamin Hedrick, a personal friend of Jonathan Worth, even as he opposed the North Carolina governor's policies, warned of the disastrous consequences of Johnson's attacks on the Republican party. "Many of the Republican politicians are just as big a scamps as are to be found," he told Worth, "but the sober industrious marrow of the North" would never accept a Democrat as an alternative. And that was how they were increasingly coming to view Johnson.[13]

Pool and many of the strait-sect unionists were already drawing away from the president because of his support of their political opponents. More striking was the growing apprehension of conservatives. William Henry Trescot had no objection to Andrew Johnson's political strategy; it was strikingly similar to his own. But Trescot and a number of southern conservatives were far less certain that Johnson possessed the political skills to make such a policy work. Unlike Johnson, who had never suffered political defeat, the South's postwar leadership saw on every hand the consequences of rash and impetuous action. Under the circumstances, it is not surprising that they sometimes responded uneasily to Johnson's politics of confrontation. "The President had badly underestimated the willingness of the Republican Party to stick together and fight," observed Trescot. Why was the president unable to see the need for exhibiting a "sensible regard for the feelings of Northern Republicans?" The best strategy, argued an increas-

12. Michael Perman, *Reunion Without Compromise: The South and Reconstruction, 1865– 1868* (Cambridge, 1973), 214–22; Wagstaff, "Johnson and the National Union Movement," 283–84; Wagstaff, "The Arm in Arm Convention," *CWH*, XIV (1968), 101–19.

13. John Pool to Thomas Settle, July 4, 1866, in Thomas Settle Papers, SHC; Benjamin Hedrick to Jonathan Worth, September 16, 1866, in Jonathan Worth Papers, NCA. For background on Hedrick, who had been a professor at the University of North Carolina, see Monty Woodall Cox, "Freedom During the Fremont Campaign: The Fate of One North Carolina Republican in 1856," *NCHR*, XLV (1968), 356–82.

ingly frustrated Trescot, was to defeat the more radical proposals by accepting the moderate provisions. After weighing public opinion in February and March of 1866 and talking with conservatives, moderates, and radical Republicans, the South Carolina conservative concluded in his report to Governor Orr: "I don't like the look of this here [in Washington]—everything bodes a storm more trying I think even than the war." The president had certainly succeeded in achieving his goal of confrontation with the radicals, reported Trescot, but his attempts to "bully" Congress would lead the Republicans to unite on a more stringent program for the South. "I fear we have not much to expect from Executive Assistance."[14]

Kemp Battle, the North Carolina conservative who had supported the Confederacy until the end, agreed. Battle had begun the new year with cautious optimism, but by April he was increasingly fearful that Johnson would become even more "sore-headed and lose his self-possession." It was far better, Battle said, for Johnson to work out an agreement with Republican moderates that would *"settle"* the issue, even at the cost of compromising some of the South's "traditions and prejudices."[15]

Battle's father was particularly uneasy over the president's growing reliance upon the Democrats, North and South. "I have little hopes of good from the Democrats—the authors of all our woes," concluded William Horn Battle in February of 1866. In that respect, the cautious response of a number of conservative newspapers to Johnson's new party reflected this uneasiness. Samuel Hayes, the editor of the Savannah *Republican*, had been caught in a difficult position in 1865 when he erroneously assumed that the president would lead a coalition of conservative Republicans, reborn Whigs, and union Democrats. By June of 1866 he was scornful of Johnson's National Union movement, but increasingly uneasy over the growing strength of the radical wing of the Republican party—"the infamous Thad Stevens and Charles Sumner and other fanatics." Why were Americans being forced, he asked in exasperation, to choose between these men and the "rotten and corrupt wing of the so-called Democracy of the North?" The only

14. A survey of northern public opinion by the New York *Tribune* particularly disturbed the cautious Trescot. On March 3, the *Tribune* had printed editorials from almost every major Republican newspaper in the nation. While many continued to support the president, they opposed his veto of congressional legislation designed to protect the freedmen. Trescot to Orr, March 6, April 20, May 6, 1866, all in Orr Papers.

15. Kemp Battle to Benjamin Hedrick, April 13, 1866, in Hedrick Papers. See Henry J. Raymond, "Extracts from the Journal of Henry J. Raymond," *HW*, XX (1880), 275–76. For some examples of the apprehensions of conservative southerners as the spring passed into summer, see J. J. Gier to Robert M. Patton, July 30, 1866, in Alabama Governors' Papers, AA; W. J. Mason to David M. Carter, March 5, 1866, in David Miller Carter Papers, SHC; Edward Jenner Warren to Alfred E. Willard, August 25, 1866, in Alfred E. Willard Papers, SHC; James Hemphill to W. R. Hemphill, August 2, 1866, in Hemphill Collection, DUL.

hope, he vainly suggested, was the creation of a "genuine Conservative Party, composed of the liberal men of all parties, and into which could be infused . . . those truly patriotic and progressive principles [of] . . . the Grand Old Whig Party of other days."[16]

Few other old-line Whig newspapers were willing to echo Hayes's criticisms of the president. (They were always intimidated by the charge of fire-eating southerners that "any Southerner who, for whatever reasons, opposes the President is a miserable tool of the Northern radicals.") But they did criticize Johnson implicitly by attacking the role of the Democratic party in the National Union movement. The "public crib cormorants" of the northern Democratic party hoped to hoist themselves back into power by embittering the South against the North, warned one old Whig newspaper editor, but the South should understand that this was "bright thin ice that covers the rapid current." The northern Democracy had learned nothing from experience, agreed the editor of the Macon *Telegraph.* If they would only "consent to abandon their organization and unite with the Republican friends of the President . . . , something might be done." As it was, the "braying of the Democrats" kept the Republicans united. The editor of the Columbus, Georgia, *Enquirer* was particularly incensed at the insistence of northern Democrats that they play a critical role in shaping the new party. Their political blindness was "ruining the country" and "amounts simply to madness."[17]

Such counsel was brushed aside by the president. Marcus Cruikshank, an antebellum Whig unionist from Talladega, Alabama, had won election to the Confederate Congress in 1863 as an opponent of the Davis administration and had spent the last eighteen months of the Confederacy publicly attacking the government on every issue and privately encouraging the growing peace movement in his northeastern Alabama district. When he traveled through the North in the late spring of 1866 soliciting food and funds as Alabama's commissioner for the destitute, he was surprised and troubled by the widespread opposition to the president from northerners of all political persuasions. Whatever their differences, he concluded at the end of his eight-week tour, northerners were agreed on two things: first, the federal government had to protect the basic civil rights of the freedmen and, second, the government was not to be entrusted to the "copperheads" of the Democratic party. When he expressed his concerns to the president in a private meeting, emphasizing the danger of alienating moderate con-

16. William Horn Battle to Benjamin Hedrick, February 6, 1866, in Hedrick Papers; Savannah *Republican,* June 16, 1866.
17. Macon *Daily Telegraph,* March 21, 1866; Columbus (Ga.) *Enquirer,* April 7, 1866.

gressional Republicans, Johnson curtly dismissed his warnings. According to Cruikshank, the president spoke "only of the danger from Radicalism," a threat that he insisted was "even greater than from Secession." Unlike the secessionists of 1860, Johnson told the apprehensive Alabamian, the radicals planned to carry out their political revolution by stealth and guile. And if the radicals should succeed, white southerners would inevitably suffer "degredation and the loss of freedom."[18]

Cruikshank put aside his misgivings. To him, as to most southern conservatives, there seemed to be no alternative between the president and the Republican party. And in a political atmosphere that was becoming increasingly polarized, no one wanted to choose the latter. Between March and midsummer of 1865, two key political figures from Georgia—Herschel Johnson and Alexander Stephens—concluded that the president would never succeed in his frontal assault on Congress. "Grant is to be the next President," Johnson told his friend, and southerners had best plan on that contingency rather than placing their faith in the Tennessean in the White House. Significantly, however, neither Johnson, Stephens, nor in fact any of their fellow conservatives made public their private fears. There was always the tantalizing possibility that Johnson would prove politically successful. All but the most pessimistic conservatives had convinced themselves that the strongest advocates of black suffrage within the Republican party had overreached the limits of northern support for civil rights and political interventionism in the South (a view shared by some cautious Republicans). Thus, even as they confided their private fears, they tended to balance such apprehensions with the hope that Johnson might succeed. With few exceptions, Johnson was able to count upon either the support or the silence of the conservative leaders who dominated the provisional regimes he had created in the postwar South.[19]

And these timid expressions of conservative caution were completely overshadowed by outspoken voices complaining that the South had been far too conciliatory already. Such opposition was often couched in partisan terms as Democrats drew back from what they believed would become a coalition of "so-called conservative" Republicans and "contemptible ex-Whigs." The July decision of the national Democratic party to support the National Union movement calmed the fears of many southern Democrats,

18. Marcus Cruikshank to Patton, July 13, August 14, 1866, in Alabama Governors' Papers.

19. Herschel V. Johnson to Alexander H. Stephens, July 5, 1866, in Herschel V. Johnson Papers, DUL; William L. Sharkey to Benjamin Humphreys, March 14, 1866, in Benjamin G. Humphreys Correspondence, Mississippi Governors' Papers, MSA; Wagstaff, "Johnson and the National Union Movement," 221; Perman, *Reunion Without Compromise*, 187–88.

but initially more than one southern Democrat echoed the suspicions of the Augusta *Daily Press*. The Whig party of the 1840s may have been a "respectable" political organization, admitted the *Daily Press*, but it had "degenerated into Know Nothingism and finally into Abolitionism and Republicanism by which it was completely swallowed up." The editor of the Mobile *Advertiser* was equally unwilling to form any alliance with "discredited remnants" of the Whig party and the "Black Republican Party." The South could be saved only if the "true Democratic Party would arouse itself. . . . Their creed contained the saving principles which would make possible the South's return to the Union on honorable grounds." Joining hands with the Republicans, on the other hand, would require southerners to "stultify and criminate ourselves and insult the ashes of our fallen brethren by admitting that we were traitors and our heroic dead died the death of felons."[20]

If white southerners, like Andrew Johnson, assumed that the Republicans would isolate themselves from the northern electorate by pushing too hard for black suffrage, it was simply another of a lengthening list of political miscalculations. For throughout the spring and summer of 1866, Republicans had moved cautiously from one piece of legislation to another—from the extension of the Freedmen's Bureau, to the Civil Rights Act, and finally to the proposed Fourteenth Amendment (the Howard Amendment), which would serve as the centerpiece of the Republican party's 1866 congressional campaigns. As it finally emerged, the proposed amendment placed (in vague terms) the Civil Rights Act of 1866 into the Constitution, safe from the danger of repeal by a future Democratic Congress; it guaranteed the United States war debt; and it reaffirmed Andrew Johnson's requirement that the Confederate debt be nullified. To the anger and disgust of Republican radicals, however, the amendment refused to guarantee the vote to the freedmen outright. Instead, its framers had skirted this politically explosive issue by barring most of the region's traditional leadership from office and giving white southerners two options on black suffrage. They could, under the terms of Section 2, give the vote to their former slaves *or* they could accept a proportional reduction in their congressional representation.[21]

20. Mobile *Advertiser and Register*, July 14, 1866; Augusta *Constitutionalist*, July 10, 1866; Charlotte *Western Democrat*, June 25, 1866; Augusta *Daily Press*, July 4, 1866; Columbus (Ga.) *Sun*, June 7, 1866; Richmond *Enquirer*, July 2, 1866; Winnsboro (S.C.) *Tri-weekly News*, n.d., quoted in the Augusta *Constitutionalist*, July 20, 1866. The *Constitutionalist* ran editorials from eight southern newspapers opposing the National Union movement on July 11, 1866.

21. *National Anti-slavery Standard*, May 26, 1866; *Congressional Globe*, 39th Cong., 1st Sess., 314.

Not surprisingly, advocates of black suffrage saw the amendment as the production of "political mountebanks" who had acted on the basis of "hypocrisy, fear and compromise." Charles Sumner remained virtually silent on the issue and other such radicals as Thaddeus Stevens defended it half-heartedly. He had hoped to purify the Constitution, the Pennsylvania Republican told his colleagues. Instead, "I find that we shall be obliged to be content with patching up the worst portions of the ancient edifice."[22]

Whatever its shortcomings as a brief for the freedmen's political rights, however, it deprived Andrew Johnson of an emotional issue that might offset the increasing uneasiness of moderate and conservative northern voters. There was nothing in this cautious document to drive the great majority of Republican voters into a new political movement which, by September of 1866, increasingly resembled the discredited Democratic party.

The passage of the Fourteenth Amendment came as a jolt to all but a handful of white southerners. Throughout the summer and fall of 1865, whites in the region commented upon the "threat" of universal manhood suffrage, but there was little panic. One southern journalist traveling through the North in the summer and fall of 1865 found, as he had expected, that the "New England States, from their mouthpiece, Boston, the hotbed of abolitionism and negro equality, insist that the blacks shall at once be elevated to an equality, civil and political with the whites." Fortunately, there was little support outside New England, he concluded, and, in fact, open hostility to the idea in most parts of the North. The advocates of Negro suffrage were hard at work, spreading atrocity stories and whipping up accounts of white disloyalty, agreed the editor of the Richmond *Times* as he surveyed national politics on the eve of the convening of Congress in December of 1865. "We of the South are fortunate that the great mass of Northern voters see through this pretext of 'philanthropy' for the political fraud that it is. No sane person can advocate granting the ballot box to an illiterate, an uninformed population one step removed from generations of servitude."[23] But when the Howard Amendment was sent to the state legislatures for action, white southerners realized that the unthinkable had become possible.

As they read of the proposed amendment, white southerners responded with hysterical exaggeration. Most critically, the amendment did not re-

---

22. The historical literature surrounding the adopting of the Fourteenth Amendment is voluminous. Joseph B. James, *The Framing of the Fourteenth Amendment* (Urbana, Ill., 1956), remains the standard account, although it should be supplemented by more recent works, such as Les Benedict's *A Compromise of Principle*, 162–87, which places the issue in the broader context of the deep divisions within the Republican party.

23. Macon *Daily Telegraph*, September 9, 1865; Richmond *Times*, November 25, 1865.

quire black suffrage, although it did make likely the continuing supremacy of the Republican party by forcing white southerners to enfranchise the freedmen on their own or accept a proportional reduction in their representation in Congress. In stark contrast to most southerners, James Lusk Alcorn of Mississippi found the proposal eminently reasonable. The prewar South had been able to count its slaves as three-fifths of the white population in calculating congressional representation. After southerners had fought a war to destroy the Union, Alcorn asked the Mississippi legislature, was it reasonable that they should reenter stronger than when they left? And the Mississippi planter also pointed out that it was particularly unseemly of the South to demand that blacks be counted in computing federal representation since every postwar state legislature had refused to count the freedmen in apportioning state legislatures.[24]

Alcorn was able to respond to the Fourteenth Amendment with equanimity because he was already reconciled to the prospect of some form of black suffrage. As early as August of 1865, he had privately expressed a willingness to consider limited suffrage for the freedmen. Though he hardly welcomed such a prospect, he told his wife, some form of suffrage based upon property or educational requirements would disarm northern radicals and prevent a racial confrontation that would leave the South "red with blood and damp with tears." Other cautious conservatives privately agreed. In North Carolina the first to suggest such a possibility were a handful of "young whigs of old whig families," claimed Samuel Phillips. In Tennessee it was also the survivors of the Whig tradition led by John Bell. V. C. Barringer, one of those North Carolinians to whom Phillips alluded, early concluded that the "political enfranchisement of the negro, both as a policy, & as a right, follows logically & inevitably from emancipation. Everything points to it."[25]

It was all very well to timidly suggest such heretical notions to friends, however, and quite another to voice them publicly. In early June of 1866, the editor of the Atlanta *New Era* suggested that Negro suffrage was approaching and would ultimately prevail "little as we relish it." In fact, suggested the *New Era*, "we shall not be surprised to see the day when females . . . will be enfranchised and admitted to the ballot." The solution was not to resist or sit sullenly on the sidelines; white southerners should "fight the devil with fire" by accepting and controlling the black vote. Although this

24. Lillian A. Pereyra, *James Lusk Alcorn: Persistent Whig* (Baton Rouge, 1966), 87–89.
25. Samuel F. Phillips to Kemp Battle, September 5, 1865, in Battle Family Papers, SHC; James Lusk Alcorn to Wife, August 26, 1865, in James Lusk Alcorn Papers, SHC; V. C. Barringer to Daniel Moreau Barringer, December 20, 1866, in Daniel Moreau Barringer Papers, SHC; Atlanta *Daily Intelligencer*, January 20, 1866.

was a position ultimately taken by a large number of white conservatives in 1867 and 1868, the *New Era*'s journalistic competitor on the Atlanta *Daily Intelligencer* led an attack so vitriolic and personally abusive that it provoked a challenge to a duel. After one month of continuous public criticism, the editor of the *New Era* retracted his "ill-advised" proposal. His political mistiming led, however, to his paper's bankruptcy in October, 1866.[26]

In the summer of 1866, there simply was no public support for a policy of expedient compliance on the suffrage issue. Nor, outside East Tennessee and parts of Louisiana, was there support for such a policy among those southern unionists who had criticized Andrew Johnson for his lenient policy toward the "rebels." Within the year Robert P. Dick and W. W. Holden of North Carolina would swallow their misgivings and accept black suffrage, but there was nothing but scorn for such a proposal in the summer of 1866. "We are willing to give a great deal," Dick told a group of supporters in a June 7 speech in Raleigh, but the granting of the vote to the freedmen would never be accepted. As long as "Southern blood shall flow in Southern hearts, we will hate and scorn the people who would humiliate and degrade us." Surely, insisted conservative Republican Samuel Hayes, his party did not want to exchange the "insolent rule of three hundred thousand Southern slaveholders for the rule of five hundred thousand Southern negroes who but yesterday were slaves and the descendants of ignorant slaves for hundreds of years."[27]

Samuel Hayes was probably correct in assuming that the majority of Republicans remained unenthusiastic over the prospect of four hundred thousand black voters in the South and frightened over the danger of a backlash by northern voters in the upcoming congressional, state, and local elections of 1866. The signal accomplishment of the white South in 1865 and Andrew Johnson in early 1866, was to force most Republicans to overcome their inhibitions. Congressman John Kelso, a Missouri Republican, bluntly faced up to the party's dilemma in the spring of 1866. He was not worried about the future of republicanism in Missouri, he told his colleagues. "We have got the Rebels under; and by the Eternal, we mean to keep them under." But the fate of the nation was bleak indeed if southern whites regained control in the Deep South. One by one Kelso reeled off the shattered illusions of "timid" members of his party. It was assumed that the "true unionists" would dominate the postwar South, said Kelso, but they

26. Atlanta *Daily Intelligencer*, March 21, 22, 1866; Memphis *Daily Appeal*, June 17, 1866; Augusta *Constitutionalist*, October 17, 1866; Joseph E. Brown to William D. Kelley, May 20, 1867, in Hargrett Collection.

27. *North Carolina Standard*, June 9, 1865; Savannah *Republican*, August 21, 1866.

turned out to be an ineffectual minority in most states. The possibility was held out that the majority of whites might be "converted" to the Republican principles of equal rights, and then there was the assurance that the president would prevent the resurgence of "rebel arrogance" and disloyalty.[28] One by one these illusions were exposed as so many "phantasmagoria," said Kelso, until they were left with one alternative: the disfranchisement of the rebels and the granting of the vote to the freedmen. It was true, he acknowledged, that there would be "evils" in the wake of the enfranchisement of "four million ignorant blacks . . . , none of whom have ever been accustomed to think or act for themselves." But someone had to vote in the South, "and for my part I would rather it should be the loyal party, though they are mostly ignorant and black." The whites, he concluded, "with all their intelligence were traitors, the blacks with all their ignorance were loyal." Watching this relentless movement toward black suffrage, a shaken Alabama conservative concluded, "I still do not believe the North is for negro suffrage." But in a footnote that summarized the wisdom to which he had belatedly come, he concluded, "They fear us as rebels more than they fear the negroes as incompetent voters."[29]

Thus in the summer of 1866, most white southerners had grimly concluded that the Republican majority was moving toward granting full suffrage to the freedmen, and only the danger of political backlash in the North would deter the party. It was this fearful awareness of Republican intentions that formed the rhetorical basis for mobilizing white southerners in the support of the president's new political party. The scenario was carefully crafted by the president's close supporters in the region, though with surprisingly little guidance from Johnson himself. The choice of delegates was absolutely critical, observed one Alabama conservative. They should be men of character, ability, and intelligence, but also individuals who had not been "very prominent or active either for or against secession." A former Union general who advised James L. Orr of South Carolina suggested that southerners choose "good old fellows against whom nothing can be laid." But whatever their qualifications, they could not be original secessionists or "fight-it-out-to-the-last men" given to fits of intemperate rhetoric, warned North Carolina's Kemp Battle.[30]

Dutifully, the president's supporters throughout the region issued the

28. Congressional Globe, 39th Cong., 1st Sess., 732, 834–35.

29. Ibid.; William Dickson to Robert M. Patton, June 19, 1866, in Alabama Governors' Papers.

30. Kemp Battle to Benjamin Hedrick, July 20, 1866, in Hedrick Papers; Albert Elmore to Patton, July 14, 1866, F. L. B. Goodwin to Patton, July 16, 1866, Henry Clay Dean to Patton, July 15, 1866, all in Alabama Governors' Papers.

call to rally behind the president. In South Carolina the movement was led by James L. Orr and Benjamin Perry. In Louisiana the key figure was W. H. C King, editor of the New Orleans *Times*; in Alabama the leaders were Lewis Parsons and Robert Patton. The resourceful Joseph E. Brown, with the support of a number of like-minded Georgians, coordinated the selection of delegates in that state. In other parts of the South, the selection process was less centrally organized, but always there was the desire on the part of the postwar leadership to stage-manage the process to reassure northerners of southern loyalty and to minimize conflict within the region.[31]

The obsession with "managing" the convention would suggest that there was always an element of duplicity in the southern reponse to the National Union movement—a desire to stage a "show" convention that would be little more than an exercise in public relations. Thus, Samuel F. Phillips, the North Carolina conservative who would ultimately join the Republican party, warned North Carolinian Kemp Battle of the danger of choosing those who had been "firebrands" in the 1850s and opponents of peace in the last years of the war. These gentlemen, he said, ought to have "sense enough to keep out of view now." The implication was clear: appearances were more important than reality. But in a crucial addition to his warning, Phillips added: The "die-hard Confederates" and the secessionists "have had their time for power—& they abused it—Now let them tarry at Jericho *till they get a new crop of beard—which we know not to be dyed, but of legitimate growth & colour.*" With very few exceptions, the southern delegates chosen for the National Union Convention were cut from the same cloth as those chosen throughout 1865. They were mostly conservative former Whigs who had opposed secession until there seemed no alternative but to go with their state.[32]

Given the bleak alternatives facing the region, the organizers of southern support for the new movement assumed that southerners would enthusiastically embrace the president's new party. They were often stunned to confront apathy. The Waynesboro, Georgia, *Times* claimed there were not enough interested people in southern Georgia to "scare up a respectable cross roads meeting." Publicly, Johnson's supporters spoke of "mass meetings" and "enthusiastic resolutions" accompanying the election of delegates to Philadelphia. Privately, they acknowledged the lack of enthusiasm. "Hereabouts, nobody seems particularly interested in the matter," admitted

31. Perman, *Reunion Without Compromise*, 214–22; Wagstaff, "Johnson and the National Union Movement," 283–84.
32. Samuel F. Phillips to Kemp Battle, July 20, 1866, in Battle Papers.

the editor of a western Georgia weekly who had tried in vain to stir up support for the new party. Despite the pleas, threats, and warnings of the local Sumter, South Carolina, *Watchman* and the Charleston *Daily Courier*, only a handful of voters attended that county's meeting to elect representatives for the Philadelphia convention. Julius Fleming, the Sumter planter, lawyer, and correspondent for the *Courier*, was not surprised by this apathetic indifference to all national politics. So many efforts had already been made to comply with the demands of the national government "and so little success has attended these efforts that the people are losing all faith in their power to effect [*sic*] in any way, the ponderous machinery of a government which allows them no votes in its councils." The best that could be said for the convention was that it would do no harm, claimed the Washington correspondent for one southern newspaper. "It will certainly do very little good." Under these circumstances, Georgia's Linton Stephens, the brother of the former vice-president of the Confederacy, spoke for more than one southern conservative when he declined to attend the Philadelphia convention on the grounds that he had "very little faith in the thing . . . —not enough to spend money or risk cholera on it."[33]

Judge Stephens' scepticism was well taken. On July 30, less than two weeks before the Philadelphia convention assembled, New Orleans policemen and a mob of angry white bystanders killed or wounded more than 150 black and white Louisianians who had gathered in the Crescent City in support of black suffrage. The president's defeat was a product of many forces, but none more important than the New Orleans Race Riot of 1866.

The roots of that riot were caught up in the complex history of Louisiana wartime politics. In 1864 a convention of Louisiana unionists had drawn up a constitution and gained its ratification by a vote of 6,836 to 1,566. With the support of President Lincoln these unionists had petitioned the Congress for admission to the Union. Congress had rejected the Louisiana convention, and the postwar elections of 1865 were only nominally under the authority of that constitution; what limited power the Louisiana governor, J. Madison Wells, and legislature possessed came from the president's suffrance. There had, however, been a provision approved at the 1864 assembly calling for the reconvoking of the delegates at the pleasure of the convention president. Though the 1864 constitution restricted the suffrage to whites, black and white opponents of the Johnson regime saw the provision as an opportunity to convene a new convention

33. Hammond Moore (ed.), *The Juhl Letters to the Charleston "Courier"* (Athens, 1974), 107; Washington (Ga.) *Gazette*, July 3, 1866; Atlanta *Daily Intelligencer*, August 15, 1866; Linton Stephens to Alexander H. Stephens, July 29, 1866, in Alexander Stephens Papers, EU; Waynesboro *Times*, n.d., quoted in Augusta *Constitutionalist*, July 22, 1866.

and approve a constitution embracing the disfranchisement of Confederates and the enfranchisement of the state's freedmen. Encouraged by the mercurial Governor Wells, a small number of delegates from the 1864 convention called for a reconvening of the convention at Mechanics Hall in New Orleans on July 30.[34]

For the next 125 years, first the participants and observers and then the historians would argue over the precise circumstances surrounding the beginning of the riot. Whatever the events that precipitated it, the end result was indisputable. At least 34 blacks and 4 whites were killed, and another 150 delegates (most black) suffered serious wounds. With the exception of the accidental shooting of two or three white members of the mob that attacked the assembly at Mechanics Hall, the victims were convention delegates and supporters. Even after members of the convention extended the white flag from the assembly hall and attempted to flee, they were shot down without mercy. Nothing could alter these facts.[35]

New Orleans was not the site of the first postwar race riot. Whites and blacks had battled in Norfolk in March of 1866 and, on a much larger scale, in Memphis in May of that year. In the Memphis riot there were more deaths than in New Orleans; forty-five blacks died and seventy-five were seriously injured. Republican newspapers had condemned the attacks by whites as "wanton, unprovoked diabolism" that made the "atrocities of the great New York anti-Negro riot seem honorable and the massacre of Fort Pillow an innocent affair." But the issues surrounding the Memphis violence did not seem so clearcut as those in New Orleans. From the Republicans' standpoint, there was the uncomfortable fact that poorly disciplined black soldiers had harassed white citizens on the streets of Memphis and, on at least two occasions, had shot down whites without apparent provocation.[36]

Three factors made the New Orleans riot different in the thinking of northerners—moderates as well as radicals. In the first place, the members of the would-be constitutional convention were, for the most part, peacefully exercising that most democratic right of convening and petitioning for a redress of grievances. White southerners would make much of the fact

34. George Calvin Rable, "But There Was No Peace: Violence and Reconstruction Politics" (Ph.D. dissertation, Louisiana State University, 1979), 229–76.
35. Rable's account should be supplemented by Peyton McCrary, *Abraham Lincoln and Reconstruction: The Louisiana Experiment* (Princeton, 1978), and Gilles Vandal, *The New Orleans Riot of 1866: Anatomy of a Tragedy* (Lafayette, La., 1983).
36. Jack D. L. Holmes, "The Underlying Causes of the Memphis Race Riot of 1866," *THQ*, XVII (1958), 195–211; Holmes, "The Effects of the Memphis Riot of 1866," *WTHSP*, XII (1958), 58–79; Joe M. Richardson (ed.), "The Memphis Race Riot and Its Aftermath: Report by a Northern Missionary," *THQ*, XXIV (1965), 63–69.

that it was an "illegal" assembly, but as the temporary military commander Absalom Baird pointed out to the mayor of New Orleans, if the convention had the "legal right to remodel the State government, it should be protected in so doing; if it has not, then its labors must be looked upon simply as a harmless pleasantry to which to none ought to object." The obligation of government in a free society, Baird had scolded the mayor, was to protect those who, "having violated no ordinance of the State, are engaged in peaceful avocations."[37]

Second, the New Orleans massacre, following closely on the heels of the Memphis riot, dovetailed with the growing conviction of even the most moderate northerners that southern whites had unleashed a reign of terror against the hapless freedmen. Furiously, white southerners denied the charges, and editors in the region filled their columns with denials and exposés of the most exaggerated accounts of racial atrocities published by northern newspapers. Privately, there was more often a frank acknowledgment of the growing level of violence directed against the freedmen. J. Floyd King, a coastal Georgia planter living in Mississippi after the war, claimed it was primarily a product of the "newer" areas of the South. Having lived among the "western planters" for nearly a year, he said, "I no longer wonder so much the dislike they . . . incite in the spirit of the Northern fanatics." They were "purse-proud, ill-educated, raw, drinking, gambling bravos," he concluded, whose violence against the blacks in their midst had been restrained before the war only by a sharp eye for property values. With that barrier removed, they struck out viciously against helpless freedmen without any concern for their humanity. "Here negroes were a speculation—with us on the coast of Ga. they were an estate."[38]

Antebellum Alabama Senator George S. Houston found a similar pattern of violence in southwestern Alabama, where "complaints of the negroes receive no attention and murderers walk about with impunity." The instigators of these acts of vengeance were men in their early twenties, he said; back from the war's excitements to face a life of poverty and toil, they spent their time "taking out their anger on the 'damned nigger.'" What was equally depressing, reported Houston, was that conservative community leaders made no efforts to restrain these young men in their "violence and absurd conduct." In fact, their only statements seemed to "countenance disorder and abuse of negroes."[39]

37. House Select Committee on New Orleans Riots, "New Orleans Riots," *House Reports*, 39th Cong., 2nd Sess., No. 16, p. 442.
38. J. Floyd King to Anne, February 19, 1866, in Thomas Butler King Papers, SHC.
39. George S. Houston, Report to Gov. Lewis Parsons, August 29, 1865, Houston to Patton, April 30, 1866, both in Alabama Governors' Papers.

Very occasionally, white southerners breached the public wall of denials and openly acknowledged the pattern of violence that had emerged in the months after the war. In a dispatch to the Charleston *Daily Courier*, a Sumter planter and local magistrate bluntly acknowledged that acts of injustice and physical abuse against the freedmen were far more common than whites wished to acknowledge. And those whites who pleaded the freedmen's cause or demanded even-handed justice were subjected to the abuse and scorn of supposedly respectable members of the community. The editor of the Augusta *Constitutionalist* agreed, ignoring complaints from whites that the recognition of white violence against blacks strengthened the radicals. To the "mortification of candid and honorable men," southern whites were mistreating the freed slaves of the South, thus committing the most "damnatory of all atrocities." These "vicious men ignore facts . . . and with crazy impotence charge windmills," he concluded. The rights of the freed population were "indisputable" and their claims upon humanity strongly defined. Unfortunately, such outspoken comments were rare and when conservatives did speak out, it was usually to complain about the effect of such atrocities upon northern public opinion.[40]

The final factor in arousing northern anger and hostility was the brutal response of white southerners to these events. To be sure, radical Republicans often took a flight from reality as they described a "preconcerted and prearranged plan of weeks for the slaughter of Union Men" and darkly hinted that the president was aware of these plots. Such idle speculation was nothing compared to the reaction of white southerners. The initial newspaper accounts sent out by southern reporters from the New Orleans *Times* and the *Picayune* were unquestionably slanted to discredit the convention organizers. But they were remarkably explicit in describing the atrocities committed by the white mob (and police) surrounding Mechanics Hall. Even as the New Orleans *Times* correspondent blamed the "radicals" for precipitating the affair, he vividly described the manner in which "fleeing and unarmed delegates were attacked and killed" one by one—like so many "mad dogs," reported a shaken *Picayune* reporter. To see the black delegates "mutilated and literally beaten to death as they sought to escape was one of the most horrid pictures it has even been our ill fortune to witness," he reported.[41]

40. Charleston *Daily Courier*, August 14, 1866; Julius Fleming to Orr, November 29, 1866, in Orr Papers; Augusta *Constitutionalist*, October 19, 1866. Charles Phillips to Kemp Battle, December 17, 1866, in Kemp Battle Papers, SHC; Atlanta *Daily Intelligencer*, January 6, 1866.

41. See the New Orleans *Times* and the New Orleans *Picayune* for July 31 and August 1–5, 1866.

Despite these vivid eyewitness accounts, the newspapers of the South responded with a barrage of self-congratulatory editorials praising New Orleans whites for giving a "salutary warning" to northerners that the southern people, though "law-abiding," would "never submit to be ruled and made strangers in their homes by Northern emissaries, a few mischievous Southern men and their negro allies." The "brave people of New Orleans have vindicated their honor and their rights," crowed the editor of the Columbus *Sun*, while his counterpart on the New Orleans *Times* took satisfaction in the fact that the riot sharpened the political issues. There was no middle course, concluded the *Times* editor, the southern states must have their "rights," or the people of the North had to cease pretending that they were free men.[42]

Timidly W. W. Holden's newspaper, the *Standard*, suggested that the bloody suppression of this assembly (albeit an "illegal body") would lead to political reprisals by the North. But the only critical public comment on the behavior of the New Orleans mob came from the Columbus, Georgia, *Enquirer*. The editor acknowledged that this was a "revolutionary" assembly, but in the understatement of 1866, he pointed out that the meeting had not been terminated in a "legal and orderly manner." There could be no substitute, he argued, for an independent investigation by a conservative and impartial panel that would "uphold the majesty of the law regardless of popular passion and prejudice." In the context of the hysteria that swept through the region, this endorsement of due process may have been courageous, but it was hardly reassuring evidence to northern moderates that southern whites could be depended upon to uphold the rights of free speech and free assembly.[43]

Even privately, few white southerners condemned the riot on grounds other than political expediency. One of this few was Kemp Battle, who called it a "horrible massacre." But even he coupled his condemnation of the "demons of passion and prejudice . . . in the Southern character" with the charge that the radicals had deliberately encouraged the convention to "goad the New Orleans folks to acts of madness." Benjamin Hedrick had not been surprised at the level of mayhem that existed in the postwar South. To the exiled North Carolinian turned Republican, the "amount of violence . . . is not greater than might be expected under the circumstances." What he found utterly astonishing was the refusal of local officials

42. Macon *Daily Telegraph*, July 30, August 12, 1866; New Orleans *Times*, July 31, 1866; New Orleans *Picayune*, July 31, 1866; Charleston *Daily Courier*, August 4, 1866; Columbus (Ga.) *Sun*, August 2, 1866; Augusta *Constitutionalist*, August 8, 11, 1866; Atlanta *Daily Intelligencer*, August 1, 7, 1866; Raleigh *Sentinel*, August 3, 1866.
43. Columbus (Ga.) *Enquirer*, August 1, 1866.

and southern leaders to condemn such outrageous mob behavior. In this respect, the riot in New Orleans marked a turning point in his own thinking. Even a riot could occur—indeed they had occurred—in the North, "but none such as this New Orleans affair could occur in the North without *some* steps being taken to punish the guilty." As Hedrick clearly understood, the failure of southerners in positions of leadership to challenge violent and lawless mobs had destroyed any chance to build political support in the North.[44]

The New Orleans affair was mentioned only in the most oblique fashion when the National Union Convention met in Philadelphia. New York's Henry J. Raymond dismissed the New Orleans and earlier riots as the "fruit of untimely and hurtful political agitation." But the repercussions of the bloody affair cast a shadow over what was supposed to be the beginning of a campaign to rally national support behind the president. The New York *Evening Post*, which had supported Johnson (albeit with increasing reluctance), abandoned him in the wake of the riot and the president's silence. As E. L. Godkin, the editor of the *Nation*, concluded ten days after the massacre, "The coolness with which he refrained from expressing one word of honest indignation . . . is perhaps the most alarming incident in this sad affair." The loss of the support of the *Evening Post* would be followed within a month by that of the New York *Times*, the New York *Herald* and a half dozen other important metropolitan dailies in the North. Moreover, though it is impossible to precisely measure the impact of the New Orleans massacre upon national public opinion, the evidence seems clear that it led to a sharp escalation in the rhetoric of radical newspapers. The president "aided and abetted the New Orleans mob . . . [and] doubly inspired the murderers," said the New York *Independent*.[45]

On August 28 Andrew Johnson began his ill-fated "swing around the circle," traveling from Washington to Chicago and back again, speaking to mass audiences from a special train in an attempt to generate support for his policies, but he and his policies were already doomed. With impotent horror, southern conservatives watched as the combative president, faced with jeers and catcalls from hostile audiences, responded with crude and undignified stump speeches. These speeches infuriated a number of southern conservatives, who realized that they would have to pay the price for his political intemperance. The kindest word Herschel Johnson could find for

44. Kemp Battle to Benjamin Hedrick, September 7, 1866, in Hedrick Papers; Benjamin Hedrick to Jonathan Worth, September 16, 1866, in Worth Papers.
45. Wagstaff, "The Arm in Arm Convention," 117; New York *Independent*, August 9, 1866; New York *Evening Post*, August 2, 1866; New York *Herald*, September 13, 1866; New York *Times*, September 24, 1866.

the president's actions was "folly." Andrew Johnson had "made an ass of himself," said Johnson. He had "parted with his official dignity, his prudence and discretion," the dejected Georgia conservative concluded. By descending to the level of shouting "blackguards," he had jeopardized any chance for the restoration of the South to the Union.[46]

William W. Boyce, the South Carolina secessionist who had become an early peace advocate in that state, had been ebulliently optimistic in the summer of 1865, but each refusal of the president to placate the Republican moderates had strengthened his apprehension that Johnson was unable to cope with the delicate task of reunion. From his law office in Washington, where he resettled after the war, he had warned his fellow South Carolinians that Johnson's stubborn refusal to compromise would lead to "revolutionary measures that only a handful of radicals now support." Well before the ballots had been cast, all but the most optimistic supporters of the president were conceding defeat. William A. Reid, owner of the Macon *Daily Telegraph*, was still optimistic as the convention came to a close, but a leisurely trip from Philadelphia to New York and back to Washington was a sobering experience for the Georgia conservative. As Boyce succinctly concluded when the first state election returns were telegraphed to Washington in September, southern conservatives had gambled everything on the success of the president and they had lost. The Republicans, he predicted gloomily, would have a decisive majority in the next Congress, and they would override the president and push through a reconstruction program that incorporated black suffrage. "The New Orleans Riot and his foolish speeches have done his business for him," a frustrated Boyce concluded. "He is a dead cock in the pit."[47]

The decisive Republican victory in 1866 meant that white southerners, particularly the leadership that had guided the postwar South, could no longer indulge the wishful assumption that Johnson might yet rally a sym-

46. Herschel Johnson to William A. Graham, September 25, 1866, in William Alexander Graham Papers, NCA.
47. Steven A. Channing, *Crisis of Fear: Secession in South Carolina* (New York, 1970), 175–76; Ezra J. Warner and Wilfred Buck Yearns (eds.), *Biographical Register of the Confederate Congress* (Baton Rouge, 1975), 27–28; William W. Boyce to Orr, May 23, 1866, in Orr Papers; Boyce to J. D. B. De Bow, October 1, 1866, in J. D. B. De Bow Papers, DUL. For the growing discouragement of Johnson backers, see the David Schenck Diary, June–November, 1866; William A. Graham to Kemp Battle, August 23, 1866, in Battle Papers; Charles L. Jenkins to Orr, September 20, 1866, in Orr Papers; Jonathan Worth to Dr. J. G. Ramsey, September 13, 1866, in James Graham Ramsey Papers, SHC; Edward Jenner Warren to Alfred E. Willard, October 7, 1866, in Willard Papers; W. J. Mason to David M. Carter, March 6, 1866, M. B. Rodman to David M. Carter, November 1, 1866, David M. Carter to John Pool, November 1, 1866 (copy), all in Carter Papers; James Hemphill to W. R. Hemphill, August 2, 1866, in Hemphill Collection; John Erskine to Joseph E. Brown, September 21, 1866, in Felix Hargrett Collection, UGL.

pathetic North. The last hope was gone, concluded a gloomy North Carolina politician. Southerners must "get out of the way . . . get into the current and ride . . . , [or] otherways be overtaken and run over by the Political storm of fanaticism that is sweeping over the land."[48] To do nothing was probably the easiest course, for the only positive action would be to offer concessions that would satisfy the Republican majority in Congress, and this almost certainly meant the acceptance of black suffrage. For that minority of ambitious strait-sect unionists who had become politically isolated from the Johnson regimes, the congressional elections removed any questions about the future course.

Even before the fall elections, there had been a handful of southern unionists ready to throw their support behind the emerging Republican congressional leadership. James Pearson Newcomb of San Antonio returned to Texas in 1866 after five years of exile in California, precipitated when a pro-Confederate mob had burned his unionist newspaper in May, 1861, and nearly lynched the twenty-four-year-old editor. He had returned ready to apply a "pure bracing radicalism" to the "infected and treason-sick State." Other southerners might hesitate at the "extreme" measures of the Republican majority, but Newcomb scolded them for their timidity. In a series of speeches, he urged that the estates of leading Texans be confiscated, and he endorsed Negro suffrage as the only hope for the future of the Republican party, the party of "liberty and progress." Privately, he might admit that he was "much prejudiced in favor of the White race," but Newcomb—like other unionists—was willing to use any weapon to break the power of the "Confederate traitors" who had persecuted him in the war.[49]

For those more radical unionists who had become politically isolated in 1865 and early 1866, the congressional elections made it possible for them to plan a political comeback *if* they were willing to accept black suffrage. Like James Newcomb, former Texas provisional governor Andrew Jackson Hamilton made his decision even before the fall elections. After the defeat of his chosen candidate for governor in the summer of 1866, Hamilton was

48. Leander Gash to Wife, March 1, 1867, in Leander Gash Papers, NCA. Gash, a state senator from western North Carolina, wrote 28 lengthy letters to his wife between February 4, 1866, and March 1, 1867, which have just been edited and annotated by Otto H. Olsen and Ellen Z. McGrew. Collectively, they are the most extensive source of information on the day-to-day operation of state legislatures during the era of Johnsonian Reconstruction. See Olsen and McGrew, "Prelude to Reconstruction: The Correspondence of State Senator Leander Sams Gash, 1866–67," *NCHR*, LX (1983), 37–88, 206–38, 333–66.

49. San Antonio *Express*, July 23, 30, August 12, 1867; James Newcomb to Simon Newcomb, August 4, 1867, James P. Newcomb, "An Appeal in Behalf of the Republicans of Texas" (1868?, 1869?), (Unpublished speech, [1868 or 1869?]), both in James P. Newcomb Papers, UTA; Dale A. Somers, "James P. Newcomb: The Making of a Radical," *SwHQ*, LXXII (1969), 460–63.

beset by financial and personal problems. (He was an alcoholic.) He had become a politician without a political base and a lawyer without clients. First reluctantly, and then with increasing enthusiasm, the Texans who had sworn to maintain a white man's government embraced the Fourteenth Amendment and turned on the president. In early September he led southern delegates at the Philadelphia "Loyalist" convention, which had been convened to focus national public opinion on the plight of southern unionists. Later that month he served as member of the "truth squad" that followed President Johnson on his swing around the circle. And yet the very solicitude with which northern Republicans treated a distinctly minor figure like Hamilton reflected the marginal political position of most of the southern unionists who had rejected Johnson in early 1866. Far more significant was the wave of defections by southern unionists that followed the elections.[50]

North Carolina's W. W. Holden was one of the first important figures to shift his allegiance from the president to the Republican congressional leadership. Embittered by his failure to gain election in the fall of 1865, Holden had become increasingly vitriolic in his attacks on his successor, Jonathan Worth. By the late spring of 1866, the rhetoric of Holden and his newspaper had steadily escalated. The state was in the hands of "monsters of moral iniquity" who had starved and tortured Union soldiers during the war, claimed Holden. Worth and his minions were as "groveling and cowardly" as they were "mean and traitorous." In terms of policy toward the freedmen, however, there was little difference between the Holden and Worth factions. Throughout the spring of 1866, Holden backed Johnson and argued that his political opponent, Governor Worth, was insufficiently supportive of the president. He had endorsed Johnson's veto of the Civil Rights and Freedmen's Bureau bills, and he had accepted the right of the freedmen to testify with great reluctance. As late as September of 1866, he continued to oppose black suffrage. When a convention of black North Carolinians met in Raleigh in the early fall of 1866 to petition for expanded educational opportunities and to ask for the right to vote, Holden warned them against seeking political rights. They were "unfit" for such activities, he insisted.

In the weeks after the fall elections, however, Holden's newspaper abruptly ended the publication of antiblack letters and articles, ignored Andrew Johnson, and reprinted without comment editorials from northern

50. New York *Times*, August 21, 31, 1866; Andrew Jackson Hamilton, *An Address on "Suffrage and Reconstruction": The Duty of the People and Congress* (Boston, 1866), 2–4; John L. Waller, *Colossal Hamilton of Texas: A Biography of Andrew Jackson Hamilton, Militant Unionist and Reconstruction Governor* (El Paso, Tex., 1968), 94–99.

conservative newspapers arguing that some form of black suffrage was essential before the South could be readmitted to the Union. On December 25, 1866, he began an editorial endorsing the proposed Fourteenth Amendment with a reference to "all our Union people, white and black." A week later Holden spoke at a black church in Raleigh, endorsing the disfranchisement of "disloyal" whites and a revised suffrage based upon only those who were "loyal white and black citizens." Within ten weeks he had formally announced his allegiance to the Republican party.[51]

It was one thing for Hamilton or Holden and his North Carolina supporters to embrace the new political order; it was far more traumatic for those conservatives who had generally been successful in controlling the Johnson program. But many of those southerners with ambitious plans for postwar economic development were at least willing to consider endorsing the Howard Amendment if it might settle the issue. The common theme, whatever their differences on specific points, was a desperate desire to end the unsettled political affairs in the postwar South.

Of course the Howard Amendment was a "crude act of political chicanery" by the Republicans, a North Carolina conservative concluded. But it did no good to "stand out upon an assumption of right & a supposed point of honor," Edward Warren told a South Carolina textile manufacturer. "I want action which will harmonize our people, revive patriotism and make the state inviting to capital & enterprise," he argued. If that were ever to be possible, the "Howard amendment must be adopted without too much grumbling or the present state government will be blotted out and a new one constructed upon the basis of more serious test oaths than we have yet dreamed of." The question was "not whether we like the medicine which is prescribed."[52]

Barton Jencks, a Baltimore businessman, agreed that the proposed constitutional amendment was a "disgrace and a fraud." Nevertheless, he told South Carolina's governor James Orr, the acceptance of the Fourteenth

51. *North Carolina Standard*, June 9, 26, December 25, 1866, January 9, March 13, 20, 1867. The shift among North Carolina unionists (and others throughout the South) is much more complicated than this brief summary implies. Some of Holden's supporters (Thomas Settle and John Odom, for example) cast their lot with the Republicans early in 1866; others, such as R. P. Dick, John Pool, Edward Conigland, and Alfred Dockery, rejected Johnson but agonized over the prospect of accepting black suffrage. See, for example, John B. Odom to Thomas Settle, May 18, 1867, John Pool to Thomas Settle, July 4, 1866, both in Settle Papers; Edward Conigland to Wife, October–November, 1865, *passim*, in Edward Conigland Papers, SHC; Louis Hanes to Jonathan Worth, May 17, 1866, in Jonathan Worth Perrin Papers, NCA; Perrin Busbee to Benjamin Hedrick, January 8, 1867, in Benjamin Hedrick Papers, DUL.

52. Edward Jenner Warren to Alfred E. Willard, August 25, October 7, 1866, September 21, 1867, all in Willard Papers.

Amendment and the granting of black suffrage would be a "finality" that would "put an end to the utter uncertainty that has been hanging over the future of the Country." Almost any settlement, he argued, would be preferable to the "discord and strife" that were paralyzing the will and energies of the southern people and creating an unfavorable business climate in which "timid capital dare not invade."[53]

"Business of all kinds . . . is suffering under suspense and uncertainty," complained R. H. Bigham, the president of the Chattahoochee Textile Manufacturing Company. An acceptance of congressional terms, including forced enfranchisement of the freedmen, was the only action that would relieve the South from a political "incubus" so "stifling to hope, inimical to happiness & detrimental to prosperity." It was true, conceded L. F. Mellen of the Bank of Selma, that the "passions of the people" had been aroused in opposition to further concessions. These passions, he glumly noted, had been unwisely exacerbated by Andrew Johnson. But most southerners were simply too "uninformed" to realize that the business interests and welfare of the state required the abandonment of political aspirations and "personal prejudices."[54]

Of all the southern governors, Robert Patton received perhaps the most extensive advice from conservative leaders around the state debating the merits of accepting or rejecting the Fourteenth Amendment, and he was more than receptive to such advice. Throughout late 1865 and early 1866, his politics on the critical issue of civil rights had been conventional, tempered primarily by his concern for northern sensibilities. After his election in 1865, he had urged fellow Alabamians to grant all civil rights to the freedmen, but he assured them he would never consent to the "absurd project of conferring the right of suffrage upon an ignorant and semi-barbarian population of suddenly emancipated slaves." Alabama was to be forever a "white man's state" with a "white man's government." Throughout the summer and fall of 1866, however, he grew increasingly restive over the division between Johnson and the Congress, sharing his brother-in-law's view that the most important thing was to "retain sufficient influence with the members of the dominant party." After first urging the Alabama legislature to reject the proposed constitutional amendment in November, 1866, upon sober reflection, he reversed himself. There were many factors in his decision, but he seems to have been particularly influenced by the

53. Barton Jencks to Orr, March 9, 1867, in Orr papers. Orr received similar advice from others. J. N. Morris to Orr, December 22, 1866, James Farrow to Orr, March 23, 1867, C. W. Dudley to Orr, December 31, 1866, all in Orr Papers.
54. R. H. Bigham to Patton, March 4, 1867, L. F. Mellen to Patton, January 27, 1866, both in Alabama Governors' Papers.

trip he made to New York in an effort to obtain loans for the state and for his business investments. The "banking and monied men" of New York frankly told him, Patton confided to his secretary, that nothing could be done until the political situation was stabilized in the South. The president might continue to urge southerners to "resist and stand firm," said a scornful Patton. That was "foolishness." In early December, Patton told the Alabama legislators to ratify the amendment on the grounds that "necessity must rule." His good friend and predecessor, Lewis Parsons, counseled against Patton's endorsement of ratification but only "to give time enough for us to consider what we ought to do when we find there is no hope of receiving our rights in that way [by backing the President.]"[55]

There was at least the potential for a common ground between those Johnsonian conservatives who looked timidly toward an economically transformed South and the yeoman small-farmer constituency that supported men like Holden in North Carolina. Thomas Settle of Rockingham, North Carolina, had served in the legislature from 1854 to 1859 as a Democrat, then a Whig, and finally as a Democrat again. In a burst of patriotic enthusiasm, he had enlisted in the Confederate army as a captain. Later, as state solicitor, he had vigorously and successfully prosecuted unionists and "slackers" like one of North Carolina's most consistent unionists, the Reverend George Welker, who delivered a pro-Union speech in 1862. By late 1863, however, he had begun to have second thoughts about the Confederacy and to angrily condemn the "follies and crimes of the Richmond government." In the summer of 1865 he won election as a "faithful Johnson man" to the constitutional convention, of which he was a prominent member, and he later served as speaker of the first postwar senate.

But Settle soon became estranged from Johnson primarily because he felt that the president had supported the state's "old fogies," who were blind to the economic potential of the state of North Carolina and the region. Unlike many of his fellow politicians, who sought the shelter of the Republican party because they had no alternative, Settle made a conscious

55. Among the dozens of letters Patton received from November, 1866, to April, 1867, was one from former secessionist governor A. B. Moore praising him for his endorsement, which would promote a "speedy advancement of our material interests," and two from southern newspaper editors who praised Patton privately even as they publicly counseled resistance to the amendment. A. B. Moore to Patton, March 17, 1867, Salem Dutcher to Patton, January 11, 1867, William L. Scruggs to Patton, January 12, 1867, all in Alabama Governors' Papers. Perhaps the most striking example of the inconsistency between public and private statements was the public insistence of former provisional governor Lewis Parsons that he would "stand firmly by the President" (Richmond *Enquirer and Sentinel*, January 4, 1867) even as he secretly agreed with his successor, Patton, that the president was to be abandoned as soon as it was expedient. Parsons to Patton, December 17, 1866, in Alabama Governors' Papers.

decision to join the party because it offered a blueprint for the region's economic and social salvation. The North, he told a Rockingham audience in March of 1867, had far surpassed the South despite its disadvantages. Why did the "bleak and naturally barren hills of New England bloom like gardens," Settle rhetorically asked, while southern fields were covered with weeds and broom sedge? Why did churches, schoolhouses, railroads, canals, steamboats, factories, workshops, cities, small towns, beautiful villages, and "neat farm houses" flourish in the North, "while poverty and pride constitute our fortune here?" The answer was obvious, he declared. "The one is the result of free labor, the other of slavery." What was needed was "Yankees and Yankee notions . . . to build factories, and workshops, and railroads, and develop our magnificent water powers." This would never be possible, concluded Settle, until southerners were willing to bury a "thousand fathoms deep" the ideas and principles that had shaped the old South. And this meant the acceptance of black suffrage, the one great issue dividing the South from the North.[56]

But few conservatives were willing to bluntly attack the president even if they were willing to join Settle in accepting Congressional Reconstruction as the price of readmission. The political dilemmas of Joseph Brown of Georgia reflect the peculiar difficulties of those postwar conservatives. Brown had made a similar assessment of the future in his month-long trip to Washington in January of 1867. Brown had gone to Washington to meet secretly with officials of the Treasury Department to pass on confidential information concerning Confederate property that a Georgia railroad company had squirreled away at the end of the war. As an informant, Brown was entitled to a percentage of the property seized by the federal government. During the course of his stay, Brown talked with the president and with key members of the Republican party, including James A. Garfield and William D. Kelley. Already certain of the futility of supporting the president, he was convinced from his conversations that, at best, there would ensue a long period of political uncertainty and, at worst, a revolutionary setting in which all but a handful of whites might be disfranchised and the dread issue of confiscation be raised once again. In correspondence with several close supporters, he outlined his conclusions and announced his intention to support Congressional Reconstruction as the "lesser of evils."[57]

56. *Dictionary of American Biography*, XVI, 598–600. Thomas Settle, Speech, March [?], 1867, Settle Papers.
57. William E. Chandler to David Patterson, December 29, 1866, Patterson to Joseph E. Brown, January 11, 1867, both in Hargrett Collection; Joseph E. Brown to Joseph H. Lumpkin, February [?], 1867, James Lumpkin to Joseph E. Brown, February 21, 1867, both in McLeod Collection, UGL.

One week after his return from Washington, he publicly announced his support for the Fourteenth Amendment and an acceptance of whatever terms the Congress might offer. The South had entered a new era, he argued. "We need capital and labor. Neither will come till our difficulties are settled and our political status defined." Without referring to his own considerable financial interests, Brown described a state "teeming with rich resources" and on the edge of economic wealth that would far eclipse the "false prosperity" of the old slave South. The region had lost immensely; was it "wise to stubbornly sacrifice the little that is left of us?" The only hope for the South was to "agree with thine adversary quickly." As one of his supporters acknowledged, the acceptance of the Fourteenth Amendment and universal suffrage would be humiliating, but it was too late to talk about degradation and dishonor. Compliance would have the practical effect of saving the region from political chaos and economic collapse, and it would "take the wind out of the sails of the extreme radicals."[58]

"Our poor butchered people want peace," agreed a Bennettsville planter in urging fellow South Carolinians to accept the proposed constitutional amendment and black suffrage. Like other apprehensive men of property, he was able to conjure a nightmarish scenario in which continued defiance would rekindle national support for confiscation and even more radical disfranchisement measures. If southerners kept insisting that the danger had passed, said Bartholomew Moore, the result would "assuredly be 'confiscation.'" The "bitter cup" facing the white South was "one not of our choice but one of compulsion," concluded an Alabama planter. The choice was either to accept the conditions imposed by Congress or face continuing unrest that would eventually lead to rule by a "band of desparadoes [*sic*] that will inaugurate a reign of terror, and every respectable man will have to flee the country a beggar to save the lives of himself and family." The president might believe that, by some "fortunate shaking of the dice, the radicals could still be thwarted," warned C. W. Dudley. "But remember, we have been shaking the dice for the last five years & we have shook out only blood & suffering."[59]

Such arguments of economic calculation and political expediency were doomed. It is conceivable (though not likely) that the postwar conservative

58. Brown's letter appeared in full in the Atlanta *New Era*, the Atlanta *Daily Intelligencer*, and the Milledgeville *Federal Union* on February 26, 1867. Brown, like Patton and Parsons of Alabama, hesitated nearly a year, however, before formally joining the Republican party.

59. Bartholomew F. Moore to Kemp Battle, May 8, 1867, in Battle Papers; C. W. Dudley to Orr, December 31, 1866, in Orr Papers. See also "Memorandum, March 28, 1867," in John Arrington Papers, SHC; William Henry Trescot to Orr, December 13, 1866, in Orr Papers; Thomas A. Belser, Jr., "Alabama Plantation to Georgia Farm: John Horry Dent and Reconstruction," *GHQ*, XXV (1963), 144.

leadership might have been able to mobilize majorities for the Fourteenth Amendment *if* the president had agreed to stand aside quietly; and *if* the Republican majority had been willing to make the amendment a "final settlement" of the requirements for reunion. But neither condition existed. The president was unwilling to encourage the southern legislatures to accept the congressional amendment. The elections, far from convincing him of the need for conciliation, only strengthened him in his opposition to any concessions. The proposed amendment would never be ratified unless the Republicans legislated military coercion and explicit black enfranchisement, reasoned Johnson. And the overt endorsement of black suffrage, unlike the duplicitous language of the constitutional amendment that had duped northern voters in 1860, would lead to the radicals' political downfall at the next national elections.[60]

Nor was there any likelihood that the congressional majority would agree that the Fourteenth Amendment was a finality. The Congress had readmitted Tennessee in July of 1866 after that state ratified the Fourteenth Amendment, and a number of key Republican moderates believed that endorsement should lead to readmission to the Union. New York and Michigan Republicans had even made this commitment a part of their 1866 platform. But the radicals—who had been proved right on so many occasions in the past—would have none of it. No guarantees were to be made, insisted Charles Sumner; the amendment was "only an installment, not a finality."[61]

Under the circumstances, it is hardly surprising that the mixed message that the Republican party conveyed in 1866 and 1867 only strengthened opponents of the amendment. White southerners who had consistently argued against concessions after 1865 were reinforced in their conviction that such "conciliation" only provoked further demands. They had acted in a "manly and honorable fashion" in 1865, only to be "tricked and betrayed by unscrupulous Republicans," argued one Deep South editor. They had been told to abolish slavery, to acknowledge the supremacy of the Union, and to repudiate wartime debts, said the editor of the Augusta *Constitu-*

60. Albert Castel, *The Presidency of Andrew Johnson* (Lawrence, Kans., 1979), 100–101. Though Johnson once again miscalculated, he was not entirely mistaken in his assumptions. The Republican defeats in 1867 did reflect a growing backlash among white voters in the North. In Ohio, where a black suffrage amendment had been placed on the ballot, it went down by a decided majority with many of the still-Republican areas returning majorities against black suffrage. Felice A. Bonadio, "Ohio: A 'Perfect Contempt for All Unity,'" in James C. Mohr (ed.), *Radical Republicans in the North: State Politics During Reconstruction* (Baltimore, 1976), 90–93.

61. Charles Sumner to F. W. Bird, January 10, 1867, in Edward L. Pierce, *Memoir and Letters of Charles Sumner* (London, 1893), IV, 311; Les Benedict, *A Compromise of Principle*, 211–16.

tionalist. But when the region had elected its most "conciliatory" leaders, they had "presented themselves at the doors of the National Temple—only to be scorned and insulted." Each time southerners had tried to reenter the Union, they had been "shown the path by the forcible application of a well-booted foot." And now the "conciliators" insisted that, if only the South would accept the Howard Amendment, the crisis would end. "They *lied,*" said the *Constitutionalist,* "when they claimed that even the wages of this abasement—the poor bribe of misrepresentation—will be paid." The radicals at least were frank enough to acknowledge that there was no limit to their demands short of the disfranchisement of white southerners and unconditional suffrage for the freedmen. "Of the honesty of the several parties, we have more respect for the Radicals than those who are neither fish, fowl or good Red Herring." Any attempt to reason with the Republicans—who cared about nothing except the continuing supremacy of their party—was futile.[62]

As they tried to cajole and persuade their fellow southerners to accept the Fourteenth Amendment, this dwindling band of conservative whites was locked in a rhetorical battle it was bound to lose. The great majority of white southerners simply had no sympathy for the arguments of expediency and economic calculation. The timid conservatives who sought to persuade the white South into endorsing Congressional Reconstruction had misinterpreted the mood of white southerners, argued South Carolina's Benjamin Perry. They kept whining of the danger of losing our property, sneered Perry, but "as a friend of mine said the other day, 'we have only got two dollars and a half a piece,' and why should we sacrifice our honor to save that."[63]

When Perry used the word *honor* he reached back to the same emotions that had united—if only briefly—the overwhelming majority of white southerners in 1860 and 1861: the fear of losing their manhood. The warnings against shameful self-abnegation that had appeared during the constitutional conventions of 1865 had become more insistent in the months that followed. Even when southerners were asked to compromise on issues of form rather than substance, they bridled. In the debate over whether or not to send delegates to the National Union Convention in the summer of 1866, most white southerners acknowledged that the convention was de-

---

62. Augusta *Constitutionalist,* October 17, 1866. For similar arguments that the white South had been "duped" with misleading conditions, see Columbus (Ga.) *Sun,* March 31, July 4, 1866; Waynesboro (Ga.) *Times,* n.d., quoted in Augusta *Daily Constitutionalist,* July 22, 1864.

63. Benjamin Perry to F. Marion Nye, May 25, 1867, in Benjamin Perry Manuscripts (Microfilm, 2 reels, SHC, 1967).

signed to serve purely cosmetic purposes, but they seemed unable to accept even the sham of voluntary acquiescence and repentance. Of course the South would not resist emancipation, nor would it attempt to revive the doctrines of secession, the editor of the Augusta *Constitutionalist* had argued, but there was always the danger that northern delegates would expect them to "glory in the defeat of the Confederate cause" (which they did not) and "praise the blue jacketed soldiers who left a trail of fire and blood through the South." Southern delegates under the circumstances would be placed in a situation in which they had a choice between signing a party platform that would change nothing politically but would require them to "curse the memories of our dead soldiers" and "confess that we were rebels, traitors and murderers." If they refused to sign, on the other hand, it would furnish "propaganda grist for Northern radicals."[64]

The Atlanta *Daily Intelligencer* editor had reluctantly endorsed the Philadelphia convention because of his loyalty to President Johnson. Nevertheless, he also expressed concern that northerners—even conservative northerners—would insist that southerners should once more profess their "love for the union." It was true, said John Steele, that the "Bible requires we should kiss the hand of almighty God when he smites us; there is no similar injunction as to man." The South was a land of widows and orphans, with men crippled and demoralized, farms laid waste, and towns still bearing the fresh scars of the war. And everywhere there were the fresh graves of tens of thousands of southern men. The southerner could be a loyal and obedient citizen of the government; to ask him to love the government that had presided over this enterprise was to ask only for "dishonorable hypocrisy." A. W. Bradford wearily conceded to J. D. B. De Bow that he was ready to swallow his pride and go to the convention and sign a pledge of "sin no more." Most southerners were not.[65]

To northerners, the shifting emphasis of southern spokesmen from the language of expediency and submission to the angry vocabulary of "manhood" and "Southern rights" evoked echoes of the 1850s and aroused fears of a resurgent rebelliousness on the part of white southerners. There was such a shift, but it did not so much reflect a dramatic change in regional attitudes as it exposed the limits that had always existed on the compliance of white southerners. In the struggle to shape postwar policies toward the North, the conservative leadership sought to balance the demands of the victorious North with the "sensibilities" of the defeated

---

64. Augusta *Daily Constitutionalist*, July 10, 25, 1866; Augusta *Daily Press*, July 4, 11, 1866; Sandersville *Middle Georgia News*, n.d., quoted in Montgomery *Advertiser*, July 20, 1866.

65. Atlanta *Daily Intelligencer*, February 10, June 13, 1866; A. W. Bradford to J. D. B. De Bow, July 9, 1866, in De Bow Papers.

South, to weigh the psychic pain of submission against the very real financial costs of continued exclusion from the Union and political and economic unrest. By mid-1866 the limit of their support from the great mass of southern whites had been reached, and opponents of further concessions were able to reach back to far more potent emotional briefs than the tepid arguments of expediency.

We are told to be "conciliatory," to "promote harmony," said Raleigh attorney Thomas Richardson sarcastically. White southerners had been conciliatory enough. He had bitterly opposed secession, and he was anxious to return to the Union, he told his good friend Thomas McDowell, but "not if it requires that we stoop to kiss the toe of the Great High Priest, Thad Stevens." He added, "I for one am determined to put no more sack-cloth and ashes upon . . . [the South] in order to humiliate her to the proper level of radical favor."[66]

As early as March of 1866, William L. Sharkey had thought it possible that the president would be defeated by the Republican radicals. When that time came, said Sharkey, "I shall . . . like the girl on her wedding night, lie flat on my back, trust to Providence and take whatever comes." Sharkey's crude metaphor of feminine passivity betrayed the weakness of conservative advocates of compliance—even cosmetic compliance—with Republican demands far better than most contemporaries or later historians realized. The South had surrendered with dignity, said William A. Reid of Macon. But "he who surrenders his sword should remember that, in relinquishing the weapon of a man it does not become him to have recourse to a woman's tongue." The South was at the mercy of the North. Did this mean "I am therefore to sing hosannas to his honour and forthwith model myself in all ways possible after the fashion of my master?" Many of his fellow southerners were so lacking in manhood and honor that they were willing to give any assurances, make any concessions and even "mimic the principles of the Yankee." Someday, said Reid, the sons would look back in shame upon their fathers' "systematic crawling upon bellies and methodical eating of dirt." The South was beaten. "Beyond that declaration do not go."[67]

However one might define honor, it would never embrace the cowardly and pusillanimous behavior of men like Joseph E. Brown. The response to Brown's cautious political recommendation was itself a chilling example of how such rhetoric could be used to silence those who advocated conciliation. By counseling acquiescence Brown had urged the white men of the

66. Thomas Richardson to Thomas Davis Smith McDowell, May 30, 1866, in McDowell Papers, SHC.
67. William L. Sharkey to Benjamin Humphreys, March 14, 1866, in Humphreys Correspondence, Mississippi Governors' Papers; Augusta *Constitutionalist*, August 12, 1866.

South to "fall down and embrace terms which stand unparalleled in history for their humiliation and their debasement," claimed the Mobile *Advertiser*. Brown wanted to add "stultification and disgrace" to the region's political and economic ruin. Dishonorable men are "given to crawling and to slime, and we are therefore not surprised to see Governor Brown on his belly and calling on ten millions of Southern people to get on their bellies too, to thank Congress for its cruelty and beg its forbearance." At political rallies in Atlanta in June of 1867, several hundred Georgians condemned Brown for offering a "poisoned chalice" that would "sink us below the legal status of our former slaves." Georgians might have to accept the Howard Amendment, but to give it legitimacy through ratification would do more than simply dishonor those who had survived the war, it would "stigmatize, anathematize and forever defame, degrade, disown, damn and dishonor the immortal heroes who surrendered their lives." Even Sharkey, for all his talk of accepting the inevitability of "radical" rule, refused to join the Republican party.[68]

From the time that the Fourteenth Amendment was first proposed, William M. Browne of Georgia had argued that it was "more infamous than Stevens's subjugation or Sumner's compulsory nigger suffrage scheme" because it "affects benevolence and invites us to eat dirt to please the radicals." He argued bitterly, "If I have to eat it, I want to be compelled to do it, not to be hospitably invited to it as a desirable meal." "We are conquered, conquered by our own folly," agreed Robert Toombs, a man as responsible for that folly as any southerner. "Let us stand . . . whatever these people put upon us, but do not let us stultify ourselves."[69]

In November of 1866 one North Carolina state senator reported that twenty to thirty of his two hundred colleagues in the state legislature favored ratification of the Fourteenth Amendment if they could be reasonably sure that this was the "final demand" upon the South. By the time that the vote was taken in January, however, their number had dwindled to eleven. The refusal of the Republicans to commit themselves to final terms and the president's no-compromise policy probably influenced that reduction, but proponents of compromise were far more handicapped by the fact that the limits of voluntary acquiescence had been reached in the white South. In an editorial in late September of 1866, the editor of the New York *Herald* in-

68. Mobile *Advertiser and Register*, March 3, 1867; Milledgeville (Ga.) *Federal Union*, March 7, 1867; Atlanta *Daily Intelligencer*, June 24, July 16, 18, 1867; Savannah *Republican*, July 18, 1867.

69. William M. Browne to Howell Cobb, March 28, 1866, Robert Toombs to Alexander Stephens, December 15, 1866, both in Ulrich Bonnell Phillips (ed.), *The Correspondence of Robert Toombs, Alexander Stephens, and Howell Cobb* (New York, 1970), 675–78.

sisted that the Fourteenth Amendment could be easily ratified if only the president would act. "A little pressure upon the Governors of the Southern states concerned by the President, like that which was applied in behalf of the Constitutional Amendment abolishing slavery, will do the work." But the editor of one Georgia newspaper noted a critical difference. Emancipation had been the goal of a substantial minority of Americans for more than a generation, and even it had been achieved only at the cost of a bloody civil war. Suffrage, on the other hand, was seldom discussed and then not very seriously until after the end of the war.[70]

One by one the southern states rejected the proposed Fourteenth Amendment—usually by overwhelming majorities—and accompanied each rejection with a long-winded constitutional explanation pointing out the fact that it was discriminatory in affecting only the South or mocking the absurdity of requiring ratification from illegal and nonexistent state governments. But most white southerners had long since convinced themselves that it was fruitless to appeal to the radicals on the basis of reason, fairness, or constitutional principles. "Talk of the Constitution!" sneered James Randall of Augusta. "One might as well try to explain the decalogue to a gorilla."[71]

The introduction of the Reconstruction Acts in the spring of 1867 gave further strength, if any was needed, to the arguments of those who had counseled against further concessions. The argument that the passage of the Fourteenth Amendment and a reduction of congressional representation would satisfy the Republicans had been exposed as wishful thinking. The rhetorical warning of dishonor was given additional strength by the fact that the Republican program was clearly not simply a matter of symbolic acquiescence. For what could be more substantive—and "degrading"—than the handing of the power of the ballot to a million former slaves?

By the end of 1866, one South Carolina up-country newspaper expressed a willingness to simply close down the legislature without waiting for Congress to act. "Never before . . . have we seen the law-making power of the State entrusted to such feeble hands as now compose a large portion of that body," concluded the Yorkville *Enquirer*. The newspaper found this

70. Leander Gash to Wife, November 25, 1866, in Gash Papers; New York *Herald*, September 27, 1866; Augusta *Constitutionalist*, October 7, 1866. Unfortunately, Joseph B. James's *The Ratification of the Fourteenth Amendment* (Macon, 1984), appeared too late to be used in this study.

71. Macon *Daily Telegraph*, October 2, 1866; Augusta *Constitutionalist*, October 17, 1866; Joseph B. James, "Reaction to the Fourteenth Amendment," *JSH*, XXII (1956), 493–97.

perfectly understandable since the pervasive apathy meant that competent and forceful individuals had neither the desire nor the will to commit themselves to the political arena.[72]

At times diarists who had read too many nineteenth-century novels expressed the depression of postwar southerners in melodramatic language. Defeat seemed particularly overwhelming to southern women, who had substituted fierce emotional attachment to the Confederacy for their inability to take up arms for the cause. "I was so crushed by the fall of our country that I took to my bed and was inconsolable for a long, long time," recalled one Mississippi woman. There had to be some reason, some purpose behind the death and suffering of the war, wrote Sarah Wadley, "God does not act capriciously." Eventually she would be reconciled, "but now, Oh God, help me. It seems so hard to bear."[73]

If it was simply a grief-stricken reaction to the loss of the Confederacy, however, it was also caught up in the deadening struggle for survival that followed in the months after Appomattox. In the summer of 1865, Grace Elmore of Richland County, South Carolina, watched painfully as her father tried unsuccessfully to rearrange the family finances so that they could save their home, the farm where she had spent the sixteen years of her life. In the late summer her father finally gave up and sold out everything to two army officers eager to try their hand at cotton planting. "My home was beautiful," she wrote in her diary the night after she had loaded her trunk in a canvas-covered wagon and moved to Columbia, "but it was with a feeling of relief . . . that I looked my last upon the roses we had planted, the great oak trees . . . , the rooms in which I had so many happy, so many sad hours." Better, she said, to give up than to continue a hopeless struggle. Six months later, nothing had changed for her and her friends. "I long for something cheerful, I long for something to break me from the dead weight that rests upon me and upon those around me."[74]

Nor was such depression simply the emotional response of impressionable young teenagers. S. D. McConnell, a Fort Gaines, Georgia, attorney, returned from the war jobless and impoverished but with friends and connections in the little town where he planned to set up a private school. Three months after his return he confided to a close friend that he had been unable to bring himself to make any plans. He wandered listlessly, visiting first one relative and then another, paralyzed, he said, by an overwhelming

72. Yorkville (S.C.) *Enquirer*, December 20, 1866.
73. Elizabeth Brownrigg Waddell to Mrs. P. E. Bailey, January 29, 1866, in John Lancaster Bailey Papers, SHC; Sarah Wadley Diary, SHC, May 13, 1865.
74. Grace Brown Elmore Diary (Typewritten copy in SCL), September 21, 1865, March 26, 1866.

moral inanition. Returning veterans seemed particularly gripped by "tor-por and depression," observed David Swain, and a successful Georgia mer-chant admitted a similar inability to break the mood of despondency that gripped him. His economic prospects were precarious, Thomas Harrold told his brother, but he lacked the energy to sit down and write a letter, let alone plunge into the work of rebuilding his mercantile establishment. "It sometimes appears to me as if my vitality & energy were all gone & I be-lieve it is not all fancy. The *war* has broken all the bonds that connected me with the past & at present there is no future before me."[75]

What was perhaps most surprising, however, was the response of the great majority of white southerners to this turn of events. On the eve of the election of 1866, the editor of the Columbus, Georgia, *Sun* had warned that "radical victory" would lead southerners to conclude that the "car-tridge box must come to the rescue of the country and the Constitution." When that victory came, there were outbursts of anger and occasional threats, but the overwhelming reaction was one of resignation and withdrawal.[76]

Like Harrold, William Pitt Ballinger had been reconciled to the defeat of the Confederacy well before the end came. But Ballinger was paralyzed for weeks, unable to concentrate upon his work. "I feel extremely de-jected—far beyond any feelings I ever had in my life," he wrote in his diary. His good friend, William N. Broadwell of Shreveport, Louisiana, saw "nothing in the future that holds any charm . . . and but little to condone the past—except the satisfaction of knowing that I have been faithful and tried to do my duty."[77]

A handful of southerners went so far as to turn from their religious faith. "I rebelled against this most mysterious dispensation of God and my faith was crushed out," admitted one Mississippi woman. Though she claimed to have later come to accept the "inscrutable actions of divine providence," many of her friends were "sceptical still." If Elizabeth Waddell regained her faith, it is clear that others did not. "What does all this trial—this horror upon horror—mean?" asked Louis Blanding of South Carolina. Blanding, who had studied with James Henley Thornwell, the major theologian of antebellum southern Presbyterianism, was scornful of his brother's profes-sion that there reigned a God of "*mercy* & *justice*." He still wanted to be-

75. S. D. McConnell to E. M. L'Engle, June 25, 1865, in Edward McCrady L'Engle Pa-pers, SHC; David Swain to Zebulon Vance, November 1, 1865, in Zebulon Vance Papers, NCA; Thomas Harrold to Brother, July 14, 1865, in Harrold Brothers Papers, EU.

76. Columbus (Ga.) *Sun*, September 4, 1866.

77. William Pitt Ballinger Diary, UTA, May 13, 1865; William N. Broadwell to W. P. Ballinger, April 28, 1865, in Ballinger Papers, UTA.

lieve in the existence of a loving God, he said, but he found it impossible to find a justification for the death and suffering which had been visited upon his people.[78]

Well before Johnson had been overshadowed by the Republican congressional majority, Samuel Boykin of Macon expressed horror at the "criminal apathy" that characterized his contemporaries. "The philosophical historians, whose task it will be to portray to posterity the events of this time, will feel at a loss to account for this strange and freezing indifference to our most vital interests; this suicidal inaction, this moral catalepsy." However much Boykin might scold fellow southerners, he could not dispel the weariness that paralyzed George Munford of Buckingham County, Virginia. "From the bottom of my heart I wish to be quietly in some country retreat . . . far from all politics and governmental concerns," said Munford. "I am sick of everything connected with political offices." "I have done with politics," agreed a Georgia planter five months after the war had ended. "I shall vote no more; let them squabble to their hearts content; I want no further share of it."[79]

It would be easy to exaggerate this mood. There had always been a deep strain of pessimism in the thinking of white southerners, and most survivors of the war—civilian and military—insisted that their faith had been strengthened by defeat and deprivation. "I live now for the day and by the day, leaving the future and all its events in His hands without care or conjecture." Josiah Gorgas, the Confederate government's chief of ordnance, described a wealthy planter friend who was broken by the war and defeat. "The state of mind is natural and leads to despondency in his case," Gorgas concluded, "but not so in the case of most planters." More than one former Confederate showed the resilience of a fifty-five-year-old Virginia woman who brooded for two weeks after the surrender of Lee, and then when her last horse and mule were seized by Union soldiers, walked seven miles to Richmond, angrily stood down an intimidated Union officer, and returned home with her horse and mule.[80]

78. Elizabeth B. Waddell to Mrs. P. E. Bailey, January 29, 1866, in Bailey Papers; Louis Blanding to James Douglass Blanding, July 7, 1866, in James Douglas Blanding Papers, SCL; Emma Mordecai to George W. Mordecai, April 21, 1866, in George W. Mordecai Papers, SHC; Honoré Gayarré to J. D. B. De Bow, April 23, 1866, in De Bow Papers; David Schenck Diary, May 31, 1865.

79. Macon *Daily Telegraph*, September 1, 20, 1865; George W. Munford to Mrs. E. T. Munford, April 21, 1865, in Munford-Ellis Family Papers, DUL; Samuel Forwood to W. S. Forwood, November 9, 1866, in William Stump Forwood Papers, SHC; William W. Boyce to J. D. B. De Bow, July 24, 1866, in De Bow Papers; George Anderson Mercer Diary, SHC, July 6, 1865.

80. Josiah Gorgas Journal, SHC, June 15, 1865; Emma Mordecai to George W. Mordecai, April 21, 1865, in Mordecai Papers.

But something profound had happened. A Marianna, Florida, physician would later comment to his brother upon the extraordinary incidence of acute depression he encountered in the wake of the war. "Many of our wisest and best and strongest men . . . have, like a reed bent to the blast . . . snapped asunder." Occasionally there were suicides, said Ethelred Philips, but far more common was a "collapse of the spirit" and paralyzing depression characterized by acute "mental anxiety and apprehension." Philips had observed only the citizens of the little central Florida community where he lived, but the pattern existed throughout the South. At times, there was a rhetoric of mawkish self-pity, but the more common complaint was simply of constant lethargy and listlessness. "I am doing nothing for myself," wrote Henry Garrett from his Mississippi plantation; "I am constantly stricken with fatigue." Garrett believed his "inertia" was caused by "acute mental lassitude"; other southerners talked of "demoralization," "paralysis," "apathy," even "moral catalepsy."[81]

In virtually all of the elections held in the two years after the war, voter turnout declined dramatically. In North Carolina where W. W. Holden and Jonathan Worth waged a spirited campaign for the governorship in the fall of 1865, sixty thousand voters went to the polls, but that was less than 55 percent of the 1860 turnout, and in other states, the drop in the number of voters was even more precipitous. Only forty-five thousand Georgia voters bothered to vote in the fall, 1865, elections, 42 percent of the 1860 turnout. Even during the last statewide election of the war, fewer than twenty thousand voters cast their ballots in South Carolina's fall election, and the turnout in Virginia was the lowest for a statewide election in fifty years. Altogether, in the eight southern states, approximately 247,000 voters cast their ballots in statewide elections in the fall of 1865. In the election of 1860, more than 535,000 voters had gone to the polls.[82]

The fears of confiscation, of living under a government controlled by political opponents and former slaves led many southern conservatives to continue their effort to influence political choices in the postwar South. David Schenck of North Carolina—lawyer, secessionist, bitter racist, and apprehensive planter—agonized over the issue of what position to take through-

81. Henry Garrett Diary, October 8, 1865; Ethelred Philips to J. J. Philips, January 21, 1866, in James John Philips Papers, SHC; Addie Worth to William H. Bagley, May 4, 1865, in Bagley Family Papers, SHC; David Schenck Diary, May 31, 1865.
82. *Journal of the Constitutional Convention of 1865 at Tallahassee, Florida*, 132; Harris, *Presidential Reconstruction in Mississippi*, 94; "Report of the Secretary of State, Election Returns, 1865," AA; Hamilton James Eckenrode, *The Political History of Virginia During the Reconstruction* (Baltimore, 1904), 37; James Douglas Smith, "Virginia During Reconstruction, 1865–1870: A Political, Economic, and Social History" (Ph.D. dissertation, University of Virginia, 1960), 14.

out the months after the Republican victory. Continued southern resistance, he first decided, would only strengthen those northern radicals who were crying for the division of southern lands and other radical measures. Schenck even envisioned a chain of events that might lead to the nightmare of women's suffrage. On the other hand, the enfranchisement of the freedmen would strengthen the white minority that was always ready to "confiscate and divide the lands and indulge in a carnival of agrarianism." He was inclined to throw his support behind the moderate Republicans ("It would be better to trust them than some North Carolina radicals") and hope that conservative whites could control the black minority in his state. "But such is the ostracism of public opinion among white men in the State that no one dare enunciate these sentiments, without being socially condemned and ignored," he wrote in his diary. Therefore, he had decided "for peace and harmony's sake" to occupy a neutral position, to avoid all discussion on political questions, and to keep aloof from public gatherings.[83]

Unlike Schenck, David Miller Carter of Beaufort, North Carolina, first opposed secession, then accepted the state's decision and served in the Confederate army. After election to the state legislature in 1862, however, he joined the Holden wing of "peace men" and two years later supported a convention to end the war—with slavery if possible, without if necessary. Although he suffered no mistreatment at the hands of the Confederate government, the experiences of the last year of the war instilled in him a disgust for the "last-ditch disunionists" who had fought on long after any hope of victory was gone. When he saw the control of state government shift away from the 1864 "peace men" and watched Andrew Johnson drift into the arms of the "Copperhead elements" of the Democratic party, his support for Holden strengthened. He worked behind the scenes with Thaddeus Stevens late in 1866 in an attempt to gain approval for a plan that would have restored North Carolina to the Union under considerably more "lenient" provisions than were later required by the 1867 Reconstruction Acts.

But there were limits beyond which Carter simply would not go. From the first months after Appomattox he had been appalled by the western unionists, whom he regarded as "hate-filled" and "illiberal." He professed contempt for the old aristocracy that had dominated North Carolina politics, but he was horrified by the prospect of confiscation, whether undertaken by Congress or by vengeful North Carolinians. Confiscation, he told

83. David Schenck Diary, November 26, 1866, March 26, May 26, June 17, 1867, April 12, 1868.

one Holdenite, was the instrument of a "bestial" and "anarchistic society" in which class would be pitted against class.[84] Carter had led the legislative effort of North Carolina conservatives to grant broad civil rights to the freedmen out of conviction as well as expediency. Very shortly after the war, he expressed a willingness to support a qualified black suffrage, and he argued that the "acquisition of knowledge and property" would ultimately lead to universal manhood suffrage. But he was equally convinced that it was "unthinkable" to grant immediate and unconditional suffrage to the freedmen, particularly if it was accompanied by the disfranchisement of large numbers of southern whites. Thus, although he supported the Howard Amendment, when he read the text of the first of the Reconstruction Acts of 1867, which granted precisely that unconditional suffrage, he was filled with foreboding. Such legislation, he told his old friend John Pool, would mean that "half the Southern states are placed forever under the absolute sway of emancipated slaves; and an interminable vista of strife and fierce rivalry are opened before our eyes."[85]

Benjamin Gardner of Alabama, an "earnest and consistent union man" who had been "overawed" in 1861, had apprehensively watched the growing debacle of the president's policies. By the spring of 1867 he was adrift and "at a loss as to what course to pursue and what party to ally myself with." The conservatives ("as they call themselves"), with their refusal to repudiate the president, would only lead to a "final overthrow and destruction of all the privileges of Alabamaians." On the other hand, Gardner concluded, "The Republican party, I fear is too extreme in their efforts in behalf of the negroes." Thus, he concluded, "you perceive that I am in a dilemma not knowing really what course to pursue."[86]

The South had become a "strange world," one young North Carolina soldier wrote early in the war. "One does not know what to believe, or what to think. Things have all got into a sort of whirlwind, and are whirling and kicking & jumping around at such a rate, that half the time, a man hardly knows whether he is standing on his head or feet." And things had become

84. David M. Carter to John Pool, December 11, 1865, W. J. Mason to David M. Carter, March 6, 1866, both in Carter Papers; Raleigh *Standard*, December 25, 1866. For background on Carter, see Carolyn A. Wallace, "David Miller Carter," in William S. Powell (ed.), *Dictionary of North Carolina Biography* (1 vol. to date; Chapel Hill, 1971), I, 333–34.

85. David M. Carter to John Pool, November 1, 1867, John Pool to David M. Carter, August 19, September 30, November 8, 1867, M. B. Rodman to David M. Carter, February 23, 1868, all in Carter Papers.

86. Benjamin Gardner to Patton, April 14, July 3, 1867, in Alabama Governors' Papers. See also John Pool to David Miller Carter, August 19, September 30, 1867, both in Carter Papers.

even stranger after the war. Jacob Hawkins, a bewildered postwar Louisiana politician, tried to summarize the forces at work in 1865 and 1866, but he finally gave up with the confession that politics had become a "land of fog and confusion."[87]

Those politics did not end in 1866. In the months that followed the fall elections, white southerners confronted their deepest fears as the Reconstruction Acts of 1867 set in motion the creation of biracial governments, established under military rule. Benjamin Gardner would choose the Republican party and go on to become Alabama's attorney general in 1870. David Carter, without overtly breaking with his friends who became Republicans, would quietly withdraw from politics. But in that fog and confusion, that strange new world that Henry Graves encountered, the fragile unity of the postwar conservative leadership was shattered. Like Gardner and Carter, thousands of white southerners would decide whether to acquiesce in the new order, to continue to resist, or to passively retreat into a world separated as much as possible from the contamination of politics. Such choices would be shaped by class background, wartime experiences, emotional temperament, political ambition, economic calculation, or family pressures. These choices were not the product of any group consensus, however, but of individuals seeking to survive in a political system that had undergone a revolution.

For the men who lived through these critical months (and for the historians who have studied them) there soon emerged a sense of lost opportunities, a feeling that a critical moment in the shaping of a less rancorous and more just postwar settlement had slipped away. From the perspective of Republican journalist Whitelaw Reid, that moment had come in the months of May and June of 1865 when there were "no conditions" the defeated South would not have accepted—even black suffrage. They might have been shocked, claimed Reid, but "if the Government [had] required it, they were ready to submit." The "whole body politic was as wax. It needed but a firm hand to apply the seal."[88]

Benjamin Harvey Hill, one of the postwar conservatives who had attempted to guide the South back into the Union, also believed there was a lost opportunity, but like most white southerners—conservative and fire-eater alike—he blamed the congressional Republicans. The old Whigs and union Democrats would have controlled the South after the war, claimed Hill, and brought with them "stability, economic progress and prosperity"

---

87. Henry Graves to Aunt Sibbie, September 4, 1861, in Graves Family Papers, SHC; Jacob Hawkins to James Govan Taliaferro, September 22, 1865, in James G. Taliaferro Papers, LSU.

88. Whitelaw Reid, *After the War: A Southern Tour* (Cincinnati, 1866), 219, 296–97.

if given a free hand. Instead, the Congress had "lumped the Old Union Democrats and Whigs together with the secessionists and said they would punish all alike and would put us all under the negro." The inevitable result, he argued, was belligerent resistance and the racial solidarity of whites.[89]

But the conclusions of both Reid and Hill rest upon flawed assumptions. In light of a century of racial tension and conflict, it is appealing to endorse Reid's argument that firm demands on the part of the North would have forestalled southern white resistance and minimized the racial oppression that soon developed. The difficulty with Reid's position is that these "demands," limited as they were, were themselves a consequence of white resistance. Before the events of 1865 had transpired, there was no consensus on the part of the victorious North to lay down "radical" demands for the South. Nor, Reid's assertion notwithstanding, was there a willingness on the part of the great majority of white southerners to accept any truly radical requirements in 1865.

Hill's desire to see a white conservative alliance created after the war is also understandable, but it is by no means certain that the policies of the men who led the postwar Johnson regimes would have brought political stability and economic prosperity. Their "New South" policies in the 1880s were hardly an unqualified success. And they certainly would not have ensured civil justice, let alone political or economic rights for the freedmen.

The events of postwar reconstruction were not inevitable; there were a range of political alternatives, North and South, after the war. But all things were not possible. As the nursery rhyme concludes, if wishes were horses, then beggars would ride. Judge O. O. Lochrane had been right in 1865 when he sadly observed that it was "difficult for men to shake down their convictions like apples from a tree." If southerners insisted on "stumbling backward over a wilderness of graves while proudly reliving the mistakes of the past," he had warned, they would reap the "bitter fruits of another generation of pride, prejudice and blind folly."[90] It would be more than one generation.

89. *House Reports*, 40th Cong., 2nd Sess., No. 26, VII, 762.
90. O. A. Lochrane, *The Present Condition of the Country: Our Duty and Prospects* (Macon, 1865), 13.

Index